Memorial Plaque of Jonathan Edwards by Herbert Adams in the Sanctuary of The First Churches Northampton, Massachusetts

THE CONTRIBUTION OF JONATHAN EDWARDS TO AMERICAN CULTURE AND SOCIETY

Essays on America's Spiritual Founding Father

(The Northampton Tercentenary Celebration, 1703-2003)

Edited by
Richard A. S. Hall

The Edwin Mellen Press
Lewiston•Queenston•Lampeter

Library of Congress Cataloging-in-Publication Data

The contribution of Jonathan Edwards to American culture and society : essays on America's spiritual founding father (the Northampton tercentenary celebration, 1703-2003) / edited by Richard A.S. Hall.
   p. cm.
  ISBN-13: 978-0-7734-5060-8
  ISBN-10: 0-7734-5060-2
  1. Edwards, Jonathan, 1703-1758--Influence. 2. United States--Civilization. I. Edwards, Jonathan, 1703-1758. II. Hall, Richard A. S.
  BX7260.E3C645 2008
  285.8092--dc22
                              2008041351

hors série.

A CIP catalog record for this book is available from the British Library.

Front cover: Stained glass window of Jonathan Edwards, executed by Charles J. Connick Studios
        Courtesy of the United Congregational Church of Holyoke, Massachusetts

Copyright © 2008 Richard A. S. Hall

All rights reserved. For information contact

The Edwin Mellen Press	The Edwin Mellen Press
Box 450	Box 67
Lewiston, New York	Queenston, Ontario
USA 14092-0450	CANADA L0S 1L0

The Edwin Mellen Press, Ltd.
Lampeter, Ceredigion, Wales
UNITED KINGDOM SA48 8LT

Printed in the United States of America

The beauty of the world consists wholly of sweet mutual consents, either within itself, or with the Supreme Being. As to the corporeal world, though there are many other sorts of consents, yet the sweetest and most charming beauty of it is its resemblance of spiritual beauties. The reason is that spiritual beauties are infinitely the greatest, and bodies being but the shadows of beings, they must be so much the more charming as they shadow forth spiritual beauties. This beauty is peculiar to natural things, it surpassing the art of man.

–Jonathan Edwards

Preface

This volume contains select papers delivered in October of 2003 at the First Churches of Northampton, Massachusetts, in celebration of the tercentenary of the birth of Jonathan Edwards. The First Churches is the successor to the church Edwards served for almost a quarter of a century and is situated on the same site. The Northampton Tercentenary of 2003 is in continuity with the conference held in the same building in June of 1900 to mark the sesquicentenary of Edwards' dismissal from his church, and the anticipated conference to be held in the same place to honor the quadricentenary of his birth in 2103.

Contents

Acknowledgements x

PART I: INTRODUCTION

The Historical Background to the Edwards Tercentenary 1
    –Richard A. S. Hall

Banquet Address: J. Edwards Conference 57
    –Huston Smith

PART II: EDWARDS AS SOCIAL & POLITICAL PHILOSOPHER

Why Is Jonathan Edwards America's Spiritual Founding Father? 65
    –Herbert Richardson

The Mind of Jonathan Edwards: Beyond America 73
    –M. Darrol Bryant

"One vast and ecumenical holding company": Edwardsean Millennial Themes in Nineteenth- and Twentieth-Century Dystopian Fiction 89
    –James Hewitson

PART III: EDWARDS AS INTERPRETER OF NATURE

Edwards, Swedenborg, Emerson: From Typology to Correspondence 109
    –Devin P. Zuber

From Edwards to Emerson to Eddy: Extending a Trajectory of Metaphysical Idealism 125
    –David L. Weddle

Edwards—Thoreau—Dillard: Reading/Writing Nature and the Awakened/
    Awakening Self 153
        –Michael G. Ditmore

PART IV: EDWARDS & AMERICAN PHILOSOPHY
Experience as Religious Discovery in Edwards & Peirce 201
        –Roger Ward
**Jonathan Edwards as Proto-Pragmatist and John Dewey as Post-Theological
    Calvinist** 219
        –Stuart Rosenbaum

PART V: EDWARDS IN HIS CONTEXT
Bishop Butler and Jonathan Edwards 233
        –David White
Doing Metaethics with Kant and Edwards 243
        –Charles Don Keyes

PART VI: EDWARDS & THEOLOGY
Satan and his Maleficium in the Thought of Jonathan Edwards 259
        –Scott D. Seay
**Jonathan Edwards' Trinitarian Theology in the Context of the Early-
    Enlightenment Deist Controversy** 281
        –Steve Studebaker

PART VII: MISCELLANEOUS THEMES IN EDWARDS
**Jonathan Edwards, Children, and Young People: Less of Earth and More of
    Heaven** 305
        –Charles Pierce

Edwards' Contribution to the Missionary Movement of Early Baptists....319
　　–Michael D. Thompson
Edwards as Mystic **327**
　　–Richard A. S. Hall
"Heaven Is a World of Love" **347**
　　–Ronald Story

Appendix **357**
　Tercentenary Celebration Conference Program, 2003
　Program of Commemorative Concert
　Music Scores
　　The Bow of God's Wrath, An Anthem for SATB Chorus, A Cappella
　　　–David Kidwell
　　Pilgrim's Blues, Trio for Violin, Piano, & Cowbell
　　　–Keith Dippre
　　Parting Words, A Cantata for Mixed Voice, Tenor Solo, and String Quartet
　　　–Clifton J. Noble, Jr.
　　Conversing with Some One Invisible, String Quartet Number Two
　　　–Daniel Pinkham
　Program of Conference
　Bulletin of Jonathan Edwards' Tercentenary Worship Service
　Gallery
　　　–Darren Pierce

Acknowledgements

A debt of gratitude is owed to the following persons and institutions without whose generosity and efforts the Northampton Jonathan Edwards Tercentenary Celebration would not have been possible:

To Herbert Warren Richardson, a long-time student and teacher of Edwards, whose inspiration it was to hold this Tercentenary Celebration, and who gave unstintingly of his resources during the planning of the event.

To John Rupnow and other staff of the Edwin Mellen Press for their financial and logistical support.

To Rev. Peter Ives and the staff and congregation of the First Churches in Northampton, Massachusetts, for graciously providing the use of their sanctuary for the event; in particular, special thanks are owing to Kathryn Gabriel, church archivist, for her meticulous behind-the-scenes organization of the conference and for her display of Edwards memorabilia and other eighteenth-century artifacts; and to Jaya Reddy, secretary, and Wendy Williams, custodian.

To the Reverend Peter Kakos and the congregation of the Edwards Church for kindly allowing the use of their sanctuary, choir, and organist for the Tercentenary concert.

To the staff of the Forbes Library of Northampton for providing archival material for display at the conference.

To Carol Hutter whose superb networking and organizational skills made the concert possible.

To the staff of Methodist University in Fayetteville, North Carolina; in particular, to Deborah Melot, formerly of Methodist University, and Candace

Fellows, of Fayetteville State University, in Fayetteville, North Carolina, for their indispensable secretarial services. To Dr. Elton Hendricks, president of Methodist University, and Dr. T. J. Bryan, former chancellor of Fayetteville State University, for generously providing their resources in support of the Tercentenary. And, of course, the conferees and musicians who convened in Northampton to celebrate the thought, work, and life of Jonathan Edwards.

To Darren Pierce of Hawkeye Photography, Northampton, Massachusetts, for photographing the events.

To Suzan Flanagan for her invaluable editorial work on the Proceedings in preparation for the press.

To Keith Dippre and Clifton J. Noble, Jr. for their respective scores *Pilgrim's Blues,* Trio for Violin, Piano, & Cowbell; and *Parting Words,* A Cantata for Mixed Voices, Tenor Solo, and String Quartet. Also to David Kidwell who permitted the reproduction of the first page of his score *The Bow of God's Wrath,* An Anthem for SATB Chorus, A Cappella.

And to Ione Press, Inc., a division of ECS Publishing, Boston, Massachusetts, for granting permission to reproduce Daniel Pinkham's score *Conversing with Some One Invisible,* String Quartet Number Two, © 2003 by Ione Press.

PART I

INTRODUCTION

The Historical Background to the Edwards Tercentenary

Richard A. S. Hall

Edwards' Life

Born in 1703, Jonathan Edwards belongs to the fourth generation of Puritans who first landed on the coast of the Massachusetts Bay Colony in 1620. During his precocious adolescence he embarked on bold metaphysical speculations and underwent intense spiritual struggles, culminating in a conversion to a mystical Calvinist orthodoxy. In 1723 he was awarded the Master of Arts degree from Yale College. After serving briefly as pastor of a Presbyterian church in New York City, and then a short stint as a tutor at Yale, Edwards was called in 1726 to assist his aging maternal grandfather, Solomon Stoddard, in his pastoral duties at the church in Northampton. Because of his enormous authority, prestige, power, and popularity, Stoddard had earned himself the sobriquet "Pope Stoddard." In 1728, after fifty-seven years of faithful service to his church, Stoddard died and Edwards replaced him.

Between 1734 and 1735 a wave of religious revivals swept through Northampton. Edwards carefully documented these "surprising conversions" and analyzed them in his *A Faithful Narrative* of 1736. This episode was the first act of a spiritual development whose effects would be felt throughout the subsequent course of American history. In 1740 an itinerant English evangelist, George Whitefield, visited the American colonies. Whitefield preached revivals up and down the eastern seaboard and a fire of religious enthusiasm swept over America. Edwards observed remarkable changes in the people of Northampton as a result of Whitefield's revivals. The changes Edwards observed included people

(1) exhibiting serious concern for their spiritual state, (2) relinquishing immoral behavior, and (3) engaging in fervent prayer. Many were thrown into spiritual ecstasies through their deeper communion with God. Even young people were affected. In droves, they left off their bouts of drunkenness, debauchery, and general rowdiness to engage in private prayer meetings and conversations on religious subjects. Children as young as five reported having had extraordinary religious experiences. Religion became the chief business of the people's lives. This revival of religion was called the "Great Awakening."

Edwards now sought to arouse the spiritually dead with sermons like "Sinners in the Hands of an Angry God," preached in 1741 at Enfield, Connecticut. This sermon was destined to enter the annals of America as a classic of its kind. Edwards rejoiced in the revivals, believing them to be a harbinger of the Second Coming (which he thought was imminent and would occur in the New World). He meticulously documented, described, and analyzed these revivals in *The Distinguishing Marks of a Work of the Spirit of God* (1741) and *Some Thoughts Concerning the Present Revival* (1742). By 1741, Edwards was at the height of his powers, prestige, and influence. He was becoming another Solomon Stoddard.

But things began going terribly wrong. There now were outbreaks of virulent fanaticism. In one such case, James Davenport, a Connecticut revivalist, escorted his congregation to the wharf in Bridgeport and ordered them to strip off their finery, which he then burned (he was subsequently incarcerated for insanity). During another revival, Edwards' uncle, Joseph Hawley, slit his throat in a bout of depression induced by a concern about his spiritual estate.

The Congregational and Presbyterian clergy split over the Great Awakening. Charles Chauncy, minister of Boston's old First Church, denounced these revivals as spurious forms of religiosity. The heart of his complaint was that they fanned the fires of undisciplined emotion while extinguishing the light of reason. Chauncy went so far as to attack Edwards personally. He accused him of "enthusiasm," the worst insult that could be hurled at an ecclesiastical opponent.

Edwards, a staunch advocate and instrument of the revivals, was forced to defend them.

Because so many had been deceived about the genuineness of the mass conversions occurring during the Great Awakening, Edwards decided to establish criteria to determine whether conversions were genuine. He published these as *A Treatise on Religious Affections*. In this book, Edwards described twelve signs, centered on their emotions, which persons could use to decide whether they were truly converted or not. Among the most important criteria Edwards identified were (1) a purely disinterested love for God motivated principally by the beauty of his holiness, a new sense of which is imparted by saving grace; and (2) daily conduct inspired by and exemplifying such love.

By helping people to reform themselves spiritually at the personal level, Edwards hoped to effect a reformation of sorts in the local church. He sought to make his church a congregation of the converted. He tried to get them to give *visible evidence* of their conversion in every facet of their lives, particularly in their speech, emotional dispositions, and behavior. To do this, Edwards stiffened the requirements for church membership. In so doing, he revoked the so-called "Half-Way Covenant," which had been instituted by his predecessor, Solomon Stoddard.

In 1677, Stoddard had instituted the Half-Way Covenant as the basis of church membership. Under this covenant, all one had to do to become a full member of the church was to have led a conventionally moral life and pledge to be open to a possible future conversion. One need not have been actually converted nor make a profession of faith to be a member under the Half-Way Covenant. Stoddard's Half-Way Covenant had the effect of swelling the church rolls, and this had two advantages. The advantage for Stoddard was that he could now exercise greater theocratic control over a larger segment of the town's population. The advantage for the townspeople was that, since the franchise depended on church membership, more men could enjoy the privilege of voting. Through the Half-Way Covenant,

Stoddard hoped to realize in Northampton the theocracy the Pilgrims had hoped to achieve.

Edwards had serious misgivings about the Half-Way Covenant. In the early years of his Northampton ministry, he tolerated it, partly out of deference to his revered grandfather and partly as a concession to a popular custom. But in the aftermath of the Great Awakening, with the rampancy of false forms of religiosity and backsliding, Edwards resolved that it was time to take decisive action. He revoked Stoddard's Half-Way Covenant.

Now for Edwards, it was not sufficient that members of the church live conventionally moral lives and be open to conversion at some future time. For Edwards, church members had to be in a state of *actual* grace. As Edwards understood the matter, church members had the privilege of receiving the Lord's Supper. But Edwards did not consider this ordinance to be a means of obtaining grace (a converting ordinance) but rather as a sign of the saving grace that the communicants had received at their conversion. Edwards contended that for the unconverted to partake of communion was to pretend to a faith that they lacked. Edwards stipulated, therefore, that to qualify for full church membership (and so for communion) persons should examine themselves to determine whether they were truly converted. They should use the criteria of genuine conversion that Edwards had laid out in *Religious Affections*. If they determined that they were indeed recipients of saving grace, then they would make a public profession of their faith to the congregation. It was then up to the church elders to decide whether the "professors," on the basis of their profession and their overall conduct, were eligible for full church membership together with all its privileges.

Needless to say, Edwards' revocation of the Half-Way Covenant did not sit well with the townspeople. They perceived it as an insult to Stoddard's memory. Some even thought that Edwards was illegitimately arrogating to himself the authority of separating the sheep from the goats. Therefore, in protest against him, not a single applicant for full membership came forward between 1744 and 1748.

When an applicant finally did come forward in December of 1748, he refused to make the profession of faith Edwards required. In 1749, Edwards published a rigorously reasoned *apologia* for his position, *An Humble Inquiry*. Since no one in Northampton was willing, or able, to dispute with Edwards over the issue of qualifications for communion, his work was ignored by those to whom it was addressed. Edwards' revocation of Stoddard's Half-Way Covenant proved to be the proverbial last straw. Public sentiment against Edwards had been brewing for some time. So on June 22, 1750, Edwards' congregation, on the recommendation of a council of local churches convened expressly to advise them, voted for his dismissal.

In the summer of 1751, after rejecting offers of pulpits in Canaan, Connecticut, and Lunenburg, Virginia, and even of one far away in Scotland, Edwards moved with his family to the frontier town of Stockbridge. He was to be a missionary to the Houssatonic Indians, a post for which he was by temperament singularly unsuited. Here he preached and taught in the Indian school. Nevertheless, he had the leisure there to produce four great theological works in quick succession: *Freedom of the Will* (1754); *The Great Doctrine of Original Sin Defended* (1758); the twin dissertations, *Concerning the End for Which God Created the World* and *The Nature of True Virtue* (both published posthumously in 1765); and his uncompleted summa, *A History of the Work of Redemption* (published posthumously in 1774). These works together constitute a massive assault on Arminianism and Deism in their various guises, and a rigorous and consistent defense of divine sovereignty in all its aspects.

In 1757, the presidency of the College of New Jersey (the future Princeton University) came open upon the death of its incumbent, Aaron Burr. The trustees of the college offered the post to Burr's father-in-law, Jonathan Edwards, whose reputation had greatly increased during his Stockbridge years. Edwards was initially reluctant to take the position. However, Edwards finally relented, and in February of 1758, at the age of fifty-four, he arrived in Princeton to take up the presidential duties of its college. At the height of his intellectual powers and finally receiving the public recognition and appreciation he deserved, Edwards should have enjoyed many more years of productive work. Yet this was not to be. A few months before his arrival, an epidemic of smallpox had broken out in Princeton. Edwards took the precaution of being inoculated against the disease. But, the effects of the inoculation proved deleterious and, on March 22, 1758, Edwards succumbed to infection and died. He is buried in Princeton. He had been president of the college for only five weeks.

Edwards' Legacy

Edwards' relationship to the subsequent American culture that he helped shape is complex and fraught with ironies. That relationship takes two forms: (1) his demonstrable and enormous influence, either direct or indirect, on American religious movements and institutions; and (2) the deep and abiding affinities between the pattern of his thought and that of later American philosophers and men of letters.

Edwards directly influenced a group of men who developed and perpetuated his theology. Joseph Bellamy and Samuel Hopkins studied under Edwards, and Jonathan Edwards, Jr., his youngest son, in turn studied under Bellamy and Hopkins. They, together with Nathaniel Emmons and other fellow travelers, were called the "New Lights"; they formed the nucleus of a theological movement known as the "New Divinity." Like Edwards, they were orthodox in their beliefs, insisted on conversion as a criterion of church membership, and encouraged revivals. The New Divinity helped foment the Second Great Awakening and links Edwards' Puritanism with the American Protestant theology of the nineteenth century.

In spite of the valiant efforts of the New Divinity men to preserve Edwards' theological legacy, "the Edwardsean spirit was really never infused into the life and thought of his church," according to Sidney Ahlstrom, but "remained a kind of perpetually misunderstood stranger." Ahlstrom gives two reasons for this: One is the unavailability of the complete corpus of Edwards' works (still a problem today, incidentally). A second reason is that Edwards' available texts did not display that unity of thought that may have existed in his own mind.[1] A third reason, perhaps, is that the New Divinity hardened into a shell of Protestant scholasticism from which whatever was vital in Edwards' own thought had long fled. The New Divinity men in their fidelity to the letter of Edwards' theology were not animated by its vivifying spirit.

Evidence of Edwards' less direct influence is the Second Great Awakening (1797–1831), which, no less than the earlier one, was a signal event in American history. It received impetus from the New Lights and Timothy Dwight, Edwards' grandson and the illustrious president of Princeton University.

Among the practical fruits of this second awakening was the formation of a multitude of voluntary associations, with mainly lay membership and leadership, dedicated to the improvement of society. These associations—which so impressed Alexis de Tocqueville—promoted missionary work and Christian education, worked for reforms in the treatment of the insane and the physically handicapped, fought for the abolition of slavery, and sought to raise the moral tone of society, among other such endeavors. This huge army of volunteers created institutions, some of which are still extant, such as the American Home Missionary Society (1826), the American Bible Society (1816), the American Tract Society (1823), the American Education Society (1826), and the American Temperance Union (1836). Furthermore, the Second Great Awakening helped lay the groundwork for a veritable social revolution. The various voluntary associations particularly attracted women. By thus giving scope to their ambitions, the opportunity to organize themselves, and practice in promoting social and political causes, these associations fostered the growth of the women's rights movement, whose continuing impact continues to be felt in the twenty-first century.[2]

The myriad social and political reforms spawned by the Second Great Awakening, then, can be traced through the evangelism of the New Lights right back to Jonathan Edwards, their distant progenitor. It is interesting to note that Edwards himself pioneered the formation of voluntary associations. One such association was the so-called "concert of prayer," a body of people who would meet regularly to pray in unison for the advancement of God's Kingdom.

Edwards' incalculable impact on the history of American theology and religion, and indirectly on the social and political movements they inspired, is both demonstrable and incontrovertible. Can the same be said of Edwards' influence, if any, on the subsequent course of American philosophy?

Edwards' reputation as a philosopher of distinction was established early on. An early recognition of Edwards' philosophical genius came from the Scots philosopher, Dugald Stewart, who wrote of Edwards that he "in logical acuteness and subtility does not yield to any disputant bred in the universities of Europe."[3] Stewart's high estimate of Edwards was later echoed by both European and American thinkers throughout the nineteenth century. Given Edwards' lustrous reputation as a philosopher, his influence on subsequent American philosophy would expectedly have been as great as his influence on American theology and religion. Indeed, the English cleric and philosopher, Frederick D. Maurice, expected as much. In 1872, Maurice declared, "In his own country Edwards remains, and must always remain, a great power. We should imagine all American theology and philosophy, whatever change it may undergo, and with whatever foreign elements it may be associated, must be cast in his mould."[4]

But no distinctively "Edwardsean" school of philosophy emerged comparable to the New Divinity. Surprisingly, Edwards seems to have had no significant impact on any of America's classic philosophers—Charles S. Peirce, William James, Josiah Royce, John Dewey, and George Santayana. James does cite him by way of illustration in his *Varieties of Religious Experience,* but does not acknowledge Edwards as possibly his only peer in the psychology of religion. And

Royce ranked Edwards "in order of time, the first of our nationally representative philosophers,"[5] along with Emerson and James whom he ranked as the second and third respectively. Edwards, it seems, had no influence on these men, or, if he did, they do not acknowledge it. Edwards' apparent lack of influence is especially odd given that his stock as a philosopher was high at least as early as 1829.

One reason perhaps that Edwards did not give rise to a distinctive philosophical school or have any obvious influence—and this is purely speculative—is that the philosophical movement dominant in American higher education up until the middle of the nineteenth century was Scottish Common Sense Realism. Now Common Sense Realism, as its name suggests, was antithetical to idealism of any sort, of which Edwards' philosophy was a spectacular example. John Witherspoon, who was chiefly responsible for establishing the Realism of his native Scotland at Princeton when he became its president in 1768, was implacably opposed to Berkeley's idealism, which, incidentally, he misunderstood. Furthermore, he was a traditional Calvinist who had no sympathy for the New Divinity, Edwards' direct theological legacy. And when the hegemony of Scottish Realism in America was finally broken up in the middle of the century by the importation of various forms of German idealism and the emergence of Transcendentalism, American idealists like William Torrey Harris and Josiah Royce took their cue from Kant, Hegel, and Schopenhauer, not from Edwards.

Another possible reason for Edwards' lack of philosophical influence is that his early metaphysical speculations, the bulk of his philosophy, were not published until well into the nineteenth century. It was only then his reputation as an idealist who ranked with Berkeley began to emerge.

Nevertheless, though no later American philosophers admit to being influenced by Edwards, Bruce Kuklick in his recent study, *Churchmen and Philosophers: From Jonathan Edwards to John Dewey*, detects Edwards' influence on one American philosopher, John Dewey. Kuklick argues "that there are continuities that take us from Edwards to Dewey."[6] Thus, Edwards directly influenced the

New Divinity, and the "Progressive Orthodoxy" that emerged from it was part of Dewey's intellectual background.

Although Kuklick confines himself to tracing the continuities between Edwards and Dewey, similar continuities might be traced between Edwards and both Josiah Royce and William James. Royce's formative years were spent in an evangelical Calvinist household, and James' father, Henry James, Sr., spent his life reacting creatively against his own father's Calvinism. American Calvinism, which bore the unmistakable stamp of Edwards and the New Divinity, was part of the intellectual and spiritual heritage of Royce and the younger James.

However, whatever the truth may be regarding Edwards' philosophical influence, there can be no doubt about the deep intellectual kinships and thematic continuities between Edwards and those American philosophers who flourished in the late nineteenth and the early twentieth centuries. Some of these kinships and continuities are to be found in their common preoccupation with religion, their idealism, and even their pragmatism.

Like Edwards, James, Royce, and Dewey were preoccupied with religious questions. They were alike deeply sympathetic with religion and sought to defend it against its detractors. All three attempted to resolve the conflict between religion and science that had intensified since the seventeenth century. Edwards sought to reconcile religion with Newtonian mechanics, whereas James, Royce, and Dewey in their respective ways sought to reconcile religion with Darwinian evolution. All three endeavored to explain the essential nature of religion. James found the essence of religion in the mystical experiences of individuals, while Royce and Dewey found it in the social dynamics of the community of faith. Edwards, interestingly, found it in both. He believed that true religion must spring from the spiritual experiences of individual persons but must take social form as the church.

By the mid-nineteenth century, German idealism had displaced Scottish Common Sense Realism as the dominant strain of American philosophy.

Hegelianism flourished in St. Louis through the advocacy of William Torrey Harris and his associates. The ancestral idealism of Plato and the critical idealism of Kant informed the thought of Emerson and other Transcendentalists in New England. Whereas both Hegel's objective idealism and Schopenhauer's voluntarism were fused in Royce's thought. As idealists these and many other American philosophers moved, though distantly, in Edwards' orbit.

Pragmatism, indigenous to America and perhaps her most distinctive philosophy, evolved out of American idealism. The young Dewey espoused Hegel's absolute idealism, and Royce's system is a hybrid of German idealism and pragmatism. Pragmatism is what distinguishes the Golden Age of American philosophy as represented by Peirce, James, Royce, and Dewey. Yet a nascent pragmatism can be found in Edwards' insistence that the best proof of the truth of religion is to be found in its practical fruits, in the positive differences it makes in the world.

Maurice's assessment of Edwards has proven prophetic, but not in the ways he perhaps imagined. In retrospect, we can see that American theology and philosophy has indeed been cast in Edwards' mould, however unintended, accidentally and in some respects ironically. And Maurice was also right in predicting that Edwards would remain a great power in American thought. Edwards' abiding power is evident in the fascination that he has held for generations of Americans, and in the endeavors of many Americans of different temperaments and outlooks to come to terms with his thought. These endeavors to understand Edwards and his significance for American culture and to discover the "real" Edwards in his literary remains have produced the torrent of Edwards scholarship that began in the late nineteenth century.

However, the real Edwards, or what he really thought, has been frustratingly elusive. There are perhaps three reasons for this. First, Edwards' philosophical theology is complex and multifaceted drawing from many different and sometimes incompatible sources. Edwards was an intellectual amphibian who inhabited uneasily the contrasting domains of Reformed theology and Enlightenment philosophy. Second, Edwards died before he could put the capstone on his system of thought in the form of the *History of the Work of Redemption*. And third, Edwards commentators come from different generations and so read Edwards through the ideological lenses of their own times.

Edwards' Thought

A Brief History

The history of Edwards' reception as a thinker exhibits three main periodic phases. These phases are both chronological and thematic. They are chronological insofar as they occur within certain historical periods. Though the beginnings and endings of these phases cannot be precisely determined, it is convenient to mark the beginning of each phase with the publication date of some text, followed by published responses to it or discussions from the press of ideas initiated by it, which collectively appear to represent a period. These phases are thematic insofar as they may be characterized and even typified by distinctive interpretive themes. However, this thematic characterization is by no means clear-cut. An interpretive theme dominating one phase may, like a recessive gene, re-emerge in a later one dominated by another theme. On the other hand, a theme muted in an earlier phase may come to the fore in a later one. Each phase is initiated by an event, typically the publication of a text, which gives impetus and direction to what follows. The interpretations of Edwards characterizing each phase reflect the climate of opinion in the larger intellectual and cultural spheres, particularly contemporary developments in philosophy and theology. Further, the phases are typically marked by a dominant pair of interpretations, or intellectual portraits, of Edwards that are in tension with one another, if not in conflict.

The first phase in the history of the interpretation of Edwards, roughly from 1769 to 1864, might be styled the theological phase. His commentators during this period dealt principally with the theological issues he raised; they sought to appropriate his thought to meet their theological demands. The second phase, from around 1871 to 1903, might be characterized as the philosophical phase. This is a more complex phase insofar as Edwards as philosopher, mystic, and poet now attracts the attention of scholars. Finally, the third phase in the interpretation of Edwards, occurring from about 1907 to the present may be described as principally the historical phase. What most distinguishes this third period is the contextualization of his thought, embedding it in its time and place.

The Theological Phase

This phase begins eleven years after Edward's death, with the 1769 publication of John Smalley's defense of Edwards' *Freedom of the Will* under the title, *Consistency of the Sinner's Inability . . . with his Inexcusable Guilt*, and ends about 1864 with the appearance of Rowland G. Hazard's *Freedom of the Mind in Willing*, a critique of Edwards' determinism. In retrospect, the 1769 publication of Smalley's two sermons defending Edwards on the will might be taken as the fillip for the works that make up the first phase. Promptly following the next year was James Dana's *An Examination of . . . Edwards,* a critique of Edwards' doctrine of the will and so a rejoinder to Smalley. But this did not go unchallenged, for in 1772 Stephen West published his *Essay on Moral Agency,* to which Dana replied from the press the next year. And so it went, back and forth, for almost a hundred years. During this period, Edwards was the subject of over twenty books and many tracts and essays authored by men from a variety of professions and walks of life.[7]

A possible reason for this spate of interest is that for representatives of the New England Theology throughout its various stages, Edwards was not simply an antique figure of purely scholarly interest. He was a living presence with whom they had to come to terms. As St. Thomas deferentially referred to Aristotle as "the Philosopher," so the New England Theologians with equal justice might have referred to Edwards as "the Theologian." It is Edwards the polemicist and apologist for Calvinism, revivalism, and experimental religion who takes center stage during this first phase.

Edwards' successors (the "Edwardseans") who created the New Divinity were of two sorts. There were the expositors of Edwards such as Jonathan Edwards, Jr. and Joseph Bellamy who produced digests of Edwards' thought like Bellamy's *True Religion Delineated*. Then there were the developers of Edwards' thought such as Samuel Hopkins and Nathaniel Emmons and the many others who set out to address what they perceived as inconsistencies and other outstanding problems in his theology. In particular, they sought to bridge a series of uncompromising dualisms that Edwards had bequeathed to them: between God and man, nature and grace, and human freedom and divine sovereignty. These theologians were especially exercised over the issue of free will, seeking to square divine sovereignty with that degree of volitional freedom necessary for moral responsibility. Consequently, in their persistent investigations into the mysterious and elusive workings of the human will they happened to produce an impressive literature in the psychology of religion,[8] which, curiously, anticipated William James' *The Varieties of Religious Experience*—though this work apparently owes no intellectual debt to that literature.

However, this first phase was not unmarked by dissent. The Old Calvinists, like Ezra Stiles, had been alarmed by the revivals of the Awakening with their outbursts of enthusiasm and the sectarianism they spawned. They opposed the New Divinity (the name they coined for the Edwardseans) and bypassed Edwards by championing the old Puritan covenant theology. Stiles was not sympathetic to systematic theology; it was he who once prophesied that Edwards' "valuable Writings in another Gener[ation] will pass into as transient Notice perhaps scarce above Oblivion . . . ; and when Posterity occasionally comes across them in the Rubbish of Libraries, the rare Characters who may read & be pleased with them, will be looked upon as singular & whimsical."[9] Ironically, Stiles himself perhaps will be best remembered for this remark, and not for anything else he wrote. Yet others, such as Edwards Amasa Park and Parsons Cooke dissented from the New Divinity, not because it followed Edwards, but because they thought it had departed from him.

This theological phase in the interpretation of Edwards, though, was hampered by parochialism. Its discussion of Edwards was largely an in-house affair that could have little interest outside the narrow world of New England Congregationalism.

The Philosophical Phase

In this period of engagement, Edwards ceased to be merely a parochial theologian picked over by the men of the New Divinity and their opponents. He became the preserve of religious liberals who esteemed him less as a theologian but more broadly as a philosopher and mystic, and even as a poet, and who regarded him as a world figure brooking comparison with major European thinkers. What during the last quarter of the nineteenth century might explain this sea change from the theological to the philosophical and aesthetic interpretations of Edwards?

One reason perhaps is that the traditional New England Theology (and with it the New Divinity) had become defunct, and so too, of course, the theology of Edwards that had engendered it. Oliver Wendell Holmes compared it in a poem to a "one-hoss shay," which being "built in such a logical way" then "went to pieces all at once."[10] The explanation for its demise lies in a radical shift in the American climate of opinion during the second half of the nineteenth century. The Higher (historical) Criticism of the Bible blew in from Germany, and Darwinism from England. During this period the old orthodoxy was replaced by the New Theology or Progressive Orthodoxy, and this was particularly true at the Andover Theological Seminary and the Episcopal Theological School.

Now Alexander V. G. Allen, Egbert Coffin Smyth, George Park Fisher, and William Harder Squires who helped shape the philosophical interpretation of

Edwards were theological liberals. They espoused the New Theology. Allen reacted against the evangelical party in the Episcopal Church. He would have abandoned the faith altogether, but for his reading of Coleridge (the broker of German idealism to James Marsh and Emerson). Allen eventually joined the faculty at the Episcopal Theological School.[11] Smyth, as a church historian, used the historical rather than the dogmatic method. When he came to Andover in the early 1880s, he was opposed by Edwards Amasa Park, a defender of the old New England Theology and a devotee of Edwards. Smyth was temporarily removed from his teaching position at Andover because of the liberal tendencies of some articles he had contributed to the *Andover Review*.[12] Both Fisher of Yale and Squires of Hamilton College had studied in Germany, a source of the new liberal ideas in philosophy and theology that shook up the old orthodoxy. Squires took the doctorate from the University of Leipzig where he wrote his dissertation on Edwards under the tutelage of the great experimental psychologist, Wilhelm Wundt.[13] It is little wonder, then, that these men, in their engagement with Edwards, distanced themselves from his Calvinist theology.

Another reason perhaps these scholars were so preoccupied with Edwards the philosopher as opposed to the theologian is that the prestige and autonomy of philosophy during the 1860s in America were increasing. Philosophy was less and less yoked with theology in the apologetic task of providing a rational defense of the faith. Philosophy was becoming secular, and if it were a handmaiden to anything, it was not to theology, but to science.

Further, there may have been a nationalistic motive behind these commentators' concern with the philosophical Edwards. Emerson, in "The American Scholar," America's declaration of intellectual and cultural independence, exhorted his listeners, "We have listened too long to the courtly muses of Europe."[14] What better than to find, in the colonial period no less, a homegrown American philosopher, and one, moreover, worthy to take his place with the best philosophers of Europe.

Edwards as Metaphysician.—Edwards the metaphysician dominated the thinking of those scholars whose studies constitute the second phase in the history of the interpretation and reception of Edwards. They include Georges Lyon, H. Norman Gardiner, Frederick J. E. Woodbridge, and I. Woodbridge Riley, along with the above-mentioned Allen, Smyth, Fisher, and Squires. They variously classified Edwards as an idealist, mystic, and pantheist.

Interest in Edwards as an idealist may be dated from 1871 with the publication that year of Alexander Campbell Fraser's *The Life and Letters of George Berkeley* where he was the first to propose that Edwards "adopted" and defended Berkeley's idealism. Following Fraser, Lyon in *L'Idéalisme en Angleterre au XVIII Siècle* (1888) attempted to demonstrate that Edwards' early idealism was indeed derived from Berkeley. Although Lyon proved to be wrong, he did succeed in focusing the main topic of Edwards scholarship for years to come. Lyon set subsequent scholars on the track of clarifying and tracing the sources of Edwards' idealism. One in particular was Gardiner who argued in "The Early Idealism of Jonathan Edwards" (1900) that Edwards' idealism was an original conception with him and lay at the very heart of his whole system of thought.[15]

However, some scholars interested in Edwards the metaphysician, such as Mattoon M. Curtis and Squires, went further afield and linked Edwards with some German philosophers. Curtis, in his "Kantean Elements in Jonathan Edwards,"[16] and Squires, in his "A Passage from Edwards' Speculative Metaphysics," noted intriguing similarities between Edwards and Kant such as their similar conceptions of space. Squires went even further by discerning a profound kinship between Edwards and both Schopenhauer and Wundt with respect to the will. According to Squires, Edwards is fundamentally a voluntarist who anticipates both the metaphysics of Schopenhauer and the psychology of Wundt.[17]

Curtis' and Squires' efforts to link Edwards with Kant's critical idealism, and with both Schopenhauer's metaphysical and Wundt's psychological voluntarism, are particularly significant insofar as they serve to bring Edwards into some main currents of nineteenth-century American philosophy: namely, the Platonic idealism of the Transcendentalists; the absolute idealism of the St. Louis Hegelians; and the voluntarism of both Royce and James.

This period's interest in Edwards' metaphysical idealism may be explained by three factors: the residual influence of the philosophical idealism underpinning the New Divinity; the availability of Edwards' early philosophical writings by 1830; and the tremendous impact of German idealism in America after 1830.

Metaphysical idealism had long been in the air. The New Divinity men worked within its framework. The philosophical foundations of their theology were set by such as Malebranche and Berkeley. Indeed, Joseph Periam, a tutor at Princeton during the 1760s, exposited Berkeley.[18] And though Edwards' own brand of idealism as contained in his early writings were not published until the end of the third decade of the nineteenth century, it is not impossible that Bellamy, Hopkins, and Jonathan Edwards, Jr.—all of whom knew Edwards personally—received some hint of it from the horse's mouth, so to speak.

Significantly, the years 1829 and 1830 saw the posthumous publication of Edwards' early writings. They were published by Edwards' great-grandson Sereno Dwight as part of a complete edition of Edwards' works.[19] They included Edwards' earliest essays, "The Mind" and "Of Being," which contain the substance of his idealist metaphysics. Edwards' earliest philosophical writings were now in circulation. Later in the century, Alexander B. Grosart took the manuscript of "The Mind" to Scotland, perhaps to publish it there, only to have it mysteriously disappear.[20] But Edwards' philosophical idealism was kept before the public's eye with the republication in 1895 of "Of Being," along with others of Edwards' early essays, under the title, "Some Early Writings of Jonathan Edwards, A.D. 1714–1726," in the *Proceedings of the American Antiquarian Society*.[21] Interestingly, they had been collated and edited by Smyth, one of Edwards' chief commentators during this second period in the interpretation of his thought.

Furthermore, philosophical idealism of one sort or another was regnant in the American academy after the Civil War, having usurped the position once enjoyed by Scottish Common Sense Realism. Curiously, the emergence of philosophical idealism in America coincides with the publication of Edwards' early philosophical writings and the scholarly interest taken in them. Thus, in 1829, the year Dwight began publishing Edwards' early philosophical essays, James Marsh, the Congregationalist president of the University of Vermont, published the first American edition of Samuel Taylor Coleridge's *Aids to Reflection,* together with an introduction from his own hand,[22] which had such an influence on Transcendentalism—incidentally, Emerson read it the year it came out. A scant seven years later, the Transcendental Club was formed in Concord and Emerson brought out his *Nature*. And in 1866, William Torrey Harris and Henry C. Brokmeyer founded the St. Louis Philosophical Society, dedicated to the promulgation of Hegelianism; the next year Harris established the *Journal of Speculative Philosophy*.[23] Exactly contemporary with Edwards' philosophical interpreters like Gardiner, Squires, and Riley was a constellation of distinguished American idealists including Royce, George Holmes Howison, Borden P. Bowne, and James E. Creighton. These circumstances form part of the intellectual background to the second phase in the interpretation of Edwards, and would partly explain the interest of such as Gardiner and Squires in Edwards' philosophy, and more particularly in his own form of metaphysical idealism. Kuklick writes, "At the end of the century Congregational theologians would find in philosophy only German ideas, and philosophers themselves, as they gained new respect, would enunciate varieties of idealism."[24]

Edwards as Mystic.—Typically, those commentators preoccupied with Edwards' idealism also discerned a deep strain of mysticism in Edwards that they believed informed not only his idealism but his determinism and alleged pantheism as well. Thus, according to Allen, whose magisterial *Life and Writings of Jonathan Edwards* (1889) served as the *locus classicus* for Edwards scholarship until the publication of Perry Miller's work, Edwards is best understood as fundamentally a mystic. Riley, citing Allen, demonstrated in his *American Philosophy: The Early Schools* (1907) how mysticism explains Edwards' central doctrines. It is noteworthy in this context that Riley himself, a pragmatist, was a follower of William James and sympathetic with mysticism.[25] And for Smyth, in his "The Theology of Edwards" (1904), it is Edwards' intense and abiding awareness of God's presence and agency that illuminates all his work.[26] Edwards' ecstatic "God-consciousness," so reminiscent of Spinoza, identifies Edwards as a mystic.

The interest taken in the mystical quality of Edwards' thought by his late nineteenth-century interpreters reflects the spirit of the times. It should be remembered that in the cultural background of these men lay Emerson's pantheistic "nature" mysticism and Whitman's more expansive "cosmic" mysticism. Moreover, exactly contemporary with them were those like William James and Richard M. Bucke who undertook the psychological study of mystical experience and thereby provided a philosophical apologetics for it. It should be noted that Bucke's *Cosmic Consciousness* came out in 1901, and James' *The Varieties of Religious Experience* (which Bucke greatly influenced) in 1902. For such as Emerson, Whitman, Bucke, and James, the experience of God was conceived of more broadly as the experience of the divine—however conceived, whether theistically, pantheistically, or naturalistically. Bucke called the highest form of this experience of the divine "cosmic consciousness," which he defined as a consciousness "of the life and order of the universe."[27] This for James represents the highest grade of mysticism, which he identifies as the essence of religion.[28] Now Edwards, with his consciousness of being in general, and his overwhelming sense of the fundamental harmony of all things, would certainly qualify as one who had attained to cosmic consciousness, much as Emerson and Whitman, among others whom Bucke cited, as having done so. Moreover, the experience of the divine as conceived of by Bucke and James did not require the intervention of a supernatural agent like the Holy Spirit as in the traditional Calvinist account of conversion. It was only natural, then, that Allen, Riley, and Smyth should think of Edwards as a mystic, indeed, as an eighteenth-century prototype of Emerson and Whitman, especially if they sought to rehabilitate Edwards' reputation tainted as it was by the *odium theologicum*.

Edwards as Aesthete.—Edwards scholars of the second period were drawn not only to Edwards the metaphysician and mystic, but no less to Edwards the poet. Allen and Squires both recognized the kinship between Edwards and Dante. Indeed, for Allen, Edwards in temperament and outlook more resembles Dante than Augustine and Calvin.[29] It is as a poet, and more broadly as a religious thinker like Royce and James, that Edwards' true stature is revealed.

Curiously, one who early on recognized the aesthetic significance of Edwards' thought was Harriet Beecher Stowe. The protagonist in her novel, *The Minister's Wooing,* is Samuel Hopkins, Edwards' erstwhile student and disciple. Her semi-fictional portrait of Hopkins could as well serve as a portrait of Edwards himself; she describes Hopkins as if he were Edwards reincarnated. Referring directly to Hopkins, and more obliquely to Edwards, she writes, "These hard old New England divines were poets of metaphysical philosophy, who built systems in an artistic fervor, and felt self exhale from beneath them as they rose into the higher regions of thought."[30]

Allen's and Squires' preoccupation with Edwards' aesthetic sensibility and the poetic qualities of his writings, which resulted in his portrait as an artist, reflects movements in the larger culture. In the period roughly from 1859 (interestingly, the year of both the completion of Wagner's *Tristan und Isolde* and the publication of Darwin's *Origin of Species*) to 1914 (the collapse of the *fin de siècle* culture after the Great War), the prestige of religion, particularly the conventional religiosity practiced in the churches, declined precipitously. This ebbing away of traditional faith during this period was given poignant expression in Matthew Arnold's *Dover Beach*—"The Sea of Faith / Was once, too, at the full, and round earth's shore . . . But now I only hear / Its melancholy, long, withdrawing roar."[31] The eclipse of God at this time was hastened by, among other things, the challenge of evolutionary biology and the allied sciences, and the trenchant critiques of Christianity and religion in general mounted by Nietzsche and Freud respectively.

Into the void left by the departure of religion burst art. Art—the visual arts, literature, and music—did not so much supplant religion as it became itself an ersatz religion. Masterpieces of fine art were venerated as virtual relics and sacraments providing the means to grace. Art as religion took basically two "denominational" forms. One form it took, particularly in England, was the Aesthetic Movement, whose mantra was "art-for-art's sake," and whose apostles were Oscar Wilde and Walter Pater. Art was its own excuse for being, and the purpose of life, and that which made life tolerable, was the maximum enjoyment of beauty—"To burn always with this hard, gemlike flame, to maintain this ecstasy, is success in life,"[32] in Pater's words. In France, the ideal of art being its own justification was lived out by the Symbolists, the chief among them being the poets Mallarmé and Verlaine who believed that the world existed only to be translated into poetry. The purpose of poetry, and art in general, was to suggest with the utmost subtlety the ineffable. Another form taken by the cult of art was the Pre-Raphaelite Brotherhood in England that regarded art as essentially didactic, as a moral force that could ring in a more just and free society. This utopian ideal of art, already implicit in Schiller's *Aesthetic Education of Man,* was pithily implied in Shelley's dictum that poets should be the unacknowledged legislators of the world, and lay behind Matthew Arnold's conception of poetry as the criticism of life. In Germany, Richard Wagner harbored the social and political hope (deeply tinctured by German nationalism) that through the "art-work of the future," of which he thought his own music dramas were harbingers, individuals and society might somehow be redeemed. The Festspielhaus in Bayreuth, a temple consecrated to the cult of art and presided over by Wagner himself, its high priest, remains today a palpable symbol of the nineteenth-century's idealization of art.

It is especially noteworthy that the aesthetic and idealistic mysticism of Edwards' typology of nature presages that of the French Symbolists. They too believed that the natural world was embosomed in an invisible but more real noumenal order that could at best only be represented through the poetic ordering of symbols (what Edwards called "types"). Moreover, Edgar Allan Poe was a precursor of French Symbolism and was acknowledged as such by Mallarmé. For this reason, Edwards might be associated with Poe.

Further, this kinship between Edwards and the Symbolists furnishes a clue as to why Allen and Squires compared Edwards specifically to Dante and not, say, to Milton. Milton would have been the more obvious choice. Milton, after all, wrote the founding epic of Protestantism (as Dante wrote the founding epic of Catholicism). Milton dealt poetically with the great themes of creation and redemption, which Edwards dealt with philosophically and theologically. And, not insignificantly, Edwards had a familiarity with this poet. So, what accounts for the comparison of Edwards with Dante? *The Divine Comedy* is a thoroughly symbolic or typological poem—it may be read as nothing less than a typology of St. Thomas' *Summa*. Edwards, of course, developed a complex typology through which he interpreted nature and history morally and spiritually. Edwards' types tie in with Dante's symbols.

Significantly, all the above scholars and commentators detected a fundamental instability in Edwards' thought occasioned by its incompatible elements. Allen discerned a conflict between Edwards' mysticism and his theology. For Allen, the real Edwards was a mystic who inwardly rebelled against his ancestral Calvinism. Gardiner and Woodbridge found the major fault line of his thought lying between his Calvinist theology and his Enlightenment philosophy, which, they contended, he failed to reconcile.[33]

Some, like Fisher and Lyon, lamented that Edwards' philosophy was hampered by what they thought was an obsolete theology. Fisher believed that Edwards would have ranked with Berkeley, Hume, and Kant in the pantheon of eighteenth-century philosophy had he devoted himself single-mindedly to metaphysics. And Lyon mused that had Edwards' philosophical development not been arrested by his remoteness from the European centers of learning and by the strictures of Calvinism, he might have taken his rightful place as the greatest metaphysician between Leibniz and Kant.[34]

The same man, however, is recognizable in these apparently diverse portraits of Edwards as philosopher, mystic, and poet. It is Edwards the idealist. Idealism is what shines through these various interpretations of his thought.

Edwards was a metaphysical idealist in two distinct but complementary senses, both a "rational" idealist and a "mystical" idealist. He was a rational idealist insofar as, in the manner of Berkeley, he logically deduced the unreality of matter and the sole reality of mind in "Of Being" and "The Mind." He was a mystical idealist, like Emerson, insofar as he explained in *A Divine and Supernatural Light* and *Religious Affections* that God could be known immediately through intuition, that this intuitive knowledge is superior to a ratiocinative knowledge of God, and that partial union with God was possible. Moreover, in *A Personal Narrative* and *Images or Shadows of Divine Things* he conceives of nature typologically as a system of hieroglyphics importing moral and spiritual meanings.

Edwards' mystical idealism, however, requires further qualification. It was aesthetic, and in two senses. First, Edwards compared the mystical intuition of God, what he called the "new sense of the heart," to immediate sensory experience. Second, the object of that mystical intuition or sensation was the divine beauty, which, for Edwards, is God's supreme attribute. Finally, mystical apprehension, though cognitive, was no less affective insofar as it was accompanied by and distinguished by ecstatic joy.

The Sesquicentenary of 1900

On June 22, 1900, a century and a half after Edwards' dismissal from his Northampton pastorate, commemorative exercises were held at the First Church of Christ in Northampton, the site of Edwards' church, to mark the unveiling of a memorial plaque in his honor. Addresses were also delivered on this occasion. The following year these addresses were published as *Jonathan Edwards: A Retrospect* under the editorship of Gardiner, a professor of philosophy at Smith College and chairman of the memorial committee.

Predictably, three of the addresses were delivered by Allen, Smyth, and Gardiner, whose views are discussed above. These commemorative addresses are significant, then, because they form a synopsis of Edwards scholarship at the dawn of the twentieth century and mark symbolically the end of the second phase in the history of the interpretation of Edwards. Gardiner hoped that they would "help somewhat to bring out in true historical perspective the real Edwards." In his introduction to *A Retrospect*, Gardiner remarked on the need for a study of Edwards' philosophy as whole, a need, incidentally, that yet remains unmet at the beginning of the twenty-first century. Commenting on the authors of these addresses, Gardiner said, revealingly, that some of Edwards' "most appreciative students and ardent admirers chose to represent him less as a theologian than as a prophet of the Christian faith, an interpreter of human life, a force in religious experience, and profess to see in him less affinity with Calvin than with Dante."[35] In other words, they esteemed Edwards less narrowly as a theologian and more broadly as a religious thinker and poet.

In his address, "The Place of Edwards in History," Allen voices his judgment that Edwards is greater as "a poetic interpreter of life" than as even a theologian, and as such has a deep kinship with Dante. According to Allen, "The deepest affinity of Edwards was not that with Calvin or with Augustine, but with the great Florentine poet."[36] Allen notes that Edwards and Dante occupy similar historical positions. Dante was a precursor of the Renaissance, but no less a poetic apostle of Thomas Aquinas. He thus bound Thomism with the classical humanism of the Renaissance. Similarly, Edwards stood at the threshold of a new age. He was a precursor of the humanitarianism associated with the Enlightenment, and yet was a scion of the Reformation. Edwards infused Reformed theology with the philosophy of the Enlightenment.

It is noteworthy that Squires too found an analogy between Edwards and Dante. Like Allen, he notes that both are transitional figures. Further, Squires reads Edwards' imprecatory sermons on hell as constituting his Inferno. We might add that Edwards' sermons on heaven constitute his Paradiso.

For Allen, Edwards, like William James, is principally a great phenomenologist of religion. Edwards "has given such a picture of the reality and rich variety of the interior life of religion as was never given before."[37] Not surprisingly, Allen thinks that Edwards' works dealing with the varieties of religious experience have more permanent value than his theological productions concerned with free will and original sin. Allen regarded *Religious Affections* as Edwards' greatest work.

Smyth's address, "The Influence of Edwards on the Spiritual Life of New England," is a panegyric on what he takes to be "Edwards' transcendent spiritual personality." Smyth, like Allen, sees Edwards' chief value in his phenomenology of religious experience. He consequently gives special attention to the treatise on *Religious Affections* and the sermon, *A Divine and Spiritual Light*. For Smyth, Edwards is pre-eminently a "synthesist."[38] Edwards assimilates the affections to the will, ties the will to the understanding, and conceives of these twin faculties to be capacities exercised by a unified self. A consequence of Edwards' conception of a unified self is an expanded idea of reason allowing for spiritual perception, a sense of the heart, which combines cognition with emotion. Among others of Edwards' merits, according to Smyth, is his reconciliation of faith with reason, his fusion of religion with morality, and his tying of faith to works.

George A. Gordon, in his contribution to the commemorative exercises of 1900, "The Significance of Edwards for To-day," pays "critical homage" to Edwards. Gordon recognizes that in the thought of any great thinker, and he specifically cites Plato and Dante as examples, there is much chaff mixed in with the wheat, and it is the job of modern commentators to separate them. This is no less true of Edwards' thought. "The truth in him [Edwards] is massive and precious, but it lies as gold lies in the rock. It must be delivered from encompassing error, set free, purified and brought to its full value through the fires of a happier experience. He is not a temple, he is a quarry." Gordon acknowledges Edwards' greatness as a philosopher and theologian. He contends that "the absoluteness of God is the heart of Edwards' thinking."[39] Gordon's chief demurral on Edwards is that his theology overshadows his anthropology—he exalts God, but at the expense of man. Gordon finds potential value in Edwards for the church at the turn of the twentieth century. He believes that Edwards might help bridge the gap between the Trinitarian and the Unitarian, between the conservative and the liberal in theology. Finally, it is noteworthy that Gordon agrees with Allen and Squires that Edwards is the American Dante.

The topic of Gardiner's address, "The Early Idealism of Edwards," is Edwards' early metaphysical speculations. Gardiner states the views summarized above in connection with Edwards' idealism, namely that it "was with him an original expression of personal insight, and that there is no reason to suppose that he ever abandoned it; that in short it was no mere accidental product of youthful fancy, or echo of another's teaching, but was intimately connected with the deepest and most permanent elements of his speculation."[40] Gardiner demonstrated that Edwards' idealism was not derived from Berkeley, but was original with him and perhaps suggested by his reading of Locke, Newton, and Ralph Cudworth—sources available as well to Berkeley. Gardiner's judgment as to Edwards' independence of Berkeley in this respect has been subsequently vindicated.

It is of interest to note, in passing, who did not attend the commemorative exercises held in Northampton in June of 1900, or at least did not address the conference. Conspicuous by their apparent absence were Josiah Royce and William James, both of whom were teaching at Harvard at the time and were no further away than Allen, who was teaching at the neighboring Episcopal seminary in Cambridge. Royce's absence is especially strange given the high praise he had for Edwards. Squires' apparent absence is also puzzling, for in October of 1903 he would bring out his quarterly periodical, *The Edwardean,* to honor the bicentenary of Edwards' birth. Squires was as much concerned with commemorating Edwards as Gardiner et al. He was not far away since he lived in Clinton, New York, where he taught at Hamilton College.

The Historical Phase

The lines of inquiry opened up by the first generation of Edwards scholars and their subsequent interpretations of him were continued and extensively developed by their twentieth-century successors. The various intellectual portraits of Edwards sketched by his nineteenth-century commentators were fleshed out with brighter colors and finer details by their counterparts in the next century. Nevertheless, a new note was sounded.

What most distinguishes this third and ongoing phase of the reception and interpretation of Edwards is the attempt to see him for what he really was in terms of his time and place. Commentators now, by and large, did not critically appropriate and develop Edwards' thought, as did the New Divinity men, or recast it in the image of the popular philosophy of the day, as did the liberal scholars of the second phase, but instead they aimed at contextualizing and embedding it in the larger culture. Some of the most significant studies of Edwards from this period go some way in putting him in his historical context. In this respect, many Edwards scholars in the twentieth century reflected the historicism regnant in the academy during that time. They were engaged in the quest for the historical

Edwards. The twentieth century and beyond, then, marks the historical phase in the interpretation of Edwards.

Three events were critical in providing impetus to the historical contextualization of Edwards' thought. One was the publication in 1907 of Frank Hugh Foster's *A Genetic History of the New England Theology,* which, in retrospect, may be taken as inaugurating the historical phase of the interpretation of Edwards. For Foster, Edwards was essentially a Calvinist theologian, though not unoriginal. He emphasizes Edwards' theory of the will, his voluntarism, in contrast to his idealism. He sets Edwards against the crisis underwent by New England Calvinism during the first half of the eighteenth century. The crisis was precipitated by the challenges to Calvinist orthodoxy from Arminianism and Deism. According to Foster, Edwards was the man who met these challenges philosophically and theologically by grafting the best in the new way of ideas represented by the Enlightenment into the body of Reformed theology so as to revitalize it.[41]

The work of historicizing Edwards begun by Foster was continued and abetted by Perry Miller in his landmark studies dating from around the mid-century. Miller embedded Edwards in the context of eighteenth-century philosophy and science by showing his deep indebtedness to the empiricism of John Locke. He saw Edwards as grappling with Locke's leading ideas so as to adapt them to his own purposes.

However, the project that more than any other laid the foundation for the historical study of Edwards was the continuing publication, beginning in 1956, of *The Works of Jonathan Edwards* by Yale University Press. This, when completed, will be the first scholarly and critical edition of the complete Edwards corpus and has so far proven indispensable to those scholars committed to the historical study of Edwards. The Yale volumes provide accurate and annotated texts with lengthy editorial introductions describing Edwards' sources and the historical circumstances that prompted him to write them.

The following discussion of the historical phase in the interpretation of Edwards does not pretend to be a complete review of the secondary literature on Edwards, the items of which now number in the thousands, but instead a cursory description of its major trends. Those works of scholarship are included that either continue insightfully and vigorously lines of investigation begun in the nineteenth century or blaze new paths of inquiry.

Two early commentators from the first half of the twentieth century agreed with such as Allen, Gardiner, and Woodbridge that Edwards' thought is riven by a fundamental and irreconcilable division or conflict. Consequently, they cast him in the role of tragic hero. According to Ola E. Winslow in *Jonathan Edwards, 1703–1758: A Biography* (1940), Edwards' profound religious insights were stifled by an obsolete and dogmatic Calvinistic system. He was like a butterfly that failed to break quite free of its chrysalis. For Vernon L. Parrington in *Main Currents in American Thought* (1927), Edwards naturally was inclined towards mysticism and a nascent form of transcendentalism, but was arrested in their pursuit by his youthful conversion to Calvinism. Edwards sought to reconcile a conservative theology with a liberal philosophy, but failed, and therein lay his tragedy.

One ongoing inquiry has been into determining the "real" Edwards, an inquiry prompted and made more difficult given Edwards' amphibious relationship to both the Reformed tradition and the Enlightenment: Was Edwards fundamentally a philosopher with modern, even radically modern, tendencies who tragically was hobbled by the trammels of his inherited Calvinism? Or was he, instead, nothing of the sort, but in reality an orthodox enough theologian, dedicated to Anselm's mission of faith-seeking understanding, who used the natural and moral philosophy of the Enlightenment simply to shore up his inherited Calvinism? Or, perhaps, at heart he was neither, but instead a mystic and poet.

Another inquiry, related to the above, has been into both the influences on Edwards and the influences from him on subsequent American thinkers, or at least into continuities and similarities between him and them. Interestingly, those scholars most impressed by Edwards' modernism were also among those intent on tracing his ideas to Locke and Newton, the twin architects of the Enlightenment, as if to validate his philosophical pedigree.

Another inquiry has been made into Edwards' vibrant aesthetic sensibility. Allen and Squires had celebrated Edwards as Dante *redivivus*. However, their twentieth-century counterparts see in Edwards' prose more than a practicing poet. They have demonstrated, and to some extent reconstructed, the coherent aesthetic theory implicit in his system. Edwards has lately been revealed as a theoretical aesthetician as well as a poet, like Friedrich Schiller and George Santayana.

Twentieth-century commentators have also opened up new fields of investigation such as those into Edwards' social and political thought and its impact on American culture at large from which new themes have emerged.

The quest for the "real" Edwards gave rise to some of the most important twentieth-century studies and set the tone for others. Like Allen, Gardiner, and Woodbridge in the previous generation, Harvey Gates Townsend, Miller, and Sang Hyun Lee focus on Edwards the metaphysician and philosopher. Townsend, in *Philosophical Ideas in the United States* (1934), extols Edwards as chiefly a metaphysician: "The metaphysical and logical writings of Edwards are of greater philosophical importance than all the remainder of his work."[42]

Miller, in his groundbreaking *Jonathan Edwards* (1949), reveals two "Edwardses"—Edwards the Calvinist theologian and Edwards the boldly unorthodox philosopher. Indeed, he goes so far as to claim that Edwards' work must be read as a vast cryptogram whose actual meaning must be sought between the lines. Miller asserts, controversially, that the "real" Edwards was a philosophical naturalist. For Miller, Edwards was essentially a modern thinker who, incredibly, anticipated Freud and Einstein. He was not only in advance of his own enlightened age but even of the twentieth century, which, Miller thinks, has scarcely caught up with him.

According to Sang Hyun Lee in *The Philosophical Theology of Jonathan Edwards* (1988), Edwards was engaged in nothing less than a radical reconstruction of metaphysics. Instead of conceiving of reality through the traditional categories of substance and form inherited from Aristotle, Edwards reconceived it as a matrix of active dispositions or habits. Edwards' dispositional, dynamic, and relational ontology provides the interpretative key for unlocking the fundamental unity of Edwards' thought. Further, Edwards' metaphysical reconstruction, by representing a *via media* between classic theism and process theology, reveals his relevance for contemporary philosophical theology.

However, some revisionist scholars have taken exception to the above portrait of Edwards as a preternaturally modern philosopher ill at ease with his Calvinist heritage. Like Foster in the previous century, they have limned an alternative portrait of Edwards as a rock-ribbed Calvinist theologian.

Thus, Conrad Charles Cherry, in *The Theology of Jonathan Edwards: A Reappraisal* (1966), interprets Edwards through the latter's doctrine of faith and concludes that he is first and last a Reformed theologian. Edwards' only interest in the philosophy and science of his day was as a quarry of ideas with which to rebut the Arminians and Deists and to recast and buttress the faith of his fathers.

William J. Scheick, in *The Writings of Jonathan Edwards: Theme, Motif, and Style* (1975), agrees with Cherry's overall assessment arguing that Edwards is less a modern thinker and more a traditional and orthodox one who derived his primary inspiration from his Puritan past. He simply refashioned the advanced ideas of the Enlightenment to bolster Puritan dogma.

Other revisionists, moreover, have gone further by objecting to the mostly humanistic tenor of Edwards scholarship, which has colored it from its inception. Richard C. DeProspo, in *Theism in the Discourse of Jonathan Edwards* (1985), scores the humanistic interpretations of Edwards for being entirely at odds with Edwards' radical theocentrism.

Two of the most extreme revisionists are Iain H. Murray and John H. Gerstner. Murray, in his hagiographic *Jonathan Edwards: A New Biography* (1987), hopes to redeem Edwards from the "preserve of academics" who are in thrall to an "anti-supernatural animus" and reclaim him for the church. In the multivolume *The Rational Biblical Theology of Jonathan Edwards* (1991–1993), Gerstner provides a systematic and encyclopedic digest of Edwards' theological doctrines in completion of the task that Edwards had set himself in "A Rational Account" but did not live to complete. Gerstner writes as if Edwards had uttered the last word in divinity. Oddly and perhaps unwittingly, he gives a Gnostic gloss on Edwards by affirming that he came closer than anyone else did to reading the mind of God through the lenses of reason and biblical hermeneutics. Gerstner retrospectively sees in Edwards a defender of the Fundamentals of the faith, and so an apologist for Christian Fundamentalism two hundred years or so in advance of that reactionary movement.

Vincent Tomas, in John Opie, Jr.'s *Jonathan Edwards and the Enlightenment* (1969), also disputes the portrayal of Edwards as a modern thinker and heir to the Enlightenment, but not as the above revisionists do in order to rehabilitate Edwards the orthodox theologian, or to restore Edwards the prophet to his rightful place as one who speaks truth to the contemporary church. Rather, Tomas dismisses Edwards as essentially a medieval thinker and little else.

Douglas J. Elwood, in *The Philosophical Theology of Jonathan Edwards* (1960), attempts to harmonize these contrasting portraits of Edwards and to mediate the oft-remarked conflict between Edwards' theology and his philosophy. According to Elwood, Edwards synthesized the classic theism of Calvinism with the pantheistic elements of Neo-Platonism to produce the hybrid panentheism, the doctrine that holds together both God's immanence and transcendence. Furthermore, Elwood finds Edwards' ongoing relevance is his emphasis on God's immediacy in human experience, a facet of divine immanence.

Tracking Edwards' ideas to their seventeenth- and eighteenth-century sources and tracing their influences on or continuities with nineteenth- and twentieth-century American thinkers were major undertakings of Edwards scholars throughout the twentieth century and resulted in some landmark studies.

Lyon's pioneering effort to find Edwards' philosophical patrimony continued with increased vigor and precision in the twentieth century. However, Lyon's successors believed that Edwards' thought derived not from Berkeley but from Locke and Newton.

Miller led the way in several studies, which, in addition to his earlier *Jonathan Edwards,* included *Errand into the Wilderness* (1956) and his *Images and Shadows of Divine Things by Jonathan Edwards* (1948). As did Lyon, Gardiner, and Townsend, Miller finds the key to Edwards in his youthful philosophical and scientific writings. As Hume would awaken Kant from his dogmatic slumbers, so Locke, according to Miller, performed a similar office for Edwards by making him an empiricist. Further, Edwards adopted Locke's distinction between word and idea. Edwards' great discovery, in Miller's view, was that ideas have both cognitive and affective value, i.e., they not only lodge in the understanding but necessarily draw out from us an emotional response in the form of some degree of either love or hate. To know something only by its signs or words is not really to know it at all; but to know it as an idea is to know it all.

Herbert Warren Richardson, in his doctoral dissertation, "The Glory of God in the Theology of Jonathan Edwards: A Study in the Doctrine of the Trinity" (1962), follows Miller in finding that Edwards built on the foundations of Locke and Newton. According to Richardson, Edwards developed Locke's epistemology as Newton developed Robert Boyle's physics. A problem common to both Locke's theory of ideas and Boyle's atomism was the ontological status of relations. Newton's theory of gravity was the solution to the problem raised by Boyle's physics, i.e., the relations of atoms. In Newton's theory of gravity, Edwards found clues for solving the problem raised by Locke's epistemology, i.e., the relations of simple ideas. Edwards' solution is his theory of consent (excellency or beauty), which is isomorphic with Newton's theory of gravity. On Richardson's account, Edwards applied his theory of relations of ideas to recast the doctrine of the Trinity. Incidentally, Leo Sandon, Jr. has hailed Richardson's dissertation as "definitive" a study of Edwards' theology as Perry Miller's work was of Edwards' thought in general.[43]

James Pearce Carse, in his *Jonathan Edwards and the Visibility of God* (1967), agrees with Miller that Edwards follows in Locke's footsteps, but not in lockstep. Carse thinks that Edwards' thought is driven by his critique of Locke. Locke made a sharp distinction between appearance and reality—between our ideas derived from sensory experience that we know and the *substratum* producing them that, in principle, we can never know. According to Carse, the decisive moment in Edwards' philosophical development occurred when he collapsed Locke's metaphysical distinction. For Edwards, "things are what they appear to be" or "appearances are all there are." Thus, reason cannot carry us beyond the phenomenal world to some presumed noumenal world of things-in-themselves as they really are since there is nothing beyond the world of appearances. Consequently, God must be visible, if anywhere, in the world of phenomena. Carse, then, characterizes Edwards as a philosophical and theological phenomenalist.

Wallace Earl Anderson, in his introduction to the fifth volume of the Yale edition of Edwards entitled, *The Philosophical and Scientific Writings* (1977), searches out the roots of Edwards' thought. Like Miller, Richardson, and Carse, he discovers these roots in Locke and Newton. However, he also acknowledges the influence of the Cambridge Platonists, in particular Henry More. It is noteworthy, moreover, that Anderson's introduction is the most thorough and comprehensive survey of Edwards' scientific thought to date.

Emily Stipes Watts in her doctoral dissertation, "Jonathan Edwards and the Cambridge Platonists" (1963), makes specific the manifold influence of the Cambridge Platonists on Edwards. She contends that Edwards derived his idealism from Ralph Cudworth, his conception of true virtue from Henry More, his understanding of religious experience from John Smith, and his typology and philosophy of history perhaps from Theophilus Gale.

On the other hand, William S. Morris, in his doctoral dissertation, "The Young Jonathan Edwards: A Reconstruction" (1956), identifies the Dutch scholastic logicians Heereboord and Burgersdijck as major sources of Edwards' metaphysics.

Other scholars, for example, Harold P. Simonson and Paul Helm, have disputed Edwards' dependence on Locke, and have even suggested that Edwards was not an empiricist at all. Thus, Simonson, in *Jonathan Edwards: Theologian of the Heart* (1974) claims, *contra* Miller among others, that Edwards' "sense of the heart" is not ultimately reducible to Lockean sensationalism or aesthetic sensibility, but it is rather a capacity through faith actually to experience God's glory and to understand that it is the end of creation.

Norman Fiering in *Jonathan Edwards's Moral Thought and Its British Context* (1981), as his title suggests, continues the work of others of embedding Edwards' thought in its time and place. According to Fiering, Edwards had to meet the challenge of the new naturalistic ethics that was variously developed by Samuel Clark, Anthony Ashley Cooper (Third Earl of Shaftesbury), Francis Hutcheson, Joseph Butler, David Hume, et al. Edwards met this challenge by first mounting a trenchant critique of this new moral philosophy on its own terms. He then constructed his own systematic ethics out of the refurbished ideas of the British moral philosophers, with whom he was sympathetic, but in the spirit of the seventeenth-century Continental rationalists like Spinoza, Malebranche, and Leibniz. Fiering considers that ethics is the best and most enduring part of Edwards' thought since he shows what religion contributes to the moral life.

Like Fiering, Michael J. McClymond shows that Edwards entered the lists in some of the major intellectual disputes of his day where he acted as a mediator. In *Encounters with God: An Approach to the Theology of Jonathan Edwards*

(1998), McClymond presents a synoptic view of Edwards by integrating the multiple facets of his thought and embedding it in its eighteenth-century context. He understands Edwards to have been principally engaged in mounting an apologetics for the Christian faith by appropriating and adapting the Enlightenment ideas stemming from Newton and Locke. McClymond thinks that Edwards has particular significance for us today insofar as he mediated between the metaphysical extremes of supernaturalism and naturalism, and thus between the liberal and conservative tendencies evident in religion to this day.

Some twentieth-century commentators have investigated Edwards' possible influence on American thinkers who came after him, but not nearly to the same extent or with the same success as they have inquired into the influences on him. Mention has been made above of Ahlstrom's and Kuklick's tracing Edwards' influence on the New Divinity theologians, and on Kuklick's tracing it down even further to Dewey. Royce, as mentioned earlier, though professing his philosophical kinship with Edwards, did not acknowledge that Edwards had influenced him. I know of only one thinker of any stature who has publicly attested to Edwards' influence on him, and that is H. Richard Niebuhr. In *The Kingdom of God in America* (1937), Niebuhr reveals his intellectual debt to Edwards in helping to shape his theology of radical monotheism.

However, commentators have been more convincing and successful in revealing continuities and similarities between Edwards' ideas and those of later thinkers. A pioneer in this regard is Miller again who, in *Errand into the Wilderness,* revealed intellectual and spiritual continuities between Edwards and Emerson. William A. Clebsch, in *American Religious Thought: A History* (1973), links Edwards not only with Emerson and but also with William James as advocates of an aesthetic spirituality in contrast to a prosaic moralism.

Several twentieth-century studies have added detail and depth to Allen's and Squire's portraits of Edwards as artist by revealing him to be also an important philosophical aesthetician. In agreement with his nineteenth-century predecessors,

Miller characterizes Edwards as an artist whose medium was not tones or paint but words. Roland Andre Delattre went further. In his landmark *Beauty and Sensibility in the Thought of Jonathan Edwards: An Essay in Aesthetics and Theological Ethics* (1968), Delattre argues that the aesthetic categories of beauty and sensibility inform the whole of Edwards' thought. Beauty, as the first principle of being, is the central category of Edwards' ontology and, as the objective basis and measure of goodness, beauty is the central category of his axiology or general theory of value. According to Delattre, Edwards elevates beauty to first place among the divine attributes. Beauty is Edwards' "primary model of order," the model for God's governance of the world, and both the goal and means of redemption.

Terrence Erdt, in his *Jonathan Edwards: Art and the Sense of the Heart,* puts Edwards' aesthetics in historical perspective. He traces the sense of the heart, the "cornerstone" of Edwards' aesthetics, not to Locke's sensationalist psychology but to Calvin's *sensus suavitatis.* The saint's sense of the heart is awakened to spiritual beauty, the images of which she discerns in the beauties of nature and art. By thus relating the beauty of spirit to that of nature and art Edwards may have sired the theories of moral beauty found in later American writers.

Richard Cartwright Austin, in *Beauty of the Lord: Awakening the Senses,* links Edwards' aesthetics with his ethics by finding in Edwards' theory of beauty a foundation for an environmental ethics.

A new note was sounded in twentieth-century commentaries on Edwards in the form of studies devoted to the socio-political implications of his thought for the larger culture and its history.

The pioneer study of Edwards and his impact on American culture was undertaken by Miller's student, Alan Heimert. In his *Religion and the American Mind: From the Great Awakening to the American Revolution* (1966), Heimert considers the socio-political implications of Edwards' thought. Heimert's thesis is that Edwards provided the American colonies with a radically democratic and nationalistic polity. Edwards' eschatology promised a new age where America would play a major role. Further, Heimert gives a Roycean interpretation of Edwards by contending that Edwards' God is nothing other than "a supremely excellent Christian commonwealth."

Contrary to Heimert, however, M. Darrol Bryant argues, in his *Jonathan Edwards' Grammar of Time, Self, and Society: A Critique of the Heimert Thesis* (1993), that Edwards was a prophet of a transcendent, not secular, kingdom and provides, not a rationale for American nationalism, but rather a critical commentary on it and other nascent tendencies emerging in colonial American culture.

Richard A. S. Hall, in *The Neglected Northampton Texts of Jonathan Edwards: Edwards on Society and Politics* (1990), argues from these texts dating from the last three years of Edwards' Northampton pastorate that Edwards, contrary to those who denied it, did indeed have implicitly a coherent social and political philosophy. Hall shows, among other things, that Edwards' ideal of citizenship is a "radical public-mindedness"; that his ethics is fundamentally social in character insofar as he defines "true virtue" as loyalty to or solidarity with the most inclusive community of persons; and that Edwards sought to implement his social ideal by turning his congregation into an "exclusive society of the visibly benevolent"—a deeper reason, Hall contends, for his dismissal from his pulpit.

Gerald R. McDermott, in *One Holy and Happy Society: The Public Theology of Jonathan Edwards* (1992), derives the social and political implications of Edwards' thought from a close reading of some of Edwards' occasional sermons. These sermons were in effect jeremiads that subverted any nascent ambitions of manifest destiny. McDermott shows that Edwards' postmillennialism embraced the whole of humanity, not any particular nation or state, thereby strengthening Bryant's argument against Heimert. Edwards' concepts of citizenship and magistracy were liberal and subtle, and not designed to safeguard the powers and privileges of the powerful. McDermott, then, represents Edwards as something of a Social Gospeller who was solicitous of those marginalized by society, and whose signal contribution was to show the relation of individual piety to the social and political spheres.

Some recent studies are difficult to classify since they intensively focus on a single topic in Edwards, yet in so doing illuminate other topics and link him with thinkers who preceded or succeeded him. Three such studies are in-depth inquiries into Edwards' typology, a theme, incidentally, broached early on by Miller who claimed that Edwards, inspired by his reading of Locke and Newton, expanded the range of biblical typology.

Following Miller's insights, Mason I. Lowance, in *The Language of Canaan: Metaphor and Symbol in New England from the Puritans to the Transcendentalists* (1980) and elsewhere, argues that Edwards broadened the scope of traditional Puritan typology by applying it as a hermeneutic principle with which to interpret both nature and history. By thus allegorizing natural phenomena so as to unlock their spiritual import, Edwards reconciles the book of nature with scripture. Furthermore, Lowance attributes to Edwards an "original epistemology," based on Locke's empirical psychology, through which to discern God in nature. As did Miller earlier, Lowance sees in Edwards' theory of types an anticipation of Emerson.

Conrad Cherry, in *Nature and Religious Imagination from Bushnell to Edwards* (1980), explains the relationship between Edwards' conception of nature and his religious epistemology and its bearing on nineteenth-century American religious thought and practice. Specifically, he shows how through his theory of language and epistemology Edwards construed the world as a symbol freighted with divine meaning, an idea that Bushnell would rehabilitate.

Paula M. Cooey, in *Jonathan Edwards on Nature and Destiny: A Systematic Analysis* (1985), considers Edwards' theory of types in the context of his theology of nature. According to Cooey, Edwards conceived of nature eschatologically as the medium through which God communicates his purposes, and as such, nature is the key to understanding the unity of his thought.

Thus, the scholarship on Edwards since 1769 has exhibited a remarkable thematic continuity and development. As we have seen, the three phases of Edwardsean interpretation that are identifiable and distinct chronologically, nonetheless, do overlap thematically. For example, the philosophical interpretation of Edwards regnant in the second period survived in the studies of Miller and Lee in the third period. The strictly theological interpretation dominant in the first period was revived by Foster in the second, and by such as Cherry and Gerstner in the third period. And the aesthetic interpretation of Edwards by Allen and Squires in the second period was continued and enriched by Delattre, Erdt, and Austin in the third period.

In retrospect, we can see that Miller's groundbreaking studies on Edwards is as significant for the reception and interpretation of Edwards in the twentieth century as Dwight's publication of Edwards' early writings was for that of the nineteenth century. Miller is a pivotal figure: he is a Janus who looks both backwards and forwards. On the one hand, he is the culmination of the second phase of Edwards scholarship. He put the finishing touches to the composite portrait of Edwards that was unveiled in the late nineteenth century, that of a modern philosopher who expressed himself as an artist. On the other hand, he heralds the historically minded third period with his endeavor to find the sources of Edwards' thought and its family resemblances to that of later American thinkers. As Whitehead characterized the history of philosophy as so many footnotes to Plato, so the history of Edwards scholarship since 1945 may be characterized as so many footnotes to Miller. Like any founder, though, Miller is nothing if not controversial. Miller's scholarship "has been praised and damned, but it has left no one indifferent."[44] He was, as Bertrand Russell said of Kant, great even in his mistakes, but these may have been more overstatements and sins of omission. His critics honor him by seeing him as someone worthy of their criticisms.

Edwards' stature as both an original philosopher and a theologian has steadily increased and has been better understood and appreciated. His intellectual lineage has now been more carefully and thoroughly mapped out, and shown to have roots traceable to not only Locke and Newton, but also to the Cambridge Platonists and perhaps even some of the Continental rationalists as well. Edwards' influence on, or at least kinship with, later American thinkers has been investigated and to some extent established. His much-vaunted aesthetic sensibility is now understood as part of a larger aesthetic conception of reality. Further, new lines of inquiry were opened such as those into Edwards' socio-political philosophy and his impact on American culture, and his typology.

Moreover, the historicizing of Edwards throughout the twentieth century may be the means of resolving that intractable conflict some have detected in his thought. For Allen it is a conflict between theology and mysticism; for Gardiner and Woodbridge, it is the conflict between theology and philosophy; and for Miller the conflict is more profound since it is between what Edwards said in public and what he believed in private, the two things being opposites. The perception of a conflict in Edwards' thought presupposes that it is all of a logical piece like Holmes' "one-hoss shay," that all of his subsequent works are simply workings out of ideas first articulated in his early essays, much as a fugue is the working out of the contrapuntal implications of a single, simple theme. However, Bryant, Nancy Manspeaker, Virginia Peacock, Hall and others in studying Edwards under Richardson's direction in Toronto during the 1970s and early 1980 paid close attention to Edwards' texts in their historical contexts. As a result, they found textual evidence that over time Edwards did change his mind, and his thought certainly developed, partly to meet new exigencies posed by his culture and partly as the expression of his own ranging mind. Edwards' thought, then, resembles more a sonata in which contrasting themes develop and actually come into dramatic conflict. In this respect, Edwards resembles Bertrand Russell who was notorious for changing his mind over a long career. To dismiss philosophers for changing their minds is to commit a form of the *tu quoque* fallacy.

The Northampton Tercentenary of 2003

Between October 3 and October 5 of 2003, the Tercentenary Celebration of Edwards' birth was held at the First Churches of Northampton, the very site of the conference held on June 22, 1900, to commemorate the sesquicentennial of Edwards' dismissal. The papers presented at the tercentenary celebration, like those delivered at the conference of 1900, provide a glimpse at the state of Edwards scholarship early in the twenty-first century. As might be expected they follow some of the same lines of inquiry that mark the first century and a quarter of Edwards scholarship. Interestingly, they recapitulate, thematically if not chronologically, the theological, philosophical, and historical phases described above. Further, the papers reveal the multifacetedness of Edwards' thought. Edwards was a polymath—pastor, theologian, natural and moral philosopher, mystic, and poet—and thus has been appropriated by a variety of academic disciplines—church history, theology, philosophy, literature, and the history of science. Most of these papers naturally cluster themselves into distinct groups based upon their thematic continuities.

It is interesting that these papers should spontaneously exhibit these thematic continuities and comfortably belong to one or another of the three phases of Edwards scholarship, especially so since our call for papers prescribed for them no topical plan but left open what their authors would choose to address.

The collection opens with the banquet address by Huston Smith, chairman of the Tercentenary Celebration. We were delighted when he accepted our invitation to chair the conference. It was appropriate that he do so since he is the foremost living scholar in comparative religions and their history. It was a high honor to have him in attendance. Smith reminisces nostalgically about going to Methodist revival meetings on the Great Plains, a peculiarly American form of religiosity. This is especially appropriate given the subject of this tercentenary. Revivalism was a fruit of both the Great Awakening and the Second Great Awakening to which Edwards was either directly or indirectly a stimulus.

In the first group of papers, Herbert W. Richardson, M. Darrol Bryant, and James Hewitson consider Edwards as a social and political philosopher and as a critic of culture and ideologies, and variously describe his conception of the good society.

According to Richardson, there is an unacknowledged founding figure in the history of the American Republic. Along with the well-known political founding fathers—Washington, Jefferson, Adams, et al.—and no less important culturally, there stands another, Jonathan Edwards, who ranks as America's spiritual founding father. Richardson links Edwards with Abraham Lincoln, which is appropriate enough if for no other reason than that Lincoln is, as it were, the founding father of the federal state forged in the crucible of the Civil War. In his essay "Why is Jonathan Edwards America's Spiritual Founding Father?" Richardson answers that question by taking his cue from Lincoln's Gettysburg Address in which Lincoln identifies four ideas foundational to the American Republic that he expresses in key phrases: "upon this continent"; "a new nation"; "conceived in liberty"; and, "dedicated to the proposition that all men are created equal." Richardson shows correspondences between these ideas of Lincoln and those of Edwards.

Bryant, in "The Mind of Jonathan Edwards: Beyond America," iterates his critique of Heimert's politicizing of Edwards, playing further variations on the theme of his *Jonathan Edwards' Grammar of Time, Self, and Society: A Critique of the Heimert Thesis*. Heimert portrays Edwards as a proto-revolutionary who, at least implicitly, provided pre-revolutionary America with a radical social and political ideology with democratic and nationalistic overtones. In opposition to Heimert's thesis, Bryant argues that Edwards is no prophet of American republicanism, and certainly no would-be apologist for American nationalism (or any form of nationalism, for that matter). Edwards' native country was the kingdom of God, not any earthly kingdom where he considered himself at best a sojourner. His mind was ever fixed on, and even transfixed by, the glory of God.

James Hewitson, in "'One Vast and Ecumenical Holding Company': Edwardsean Millennial Themes in Nineteenth- and Twentieth-Century Dystopian Fiction," considers one aspect of Edwards' influence in the history of American letters. Hewitson portrays Edwards as an arch-critic of the kind of facile optimism and crass materialism that became progressively rampant in the United States after Edwards' death. Nineteenth-century American utopians—Edward Bellamy, for example—secularized an Edwardsean postmillennialism and took it as a model for their own utopian fantasies. However, their critics recognized that postmillennialism, when loosened from its theological moorings, would as likely lead to dystopia than utopia, a point graphically illustrated in Hawthorne's *The Blithedale Romance*. The form of Edwards' postmillennialism, then, could be appropriated, paradoxically, as a blueprint for either a heaven or a hell on earth. Hewitson, then, joins Bryant in portraying Edwards as a cultural critic who roundly condemned any human scheme of political or social improvement outside a theocentric perspective.

In the second group of papers, Devin Zuber, David Weddle, and Michael G. Ditmore focus in different ways on Edwards' natural typology and thereby link him with other figures, American and European, who also are interpreters of nature.

Zuber, in "Edwards, Swedenborg, Emerson: From Typology to Correspondence," continues the project of Miller and Lowance by discussing the fascinating parallels between Edwards and Emerson with respect to their extraordinarily similar typological readings of nature. In his typology of nature, at least, Emerson seems to be Edwards reincarnated. However, no evidence of a direct influence of Edwards on Emerson can be found, and the few scattered references to Edwards in Emerson's journals do not bear on the theory of types. Zuber's original explanation for the indisputable similarities between Edwards' and Emerson's typologies is that Emerson's typological thinking was largely inspired by his reading of the Swedish polymath Emanuel Swedenborg, whose typology in turn is remarkably similar to Edwards'. Zuber looks at both Emerson and Swedenborg alongside Edwards.

Metaphysical idealism of one sort or another runs as an ongoing current through the history of American philosophy: A Berkeleian idealism is recognizable early on in Edwards and Samuel Johnson, and a Platonic idealism re-emerges in Emerson and his fellow Transcendentalists; Objective Idealism migrates to St. Louis to be extolled and put into practice by the educator William Torrey Harris and his band of followers; a form of voluntaristic idealism is exemplified in the thought of Josiah Royce, whereas pragmatism is strongly informed by Hegelianism, on which the young John Dewey cut his philosophical teeth.

Weddle, in "From Edwards to Emerson to Eddy: A Neglected Trajectory in American Idealism," latches onto this persistent movement in the history of American thought by revisiting, as have Miller and others, the striking parallels between Edwards and Emerson. However, Weddle goes beyond them in revealing the more definite parallels between Edwards and Mary Baker Eddy, the founder of Christian Science. Weddle anoints her as "the true heir of Edwards' metaphysical idealism." He shows how all three—Edwards, Emerson, and Eddy—through their common idealism imaginatively reconstructed nature as a system radiant with moral and spiritual significance.

The subject of Michael G. Ditmore's essay, "Edwards—Thoreau—Dillard: Reading/Writing Nature and the Awakened/Awakening Self," is again natural typology but in the larger context of American culture. Whereas Perry Miller traces a clean and single trajectory of typological thinking from Edwards to Emerson, with Weddle extending it from Emerson to Eddy, Ditmore traces a trajectory from Edwards that ramifies in multiple directions, extending not only to Emerson but also beyond to the less likely termini of Thoreau, Whitman, and Annie Dillard. He suggests, moreover, that typology provides, perhaps, a clue to a defining characteristic of American thought. Ditmore portrays Edwards,

Thoreau, and Dillard as essentially hyper-introspective creatures of solitude whose typological interpretations of nature were attempts to find a home in the American wilderness—a typically American quest.

Roger Ward and Stuart Rosenbaum, in the third group of papers, treat Edwards as a philosopher and further embed him in the American philosophical tradition by associating him with Peirce and Dewey and disclosing some thematic continuities among them.

Ward joins the ranks of scholars like John E. Smith, Michael Raposa, and Sang Hyun Lee who have made fruitful comparisons between Jonathan Edwards and Charles S. Peirce. In "The Architecture of Religious Experience in Edwards and Peirce," Ward argues that both Edwards and Peirce sought God in the structure of experience. Edwards analyzes the structure of authentic religious experience as a pattern of "signs" exhibited by the religious affections or emotions. These signs point to God as the ultimate source of these affections and so validate the experience as truly of and from God. Peirce analyzes the structure of human cognition and finds that God is the highest possible order of hypothesis. In other words, God is the ultimate object to which all our experience and reasoning tends and where it terminates. Nothing less than God can completely satisfy all thought and inquiry.

As Ward sees parallels between Edwards and Peirce, so Rosenbaum sees them between Edwards and Dewey. Rosenbaum, in "Jonathan Edwards as Proto-Pragmatist and John Dewey as Post-Theological Calvinist," identifies Edwards as a nascent pragmatist, an identification that has also been made by Smith and others. Rosenbaum finds Edwards' pragmatic impulse in his strenuous insistence that practice be the ultimate test of the authenticity of one's faith. In making his case for Edwards' proto-pragmatism, Rosenbaum refers to Dewey's 1892 lecture, "Christianity and Democracy," where Dewey explicitly identifies practical Christianity with democracy. Moreover, insists Dewey, we can know the meaning and truth of Christianity only by our living it out in our own lives; that is, more generally, our ideas, ideals, and values can be realized and validated only by being enacted in practice. Edwards and Dewey are pragmatists, according to Rosenbaum, insofar as they look to the practical consequences of beliefs for their validation.

The fourth group of papers by David White and Don Keyes follow Norman Fiering's line of inquiry by embedding Edwards' moral philosophy in its eighteenth-century context.

White, in "Bishop Butler and Jonathan Edwards," compares and contrasts Edwards with his distinguished contemporary, Joseph Butler. He does so in four distinct ways: as pastors, as moral philosophers, as systematic theologians, and as polemicists attempting to stem the tide of what they deemed irreligion, namely, deism, materialism, skepticism, and Arminianism. White claims that since Edwards and Butler are victims of misreading, he gives some suggestions on how to read them correctly. First, their thought should be evaluated in light of their pastoral concerns and duties since both men were pastors by profession. Second, they should be studied systematically since each worked up a system of divinity. With respect to their moral philosophies, White notes that neither Edwards nor Butler saw any inherent conflict between an enlightened self-love and benevolence—indeed, the one implies the other. They do differ, however, with respect to free will. Edwards, of course, is a thorough-going determinist, whereas Butler, though not explicitly denying determinism, nonetheless thinks, in anticipation of William James, that living as if determinism were true is impracticable since we cannot shake the conviction that we can freely deliberate over our decisions and be justly held responsible for them.

In "Doing Metaethics with Kant and Edwards," Keyes, like Curtis and Squires, brings Edwards into conversation with Kant, and with himself. Though acknowledging a fundamental difference between Kant's decisional and Edwards' dispositional ethics, Keyes nonetheless finds fundamental similarities together with further, subtler differences. Thus, their moral philosophies revolve around the central topics of the will, freedom, and beauty. For Edwards, virtue consists in the orientation of the will toward the totality of being (or God); for Kant, morality consists in the exercise of the good will constrained by the categorical imperative. However, whereas Kant makes volitional freedom the *sine qua non* of the autonomous or moral will, Edwards denies any such freedom to it; the only freedom he allows to the will is the ability to act on its own choices. And, most importantly for Keyes, both Edwards and Kant integrate the moral good and the aesthetic good, or beauty, within the framework of a general theory of value or axiology. The idea of beauty is integral to both Edwards' and Kant's systems, particularly Edwards' where it serves as an essential property of God. Indeed, for Keyes, it is precisely the aesthetic element in Edwards' thought that makes him indispensable for moral philosophy today. Keyes notes that Kant and Edwards have heuristic value for his own ethics, which he styles "meta-ethical essentialism," insofar as they imply certain objections to it thereby providing him occasion to refine it.

While in the fifth group of papers, Scott D. Seay and Steven Studebaker look at two of Edwards' theological doctrines, namely, his demonology and Trinitarianism, and consider them in the context of his time.

Seay, in "Satan and his *Maleficium* in the Thought of Jonathan Edwards," turns to an aspect of Edwards' engagement with the problem of evil, namely his treatment of Satan and his maleficence. Seay contends that, in opposition to the decline of demonology during the Enlightenment, Edwards reconceived traditional Puritan demonology in response to the Lockean epistemology he had adopted and the ecclesiastical and political conflicts regnant at the time. He believed in the supernatural reality of Satan and his minions who, in prideful rebellion against God and out of jealousy of humanity, implacably sought to subvert God's redemptive work in the world as it applied to both individuals and groups and so diminish God's glory in the created order. Although Satan and his allies are loose in the world and win some apparent victories, these victories are merely apparent since, eschatologically, God has already decisively won the war against evil. Edwards discerned Satan's work both, microcosmically, deep within the human soul—in particular, in the imagination—and, macrocosmically, in the course of human events. Seay concludes that Edwards' preoccupation with demonology necessitates our qualifying the historical judgment that a decline of interest in demonology occurred in eighteenth-century Anglo-American culture, particularly in its enlightened quarters.

Studebaker, in "Jonathan Edwards' Trinitarian Theology in the Context of the Early Enlightenment Deist Controversy," takes issue with commentators who contend that Edwards holds a social conception of the Trinity as a corrective to an over-emphasis on God's unity and simplicity in traditional Trinitarianism. Studebaker demonstrates that Edwards' doctrine of the Trinity is significantly similar to that of those who defended it against its critics of the early Enlightenment. Studebaker identifies two strategies Edwards employed to provide a rational foundation for the doctrine. First, he demonstrated that divine goodness necessarily implies a Trinitarian God, not the Unitarian God of the Deists that restricts it. Second, he deployed the *prisca theologia* to uncover a nascent Trinitarian idea in non-Christian religions and so to show, by its universality, that the Trinity is not an inexplicable mystery of the specifically Christian revelation.

The papers in the sixth and final group are not thematically linked nor do they belong to any of the above groupings. Though their topics are more specialized, they nevertheless pertain to some of the larger and pervasive themes in Edwards' thought. Charles Pierce's topic of Edwards and children is related to Edwards' persistent concern with the "testing of the spirits" that bore its fully ripened fruit in his monumental *Religious Affections*. Michael Thompson's topic is Edwards' influence on the British Baptist missionary movement that bears ultimately on his postmillennialism, another of his central concerns. Finally, Richard A. S. Hall addresses the topic of Edwards' alleged mysticism, which has larger relevance for his epistemology and metaphysics.

In "Jonathan Edwards, Children, and Young People: Less of Earth and More of Heaven," Pierce confirms what might be expected, that Edwards' view of childhood and youth conforms to that of the Puritan/Calvinist tradition that children are born evil but can be spiritually reborn or redeemed. Consequently, their spiritual development preoccupied Edwards throughout his life. Interestingly, Pierce illuminates Edwards' ideas about and dealings with children with some key events and experiences in Edwards' childhood and adolescence. Edwards as a boy was given to agonies and ecstasies of spirit, and in his *Personal Narrative,* he carefully describes and interprets his own spiritual maturation. This, according to Pierce, made him especially interested in and sensitive to the religious experiences of children and exceptionally well qualified to evaluate them psychologically. Further, Pierce makes the intriguing observation that Edwards' encouragement of young people to speak out in public on matters concerning their own spiritual lives inadvertently led them to boldness of speech and behavior in the secular realm, manifesting itself in disruptive behavior during church services and the "bad book" scandal, which contributed to Edwards' demise in Northampton. Pierce gives us a rounded picture of Edwards' childhood, his relationship as father with his own children, and his relationship as pastor to the children and youth of his congregation. Finally, he caps his discussion of Edwards' outlook on children with the observation that for Edwards children had particular theological significance since he understood them as being "types" of all converted or redeemed persons who thereby became the spiritual children of God.

Considering Edwards in the context of church history, Thompson, in "Edwards' Contribution to the Missionary Movement of Early Baptists," discusses Edwards' influence on the modern missionary movement. William Carey initiated the Baptist missionary movement in England in 1792 by setting sail for India where for forty years he missionized in the vicinity of Calcutta. However, previous to Carey's sailing, whether or not there should be any missionary activity at all was an issue hotly disputed by British Baptists. Being strict determinists, they thought that the work of salvation was entirely in God's hands, and so that it was the height of presumption, and an attack on God's sovereignty, to suppose that they could in any way influence its predetermined course by their own proselytizing. However, they underwent a sea change in their attitude toward missionary work, which they came to understand as not being contrary to God's will. They justified their change of mind by appealing to the writings of Edwards who himself was an evangelical Calvinist. Edwards, then, provided a theological rationale and so an impetus for missionary works overseas.

Edwards has earned a niche, along with such writers as Emerson and Whitman, in the pantheon of classic American mystics. However, some commentators, particularly more recent ones, have challenged his right to occupy it. They either flatly deny that he is a mystic at all or concede that he is, but only in a highly qualified sense. This dispute over Edwards' alleged mysticism has been muddled by the fact that scholars on both sides have either unclear, or different, definitions of "mysticism." In his essay, "Edwards as Mystic," Hall attempts to resolve this dispute by appealing to two complementary typologies of mysticism, viz., the psychological typology of William James and the philosophical typology of John Ellis McTaggart, which provide more adequate conceptions of mysticism than those that have hitherto appeared in discussions of Edwards' mysticism. Reading those texts of Edwards that have been used to either demonstrate or deny his mysticism in light of these typologies enables us to see that Edwards not only deserves his place in the mystical pantheon, but also shows him to be a mystic in some unsuspected ways. Edwards is a psychological mystic insofar as he describes himself as being endowed with a "new sense." He is a philosophical mystic inasmuch as he later generalizes his new sense as a "new spiritual sense" vouchsafed to anybody to whom God unites himself.

In his sermon preached on Sunday, October 5, 2003, during a church service in honor of Edwards, Ronald Story recapitulates Edwards' favorite and distinctive themes of light, beauty, and love. He makes clear that Edwards' sermon, "Heaven

Is a World of Love," is no less representative of his religious thought as the better known and imprecatory sermon, "Sinners in the Hands of an Angry God." These two sermons should be read as complementing one another.

From this collection of commemorative papers emerge the following conclusions, corroborated elsewhere in the literature: one is the deep kinship between Edwards' thought and that of subsequent American thinkers, suggesting perhaps that there is a distinctively American way of thinking about the perennial questions of existence. A second conclusion is that Edwards' thought continues to be relevant, especially to the fields of ethics, socio-political philosophy, and theology, which confirms Maurice's observation, "In his own country Edwards remains, and must always remain, a great power. We should imagine all American theology and philosophy, whatever change it may undergo, and with whatever foreign elements it may be associated, must be cast in his mould."

Yet, when all is said and done, the real Edwards remains as elusive as ever. Though the intellectual portraits with which we are now furnished are more finished, they are as varied as before, and the man behind these personae still remains hidden. An apt symbol for these multiple "Edwardses" is the current state of Edwards iconography. The various portraits of him attributed to John Smibert, Joseph Badger, Charles Wilson Peale, and Rembrandt Peale, among others, all show a different face. In some cases, the differences are so pronounced that one can scarcely believe they are of the same man. Winston Churchill's characterization of Russia applies no less to Edwards—an enigma wrapped up inside an enigma.

However, Edwards' elusiveness may not be a bad thing. Perhaps to ask for the real meaning of Edwards is like asking for the real meaning of Plato, Shakespeare, and Bach. Like them Edwards is a Protean spirit that requires successive generations to unpack his meanings. In doing so, they stand to learn as much about themselves as they do of Edwards. Reading Edwards is an exercise in the Socratic quest for self-knowledge. He reads us as much as we read him. A student once asked C. S. Lewis whether medieval literature is still relevant to the modern world. Lewis replied that the question ought to be whether we are relevant to medieval literature. Are we still relevant to Edwards? As the sesquicentenary of June 1900 served as a marker to us who observed the tercentenary at Northampton in October 2003, so may we serve as a marker to those who might observe the quadricentenary of Edwards' birth in October of 2103.

NOTES

[1] Sydney E. Ahlstrom, *A Religious History of the American People* (New Haven: Yale University Press, 1972), 311–312.

[2] Ahlstrom, *A Religious History of the American People*, 422–428.

[3] Dugald Stewart, *The Collected Works of Dugald Stewart*, ed. William Hamilton (Bristol: Thoemmes Press, 1994), 1:424. William Harder Squires takes Stewart's remark as referring to Jonathan Edwards, and its context would also indicate this. However, Stewart indexes this passage as referring to Dr. Jonathan Edwards. Jonathan Edwards did not hold the doctorate, but his son, Jonathan Edwards, Jr., did. Moreover, Edwards, Jr. also wrote on metaphysical issues like the freedom of the will. So, in the cited passage, there is a question as to whether Stewart is referring to the senior Edwards or to his son.

[4] Frederick D. Maurice, *Moral and Metaphysical Philosophy* (London, 1872), cited by William Harder Squires, "Some Estimates of President Edwards," in *The Edwardean: A Quarterly Devoted to the History of Thought in America,* ed. William Harder Squires, vol. 1, no. 1 (October 1903), Studies in American Religion, vol. 56, (Reprint, Lewiston, NY: Edwin Mellen Press), 35.

[5] Josiah Royce, "William James and the Philosophy of Life," in *William James and Other Essays on the Philosophy of Life* (New York: The Macmillan Company, 1911), 5.

[6] Bruce Kuklick, *Churchmen and Philosophers: From Jonathan Edwards to John Dewey* (New Haven: Yale University Press, 1985), xvi.

[7] Kuklick, *Churchmen and Philosophers,* 129n.

[8] Ibid.

[9] Ezra Stiles, *The Literary Diary of Ezra Stiles: President of Yale College, 1769–1795,* ed. Franklin B. Dexter, 3 vols. (New York, 1901), cited by Nancy Manspeaker, *Jonathan Edwards: Bibliographical Synopses* (Lewiston, NY: Edwin Mellen Press, 1981), 200.

[10] Oliver Wendell Holmes, "The Deacon's Masterpiece, or, The Wonderful 'One-Hoss Shay,'" cited by Kuklick, *Churchmen and Philosophers,* 216n.

[11] Dictionary of American Biography, vol. 1 (New York: Charles Scribner's Sons, 1964), 184.

[12] Ibid., vol. 9, 374–375.

[13] Richard A. S. Hall, "Introduction," *The Edwardean,* vii, xiv.

[14] Ralph Waldo Emerson, "The American Scholar," in *Ralph Waldo Emerson: Selected Essays, Lectures, and Poems,* ed. Robert D. Richardson, Jr. (New York: Bantam Books, 1990), 99.

[15] Harry Norman Gardiner, "The Early Idealism of Edwards," in *Jonathan Edwards: A Retrospect,* ed. Harry N. Gardiner (Boston: Houghton, Mifflin and Company, 1901), 117.

[16] Mattoon M. Curtis, "Kantean Elements in Jonathan Edwards," in *Festschrift für Heinze* (Berlin, 1906), 34–62.

[17] Squires, "A Passage from Edwards' Speculative Metaphysics," *The Edwardean* 1, no. 3 (April 1904): 175–192.

[18] Kuklick, *Churchmen and Philosophers,* 48–49, 69.

[19] Jonathan Edwards, *The Works of President Edwards,* ed. Sereno E. Dwight (New York, 1829–1830).

[20] *Selections from the Unpublished Writings of Jonathan Edwards,* ed. Alexander B. Grosart (Edinburgh, 1865).

[21] Egbert Coffin Smyth, "Some Early Writings of Jonathan Edwards, A.D. 1714–1726," *Proceedings of the American Antiquarian Society,* New Series, vol. 10 (1895): 212–247

[22] Kuklick, *Churchmen and Philosophers,* 121–122.

[23] Ibid., 177, 117.

[24] Ibid., 128.

[25] *Dictionary of American Biography,* ed. Allen Johnson, vol. 8 (New York: Charles Scribner's Sons, 1964), 610–611.

[26] See Egbert Coffin Smyth, "The Theology of Edwards," in *Exercises Commemorating the 200th Anniversary of the Birth of Jonathan Edwards* (Andover, 1904), 73–93.

[27] Richard Maurice Bucke, *Cosmic Consciousness: A Study in the Evolution of the Human Mind* (New York: E. P. Dutton and Company, Inc., 1969), 3.

[28] "One may truly say, I think, that personal religious experience has its root and centre in mystical states of consciousness." From William James, *The Varieties of Religious Experience: A Study in Human Nature* (New York: The Modern Library, 2002), 413.

[29] See Alexander V. G. Allen, "The Place of Edwards in History," in *Jonathan Edwards: A Retrospect,* 3–31; and Squires, "Edwards' Inferno," *The Edwardean* 1 no. 3 (April 1904): 162–74.

[30] Harriet Beecher Stowe, *The Minister's Wooing* (New York: Library of America, 1982), 541.

[31] Matthew Arnold, "Dover Beach," in *An Introduction to Philosophy through Literature,* ed. Robert C. Baldwin and James A. S. McPeek (New York: The Ronald Press Company, 1950), 305.

[32] Walter Pater, *The Renaissance: Conclusion, in Philosophy through Literature,* ed. Baldwin and McPeek, 29.

[33] See Alexander V. G. Allen, *Life and Writings of Jonathan Edwards* (Boston, 1889); Harry Norman Gardiner and Richard Webster, "Jonathan Edwards," in *Encyclopedia Britannica,* 11th ed., 9:3–6; and Frederick J. E. Woodbridge, "Jonathan Edwards," *Philosophical Review* 13 (1904): 393–408.

[34] See George Park Fisher, "The Philosophy of Jonathan Edwards," *North American Review* 128 (1879): 284–303; and Georges Lyon, *L'Idéalisme en Angleterre au XVIII Siècle* (Paris, 1888).

[35] H. Norman Gardiner, "Introduction," in *Jonathan Edwards: A Retrospect,* ed. H. Norman Gardiner (Boston: Houghton, Mifflin and Company, 1901), xiv.

[36] Alexander V. G. Allen, "The Place of Edwards in History," in *Jonathan Edwards: A Retrospect,* 16, 8.

[37] Allen, "The Place of Edwards in History," 11.

[38] Egbert C. Smyth, "The Influence of Edwards on the Spiritual Life of New England," in *Jonathan Edwards: A Retrospect,* 35, 44.

[39] George A. Gordon, "The Significance of Edwards To-day," in *Jonathan Edwards: A Retrospect,* 69, 59.

[40] Gardiner, "The Early Idealism of Edwards," in *Jonathan Edwards: A Retrospect,* 117.

[41] See Frank Hugh Foster, *A Genetic History of the New England Theology* (New York: Russell & Russell, Inc., 1963), 47–103.

[42] Harvey Gates Townsend, *Philosophical Ideas in the United States* (New York: American Book Company, 1934), 39.

[43] Leo Sandon, Jr., "Jonathan Edwards and H. Richard Niebuhr," in *Journal of Religious Studies,* 12 (1976): 101–115.

[44] Cited by Manspeaker, *Bibliographical Synopses,* 132.

Banquet Address: J. Edwards Conference

Huston Smith

You have had a demanding day. Keeping your attention on tightly reasoned papers all day is exhausting. So, if I am to stave off the drowsiness that is edging in to overtake you after this enjoyable dinner, I must do better than voice the pleasantries that are expected on such occasions: thanks to the conveners who have worked hard to put the conference together, tributes to the participants for their brilliant papers that have made the conference a resounding success, and testimonials to the happiness we all feel at this moment. As I say, if I am to keep you awake, I must do better than mouth soporific platitudes, and I'm up for the challenge.

What right have I to be here? I, who am, a generation or more, older than all of you and have long since retired from writing papers? I suspect that if you have given any thought to the matter, the answer that popped up was friendship. And, that is certainly what I assumed until, in preparing for the conference, I got deeper into Jonathan Edwards; whereupon my explanation for why I am here changed radically, and I've kept that explanation under cover to spring it on you now. My presence here is not an invitation dished out to a survivor of the academic treadmill. I am here because I belong here—actually more than the rest of you—because Jonathan Edwards has impacted my life more than yours. Not just through his writing, which all of you know better than I do, but directly, in the world that has been my life. I will explain.

You all know that my heritage is Chinese, in that I was born in China of missionary parents and raised there until I came here for college. That is half the story, but the other half of my heritage is not known to the world, not because I'm ashamed of it, but because it hasn't seemed to bear on my vocation. It took this conference, for even me to recognize how importantly this second half of my heritage has shaped my life. So get ready for the unveiling of the Huston Smith that the world hasn't known about.

The unknown half of me derives from dirt farmers in heartland America, Missouri to be precise. My father went to China as a missionary from Missouri, and our furlough summers were spent on the family farm, where he grew up and where (in addition to those furlough summers) I spent two summers, while I was attending Central Methodist College at Fayette, forty miles east.

How does this relate to Jonathan Edwards?

By the mid-eighteenth century, the evangelical fervor that came to be known as the Great Awakening, which Edwards had kicked off a quarter century earlier, began to wane. But, in what some historians refer to as the Second Awakening, the fervor revived in the early nineteenth century, thanks to the migration to America of John Wesley's followers, who by then were called Methodists. Wesley wasn't a Calvinist, but on opposite sides of the Atlantic, both men, born in the same year, were cooking up evangelical storms by arguing that the Church of England's reliance on the sacraments for salvation induced complacency. A personal decision to give up sin and adhere to that decision, which is to say the conversion to a new way of life, was required.

Heartland America in my father's day was solidly Methodist, and my father's given name was Wesley. By the time he was born, the fervor of the Second Awakening had subsided, but it left in its wake revival meetings and pockets of the camp meetings that were the signature of both the First and Second Awakenings. I want to dwell for a moment on those camp meetings.

America was primarily rural in those days, and people would converge from considerable distances in wagons loaded with blankets and food supplies, to spend two or three weeks together, meeting God. Typically, the days would pivot on three long services—morning, afternoon, and evening—interspersed with food sharing and neighborly conversation. We might think of them as forerunners of the be-ins of the flower children, a century or so later.

This is where my family history kicks in, first in the person of my paternal grandfather. I never knew him, and his name was never mentioned, for in those days, family skeletons were kept locked in closets. His grandchildren simply assumed that he died prematurely—we did not know that his life ended in a mental hospital. I might never have known that fact, had I not (while teaching at Washington University) been invited to give a talk in Fulton, Missouri, where the only mental hospital in the state was located, and two people in the audience confided that they knew the story, and had visited my grandfather in the hospital. Thus, set on the trail of our family skeleton, I wrote to my parents, who told us the full story. I still have that letter, somewhere in my files, and hope that its tissue paper (the thinnest conceivable) hasn't disintegrated.

The story was this. In mid-life, my grandfather "got religion" and whenever he got word of a camp meeting within driving distance, he would hitch up the wagon and take off, leaving the family farm in the hands of his sisters. They could milk the cows and feed the chickens and hogs, but they couldn't do the heavy work, plowing, harrowing, and the like. And, neighbors had their hands full with their own farms, and were not about to bail him out of his irresponsibility. In time, this brought the family to the brink of bankruptcy, and the mortgage on the farm would have been foreclosed, if my father and his sister, who was a missionary in Korea, had not pooled their meager missionary resources to buy off the mortgage. This brings me to myself.

Missionaries typically have furloughs every seven years, and I was six years old for my first family furlough. We would sail to the States in May, and spend that summer and the following one on the family farm, settling in a town forty miles east for the school year. That meant we would be present for the evangelical revivals that toured heartland America in the summer. July was the favored month, for with the corn knee-high by the Fourth of July, and the harvesting season comfortably in the future, July was for religion. During the week that a revivalist visited us, each evening from Sunday through the following Sunday, we would drive five miles to the chapel that served our neighborhood—Smith Chapel by name, though as far as anyone could remember, our family had not founded it. When I was six, my father would harness Bell and Trot, our farm's horses, to the buggy for the ride. When I was fourteen (my second furlough) we traveled the gravel roads in a Model T Ford, and in the summers before my freshman year at Central Methodist College, my aunts sported the Model A version.

Revival weeks were dress-up occasions. Even though Missouri in July could be hot and humid, I don't recall ever having seen the dress code broken. For men, white shirts and neckties were required, but on hot evenings, it was acceptable to carry one's pressed jacket, neatly folded over one's arm. Anticipation would mount as we approached the chapel, for remember—we were on our way to meet God. Now, I want to tell you again, folks, July in America's heartland was for religion.

The evangelistic meetings themselves are easily summarized. The chapel was invariably packed. Hymnbooks were in the racks, but they were seldom needed—we knew most of the hymns by heart. Three or four hymns would warm us up before the evangelist (once there was a team of two) took to the pulpit. The format for the sermons (they weren't harangues, but "sermon" as we now understand that word doesn't really fit) were stereotypically evangelical. One of our favorite hymns almost tells the story by itself.

> I was sinking deep in sin, far from the peaceful shore,
> Very deeply stained within, sinking to rise no more;
> But the Master of the sea, heard my despairing cry,
> From the depths he rescued me, now safe am I.
>   Love lifted me; love lifted me.
>   When nothing else could help, love lif-ted me.

As the song leader prolonged that last line with a measured outward drift of his right hand, more often than not our hearts really were opened to the divine.

A brief benediction brought the meetings to a close, and we made our way out into the cool of the summer night where tables had been set up for cellar-cooled watermelons, split into generous slices, and quickly their seeds began to splatter the grass like rain. A bit of neighborly gossip and stolen glances between teenage boys and girls, and we were on our way home, already anticipating the next evening.

Well that's it, the real story of why, unbeknownst to the conveners, I was invited to this conference. And, from the looks on your faces, I have succeeded in my objective which was to keep you awake.

HUSTON SMITH is Thomas J. Watson Professor of Religion and Distinguished Adjunct Professor of Philosophy (Emeritus) at Syracuse University (New York). Recently he has served as visiting professor of religious studies at the University of California (Berkeley). He holds twelve honorary degrees, and his fourteen books include *The World's Religions* and *Why Religion Matters*. In 1996, he was the subject of Bill Moyers' PBS Special, *The Wisdom of Faith with Huston Smith*. His film documentaries on Hinduism, Tibetan Buddhism, and Sufism have won international awards. *The Journal of Ethnomusicology* acclaimed his significant discovery of Tibetan multiphonic chanting.

PART II

EDWARDS AS SOCIAL & POLITICAL PHILOSOPHER

Why Is Jonathan Edwards America's Spiritual Founding Father?

Herbert Richardson

Shortly after the Battle of Gettysburg, President Abraham Lincoln recalled the creative achievement of America's political founding fathers: *"Four score and seven years ago, our forefathers brought forth, upon this continent, a new nation, conceived in liberty, and dedicated to the proposition that all men are created equal."*

Lincoln believed that America's political founding fathers brought into being (1) "upon this continent," (2) a "new nation," (3) which was conceived through a spiritual virtue ("liberty"), (4) for the sake of establishing a more just society where "all men are created equal."

As a heuristic for arguing that Edwards is America's Spiritual Founding Father, I shall present his treatment of these four ideas in Lincoln's Gettysburg Address.

---

1) Consider, for example, Lincoln's phrase that America was established *"on this continent."* Here is what Edwards[1] says on this subject:

> *God has made, as it were, two worlds here below, two great habitable continents, far separated one from the other. This latter is, as it were, but newly created . . . that the new and most glorious state of God's church on earth might commence [in it]; that God might in it begin a new world in a spiritual respect, when he creates the new heaven and new earth.* (I/382)

Lincoln's use of the phrase "on this continent" resonates rhetorically with Edwards' eschatological vision that the "new heaven and new earth" are to be established in America.

It was Jonathan Edwards who connected the idea of the geographical new world with the idea of the eschatological new world. Edwards' theological innovation was to interpret the New England revivals of the 1730s as first signs of the millennium (in the book of Revelation).

Previous New England divines interpreted their times as a type of ancient Israel's history, finding in the Old Testament the key to the Bible. Edwards' originality was to interpret his time as the beginning of the fulfillment of history, finding in the book of Revelation his key to the Bible.

For this reason, Edwards broke with the New England theocratic ideal. He wanted to reorganize church congregations into revolutionary "holiness cells" that embodied the form of life the future would take. (This is what got Edwards dismissed from his pulpit in Northampton.)

(2) Lincoln says that our forefathers brought forth (that is, gave birth to) *"a new nation."* A nation is a group of people who share a common progenitor—history, language, character. Lincoln is saying that even though Americans may come from many old nations, they have here become "a new nation."

Lincoln's phrase is only a political restatement of the spiritual vision of Edwards. It was Edwards, more than anyone, who felt that God was creating, in America, a new spiritual/political nation, the Kingdom of God on Earth:

> *The end of God's creating the world was to prepare a kingdom for his Son. . . . So far as Christ's kingdom is established in the world, so far are . . . the first heavens and the first earth come to an end and the new heavens and the new earth, the everlasting heavens and earth, established in their room.* (I/584) *And if these things be*

> *so, it gives us more abundant reason to hope that what is now seen in America, and especially in New England, may prove the dawn of that glorious day.* (I/383)

The "new nation" which is being born in America (Edwards always says "gradually . . . gradually") is not just one more nation like the other nations of this earth. Rather, it is a new kind of nation. On this point, both Edwards and Lincoln agree.

(3) Lincoln's third point is that this new nation is *"conceived in liberty."* (Today we would use the word "freedom.") It is this conception that makes America a nation of an absolutely new kind.

For Lincoln, the thing that has created America a nation is NOT its sharing any common ethnic ancestor, common language, or historical past. The progenitor of America (what "conceived" it) is the idea, or spiritual experience, of LIBERTY.

Behind Lincoln's phrase, "conceived in liberty," is an analogous idea of Jonathan Edwards. Edwards specifically asserts that a person is born again into the new nation in America—the Kingdom of God on Earth—when the Spirit of God imparts to his soul a divine and supernatural light. Here is how Edwards describes this experience:

> *There is, therefore, in this spiritual life, a true sense of the divine and superlative excellency of things in religion . . . not only a rational belief that God is holy, and that holiness is a good thing, but there is a sense of the loveliness of God's holiness. . . . It is implied in a person's being heartily sensible of the loveliness of a thing, that the idea of it is pleasant to his soul (which is a far different thing from having a rational opinion that it is excellent).* (II/14)

According to Edwards, the divine light that the Spirit imparts to the soul is a taste, a desire, and a love for God and His purposes. It is a feeling of affection in the heart, an experience of relishing God's beauty and holiness.

Just as, for Lincoln, anyone who has the experience of freedom becomes an American, so, for Edwards, anyone who has the experience of this "divine and supernatural light" is born (again) into a spiritual community that is different from any ethnic community to which he previously belonged.

All the members of this new spiritual community share, so to say, the "gene" of Christ, their progenitor. Edwards does not even shy away from asserting that they share the very *"glorified human nature of Christ."* (II/27) They no longer have the fallen human nature of Adam; they are changed into new kinds of human beings, men and women of the future.

(4) *"Dedicated to the proposition that all men are created equal":* Lincoln understands that the new American nation, characterized by liberty, must have some spiritual purpose. For Lincoln, this purpose is to establish (gradually, gradually) a society in which both the freedom and the equality of every member are recognized and maintained.

To establish both the freedom and the equality of every one of its citizens has been—to a large extent—the fundamental political impulse in American society. Even though these two values are in tension, Americans have never acquiesced in the "realist's" claim that striving to establish a society that is both truly free and truly equal is an impossible self-delusion. And, I myself certainly believe that—"gradually, gradually" (as Edwards never tires of saying)—we are making progress toward this goal.

But, Edwards' goal for America is even more ambitious than Lincoln's. For Edwards, the spiritual idea that is analogous to Lincoln's "liberty" is "love." But what is love? Edwards gives this conception both metaphysical and political precision.

When, according to Edwards, the Spirit of God imparts "a divine and supernatural light to the soul," that soul conceives a love for excellency. "Excellency" is Edwards' technical term for the universal harmony of all things. This love for all things in their universal harmony is, says Edwards, the only True Virtue.

Writes Edwards: *"All virtue, which is the excellency of minds, is resolved into Love to Being . . . [and] we are to conceive of Divine Excellence [that is, God's love] as the Infinite General Love which reaches all, proportionately, with perfect purity and sweetness; yea, it includes the true Love of all creatures [that is, our loves] for that is his Spirit, or which is the same thing, his Love."* (I/231)

For those who find this metaphysical vision of universal love vague, let me offer Edwards' own interpretation of what it means politically: When there is a society whose members experience universal love, *"Then shall all the world be united in one amiable society. All nations, in all parts of the world, on every side of the globe, shall be knit together in sweet harmony. All parts of God's church shall assist and promote the spiritual good of one another. A communication shall then be upheld between all parts of the world to that end; and the art of navigation, which is now applied so much to favor man's covetousness and pride . . . shall then be consecrated to God and applied to holy uses."* (I/610)

---

(5) Behind these four ideas, Lincoln and Edwards share another even deeper conviction. Both Lincoln and Edwards believe that history is a meliorative process because it is actively ruled by the Providence of God, but neither one has any delusions about the sinfulness of men when left to themselves.

Both Lincoln and Edwards clearly see the rapaciousness of the magistrate, the covetousness of the businessman, the pride of the intellectual, and the self-centeredness of the family. In fact, Edwards' NATURE OF TRUE VIRTUE is the most powerful critique of human "morality" as a mere ideological justification for selfishness and exploitation. The only true virtue, says Edwards, is the "disinterested benevolence" of God, which stands as a judgement over all our moral pretences to be virtuous.

> *The God that holds you over the pit of hell, much as one holds a spider, or some loathsome insect, over the fire abhors you and is dreadfully provoked. . . . It is nothing but his hand that holds you from falling into the fire at every moment. . . . There is no other reason to be given why you have not gone to hell, since you have sat here in the house of God, provoking his pure eyes by your sinful wicked manner of attending his solemn worship.* (II/10)

Lincoln also knows how to invoke God's judgement on sin. Compare with Edwards' sermon on the Anger of God this famous peroration from Lincoln's Second Inaugural Address:

> *Fondly do we hope—feverently do we pray—*
> *That this mighty scourge of war*
> May speedily pass away.
>
> *Yet, if God wills that it continue*
> *Until all the wealth piled by the bondsman's*
> *Two hundred and fifty years of unrequited toil*
>   *shall be sunk*

And until every drop of blood drawn by the lash
　　shall be paid by another
　　drawn with the sword,

[Then]
As was said three thousand years ago,
So still it must be said:
"The judgements of the Lord
　　are true and righteous altogether."

Both Lincoln and Edwards know that history is actively ruled over by God who, in His righteousness, is the defender of the orphans and the hungry and the oppressed. But, because both Lincoln and Edwards trust in God's Providence, they are optimistic about the future. They are liberal meliorists. They have confidence that historical progress is possible.

Both Lincoln and Edwards believe that it is worth striving to establish a society in which every citizen is free and equal; both Lincoln and Edwards believe that this world can be *"knit together in sweet harmony, . . . consecrated to God, and applied to holy uses."* (I/610)

HERBERT W. RICHARDSON received the B.A. from Baldwin-Wallace College in Ohio; the S.T.B. from Boston University School of Theology; and the Ph.D. from Harvard University. He retired from the faculties of Theology and Religious Studies of St. Michael's College in the University of Toronto, and is the founding editor of the Edwin Mellen Press. Among his many publications are the following: *Anselm of Canterbury: Complete Treatises; Nun, Witch, Playmate: The Americanization of Sex; Toward an American Theology;* and *What Do Religion, Politics and Science Contribute to the Good Society? Essays in Calvinist Social Theory.*

NOTE

[1] All Edwards citations are from the 1834 edition of his *Works* reprinted by The Banner of Truth Trust, 1986.

The Mind of Jonathan Edwards: Beyond America

M. Darrol Bryant

I. Praising Edwards

I want to begin by thanking Dr. Richard Hall for the invitation to participate in these events celebrating the birth of Jonathan Edwards in 1703.

Edwards has repeatedly been called "America's greatest mind," "the most significant thinker in America," "the greatest figure to have been produced in America." Ola Elizabeth Winslow spoke for many on the 200th anniversary of Edwards' death in 1958 when she remarked that Edwards "stands forth today as one of the great original minds of America."[1] One hundred years earlier, Edwards was not so regarded. Nevertheless, Edwards stands for many at the fountainhead of American thought. William Clebsch in his *American Religious Thought: A History,* places Edwards in such a position. Clebsch focuses on the "founders and bearers of a distinct American spirituality,"[2] beginning with Edwards—"the truly compelling religious virtuoso of American Puritanism"—moving to Emerson and ending with William James. This trio of figures so disparate in the content and sensibility of their thought are repeatedly cited in studies of the American mind. And Robert Jenson considers it a "truism that Jonathan Edwards is America's greatest theologian."[3] He builds on Perry Miller's work of the 1940s and 50s that rehabilitated Edwards and located Edwards' greatness in his reshaping of the Puritan mind in relation to Enlightenment thought. Others, such as Peter Gay, rejected such a view of Edwards and considered him a "medieval thinker" bypassed by the Enlightenment. Thus the battle for Edwards continues.

I too have come to praise Edwards. I do so by asking about the shape of that mind, Edwards' mind, its dynamics and content.

I do so by raising the question of where his mind was centered. Was it centered on America? He wrote in his notebooks in the 1740s that "the world shall be supplied with spiritual treasures from America."[4] But the word "America" seldom appears in the Edwards corpus. The reason is not merely the historical fact that "America" as the United States of America was still a thing of the future, but that "America" for Edwards was not a political entity. It seems odd, if not anachronistic, to call Edwards America's greatest mind when there was no America at the time he was writing. Not only was Edwards born seventy-one years before the American Declaration of Independence, but he died long before anyone realized that events would lead the colonies of the new world into the American Republic. Indeed, Edwards' life unfolded within a colony in turmoil and transition. Rather than "America," Edwards' mind is centered on the things of God. His was a mind that from an early age beheld the glory of God. His was a mind that later was to see that God's "work of creation" was one with "God's work of providence."[5] His was a mind that struggled to discern God's Way in the midst of the cultural turmoil of his time. This is not simply to say that Edwards was a theologian not a politician, but rather that it is crucial to see "America" in Edwards' perspective. It is crucial to see that the shape and dynamics of the mind of Jonathan Edwards always led beyond political America.

Those who have engaged in the study of Edwards all have begun their studies with certain issues swirling in their minds. My own encounter with Jonathan Edwards began in the early 1970s while pursuing doctoral studies with Professor Herbert Richardson at the Institute of Christian Thought, at St. Michael's College in Toronto. It was in a seminar with Professor Richardson that I read Alan Heimert's *Religion in the American Mind*, a study in which Edwards loomed large.[6] Though I had earlier heard of Edwards, it was this seminar that led me to delve more deeply into his writings. At that time, I was deeply uncertain about my own future as an American, though my family had come to the American colonies in 1630. The previous decade had led me to an involvement in the last event organized by Dr. Martin Luther King, the Poor People's March in Washington, D.C.[7] I had come to Canada in 1967 to teach at Waterloo Lutheran University and had been caught up in the student movement and the turmoil around the war in Vietnam. Many Americans had fled to Canada to avoid the draft. A year in Geneva in 1969–70 with the Lutheran World Federation had led me to encounter the new liberation theology that was just emerging in Latin America. Though I had been accepted at Oxford, I decided to return to Canada to study with Professor Richardson. The study of Edwards was not what I had anticipated, but I found myself deeply engaged with the Heimert study and what I increasingly felt was its dissonance with the Edwards texts I was then reading. Eventually, I wrote a dissertation on Edwards that was a critique of the Heimert thesis.

Heimert had argued that "Edwards provided pre-revolutionary America with a radical, even democratic, social and political ideology, and evangelical religion embodied, and inspired, a thrust toward American nationalism." My own more constructive interpretation of Edwards was embedded in my critique of Heimert. I came to reject Heimert's view that Edwards either "embodied" or "inspired" a thrust toward "American nationalism." Such a view politicized Edwards in ways that, in my judgment, could not be sustained by a reading of the Edwards corpus. I still hold that view. But my own study, later published, dropped like a stone and had little impact on the dominant view of Edwards, which is to regard him as the pre-eminent "American" thinker.[8]

Here I will be looking at three moments in Edwards' life, moments that reveal the shape of Edwards' mind, a mind that always moved "beyond America."

II. "Inward Sweet Delight in God & Things Divine"

Jonathan Edwards was born on October 5, 1703, in East Windsor, Connecticut, to Timothy Edwards and Esther Stoddard of the famous Stoddard family of Northampton. He was the fifth of eleven children and the only boy, and this fact shaped in Edwards a feminine spirit that loved beauty, as revealed in his writing about the life of the spider: "there are some things that I have happily seen of the wondrous way of the working of the spider. Although every thing belonging to the insect is admirable, there are some phenomena relating to them more particularly wonderful."[9] He probably wrote these words in his early twenties, rather than as a teenager, as some believe. In any case, these words reveal that it was excellence or beauty that he saw at the heart of the cosmos.

Later, in his *Personal Narrative,* he tells us that from an early age he had an "inward, sweet delight in God and divine things." And later, while walking in the pasture "and looking upon the sky and clouds, there came into my mind so sweet a sense of the glorious majesty and grace of God, as I know not how to express. . . . God's excellency, his wisdom, his purity and love, seemed to appear in every thing; in the sun, moon and stars; in the clouds and blue sky; in the grass, flowers, trees; in the water and all nature . . ."[10]

Still later, he said that prayer "seemed to be as natural to me as the breath."[11]

Edwards also acknowledged times that were difficult and not so full of this "sweet delight in God and divine things." He tells us of his struggle in relation to the "doctrine of God's sovereignty," writing that "it used to appear like a horrible doctrine to me." But then there was a breakthrough—"a wonderful alteration in my mind"—that led Edwards to write that he then had "quite another sense of God's sovereignty . . . not only a conviction but a delightful conviction. The doctrine has very often appeared exceeding pleasant, bright, and sweet. Absolute sovereignty is what I love to ascribe to God."[12] Striking here is Edwards' way of characterizing his convictions: "sweet, pleasant, and bright" in relation "to God and divine things." And he continues:

> There came into my soul, and was as it were diffused through it, a sense of the glory of the Divine Being; a new sense, quite different from any thing I ever experienced before. . . . From about that time, I began to have a new kind of apprehensions and ideas of Christ, and the work of redemption, and the glorious way of salvation by him. An inward, sweet sense of these things, at times, came into my heart; and my soul was led away in pleasant views and contemplations of them.[13]

As Edwards remarked later, "God is God . . . and exalted above all chiefly by his divine beauty."[14] These experiences are what we might call altered states of consciousness that were at the heart of Edwards' faith and mind.

Later, in *Images or Shadows of Divine Things,* Edwards would remark that it was "fit and becoming of God . . . so to order things that there should be a voice of His in His works . . . a kind of voice or language of God to instruct intelligent beings in things pertaining to Himself."[15] That "language of God" is the language of image and symbol. This symbolic language of type and antitype was embedded in the natural—and social world. Moreover, "the manifestations of the moral and spiritual glory of the divine Being (which is the proper beauty of the divinity) bring their own evidence, and tend to assure the heart."[16] And thus later in his *Dissertation on Creation*, Edwards would claim of creation that "the whole is of God, and in God, and to God, and God is the beginning, middle, and end. . . ."[17] Edwards' mind was filled with this sensibility that "the whole is of, in and to God." Its purpose is communication or communion. And the chief end of human beings, as he wrote in his *Miscellanies,* is "to behold the excellency of God and his works, and to delight and be made happy therein."[18] And again,

"God intended them [humankind] only for this happiness."[19] Where is the dour Puritan view of God and human life in this? Or, even more, where is "American nationalism" in this? What is remarkable is the extent to which Edwards was able to hold to this focus and awareness of the "excellency of God and his works" in his writings so that they continued to be the lively foundation of his soul. As he would later write, faith is "consent to being itself."

What he experienced in his life became central to his writings as well. We see something of this same sensibility in his first publication, *A Divine & Supernatural Light, Immediately Imparted to the Soul by the Spirit of God, Shown to be Both a Scriptural and Rational Doctrine*. Here, Edwards defines the saint in the following way: "The Spirit of God . . . may indeed act upon the mind of a natural man, but he acts in the mind of a saint as an indwelling vital principle. . . . He unites . . . with the mind of a saint . . . as a new supernatural principle of life and action."[20] This "spiritual and divine light" does not, Edwards argues, "consist in any impression made upon the imagination" nor in "any new truths or propositions" but rather in "a true sense of the divine excellency of the things revealed in the word of God . . . a real sense of the excellency of God and Jesus Christ, and of the work of redemption . . ."[21] This inward and spiritual sense is distinguished from "merely rationally" believing "that God is glorious" by the "sense of the gloriousness of God in his heart." It is, again, "this sense of the divine excellency of things" that was the core of Edwards' faith, the lodestar of his mind.[22]

III. True Religion and the Great Awakening

Edwards is conventionally identified with the Great Awakening, that complex of events that ravaged New England beginning in 1739. But such a reading of Edwards does not notice the development that was taking place in his thinking, a development that led to his classic *Religious Affections* in 1746. In his preface, he wrote:

> 'Tis a hard thing to be a hearty zealous friend of what has been good and glorious, in the late extraordinary appearances . . . and at the same time, to see the evil and pernicious tendency of what has been bad. . . . But yet, I am humbly, but fully persuaded we shall never be in the way of truth . . . till we do so.[23]

This statement signaled a shift in Edwards' thinking as he moved beyond a simple "yes" to the Awakening to an effort to clarify what he called "the nature of true religion."[24] Even in the Connecticut River Valley Awakening of 1733–34, Edwards had been mystified by what had occurred. He did not call his work on those events a *Surprising Narrative* . . . for nothing. And when one reads the 1733 sermons on "Justification by Faith Alone" that are said to be the sermons that gave rise to those events, one can only share Edwards' puzzlement about their effect. How are they connected to the response that he witnessed? Nevertheless, Edwards continued to long for further outpouring of God's spirit. One sees this in his 1738 sermons, the sermons that became the published *Work of Redemption* in the 1770s. But when that further outpouring occurred, Edwards felt driven to reconsider the nature of true religion. Was true religion, he wondered, to be found in these events? Or were these events and reactions mixed up with something less honorable? His answer was the latter. But it was a complex answer—and a difficult one for his readers to hear—that began with his conviction that holy affections are new principles laid down in the soul by God; they were not these raised emotions of the revivals. The first sign of "affections that are truly spiritual and gracious," he wrote, "arise from those influences and operations on the heart, which are spiritual, supernatural and divine."[25] The second sign "is the transcendently excellent and amiable nature of divine things, as they are in themselves; and not any conceived relation they bear to self or self-interest."[26] And the third is "a love to divine things for the beauty and sweetness of their moral excellency. . . ."[27] Edwards was relentless—

and consistent. His writing continually points to the divine source of the heart renewed—and to nothing else.

Edwards saw that "the affection of love is . . . the fountain of all affection." But for this love to be genuine—and this is the view that distinguished Edwards from his contemporaries—it must not be grounded in self-interest or self-love. Some say, Edwards acknowledges, that "all love arises from self-love."[28] But he argues that there is another kind of love, one which arises from "this infinite excellency of the divine nature, as it is in itself." Unlike those "whose affection to God is founded first on his profitableness to them"—a view Edwards regards as beginning at the *"wrong end,"*—the affections of "true and holy love in the saints arise in another way."[29] Edwards continues: "They don't first see that God loves them, and then see that he is lovely; but they first see that God is lovely, and that Christ is excellent and glorious, and their hearts are first captivated with this view. . . . The saint's affections begin with God. . . ."[30] Thus "true gratitude or thankfulness to God . . . arises from a foundation . . . of love to God for what he is in himself."[31] This is a hard saying, but it goes to the heart of Edwards' critique of the Awakening.

Indeed, when one reads Edwards' twelve signs that do not count as signs of true religion, one encounters a list that his contemporaries—and certainly his successors in the revivalist tradition—identified as marks of God's spirit. They are not "affections raised high," nor "great effects on the body," nor "talking of the things of religion," nor "texts of Scripture . . . brought to mind," nor disposing "persons to spend much time in religion."[32] All these—and more—do not necessarily point to true religion. Edwards is devastatingly insightful and severe in his critique, often criticizing those very characteristics found in the champions of the revival.

The problem, says Edwards, is that the Awakening had become too captive to the spirit of hubris or pride. The "delight a true saint has in God" is reversed in the hypocrite whose "joy is really a joy in themselves and not in God." He continues, "having received what they call spiritual discoveries or experiences, their minds are taken up about them, admiring their own experiences: and what they are principally taken and elevated with, is not the glory of God, or beauty of Christ, but the beauty of their own experiences."[33] Despite Edwards' powerful critique of the revival experience, in volume after volume concerning the Great Awakening, Edwards is brought forward as its champion. However, this view cannot be sustained by a careful reading of Edwards' writings. While he did support the Awakening initially, he came to have a critical view of the extent to which it exhibited an unseemly pride and hubris. With the publication of the *Religious Affections,* Edwards' fate in relation to the very movement which he had helped to bring into being was sealed. He was saying "no" to exactly what the Awakening had affirmed—self-love writ large.

If the Great Awakening gave birth to a distinctive American self, then Edwards sought to subvert that self-understanding. And this subversion continued and was deepened in his post-1746 writings, especially his *Freedom of the Will, Original Sin,* and the *Nature of True Virtue.*

In 1749, Edwards was engaged in a bitter struggle with his Northampton congregation, ostensibly over the question of the qualifications for communion. Edwards wanted access to the Lord's Supper limited to those who explicitly had declared their faith—the conflict became an occasion to say "no," to Edwards. The congregation rejected him, and he went out to become a missionary to the Indians at Stockbridge. His rejection was a rejection of that distinctive spirituality that he sought to realize. Instead of holy affections, that distinctive mode of consciousness that Edwards believed was a gift of God, his Northampton parishioners chose emotions highly raised. Instead of a will set within the context of the determining grace of God, they chose a self-determining will, their own self-will writ large.[34] And instead of the beloved community of the saints consenting to being itself, they opted for the awakened community of self-interested love.[35] What they did not understand was that Edwards sought to lift them beyond themselves to the whole that was from, in, and to God. It was here that their true happiness lay, Edwards believed. But he was soon to be a voice crying in the wilderness.

A similar point is made by Stephen Yarbrough and John Adams in their study *Delightful Conviction*, which focuses on the rhetoric of conversion. They argue that Edwards' sermons and writings were focused on conversion rather than persuasion. In their view, "he sought to prepare sinners for accepting Christ by undermining or dismantling the belief structures supporting their sense of themselves as independent, self-determined individuals."[36] But his congregation refused to give up this sense of self, and Edwards was sent out.

IV. The Work of Redemption and America

One of Edwards' big projects was his *History of the Work of Redemption*. It was a work that remained unfinished but sought to do something unprecedented, namely to move the history of redemption beyond scripture to the history of humankind. What we have of the project is a series of sermons delivered in 1739 to his Northampton congregation. Some are dated; some are not. They all have the same text from Isaiah at their head, Isaiah 51:8: "For the moth shall eat them up like a garment, and the worm shall eat them like wool: but my righteousness shall be forever, and my salvation from generation to generation." Contemporary biblical scholars see this text as part of the dramatic and moving eschatology of Second Isaiah. This scripture contains the remarkable texts on the future redemption of Zion and the promise of "the new heaven and the new earth which I will make" (Isaiah 66:22). The "doctrine" that Edwards draws from the text is that "the Work of Redemption is a work that God carries on from the fall of man to the end of the world." This text (Isaiah 51:8) and doctrine stand at the head of each of the thirty sermons. Edwards saw the work of redemption as the lodestar of history. What was unprecedented was his attempt to move that salvation history beyond the scriptural story to the history of humankind. This view reveals a mind striving for inclusivity and universality, striving to see that the whole is from, for, and to God.

The work remained unfinished, and in its unfinished form it is filled with narrowness of judgment and shaky history, especially in Edwards' comments about "Mahometans, Jews, and Popery"—and the native peoples of America.[37] Edwards simply repeats many of the pervasive prejudices of his time in relation to peoples that he little knew and even less understood. We might have hoped for something more from Edwards, especially in relation to the native peoples, since he did work among them. These sermons, however, were written prior to that period in his life. Although Edwards had indicated to the Princeton trustees, when invited to become president, that he hoped to turn again to this work, his death prevented it. His sermons, however, were published by his Scottish admirer John Erskine in 1774.

John Wilson in his introduction to the Yale edition of the *Work of Redemption* writes:

> Its publication in the 1770s helped to fuel the transference of religious convictions into the political realm that became so important with the war effort. Edwards seemed to be speaking from the grave.... Of course, Work of Redemption spoke in a religious idiom. It portrayed God's people, revitalized through the spirit, as a part of God's work through Christ to redeem the entire creation. From its perspective, the founding of the American republic could be at best a foreshadowing of the renewal of God's people at the millennium. While the work of redemption would not be completed in America ... the young republic might be the setting for a new life of the Spirit....[38]

This is the heart of the problem that I have been seeking to uncover here, the transformation of Edwards' thinking into an apology for the American republic. To see

Edwards' *Work of Redemption* as a warrant for the "new" republic or any republic is to impose an intentionality that is not there. From first to last Edwards' *Work of Redemption* is a vision of God's work of redemption.

But—and this is key—Edwards' eye was always fixed on something beyond the proximate, beyond the political, beyond the historical. That something was God's work of redemption, a work typified in Jesus Christ, anticipated in Israel and in the life of the church, and realized in the Kingdom of Heaven.

V. Beyond America: The Mind of Jonathan Edwards

So, now I come to my conclusion. We best honor the remarkable Jonathan Edwards when we hear him aright. And we do that by seeing his writings on their own terms, rather than making him an apologist for the on-going American experiment—and certainly not for the American Republic. Edwards' mind always moved beyond America to the "transcendently excellent and amiable nature of divine things." The American Republic that was to emerge years after Edwards' death was centered in itself, in its own "life, liberty and pursuit of happiness." It would pursue its "Manifest Destiny" rather than the Work of Redemption as it decimated the native peoples and made its way from "sea to shining sea." It would enslave the blacks and deny them their humanity in its Constitution. Indeed, the real successor to Edwards in relation to the Republic was Samuel Hopkins, his Rhode Island student, who wrote to the Continental Congress that it would fail in its task if it did not address the issue of slavery, "the evil we are threatened with. . . ." He saw that it was a "shocking, intolerable inconsistence" to deny liberty to "thousands of our brethren, who have as good a right to liberty as ourselves and to whom it is as sweet as it is to us."[39] The founding fathers did not hear. Instead, they would champion liberty for some in the American colonies and, later, freedom for American interests in its wars here and abroad. America would relegate to itself a divine mandate and forget that it too participates in that original sin that flaws all human enterprises, as Edwards so insightfully knew. Nowhere is the dissonance between Edwards' vision of the work of redemption and the American dream more evident than in the current president's War on Terrorism. Disregarding the necessity for consent among the nations, President Bush has poured billions into what Philip Roth, the American writer, has called an "orgy of narcissism." America, with its vaunted call for freedom, has become a war machine wreaking its will on the peoples of the world. To identify Edwards as "America's theologian" is to enlist Edwards as an apologist for the on-going drama of the American Republic. If Jonathan Edwards is "America's theologian," then he was so for an America that never came to be.

DARROL M. BRYANT received the B.A. from Concordia College in Minnesota, the S.T.B. from Harvard University, and both the M.A. and Ph.D. from St. Michael's College in the University of Toronto. He retired as professor of religion and culture at Renison College in the University of Waterloo (Ontario). His major field of study is dialogue among the world's religions. He has published widely in the areas of Jonathan Edwards, Indian religions, theology, and social ethics. Among his numerous publications are *Religion in a New Key; Woven on the Loom of Time: Many Faiths & One Divine Purpose; Jonathan Edwards' Grammar of Time, Self, and Society; To Whom It May Concern: Poverty, Humanity, Community.*

NOTES

[1] Ola Winslow, ed., *Jonathan Edwards: Basic Writings* (New York: New American Library, 1966), vii.

[2] William Clebsch, *American Religious Thought: A History* (Chicago: University of Chicago Press, 1973), xv.

[3] See Robert Jenson, *America's Theologian* (New York: Oxford University Press, 1988), 3. This fine study of Edwards is rendered problematic by Jenson's acknowledgement that "the nationalism signaled in the title does indeed characterize the entire study" (viii). It is this direct linkage of Edwards with American nationalism that I find anachronistic and unwarranted.

[4] See Jonathan Edwards' *Typological Writings*, ed. M. Lowance & D. Watters (New Haven: Yale University Press, 1993), 101. It is entry no. 147 and it probably comes from 1742.

[5] Jonathan Edwards, *A History of the Work of Redemption*, ed. John Wilson (New Haven: Yale University Press, 1989), p. 519.

[6] Alan Heimert, *Religion and the American Mind* (Cambridge: Harvard UP, 1966).

[7] My involvement in the Poor People's Campaign led to my first publication: *To Whom It May Concern: Poverty, Humanity, Community* (Philadelphia: Fortress Press, 1969).

[8] See M. Darrol Bryant, *Jonathan Edwards' Grammar of Time, Self, and Society* (Lewiston, NY: Edwin Mellen Press, 1993).

[9] Ola Elizabeth Winslow, ed., *Jonathan Edwards: Basic Writings* (New York: New American Library, 1966), 33.

[10] Winslow, 83–85.

[11] Winslow, 85.

[12] C. Faust & T. Johnson, ed., *Jonathan Edwards: Representative Selections* (New York: American Book Co. 1935), 58–59.

[13] Faust & Johnson, 59.

[14] Jonathan Edwards, *Religious Affections*, ed. John Smith (New Haven: Yale UP, 1959), 298.

[15] As quoted in Conrad Cherry, *Nature and Religious Imagination: From Edwards to Bushnell* (Philadelphia: Fortress Press, 1980), 48–49.

[16] Edwards, *Religious Affections*, 299.

[17] Jonathan Edwards, "Dissertation on the End for Which God Created the World," *Works of President Edwards* (New York: Robert Carter & Bros., 1881), 255.

[18] Jonathan Edwards, *The Miscellanies*, ed. Thomas Schafer (New Haven: Yale University Press, 1994), 267.

[19] Edwards, *Miscellanies*, 268.

[20] See S. R. Yarbrough and J. C. Adams, *Delightful Conviction: Jonathan Edwards and the Rhetoric of Conversion* (Westport, CT: Greenwood Press, 1993), 112.

[21] Yarbrough & Adams, 113.

[22] Ibid., 114.

[23] Edwards, *Religious Affections*, 85.

[24] Edwards, *Religious Affections*, 85.

[25] Ibid., 197.

[26] Ibid., 240.

[27] Ibid., 254.

[28] Edwards, *Religious Affections*, 240.

[29] Ibid., 243.

[30] Ibid., 246.

[31] Ibid., 247.

[32] Ibid., 127, 131, 135, 142, 163.

[33] Edwards, *Religious Affections*, 250–251.

[34] Here I am thinking of Edwards' treatise on the freedom of the will, which is written later and where Edwards rejects the "Arminian" notion of a self-determining will—a notion that Edwards considers ridiculous but which is largely the notion that came to dominate American Christianity. Likewise, Edwards' views on original sin were little heeded by "innocent Americans."

[35] In the *Miscellanies* in speaking about heaven, Edwards says, "'Tis evident that men were intended for society, that is, to assist each other in their interests, and chiefly to assist each other in their chief interest; and if in subservient interests, surely most of all the great happiness for which he was created . . ." Of course, that chief end was the happiness that comes from the ". . . sight of God's excellence and delighting therein . . ." (268).

[36] See S. R. Yarbrough and J. C. Adams, *Delightful Conviction: Jonathan Edwards and the Rhetoric of Conversion* (Westport, CT: Greenwood Press, 1993), xv. They also make the point that Edwards always insisted that conversion came not from the preacher, who could only prepare for the possibility of conversion, but from the Spirit of God. Their recognition of the importance of Alexander Richardson—"Puritan and Ramist"—is illuminating. They also recognize Edwards' "critique of the Great Awakening," calling it a "repudiation" (66).

[37] Jonathan Edwards, *A History of the Work of Redemption*, ed. John Wilson (New Haven: Yale University Press, 1989), 311ff. Why do I find this wonky history? Gerald McDermott, in his *Jonathan Edwards Confronts the Gods* (New York: Oxford University Press, 2000), has sought to see Edwards in a new light in relation to his writings about other religions. I eagerly read McDermott's study but I was disappointed to discover that, as McDermott acknowledges, ". . . Edwards was not really open to other religions as viable, living faiths. He was interested in them primarily because they provided both ammunition for his battles with deism and support for other polemical claims made on behalf of reformed Christianity" (12). Thus while McDermott does say that Edwards "came to acknowledge that there was something more to the salvation of the heathen than previous Reformed divines had allowed and more to non-Christian religions than most Christians had granted" (224), the existing volume of the *WOR* is exclusively focused on the Christian community and his comments on "Popery, Mahamotans, and Jews" may well be standard for his age, but they are nonetheless appalling and reveal an all too standard Christian prejudice vis-à-vis other religions. Edwards' vision is founded in a pre-critical view of scripture, Christocentric and ecclesiocentric and is not yet as fully Trinitarian and anti-millennialist as his post-1746 were to become.

[38] Wilson, 93. It is the collapse of Edwards' transcendent vision into a "foreshadowing of the renewal of God's people . . . in the republic" that I find so troubling. The reason is that it undercuts a truly political society. For the best account of a truly political society that I know see H. Richardson, "What Makes a Society Political," in *Religion & Political Society*, ed. J. Moltmann, H. Richardson, et al. (New York: Harper & Row, 1974), 100–120.

[39] See my "From Edwards to Hopkins: A Millennialist Critique of Political Culture," in *The Coming Kingdom: Essays in American Millennialism & Eschatology*, ed. M. Darrol Bryant and Donald Dayton (New York: New ERA Books, 1983), 58. Edwards himself failed to address the slavery issue, but I think that Hopkins rightly saw the implications of Edwards' writing for this issue.

"One vast and ecumenical holding company": Edwardsean Millennial Themes in Nineteenth- and Twentieth-Century Dystopian Fiction

James Hewitson

For nearly fifty years, the cultural significance of Jonathan Edwards' millennial thought has been the subject of debate. In his influential "Jonathan Edwards: A New Departure in Eschatology," C. C. Goen argues that Edwards was "America's first major postmillennial thinker"; by historicizing the millennium, Edwards established "a strong impetus to utopianism in America" and was "of a piece with the liberalizing thought which came to full flower in the following century."[1] Goen's thesis has subsequently come under much scrutiny. Without questioning the influence of postmillennialism in the nineteenth century, or the extent to which this system was associated with Edwards, John F. Wilson notes that an association between Edwards and nineteenth-century theology is difficult to substantiate. This is because the discursive context between the periods differed so dramatically. With the gradual spread of Enlightenment thought following Edwards' career, many aspects of his Christocentric theology were lost. In particular, Wilson notes a progressive narrowing, in which Edwards' New Divinity successors, such as Samuel Hopkins and Joseph Bellamy, tended to focus upon technical questions, losing what he terms the "cosmic framework" evident in Edwards' millennialism.[2] Wilson charges that they "adapted Jonathan Edwards' ideas even as they adopted them—and thereby reduced them to a broadly Enlightenment-derived frame of reference, using essentially propositional modes of thought, a position which for Edwards was embedded in a much richer and far more traditional and complex cognitive world."³ Henry F. May contends that for this reason Edwards' millennialism can be seen as representing a lost ideal: "His vision of a community dedicated to the intellectual love of God, is hardly incarnate in the United States of America. It is rather, perhaps, the greatest of American lost causes, appealing powerfully to numerous enemies of American optimism and materialism from Hawthorne and Melville to Perry Miller."⁴

While allegiance to this cause may well unite Edwards with subsequent generations, this affinity has not always been apparent to later critics of American culture. Although not writing specifically about Edwardsean millennialism, Mark Twain, for example, expresses the disgust with which Edwards' theology was commonly viewed in the nineteenth century. After reading *Freedom of the Will,* Twain writes:

> continuously until near midnight I wallowed and reeked with Jonathan in his insane debauch; rose . . . with a strange and haunting sense of having been on a three days' tear with a drunken lunatic. . . . All through the book is the glare of a resplendent intellect gone mad. . . . By God I was ashamed to be in such company.⁵

Edwards is identified as an exponent of an older and inherently destructive mentality that does not offer any alternative to the contemporary world. For this reason, continuities between Edwards and later writers are predominantly evident in the parodic possibilities made available by his millennial paradigms: specifically, they have constituted a means through which subsequent writers have satirized the very notion that society was systematically moving toward perfection. In his *History of the Work of Redemption, Notes on Scripture* and *Dissertation on the End for Which God Created the World,* Edwards represents traditional typological relationships of adumbration and fulfillment through images of complex machines, in which typological fulfillment is expressed through the rotations of wheels and gears. When removed from its mooring in this figural tradition and separated from Edwards' conception of a dynamic and self-expressing God, however, his mechanistic vision of millennial progress becomes a model for humanity's dispossession and enslavement, and a means of representing the mechanization of the human subject and its alienation from true divinity. For this reason, the framework established by Edwards' millennium became a way for authors critical of nineteenth-century assumptions of millennial progress, such as Hawthorne, Melville, Adams, and Twain, to express their dissatisfaction with American culture and the assumptions on which it rested, as well as to demonstrate how systematic attempts to build a material New Jerusalem in fact worked to transform the world into a type of hell. In twentieth-century fiction, such representations are commonplace. Although authors reiterating this paradigm would not, of course, ascribe it to Edwards; the description of a society brought into conformity with some organizing system indifferent to human good can be seen as an inverted continuation of his millennialism. At the same time, the uses to which this anti-millennialism was put—exposing the falsity and worldliness underlying many attempts at social amelioration—equally is consistent with Edwards' emphasis on the formation of a community free of hypocrisy, and predicated on the integrity and well-being of its members.

Edwards' millennialism derives from his dynamic conception of God's being.[6] In his *End in Creation,* Edwards asserts that God possesses a "communicative disposition in general," which seeks to "flow out and diffuse itself."[7] The end of creation is God's "communication of himself which he intended throughout all eternity," and it is expressed in the creature's "increasing knowledge of God, love to him, and joy in him."[8] Through this self-communication, the "creature becomes more and more *conformed* to God" and the image of divinity is made "more and more perfect, and so the good that is in the creature comes for ever nearer and nearer to an identity with that which is in God."[9] From this perspective, history can be understood as constituting the process of God's eternal emanation, or, as Edwards would say, God's self-enlargement *ad extra*.[10] Edwards' historiography applied this general emphasis on God's communicative disposition to the typological mode of biblical exegesis that dominated American Protestantism throughout the seventeenth and eighteenth centuries. Traditionally, typology consists in the sequences of adumbration and fulfillment outlined in the Bible, in which persons, institutions and events of the Old Testament are understood as foreshadowing corresponding persons, institutions or events in the New Testament. This mode of interpretation can be seen to reveal the providential nature of history by illustrating how the events of the Old Testament appear to prefigure the advent of Christ. Although Edwards' general understanding of Scriptural typology remains consistent with this paradigm, in his writings he characteristically employs typological relationships to emphasize the continuous and progressive communication of God's being to his church; he sees this function as inherent to the nature of typology itself. In his "Types of the Messiah," for example, Edwards asserts that "it has ever been God's manner from the beginning of the world to exhibit and reveal future things by symbolical representations, which were no more than types of the future things revealed."[11] Scripture, moreover, "was made obscure and mysterious, and in many places having great difficulties, that his people might have exercise for their pious wisdom and study, and that his church might make progress in the understanding of it."[12] Because of this, the meaning and structure of the types become clearer in concert with the approach of Christ's millennial kingdom. Edwards notes that "[t]here are a multitude of things in the Old Testament which the church then did not understand, but were reserved to be unfolded to the Christian church, such as the most of their types and shadows and prophecies, which make up the greatest part of the Old Testament," and that "there are many [things] now that are veiled, that remain to [be] discovered by the church in the coming glorious times."[13]

To represent the progressive nature of God's typological revelation and the understanding of the universe that it implies, Edwards figuratively employs Ezekiel's metaphor of the rider and the chariot. In the *End of Creation* he writes:

> The whole universe is a machine which God hath made for his own use, as is represented in Ezekiel's vision. In this chariot God's seat or throne is in heaven, where he sits, who uses and governs and rides in this chariot, Ezek. 1:22, 26–28. The inferior part of the creation, this visible universe, subject to such continual changes and revolutions, are the wheels of the chariot, under the place of the seat of him who rides in this chariot. God's providence in the constant revolutions and alterations and successive events, is represented by the motion of the wheels of the chariot, by the spirit of him who sits on his throne on the heavens, or above the firmament. Moses tells us for whose sake it is that God moves the wheels of this chariot, or rides in it sitting in his heavenly seat; and to what end he is making his progress, or goes his appointed journey in it, viz. the salvation of his people.[14]

The created world exists exclusively for the purposes of redemption. God is the driver, moving the universe forward, and redemption the means by which God brings about his external repetition. Insofar as redemption involves the realization of God's design, it consists of an unimpeded advancement, each revolution building upon and moving beyond the previous one. Through these revolutions the earthly church is moved forward consistently and in accordance with the divine teleology governing the world.

When represented as working together in this way, God's acts of providence appear as a series of interlocking concentric circles, so that, as Edwards notes, "the whole series of divine providence, from the beginning to the end, is nothing else but the revolution of certain wheels, greater and lesser, the lesser being contained within the greater."[15] In his "Images of Divine Things," he once again explicitly connects these revolutions—and providence generally—with the workings of a machine:

> That machines for the measuring of time are by wheels, and wheels within wheels, some lesser, some greater; some of quicker, others of slower revolution; some moving one way, others another; some wheels dependent on others and all connected together, all adjusted one to another and all conspiring to bring about the same effect, livelily represents the course of things in time from day to day, from year to year, and from age to age, as ordered and governed by divine providence.[16]

History is a collection of movements, many of which seem to have no explicit relationship to the creation of Christ's kingdom, and may even seem to tend away from it altogether. All, however, are imagined as functioning in a manner analogous to an intricate machine, and the various gears, once set in motion, proceed at a precise and inevitable pace until the Final Judgment.[17]

In nineteenth- and twentieth-century literature, the image of the machine has rarely been given a positive meaning, and is typically used to describe a form of enforced systemization through which individuals are distanced from meaning, and experience alienation and subjective disintegration. This reevaluation occurred because of differences between the ways in which the intellect and the affections were understood in Edwards' context and the Enlightenment world of the nineteenth and twentieth centuries. In Edwards' description of the relationship between the intellect and the heart in *Religious Affections*, he discusses the heart as pertaining to the affections, which are "the more vigorous and sensible exercises of the inclination and the will of the soul,"[18] and delineates the relationship between the affections and the mind's reasoning component:

> God has imbued the soul with two faculties: one is that by which it is capable of perception and speculation, or by which it discerns and views and judges of things; which is called the understanding. The other faculty is that by which the soul does not merely perceive and view

things, but is some way inclined with respect to the things it views or considers; either is inclined to 'em, or is disinclined, and averse from 'em; or is the faculty by which the soul does not behold things, as an indifferent unaffected spectator, but either as liking or disliking, pleased or displeased, approving or rejecting. This faculty is called by various names: it is sometimes called the *inclination:* and, as it has respect to the actions that are determined and governed by it, is called the *will:* and the *mind,* with regard to the exercises of this faculty, is often called the *heart.*[19]

Edwards does not view the soul's inclinations, whether expressed through the will or the heart, as being opposed to the understanding per se. Rather, they pertain to the affective qualities that ideas have when viewed by the human subject. The understanding perceives ideas, bringing them before the soul, and the way in which the soul responds to them—as either being drawn to or repulsed by them—is determined by the affective quality that the mind bestows upon them. This quality is accordingly a function of the soul's affective capacity. If the mind's inclination takes the form of action, it is considered will, but if it is mental, it pertains to the heart. In the context of the mind's actual operations, the differences between understanding and inclinations, and between will and heart, are further diminished: the affections only comprehend ideas that have been grasped by the understanding, and so acts of the will invariably involve a corresponding movement of the heart.[20] As such, inclinations are inherently bound up with the understanding and acts of will become outward signs of the heart's nature. Although the inclinations of the heart are themselves constant, in their influence, they constitute the general orientation that determines the overarching tangent of an individual's life. Because of the inclinations of the heart, the saint is moved to seek God, and make "vigorous exercises of the inclination and will, towards divine objects."[21] The nature of the affections accordingly also implies a dynamic quality, a course of development through which the motivating inclinations of the heart actuate the individual to a greater engagement with the objects of the affections.

The heart's progressive disposition means that it constantly works to bring the saint into greater proximity to divinity. In this process of gradual revelation, the millennium constitutes the fullest perception of divinity experienced by the saints in the context of their material existences. In his *Humble Attempt,* Edwards explores in substantial detail the nature of this event and humanity's perception of how divinity will be expanded. He describes it as being characterized by an outpouring of the Spirit resulting in a greater level of spiritual comprehension than has heretofore been obtained. In this text, Edwards asserts: "It is evident from the Scripture, that there is *yet remaining* a great advancement of the interest of religion and the kingdom of Christ in this world, by an abundant outpouring of the Spirit of God, far greater and more extensive than ever yet has been."[22] This outpouring will not only be expressed in an increase in the universality of Christianity, but also in an awareness of how God's glory is typified extra-scripturally, in the natural world. Edwards notes that this period is "represented as a time of vast increase of knowledge and understanding, especially in divine things."[23] In the resulting proliferation of the spirit, Edwards writes, "the very fields, trees and mountains shall then as it were rejoice, and break forth into singing."[24] This new understanding of divinity will not be restricted to the natural world but will embrace the works of culture as well, so that "holiness should be as it were inscribed on everything, on all men's common business and employments, and the common utensils of life, all shall be dedicated to God."[25]

Because the affections guide the understanding in this way, Edwards is able to assert continuity between God's redemption of individuals and what he terms the "one great work" of Redemption.[26] In the nineteenth century, however, the Romantic opposition assumed between the heart and the intellect made this relationship virtually impossible. Ralph Waldo Emerson distinguished between the understanding, which "adds, divides, combines, measures," and reason, the higher faculty, which "transfers all these lessons into its own world of thought, by perceiving the analogy that marries Matter and Mind,"[27] asserting that "[t]here is no doctrine of the Reason which will bear to be taught by the Understanding."[28] Literature reflecting these developments typically opposed the heart and the intellect, and represented the intellect as being incapable of grasping the knowledge of the heart. In "The Procession of Life," for example, Nathaniel Hawthorne writes,

> though the heart be large, yet the mind is often of such moderate dimensions as to be exclusively filled up with one idea. When a good man has long devoted himself to a particular kind of beneficence—to one species of reform—he is apt to become narrowed into the limits of the path wherein he treads, and to fancy that there is no other good to be done on earth but that self-same good to which he has put his hand, and in the very mode that best suits his own conceptions.[29]

Reformers who become convinced of a particular mode of social amelioration are represented as losing their sense of heart altogether, and as becoming, like the knowledge they seek, essentially mechanical beings. In *The Blithedale Romance,* for example, the failed reformer Hollingsworth is described as becoming a "steel engine of the Devil's contrivance,"[30] and "'[a] cold, heartless, self-beginning and self-ending piece of mechanism!'"[31] The extent to which the heart and the intellect were seen as mutually exclusive, and the degree to which intellectual knowledge was demonized, is expressed in a letter Herman Melville wrote to Hawthorne:

> I stand for the heart. To the dogs with the head! I had rather be a fool with a heart, than Jupiter Olympus with his head. The reason the mass of

men fear God, and at bottom dislike Him, is because they rather distrust His heart, and fancy Him all brain like a watch.³²

The timepiece, of course, is the image that Edwards uses to express the perfection of God's works. In this context, however, the timepiece evokes an inhuman system indifferent to humanity's good, which is oriented solely toward achieving its own mechanical perfection.

The distrust of intellectual apprehension apparent in these writers and the accompanying suspicion of engineered programs for social amelioration are reflected in the way in which the figure of Edwards himself is treated in nineteenth-century literature. In *Billy Budd,* Melville specifically links Edwards with the grotesque injustices of systems that are concerned more with their own functioning than with the good of their individual members. When Captain Vere delivers his judgment condemning Billy Budd to the crew of the *Bellipotent,* the narrator notes that Vere's "announcement was listened to by the throng of sailors in a dumbness like that of a seated congregation of believers in hell listening to the clergyman's announcement of his Calvinist text."³³

In the margin of his original manuscript for Billy Budd, Melville wrote "Jonathan Edwards."³⁴ The implication, of course, is that Vere's decision, which is predicated on the well-being of the ship and the navy of which it is a part, is as disassociated from real justice as the Calvinist doctrine that Melville saw as excluding adherents from any true understanding of divinity. The fact that Melville noted Edwards' name specifically beside this section indicates the representative value that Edwards retained at this point: Edwards signified, at least, for Melville, the fatuous assumptions about divine wrath and human sinfulness that so many subsequent thinkers saw as tormenting individuals and deforming human consciousness. As such, injustice, suffering, and the sensibility that is willing to tolerate them because of a mistaken belief in the nature of divinity are seen as the legacy of Calvinism, especially as it was represented by Edwards. More pertinently, Melville's linkage implies that systematic attempts at achieving a larger good at the expense of individuals become morally equivalent to a Calvinist doctrine that consigned large numbers of people to hell for the maintenance of the system itself.

In the twentieth century, the correspondence between systematic approaches to societal amelioration and alienation has become a convention. A classic example is Ken Kesey's *One Flew Over the Cuckoo's Nest*. The novel's narrator, Chief Bromden, a diagnosed paranoid schizophrenic, connects American industrialism and social homogenization to an entity he names the Combine, which is dedicated to transforming the world into a vast collective, maintained by technology and populated by indistinguishable individuals. When describing a factory, Bromden notes how the workers seem to be tied to their machines and pulled back to them when they seem on the verge of leaving. He remarks upon "[a]ll those spindles reeling and wheeling and shuttles jumping around and bobbins wringing in the air with string, white-washed walls and steel-gray machines and girls in flowered skirts skipping back and forth, and the whole thing webbed with flowing white lines stringing the factory together."[35] These lines seem to bind the workers to the machines and, by so doing, make them appurtenances of the machinery itself. As Bromden explores the implications of this kind of reorientation, he imagines operations in which patients are gutted and their organs replaced by gears and transistors, so that they can better fit the needs of the Combine:

> Sometimes a guy goes over for an installation, leaves the ward mean and mad and snapping at the whole world and comes back a few weeks later with black-and-blue eyes like he'd been in a fist-fight, and he's the sweetest, nicest, best-behaved thing you ever saw. He'll maybe even go home in a month or two, a hat pulled low over the face of a sleepwalker wandering round in a simple, happy dream.[36]

The doctors, nurses and administrators supervising these operations are themselves mostly machines. At another point during this fantasy sequence, a worker tending the patients suddenly seems to shut down, and when his compatriots toss him in a blast furnace, Bromden hears "the popping of a million tubes."[37]

The film *Network* ties such aggressive systemization directly to the idea of postmillennial fulfillment. Here the world is depicted as being on the brink of a fundamental transformation, in which the nature of human consciousness is to be forever altered, and many of the basic tenets of postmillennialism are made explicit in the film's discussions of progress and revelation. In one scene, the Chief Executive Officer of the television corporation imposing such controls makes a speech—in a conference room described in the script as an "overwhelming cathedral"—that identifies business practices as "the primal forces of nature,"[38] and the emergence of the multinational corporation with the earthly millennium and the fulfillment of humanity's quest for a perfect world:

> The world is a business! . . . It has been that way since man crawled out of the slime, and our children . . . will live to see that perfect world without war and famine, oppression and brutality—one vast and ecumenical holding company, for whom all men will work to serve a common profit, in which all men will hold a share of stock, all necessities provided, all anxieties tranquilized, all boredom amused.[39]

Again, as in postmillennial thought, this new world is represented as emerging out of a process of historical transformation and as answering needs and aspirations that have motivated humans since their first consciousness. The implicit sense of supernatural revelation in this scene is revealed when a witness to the speech exclaims, "I have seen the face of God!"—that is, the visible manifestation of the higher reality gradually shaping the world to its image.[40]

The adoption of postmillennial rhetoric in this film illustrates both how common it has become, and how intellectually bankrupt its conventions appeared by the late twentieth century. In Thomas Pynchon's *V.*, this analysis is extended, and the capacity for humanity to find fulfillment within mechanical structures is examined in the context of a general tendency to entropy existing in the universe as a whole. The eponymous V., who is emblematic of this process, is imagined as gradually becoming a machine:

> skin radiant with the bloom of some new plastic; both eyes glass but now containing photoelectric cells, connected by silver electrodes to optic nerves of purest copper wire and leading to a brain exquisitely wrought as a diode matrix could ever be. Solenoid relays would be her ganglia, servo-actuators move her flawless nylon limbs, hydraulic fluid be sent by a platinum heart-pump through butyrate veins and arteries.[41]

The mechanization of V.'s body occurs in stages, during which she assimilates inanimate objects into herself. V.'s experience anticipates the condition of mechanization that other characters in the novel approach through diverse processes, ranging from the affinity with and love for sports cars and motorcycles, to a character's reflections during plastic surgery that "'the highest condition we can attain is that of an object—a rock,'" and her accompanying desire to become, as she states, "'a blob, with no worries, traumas, nothing: only Being.'"[42] V.'s tendency toward the inanimate is described as a "conspiracy leveled against the animate world," and as the "establishment here of a colony of the Kingdom of Death."[43] Here as well, the final state of entropy that many of the novel's characters are moving towards is represented not so much as ending but as definitively concluding human history, and as therefore having a religious significance. In her final manifestation as the Bad Priest, V. reportedly teaches children that God is soulless, and that, as another character says, "'to be like God we must allow to be eroded the soul in ourselves. Seek mineral symmetry, for here is eternal life: the immortality of rock.'"[44] By achieving such soullessness, humanity becomes a temporal repetition of God's essence; just as in Edwards' discourse, humanity will increasingly approximate and refund God's excellence in the Christian millennium. In Pynchon's narrative, however, the millennial fulfillment offered constitutes the negation of all of its higher aspirations.

In Edwards' postmillennialism, the millennium was the product of God's cooperation with redeemed humanity, and the historical expression of God's own perfection. In much twentieth-century fiction, however, the world is described as devolving according to some system of enslavement ostensibly designed to improve life, but which in fact suffocates the individual. The system works to create a state in which individuals are divested of their singularity and reduced to socioeconomic roles, and dedicated to service the very system that was supposed to effect their liberation. As such, the revelation that these texts witness is not the millennium per se but the perfection of the system itself, which has become a prison. This conception of history could be termed dark postmillennialism: it proposes a theory of degradation in which forces inherent to human social organization are represented as compelling individuals to mechanistic conformity; it uses the rhetorical techniques and exegetical approaches of the Edwardsean millennium to describe the extent to which this systemization has usurped the ends it was designed to accomplish.

This adaptation of the tropes Edwards used to formulate and explicate his millennialism to represent this new perception of history and society can be seen marking a profound shift in the way technology was viewed, and more importantly how manifest and liminal realities were understood as cooperating. For Edwards, the spiritual and material worlds worked in concert, so that societal progress was the means by which the visible and invisible churches were drawn together. Although postmillennialism itself continued to exert a strong influence on American society throughout the nineteenth century,[45] for many later writers the heavenly and earthly spheres were seen as mutually exclusive; a system predicated on the eventual perfection of the manifest world was viewed as necessarily precluding redemptive or even meaningful experiences on the part of individuals existing within it. For this reason, the structure of the Edwardsean millennium has functioned primaily as a means of parodying and critiquing the assumptions and assurances of a society that increasingly came to be seen as concerned with its own efficiency and indifferent to the well-being of its members. Paddy Chayefsky's vision of an ecumenical corporatism subsuming the world or the dystopian conformity with matter that Pynchon describes constitute the dark converse of the progressive consent to divinity that Edwards saw as heralding the beginning of the millennium.

JAMES K. HEWITSON earned the B.A., M.A., and Ph.D. all from the University of Toronto. He is a lecturer in the Department of English at the University of Tennessee. His publications address such topics as Edwards, Hawthorne, and the connections between nineteenth-century American utopian literature and millennialism.

NOTES

[1] C. C. Goen, "Jonathan Edwards: A New Departure in Eschatology," in *Critical Essays on Jonathan Edwards*, ed. William J. Scheick (Boston: G. K. Hall, 1980), 163.

[2] John F. Wilson, "Editor's Introduction," in *A History of the Work of Redemption*, ed. John F. Wilson, vol. 9, *The Works of Jonathan Edwards* (New Haven: Yale University Press, 1989), 83.

[3] John F. Wilson, "History, Redemption and the Millennium," in *Jonathan Edwards and the American Experience*, ed. Nathan O. Hatch and Harry S. Stout (Oxford: Oxford University Press, 1988), 135–136.

[4] Henry F. May, *The Enlightenment in America* (New York: Oxford UP, 1976), 50.

[5] Mark Twain, *Mark Twain's Letters*, vol. 2, ed. Albert Bigelow Paine (New York: Harper & Brother Publishers, 1917), 719–720.

[6] For more on the dynamic nature of God's being, see Sang Hyun Lee, *The Philosophical Theology of Jonathan Edwards* (Princeton: Princeton University Press, 1988).

[7] Jonathan Edwards, *A Dissertation Concerning the End for Which God Created the World*, in *Ethical Writings*, ed. Paul Ramsey, vol. 8, *The Works of Jonathan Edwards* (New Haven: Yale University Press, 1989), 435. (Hereafter referred to as *End in Creation*).

[8] Edwards, *End in Creation*, 443.

[9] Ibid., 443.

[10] Edwards asserts that it "is God's essence to incline to communicate Himself" in No. 107(b) of "The Miscellanies" [(entry Nos. a–z, aa–zz, 1–500), ed. Thomas A. Schafer, vol. 13, *The Works of Jonathan Edwards* (New Haven: Yale University Press, 1994)], 277–278. In *The Prism of Scripture: Studies on History and Historicity in the Work of Jonathan Edwards* (Bern: Herbert Lange, 1975), Karl Dieterich Pfisterer notes that this disposition or desire thus "belonged to the nature of the Godhead itself and therefore had the same claim to generality that belonged to God as the *Summum Ens*," 294. Lee elaborates upon this assertion stating that in Edwards' thought "God, conceived as essentially a disposition, is capable of being a perfect actuality *and* an eternal disposition to repeat this actuality through further exercises," 173. As such, God is in his being fully realized, while, through his communicative disposition, constantly self-enlarging. These two aspects of God's nature are equipoised through the distinction between God's *ad intra* and *ad extra* communications—between his internal self-communications and the emanations that constitute his external communication. Janice Knight, in "Learning the Language of God: Jonathan Edwards and the Typology of Nature," in *William and Mary Quarterly* 48.4 (October 1991), notes that God's *ad extra* and *ad intra* communications provide a model for understanding the relationship between God's being and history: "The source of the ineffable, indissoluble union of these two modes is contained, though not explained, in the sacred mystery of the Trinity, which not only makes one God three but also insists that priority of existence and equality of essence are eternally joined. History can no more be severed from ontology than the idea of God can be divorced from his love," 547.

[11] Edwards, "Types of Messiah," in *Typological Writings*, ed. Wallace E. Anderson, Mason I. Lowance, Jr., and David H. Watters, vol. 11, *The Works of Jonathan Edwards* (New Haven: Yale University Press, 1993), 192.

[12] Edwards, "Miscellanies" No. 351, 426.

[13] Edwards, "Miscellanies" No. 351, 426–427.

[14] Edwards, *End in Creation*, 513.

[15] Edwards, *Notes on Scripture*, ed. Stephen J. Stein, vol. 15, *The Works of Jonathan Edwards* (New Haven: Yale University Press, 1998), 374.

[16] Edwards, "Images of Divine Things," in *Typological Writings*, 125.

[17] In his *History of the Work of Redemption* Edwards describes all of the events of history as consisting of revolutions of wheels within wheels, and as working together to realize Christ's kingdom.

[18] Edwards, *Religious Affections,* ed. John E. Smith, vol. 2, *The Works of Jonathan Edwards* (New Haven: Yale University Press, 1959), 96.

[19] Edwards, *Religious Affections,* 96.

[20] In discussing the relationship between the affections and the understanding, it is important to note that Edwards distinguishes strongly between affections and passions. He defines the passions as inclinations "that are more sudden, and whose effects on the animal spirits are more violent, and the mind more overpowered and less in its own command" in *Religious Affections,* 98. The affections denote a more extensive and yet less disruptive compunction, pertaining to the series of preferences expressed consistently by a subject and so do not involve the possible conflicts with the understanding in the same way as the passions. For a more specific explanation of the relationship between the will and the heart in Edwards' theology see Smith's "Editor's Introduction," in *Religious Affections,* 12–14.

[21] Edwards, *Religious Affections,* 100.

[22] Jonathan Edwards, *An Humble Attempt To Promote Explicit Agreement and Visible Union of God's People in Extraordinary Prayer,* in *Apocalyptic Writings,* ed. Stephen J. Stein, vol. 5, *The Works of Jonathan Edwards* (New Haven: Yale University Press, 1977), 329.

[23] Edwards, *Humble Attempt,* 338.

[24] Ibid., 340.

[25] Ibid., 338. In "Images of Divine Things," Edwards describes how technological and economic developments can be seen as facilitating God's kingdom. The telescope, for example, can be considered a type of the millennium insofar as the discoveries which it has facilitated anticipate "the great increase in the knowledge of heavenly things that shall be in the approaching glorious times of the Christian church," 101. The telescope can be considered a mechanical instance of divine providence and as both a type of the millennium and a tool for its realization; the scientific discoveries it makes possible prefigure the discovery of greater divinity, and the broader knowledge of material reality it facilitates becomes a field for further understanding of divinity. For Edwards, too, the material progress that is incumbent to economic and technological development is also part of the process through which God's kingdom will come into being: America's growing trading power "is a type and forerunner of what is approaching in spiritual things, when the world shall be supplied with spiritual treasures from America," 101. As the millennium approaches, the relationship between material and spiritual realities is expected to become more profound: the growing comprehension of divinity is to continue, and all of humanity's inventions are to stand revealed as partaking of God.

[26] Edwards, *History of the Work of Redemption,* 121.

[27] Ralph Waldo Emerson, *Nature,* in *Essays & Lectures: Nature; Addresses, and Lectures; Essays: First and Second Series; Representative Men; English Traits; The Conduct of Life; Uncollected Prose,* ed. Joel Porte (New York: Library of America, 1983), 26.

[28] Emerson, "Divinity School Address" in *Essays & Lectures,* 80.

[29] Nathaniel Hawthorne, "The Procession of Life" in *Mosses from an Old Manse,* ed. William Charvat, Roy Harvey Pearce, and Claude M. Simpson, vol. 10, *Centenary Edition* (Columbus: Ohio State University Press, 1974), 217–218.

[30] Hawthorne, *The Blithedale Romance* in *The Blithedale Romance and Fanshawe,* ed. William Charvat et al., vol. 4, *Centenary Edition,* (Columbus: Ohio State University Press, 1964), 71.

[31] Hawthorne, *Blithedale,* 218.

[32] Herman Melville, *Correspondence,* ed. Lynn Horth, vol. 14, *The Writings of Herman Melville,* (Evanston and Chicago: Northwestern University Press and the Newbury Library, 1993), 192.

[33] Melville, *Billy Budd Sailor (An Inside Narrative),* ed. Harrison Hayford and Merton M. Sealts, Jr. (Chicago: University of Chicago Press, 1962), 117.

[34] Melville, "Editors' Notes," *Billy Budd,* 184.

[35] Ken Kesey, *One Flew Over the Cuckoo's Nest* (New York: Signet, 1962), 40.

[36] Kesey, 20–21.

[37] Kesey, 80.

[38] Paddy Chayefsky, *Network* in *The Collected Works of Paddy Chayefsky: The Screenplays* vol. 2 (New York: Applause Books, 1995), 205.

[39] Chayefsky, 206.

[40] Chayefsky, 206.

[41] Thomas Pynchon, *V.* (1961) (New York: Harper Perennial, 1986), 411.

[42] Pynchon, 106.

[43] Pynchon, 411.

[44] Pynchon, 340. Pynchon's treatment of religious themes is beyond the scope of this essay. For more sustained examinations of this topic, see W. T. Lhamon, Jr., "Pentecost, Promiscuity and Pynchon's *V.*," in *Twentieth Century Literature* 21.5 (1975), 163–175; Edward Mendelson, "The Sacred, the Profane, and *The Crying of Lot 49,*" in *Individual and Community: Variations on a Theme in American Fiction,* ed. Kenneth H. Baldwin and David K. Kirby (Durham, NC: Duke University Press, 1975), 182–222; Victoria H. Price, *Christian Allusions in the Novels of Thomas Pynchon* (New York: Peter Lang, 1989); Scott Sanders, "Pynchon's Paranoid History," in *Twentieth Century Literature* 21.5 (1975), 177–192; and Marcus Smith and Khachig Tololyan, "The New Jeremiad: *Gravity's Rainbow,*" in *Critical Essays on Thomas Pynchon,* ed. Richard Pearce (Boston: G. K. Hall, 1981), 169–184.

[45] For more on the relationship between postmillennialism and American progressivism, see Ruth H. Block, *Visionary Republic: Millennial Themes in American Thought, 1756–1800* (Cambridge: Cambridge University Press, 1985); James H. Moorhead, *American Apocalypse: Yankee Protestants and the Civil War, 1860–1869* (New Haven: Yale University Press, 1978); "Between Progress and Apocalypse: A Reassessment of Millennialism in American Religious Thought, 1800–1880," *Journal of American History* 71 (1984): 524–542; and *World Without End: Mainstream American Protestant Visions of the Last Things, 1880–1925* (Bloomington: Indiana University Press, 1999); Jean B. Quandt, "Religion and Social Thought: The Secularization of Postmillennialism," *American Quarterly* 25 (1973): 390–409; and Ernest Lee Tuveson, *Redeemer Nation: The Idea of America's Millenial Role* (Chicago: University of Chicago Press, 1968).

PART III

EDWARDS AS INTERPRETER OF NATURE

Edwards, Swedenborg, Emerson: From Typology to Correspondence

Devin P. Zuber

Ever since Perry Miller published his landmark essay "Jonathan Edwards to Emerson" (1940), scholars have drawn clear and compelling connections between New England's preeminent Puritan philosopher and its most memorable transcendentalist.[1] Edwards' ideas seem closest to Ralph Waldo Emerson's when either thinker turns to the book of nature, seeking there a relationship to God and the universe. In a well-known passage from one of his typological notebooks, Edwards defiantly declares his belief regarding nature:

> I expect by very ridicule and contempt to be called a man of a very fruitful brain and copious fancy, but they are welcome to it. I am not ashamed to own I believe that the whole universe, heaven and earth, air and seas, and the divine constitution and history of the holy Scriptures, be full of images of divine things, as full as language is of words . . . there is room for persons to be learning more and more of this language and seeing more of that which is declared in it to the end of the world without discovering it all.[2]

Some one hundred and five years later, Ralph Waldo Emerson, in his first book of published essays, seems to embody one of Edwards' "persons" who is learning more and more of this divine language:

> Every natural fact is a symbol of some spiritual fact. Every appearance in nature corresponds to some state of mind. . . . Who looks upon a river in a meditative hour, and is not reminded of the flux of all things? Throw a stone into the stream, and the circles that propagate themselves are the beautiful type of all influence.[3]

The influence of Edwards on Emerson, however, is not as easy as juxtaposing these quotes and remarking on their overlapping echoes. From Perry Miller to Mason Lowance, scholars of New England intellectual history have had to grapple with an irreconcilable fact: Emerson's interest in Edwards was, in the words of the Emerson biographer Robert Richardson, "quite limited."[4] Perry Miller's first publication on the successive notion of "Edwards to Emerson" evoked a storm of controversy. Miller's later *Errand into the Wilderness* (1956) attempted to quell the criticism that he had made spurious intellectual connections by maintaining that "on the crudest of levels . . . certain basic continuities persist in a culture—in this case taking New England as the test tube—which underlie the successive articulation of ideas."[5] Mason Lowance has continued and refined Miller's project in his study of the legacy of Puritan typology, *The Language of Canaan* (1980), where he argues that a substratum of continuous New England thought can be traced not only from Edwards to Emerson, but further into the work of Robert Frost and William Faulkner. Certainly, cultural traits and attitudes subsist in a people over time; Sacvan Bercovitch and Philip Gura are other exemplary scholars who have demonstrated the ongoing impact of Puritan ideology on America's definition of itself.[6] Nonetheless, a vaguely defined cultural inheritance cannot adequately account for the particular ways in which Emerson's ideas about nature, God, and language so strongly chime with those scrawled down by Edwards in the privacy of his notebook a century earlier. The matter becomes more perplexing when one finds how little Emerson refers to Edwards throughout his vast corpus of published essays, letters, and private journals. At the most, Emerson likely read Edwards' *On the Freedom of the Will*, but anything beyond that is conjecture.[7] How, then, can we account for Edwards and Emerson's remarkable propinquity?

Part of the answer, this paper argues, lies in Emerson's reading of the Swedish mystic, Emanuel Swedenborg (1688–1772). That Emerson esteemed Swedenborg's ideas is self-evident—Swedenborg was one of his six representative men, a man "whose literary value has never been rightly estimated," and Emerson's hundreds of remarks about Swedenborg, which span thirty-two years of journaling, attest to the longevity of Swedenborg's presence in Emerson's mind. It was in Swedenborg, and not Edwards, that Emerson read typological statements like "absolutely everything in nature, from the smallest to the largest, is a correspondence to something spiritual." In Swedenborg, Emerson encountered the idea that the state of man's mind shapes the perception of nature around him and that the human form is irradiated throughout the universe in micro- and macro-cosmic paradigms.[8] In Emerson's own words, "Swedenborg, of all men in the recent ages, stands eminently for the translator of nature into thought. I do not know the man in nature for whom things stood so uniformly for words."[9]

To understand why Swedenborg could take Emerson back to an understanding of language and nature that so distinctly echoes Edwards' own, this paper aims to situate the work of Emanuel Swedenborg alongside that of Jonathan Edwards. I argue that both men were cut from the same eighteenth-century cloth: that each maintained a deep emotional piety even as he eagerly read the cutting-edge science of Newton, that each wrestled with the consequences of Lockean psychology and deistic mechanization in his respective writings on free will and the human mind, and, ultimately, that each came to view the wondrous beauty of nature as an exhilarating and ecstatic text of God. Swedenborg's claim to having received ongoing visionary revelations from heaven characterizes him as a more representative mystic than Edwards, but considerations of Edwards' own mystical tendencies raise several intriguing conjectures. Had matters gone somewhat differently, could Jonathan Edwards have taken Swedenborg's place in the mind of Ralph Waldo Emerson? Can we imagine Emerson's famous chapter from "Representative Men" devoted not to a foreign Scandinavian, but to an American from the same New England stock that Emerson grew out of? By juxtaposing Edwards and Swedenborg, we can begin to see how Swedenborg integrates Ralph Waldo Emerson into a strong tradition of American thought embodied by Edwards and thereby can connect several dynamic aspects of Puritan culture with the later symbolism of the American Renaissance.

Emanuel Swedenborg was born in 1688—fourteen years before Jonathan Edwards—the third child of a Lutheran chaplain to the Swedish royal court. Emanuel's household was extremely pious, with each day marked by prayers and devotions. It was also highly intellectual, the more so after Swedenborg's father accepted a professorship in Uppsala, the university center of Scandinavia. The Swedberg[10] home became frequented by numerous theologians and professors, under whose presence the precocious Emanuel thrived. Swedenborg wrote almost nothing concerning his early childhood years except for the following reflection, which comes from a letter written when he was eighty-one:

> From my fourth to my tenth year, I was constantly engaged in thought upon God, salvation, and the spiritual sufferings of men, and several times revealed that at which my father and mother wondered. . . . From my sixth to my twelfth year, my delight was to discourse with [a] clergyman concerning Faith—that the life thereof is love. . . .[11]

On the frontier of the Connecticut Valley, a young Jonathan Edwards also found much love and delight in religious matters. At an unspecified age before going off to college, Edwards experienced a remarkable awakening in his father's church, as he writes in his personal narrative:

> I was then very much affected for many months, and concerned about the things of religion, and my soul's salvation; and was abundant in duties. I used to pray five times a day in secret, and to spend much time in religious talk with other boys; and used to meet with them to pray together. I experienced I know not what kind of delight in religion . . . it was my delight to abound in religious duties.[12]

Edwards' delight in religion was not relegated to the meeting house or to converse with other boys; some of the most religiously ecstatic moments of the personal narrative are in the accounts of Edwards' solitary immersions in Nature as he contemplated the holy things of God. The exceeding abundance of the Divine is a sweetness beyond the grasp of Edwards' language—"I know not how to express" becomes the recurring phrase he resorts to—and the sweetness "seemed to appear in everything; in the sun, moon, and stars; in the clouds, and blue sky; in the grass, flowers, trees; in the water, and all nature. . . ."[13] Edwards would later convert the lists of such experiences into the analytic elaborations of his typological notebooks, but here in his childhood they remain encounters so keenly felt by his heart that he is simply moved to sing out loud.

Edwards' sense of the Divine as a ubiquitous sweetness, incapable of adequate expression, exhibits the pantheism and mysticism that Perry Miller finds underlying Puritan new world theology, and it certainly fits within William James' qualitative definitions of mystical experience.[14] While Swedenborg's later theological work can also be placed under James' rubric, the lack of biographical documents prevents us from establishing if the young prodigy had similar ecstatic encounters with God in the nature outside Stockholm or Uppsala, as likely as this would seem. Despite his family's intellectual and clerical prestige—Swedenborg's father came from a family of Dalecarlian farmers and miners, sturdy people with strong connections to the earth, and Swedenborg himself was noted for being an avid gardener later in life—several of his visionary works, in fact, were written in his garden's small summerhouse, surrounded by trees and flowers.[15]

The young Swedenborg and his siblings were encouraged to "read" natural phenomena closely for signs of the supernatural and were instructed by their father that angels and spirits constantly surrounded them and interacted with their daily lives. In Swedenborg's father's remarkable autobiography, even the creaking furniture could contain spiritual significance: "When one unexpectedly hears how chests and wardrobes crack," Jesper Swedberg writes, "it seems that something experiences pain within them. The utensils are anxious and sigh about the godlessness gaining ground, angering God and deceiving the angels."[16] This sort of approach to the natural world was a defining characteristic of the Puritan experience in America. At its worst in 1692, the desire to read the quotidian for symbols of a spiritual world contributed to the hysteria of the Salem witch trials, but at its best, it gave the Puritans a deeply self-reflective aspect that was both outward and inward looking, as seen in Edwards' meditations. Not only does Edwards marvel at and feel the grandeur of God, but he internalizes how the landscape he beholds reflects his own spiritual state, his need for grace within. As Perry Miller writes, the Puritan "was not insensible to beauty or sublimity, but in the face of every experience he was obliged to ask himself, what does this signify? What is God saying to me at this moment?"[17]

The same questions of divine signification pursued Edwards and Swedenborg into their respective scientific research. Both were writing at a time when Enlightenment discoveries made it increasingly difficult to bring the fruits of empirical research into the proper folds of Christian ontology. Advancements in lens technology, for example, revealed Swedenborg's father's furniture to be more than just chests and wardrobes (whose creaking signified the decline of faith!): a look through a microscope would reveal a vast terrain of porous holes and types of mold, and splinters that contained hundreds of tiny bugs and mites. The earth, the planet where God incarnated as Christ, was no longer the center of the cosmos but a single speck in a vast universe of many stars. Edwards and Swedenborg gave the natural world an attention that was empirically characteristic of their Enlightenment age, all the while maintaining a deep desire to bring what they had observed into harmony with the belief in a Creator of a perfectly ordered universe. Such desire can be seen in Edwards' famous spider letter, likely written when Edwards was around the age of twenty. He closely observes the flying spiders of New England, their webs in the sunshine and their methods for moving through the air, and concludes that the flights of the spiders "show" the abundant wisdom and goodness of God. He is not fazed by his observation that the spiders' attempts at flying appear to lead them to drown in the ocean, that these wondrous flights seem futilely doomed—rather, it is a miraculous provision that prevents the world from being overpopulated by the insects. "These wondrous animals," Edwards writes, "from whose glistening webs so much wisdom of the Creator shines."[18]

Swedenborg's early scientific work also exhibits remarkable powers of observation and the same desire to bridge his empirical findings with accepted exegesis. After returning home to Sweden from his first trip abroad, Swedenborg was inspired to build a facility for astronomical observation along the lines of what he had seen in Greenwich, England. Swedenborg scouted out a possible location on Mt. Kinnekulle, one of the taller promontories in southern Sweden, which conveniently lay only fifteen miles from his father's home at Brunsbo. As Swedenborg scrambled around the peak during August of 1715, he was greatly struck by the abundance of sandy strata that contained various marine fossils. How, he wondered, given the height of the mountain, could one account for this underwater presence? He spent the next several years studying the geographical layers of the surrounding countryside, reincorporating his earlier research on a whale fossil that a friend had excavated in the area five years before. The results were published in 1719 as *The Height of Waters, and Strong Tides in the Primeval World,* which is now regarded as the first geological description of Sweden.[19] The work argues that the waters of the earth were once much higher than suspected and that this fact confirms indubitably the teachings of the biblical flood from Genesis chapter seven.

Just as Edwards' intellectual development came to be heavily colored by his reading of Locke at Harvard, Swedenborg's university years at Uppsala were imbued with the ideas of Descartes, who had been invited to teach there by Queen Christina at the end of his career. One of Swedenborg's most important scientific works, *The Principia* (1733), is strongly grounded in the Cartesian mechanistic principles he had learned as a young man, and it attempts to explain the origin and existence of the universe from pure mathematics.[20] *The Principia* also maintains a philosophy of relation-in-likeness, the idea that the structure of something can be a micro- or macro-cosmic representation of larger and smaller entities. Swedenborg had read this ages-old idea in several places; perhaps most notably for us, it appeared for him and Jonathan Edwards in Newton's *Opticks*.[21] *The Principia* argues if one can prove that part of nature obeys the laws of Cartesian geometry, then everything in the universe must be explicable geometrically, even the soul. The one who holds the right mathematical keys is able to unlock the deepest mysteries of man.

Eleven years before Swedenborg's *Principia* was first published, Edwards also grounded his work on "the mind" in mathematics. Edwards' tract opens with a speculative definition of what makes something "excellent," or pleasurable, to human perception. Edwards starts with basic geometry. He draws a variety of lines and shapes which attempt to illustrate that proportion is innately pleasing while disproportion is conversely unpleasant. At their most basic level, Edwards' pictures are an attempt to reproduce for the reader the feeling of an aesthetic experience. This foundation of "felt" geometry ultimately builds up not to a nebular hypothesis, but to a theory of beauty that also hinges on the idea of relation:

> All beauty consists in similarness, or identity of relation. In identity of relation consists all likeness, and all identity between two consists

in identity of relation . . . and so in every case, what is called correspondency, symmetry, regularity and the like, may be resolved into equalities; though the equalities in a beauty in any degree complicated are so numerous that it would be a most tedious piece of work to enumerate them.[22]

The highest relations for Edwards and Swedenborg were those that were spiritual: the beautiful signs in nature that symmetrically corresponded to truths in God's Word. Edwards' and Swedenborg's empiricism altered their perceptions of the natural world in such a way that they both had to adjust their respective approaches to sacred scripture and revelation, and yet, if each had remained doctrinaire Cartesians or blind adherents of Lockean psychology, neither would have been able to produce theories of type or correspondence which later became so important for the development of symbolic structures in the American Renaissance. It was necessary for each to alter the standard Enlightenment epistemology before he could achieve his union of soul and nature, matter and spirit.

Swedenborg's confident mechanism of *The Principia* soon met an impasse. His next major project—published as *Regnum Animale* (1744–45)—attempted to locate the soul in the human body, to find the precise position where the spiritual met with the natural.[23] Swedenborg found that his previous Cartesian mathematics were insufficient for this purpose; they could not adequately account for the organic nature of the universe nor for God's transcendence beyond our natural perception. As Swedenborg immersed himself in studies of human anatomy, he refined two important concepts into a new methodology. The first was something he designated as the *archeus,* or creative primal energy, that lay behind all things. Every aspect of nature was constantly in a state of becoming because of a higher, immanent world of being that causally lay behind it. The world of our senses was not perfectly ruled by geometry, but under the influx of perpetual creation via the *archeus.* The German scholar Ernst Benz has written that this aspect of Swedenborg's science—which carries over into the distinction between the natural and spiritual worlds of Swedenborg's later theology—places Swedenborg in the great tradition of mystical *Naturphilosophie* which ranges from Paracelsus to Jakob Boehme, from Robert Fludd to Henry More.[24] The *archeus* also distinguishes Swedenborg from his predecessor, Newton, who had seen the motion and energy of the universe as inexorably slowing down into decay.[25] The second idea Swedenborg developed is closely related to the *archeus*. Swedenborg termed it the *anima*, and defined it as the most subtle of fluids, connected through all the major organs and vessels of the human body. The *anima* was at the same time a spiritual substance, a flowing connection to the *archeus*, the link to the Divine source of all life. The *anima* was the drive behind the shape of all our thoughts, lying before and above reason—and here, Swedenborg significantly shifts from the mechanical perspective of the earlier *Principia*. Rather than elevating the understanding as the supreme faculty, man's reason is preceded by the *anima*, and becomes lower in the ordering of the soul. Before we begin to formulate thought, our impulse is preceded by intuition, by will—what Jonathan Edwards might have called "the sense of the heart."

This is not to suggest that Swedenborg dispenses with the understanding or conceives of will and rationality as in opposition. A mutuality between the two is essential for a soul's health. However, like Edwards—and Jean Jacques Rousseau—Swedenborg writes against the dry rationalism of his age when he emphasizes the importance of the will. In one of his more memorable encounters with spirits in the afterlife, Swedenborg watches angels at a gate inspecting people who have recently died and want to go to heaven. While the people are intelligent—among them are naturalists, a politician, and an articulate priest—because they had not developed genuine religious affections in their wills, the angels turn these spirits around and discover that the backs of their heads are completely hollowed out and force them to leave. Swedenborg concludes with a statement that reflects his earlier anatomical research and explains the reason for the hollowing:

human beings have two brains, one in the back of the head, which is called the cerebellum, the other in the front of the head, which is called the cerebrum . . . when the thought of the understanding does not guide the love of the will, the inmost regions of that person's cerebellum, which are in themselves heavenly, collapse; this causes the hollowing out.[26]

In *A Treatise Concerning Religious Affections* (1746), Edwards also illustrates the dangers of an empty will with references to the human head: "He who has no religious affection, is in a state of spiritual death . . . where there is a kind of light without heat, a head stored with notions and speculations, with a cold and unaffected heart, there can be nothing divine in that light, that knowledge is no true knowledge of divine things."[27] Later in the same treatise, Edwards outlines the changed perception of someone who has been regenerated by God in a direct re-adjustment of Lockean psychology. The saints are given "a new inward perception or sensation, entirely different in its nature and kind, from anything ever that their minds were the subjects of before. . . ."[28] Ideas must still be built up through the senses, but thanks to the grace of God, a new ability is imparted to perceive His presence feelingly. Edwards' "sense of the heart" is a gift apart from what the understanding can comprehend—it is "vastly above any sensation which 'tis possible a man should have by any natural sense or principle, so that, in order to have them, a man must have a new spiritual and divine sense given him, in order to have sensations of that sort."[29] As the *anima* did for Swedenborg, Edwards' elevation of the will into a supernaturalized category of perception allows him to bridge spiritual ontology with empirical science.

Religious Affections was not the first place where Edwards modified Lockean psychology for the Puritan mind. In the earlier sermon *A Divine and Supernatural Light* (1734), Edwards announced that "there is such a thing, as a spiritual and divine light, immediately imparted to the soul by God, of a different nature from any that is obtained by natural means."[30] Here, spiritual knowing comes independent of natural reason and the five senses, but since Edwards had read Newton's *Opticks* as keenly as Swedenborg, this light can be fully understood by the elect mind, following the same laws as those that guide the rays of light and order the colors of the rainbow. "Reason indeed is necessary in order to it," writes Edwards, "as 'tis by reason only that we are become the subjects of the means of it. . . ."[31] Some ten years after Edwards wrote these words, Emanuel Swedenborg began to undergo a transformative spiritual crisis. In addition to vacillating between extremes of enthusiasm and despair, Swedenborg found that when he entertained certain ideas of his research on the human soul, he perceived an inexplicable sensation of light flickering through his interior. Swedenborg remarks in his diary from this period that this was like "a sign . . . a certain cheering light and joyful flash . . . a certain mysterious radiation—I know not whence it springs—that darts through some sacred temple of the brain."[32] The searching for words here, the fumbling for the correct phrase, indicates an experience beyond language. Swedenborg's divine and supernatural light culminated in visions of Christ between 1744 and 1745 and thereafter; the Swedish scientist was to spend the remainder of his life writing theological works that were based on close biblical exegesis and the experience of his ongoing visions—the empirical data of things he had "seen and heard," as he frequently writes, in the spiritual worlds of heaven and hell. Again, it is useful to recall William James' definition of mystical experience. Swedenborg's inexplicable sensation of flickering light—his extremes of exhilaration and despair—the culminating certitude with which he claims to have seen and talked with Christ, after finding himself violently thrown to the floor of his bedroom—all exemplify James' four characteristics. They are initially ineffable (beyond language), noetic (making an epistemological claim to truth), transient and passive (losing the individual will in abeyance to something vastly superior).[33] Edwards' mystical proclivities are not as pronounced as Swedenborg's and probably only qualify under the first two criteria (which James stated were the most important of the four), which emphasize the large differences between the two men.

Still, the gulf between Edwards' Calvinism and Swedenborg's new dispensation of Christianity should not sunder the closeness between Swedenborg's correspondence and Edwards' typology. There is not room left to embark on a comparative discussion of the nuances distinguishing a Swedenborg correspondence from an Edwards type; it suffices to point out that they allowed Edwards and Swedenborg to read the facts of the physical world as shadows of a superior spiritual world and that to know this universal language was to communicate with the Divine. Edwards writes that if "we look on these shadows of divine things as the voice of God . . . we may as it were hear God speaking with us," and Swedenborg states that to comprehend a correspondence in nature is to bring our spirit into the company of angels.[34] Both Edwards and Emerson expanded their typologies and correspondences far beyond the traditional realm of scriptural exegesis, into the natural world and human history (and it is this expansion, Miller argues, and not its signification, that makes Edwards' typology noteworthy).[35]

That Edwards' and Swedenborg's typologies overlap is not all that surprising considering that their literary digests shared more than Newton. Each appears to have been familiar with the typologies of Henry More and the Cambridge Neo-Platonists. Edwards also read parts of the Cabala, and ever since Jose Luis Borges pointed it out, scholars have been intrigued by the suggestive parallels between some of Swedenborg's ideas (his statements on the Hebrew language, for example, and the idea of a "universal grand man" structuring the cosmos) and several Cabalistic concepts.[36] Pursuing any of these strands of mutual influence might further clarify the distinctions between Swedenborg's correspondence (as Emerson understood and used it) and Edwards' tropes and types and illuminate to what extent Emerson was drawing upon inherent New England symbolic tendencies and to what degree he was using Swedenborg to arrive at a place which Edwards himself once occupied.

DEVIN ZUBER earned the B.A. from Bryn Athyn College (Pennsylvania); the M.A. from Queens College, City University of New York; and the M.Phil. and the Ph.D. both from the Graduate Center, City University of New York. He is assistant professor of American studies at the University of Osnabrueck (Germany). His research interests include Romanticism, ecology, and aesthetics, and his articles have appeared in *American Quarterly, Variations,* and several scholarly anthologies.

NOTES

[1] Perry Miller, "Jonathan Edwards to Emerson," *The New England Quarterly* 13 (1940): 589–617.

[2] Jonathan Edwards, *Typological Writings,* ed. Wallace E. Anderson, Mason I. Lowance, and David H. Watters, vol. 11. (New Haven: Yale University Press, 1993), 152.

[3] Ralph Waldo Emerson, "Nature," *Essays and Poems* (New York: Library of America, 1996), 20–21.

[4] Robert Richardson, *Emerson: The Mind on Fire* (Berkeley: Los Angeles Press, 1995), 594.

[5] Perry Miller, *Errand into the Wilderness* (Cambridge: Belknap Press, 1984), 185.

[6] Mason I. Lowance Jr., *The Language of Canaan: Metaphor and Symbol in New England from the Puritans to the Transcendentalists* (Cambridge: Harvard University Press, 1980). See also Sacvan Bercovitch, *The Puritan Origins of the American Self* (New Haven: Yale University Press, 1976), and Philip Gura, *The Wisdom of Words: Language, Theology, and Literature in the New England Renaissance* (Middletown: Wesleyan University Press, 1981). My argument most closely aligns with Gura's, whose judicious tracing of New England theology includes Swedenborg as a vital contributor. Lowance, on the other hand, despite his focus on typology, does not acknowledge the importance of Swedenborg's correspondence theory for the Transcendentalists.

[7] See Richardson's brief discussion, 594. Emerson's journal references to Edwards are few and far between. Fascinatingly, in one of Emerson's only references to Edwards' *Freedom of the Will,* he brackets Edwards with a book by Samson Reed, the Swedenborgian who first introduced Emerson to Swedenborg's ideas in 1821: "Pray don't read American. Thought is of no country. . . . What hinders the action of Contemplative Spirit here? The little book called 'Observations on the Growth of the Mind' is the only book this country has produced since Edwards on the Will, that is a work of reason saving sermons and periodical literature." *The Journals and Miscellaneous Notebooks of Ralph Waldo Emerson,* vol. 12 (Cambridge: Harvard University Press, 1960), 40.

[8] Emanuel Swedenborg, *Heaven and Its Wonders and Hell: Drawn from Things Seen and Heard* [1758], trans. George Dole (West Chester, PA: Swedenborg Foundation, 2000). See nos. 106, 485–490, 90–97. In the tradition of Swedenborg scholarship, all reference numbers are to paragraphs.

[9] Emerson, "The Poet," *Essays and Poems,* 464.

[10] Emanuel Swedenborg's family name was Swedberg until 1719, when the family became ennobled by Queen Ulrica Eleonora. Thereafter the children of Jesper Swedberg took Swedenborg as their last name.

[11] Alfred Acton, compiler, editor, trans., *Letters and Memorials of Emanuel Swedenborg*, 2 vols. (Bryn Athyn, PA: Swedenborg Scientific Association, 1955), 2:696.

[12] Jonathan Edwards, "Personal Narrative," *A Jonathan Edwards Reader*, ed. John E. Smith, Harry Stout, and Kenneth Minkema (New Haven: Yale University Press, 1995), 282.

[13] Edwards, "Personal Narrative," 285.

[14] Miller writes that "there was in Puritanism a piety, a religious passion, the sense of an inward communication and of the divine symbolism in nature. . . . At the core of the theology there was an indestructible element which was mystical, and a feeling for the universe which was almost pantheistic . . . ," *Errand into the Wilderness*, 192. For James' useful definitions of mystical experience, see the discussion at the end of this essay.

[15] For an account of Swedenborg's garden on Hornsgatan, see chap. 28, "Green Things Growing," in Cyriel Odhner Sigstedt, *The Swedenborg Epic: The Life and Works of Emanuel Swedenborg* (New York: Bookman Associates, 1952), 237–246.

[16] Qtd. in Ernst Benz, *Emanuel Swedenborg: Visionary Savant in the Age of Reason*, trans. Nicholas Goodrick-Clarke (West Chester, PA: Swedenborg Foundation, 2002), 12–13.

[17] Perry Miller, "Introduction" to *Images or Shadows of Divine Things*, by Jonathan Edwards (New Haven: Yale University Press, 1948), 4.

[18] Edwards, "The Spider Letter," *A Jonathan Edwards Reader*, 8.

[19] Sigstedt, *The Swedenborg Epic: The Life and Works of Emanuel Swedenborg*, 59.

[20] Emanuel Swedenborg, *The Principia: or, The first principles of natural things, being new attempts toward a philosophic explanation of the elementary world* [1734], trans. Augustus Clissold, 2 volumes (London: W. Newbury, 1845–1846).

[21] For example: "Now, as in the great Globe of the Earth and Sea, the densest Bodies by their Gravity sink down in Water, and always endeavor to go towards the Center of the Globe; so in Particles of Salt, the densest Matter may always endeavor to approach the center." Sir Isaac Newton, *Opticks: or, A treatise of the reflections, refractions, inflections & colours of light* (New York: Dover Publications, 1979), 386.

[22] Jonathan Edwards, *Scientific and Philosophical Writings*, ed. Wallace E. Anderson, vol. 6 (New Haven: Yale University Press, 1980), 334–335.

[23] Emanuel Swedenborg, *The Animal Kingdom: Considered Anatomically, Physically, and Philosophically* [1744–45], trans. J. J. Wilkinson (London: Newbery, 1843–1844).

[24] Benz, 131.

[25] "Motion is much more apt to be lost than got, and is always on the decay . . . ," Newton writes in the *Opticks*, "Seeing therefore the variety of Motion which we find in the World is always decreasing, there is a necessity of conserving and recruiting it by active Principles. . . . And if it were not for these Principles, the Bodies of the Earth, Planets, Comets, Sun, and all things in them, would grow cold and freeze, and become inactive Masses; and all Putrefaction, Generation, Vegetation and Life would cease, and the Planets and Comets would not remain in their Orbs." Newton, *Opticks*, 398–400.

[26] Emanuel Swedenborg, *True Christian Religion* [1771], trans. John C. Ager (West Chester, PA: Swedenborg Foundation, 1996), no. 160.

[27] Edwards, *A Treatise Concerning Religious Affections*, in *A Jonathan Edwards Reader*, 148.

[28] Ibid., 160.

[29] Ibid., 163.

[30] Edwards, *A Divine and Supernatural Light,* in *A Jonathan Edwards Reader,* 104.
[31] Ibid., 121.
[32] Emanuel Swedenborg, *Diarium Spiritualis [Spiritual Diary],* unpublished by Swedenborg, 5 vols., trans. G. Bush, J. Smithson, and J. Buss (London: James Speirs, 1883–902), no. 2951.

[33] William James, *The Varieties of Religious Experience: A Study in Human Nature* (New York: Penguin, 1982), 380–381.
[34] Edwards, *Typological Writings,* 74; Swedenborg, *Heaven and Hell,* no. 114.
[35] See Miller, "Introduction" to *Images or Shadows of Divine Things,* 27.
[36] Jose Luis Borges, "Emanuel Swedenborg, *Mystical Works,*" in *Selected Non-Fictions,* ed. Eliot Weinberger, trans. Esther Allen, Suzanne Levine, and Eliot Weinberger (New York: Penguin, 1999), 456–457.

From Edwards to Emerson to Eddy: Extending a Trajectory of Metaphysical Idealism

David L. Weddle

The dawn of civilization was the twilight of nature's sovereignty over its own domain. Henceforth, what nature signifies is determined by human need and desire, by the rational calculation of human benefit and imaginative reconstruction of the elements of nature. Thus, Collingwood wrote, "No one can answer the question what nature is unless he knows what history is."[1] Constructing an idea of nature is our way of containing its unimaginable age and indifferent forces within a more familiar human story. What began with the shaping of the first tool leads to interpretations of nature as the reflection of consciousness. Metaphysical idealism achieves a triumph of mind over matter, spirit over nature, through an appropriation of the natural world for moral guidance and spiritual inspiration. This essay will argue that the trajectory of metaphysical idealism in American religious thought that begins in Jonathan Edwards extends through Ralph Waldo Emerson to Mary Baker Eddy.

The metaphysical idealism of Edwards, developed in early essays on being and mind, was still evident in his late treatises on creation and virtue.[2] He drew the conclusion that all reality is grounded in the eternal mind of God from his devoted reading of Calvin's doctrine of divine sovereignty. Further, Edwards' own experiences of illumination by direct communication of the divine Spirit convinced him that God was not the remote origin of the world in the distant past, but the continuing power of being and source of goodness. As all that is originated in the mind of God, so it is sustained by the presence of God, and will be consummated in the purpose of God. Metaphysical idealism is a theological translation of the biblical hope that when the end comes, "God may be all in all" (1 Corinthians 15:28).

But does Edwards' idealism constitute incipient pantheism? Perry Miller traced a connection between Edwards' reflection on the presence of the divine in nature and Ralph Waldo Emerson's transcendentalism. In Emerson's *Nature* Miller finds a suppressed strain of Calvinist piety: "the incessant drive of the Puritan to learn how, and how most ecstatically, he can hold any sort of communion with the environing wilderness."[3] Freed from the restraints of Calvinism, Emerson inspired others who saw nothing to prevent them "from identifying their intuitions with the voice of God, or from fusing God and nature into the one substance of the transcendental imagination."[4] Thus, for Miller there is a line from Edwards to Emerson running through their interpretations of the relations of God, nature, and human consciousness.

Edwards and Emerson, however, maintain a dialectical tension between mind and nature that Miller does not fully acknowledge. The project of "fusing God and nature" without remainder is accomplished by neither of them, but by a thinker to whom Miller paid little attention: Mary Baker Eddy. Eddy extended metaphysical idealism with utter consistency to the conclusion that the world is nothing but the reflection of divine mind. Since there is no power in what we perceive as material substance to distort or resist God's perfect idea, disease and evil are mere illusions: "God is All-in-all . . . God, Spirit, being all, nothing is matter."[5] For Eddy, St. Paul's phrase is not rhetorical flourish but literal truth. We will first examine Miller's essay and then consider how each of our figures construes the relation of God to the natural world.

I.

Perry Miller was apologetic for daring to suggest continuity between the champion of Calvinism and the exponent of Transcendentalism, so contrary were their convictions about the nature of God and the world. He located the sharpest difference in their assessments of human character: Edwards insisting on total depravity as the legacy of Adam's fall; Emerson defending the possibility of moral perfection. Thus, they turned to nature with different expectations. Edwards saw in natural phenomena only "shadows," images of the Creator made indistinct by blurred human vision.[6] Further, sinfulness alienates us from God and his creation so that we have no immediate intuition of the truth inscribed in natural objects and must rely on interpretation that is inevitably flawed. For Emerson, however, "there is no inherent separation between the mind and the thing . . . in reality they leap to embrace each other."[7]

Puritans also believed that regenerating grace filled the soul with divine light and in their devotional writings there is a current of mystic aspiration. Yet they never lost sight of the horizon, the sharp difference between heaven and earth, between the sovereign God and his impotent creatures. Miller observes, "Whatever difficulties were involved in explaining that the universe is the work of God but that we do not meet God face to face in the universe, Puritan theologians knew that the distinction must be maintained. . . ."[8] Consequently, they strenuously opposed all forms of mysticism and pantheism.[9] Yet Miller argues that in Edwards' later treatises, "though still in the language of logic and systematic theology, the other half of the Puritan heritage—the sense of God's overwhelming presence in the soul and in nature—once more found perfect expression."[10] The means of that expression was Edwards' typological phenomenology as his method of total engagement with nature, from raw sensation to thoroughly cooked interpretation.

Claude Lévi-Strauss, in his famous argument for the power of reflective thought in archaic cultures, described the "savage mind" as composed of "consuming symbolic ambition" and "scrupulous attention directed entirely towards the concrete."[11] It is hard to image a more precise delineation of Edwards' primary disposition toward nature. Unlike the subjects of Lévi-Strauss' ethnographic studies, however, Edwards was an individual in the modern sense of the word, with a sophisticated grasp of the scientific work of his own time. He was theologically indisposed to myth and ritual, with a spare Protestant preference for language as medium of spiritual experience. Yet, even as he sat quietly in his candle-lit study, collar buttoned to the neck and eyes fastened on the paper his quill moved relentlessly across, Edwards was driven by a primordial "symbolic ambition" to render all existent beings into media of divine presence.

A Dissertation Concerning the End for Which God Created the World is the key text for Miller's understanding of Edwards' interpretation of the doctrines earlier divines found verging toward pantheism: "doctrines of inward communication and of the divine in nature."[12] Edwards uses the imagery of "emanation of light" to describe God's relation to the world and for Miller that "betrays" his disposition toward mysticism. The only obstacle to his accepting pantheism that Miller can detect is Edwards' steadfast commitment to "orthodox theology, supposedly derived from the Word of God, which taught that God and nature are not one, that man is corrupt and his self-reliance is reliance on evil. But take away the theology, remove this overlying stone of dogma from the wellsprings of Puritan conviction, and both nature and man become divine."[13]

But is the matter quite that simple? Is Edwards so limited in theological vision and courage that he cannot venture beyond the confines of the Westminster Confession? Or does his reluctance to merge God, humanity, and nature stem from profound religious motives? At a depth Emerson's sensibility did not reach for all his perusal of the *Bhagavad-Gita,* Edwards intuitively grasped the old problem posed in the Hindu *bhakti* tradition: the one who becomes the sugar can no longer taste the sugar. If, as the Westminster Shorter Catechism puts it, "Man's chief end is to glorify God, and to enjoy him forever," then merging with the divine would defeat the purpose. The ontological unity of self and God makes worship, and all its pleasures, impossible. Thus, it was as much from his passionate devotion, as from an obdurate attachment to tradition, that Edwards rejected pantheism.

II.

For Edwards, nature is the realm of "shadows and images of divine things," reflections of the will and purpose of her Creator with messages inscribed in every object and event. While the relation between God and the natural world is as intimate as that between the sun and the light that radiates from it, however, that intimacy never reaches ontological consummation. Edwards insists on the essential distinction between God and the world. In a fragment of an unpublished letter Edwards refers to "holiness" as the divine quality in which believers participate.

> And this is that in his nature which he communicates something of to the saints, and therefore is called by divines in general a communicable attribute; and the saints are made partakers of his holiness, as the Scripture expressly declares (Heb. 12:10), and that *without imparting to them his essence.*[14]

But what Edwards denies as doctrine, he entertains as metaphor in the next paragraph. He concedes that light and heat may "in a special manner be said to be the proper nature of the sun; yet none will say that everything to which the sun communicates a little of its light and heat has therefore communicated to it the essence of the sun, and is sunned with the sun, or becomes the same being with the sun, or becomes equal to that immense fountain of light and heat."[15]

But is it so obvious that none would make that connection? Is Edwards confusing quality and quantity? To have the same quality of light as the sun does not require an object to become equal in size to the sun; it only requires that the object participate in the same light that issues from the sun. To that extent it becomes a partaker in the solar nature, just as the Bible declares believers to be "partakers of the divine nature" (2 Peter 1:4). The imagery of light is tricky and Edwards concedes in the next sentence that, if a crystal reflects sunlight with a brightness "immensely less in degree" than that of the sun itself, "yet it is something of the same nature." But what is the difference between "something of the same nature" and "of the same nature"?

Edwards begins his treatise on God's ultimate end in creating the world by consideration of "what reason teaches." The reason he consults is shaped by the conciliar tradition of Christian theology and assumes without question the premise that God is self-sufficient and immutable. Therefore, according to "the dictates of reason," God could not seek anything from creation nor be enhanced in any way by creatures.[16] Therefore, it is appropriate that in the creation of the world God has "supreme regard for himself."[17] But God not only encompasses the "infinite fullness of all possible good," he also "is capable of communication or emanation *ad extra*."[18] It is the emanation of divine fullness as the supreme good *in itself* that "excites" God to create. There is "a disposition in the fullness of the divinity to flow out and diffuse itself," prior to any interest in creatures that communication might imply.

Edwards' intention is to preserve the primacy of God as source and end of all that is, yet he must acknowledge that his own metaphors of rising sap and radiating sunlight imply actions that bring their sources into their "most complete" states. Thus it follows that "God looks on the communication of himself . . . as though he were not in his most complete and glorious state without it"[19]—just as the "fullness of Christ" is completed in the church, "which is his body, the fullness of him who fills all in all" (Ephesians 1:22–23). The parallel is startling: as Christ is fully present only in the church, so God is fully realized only in the world.

In the economy of redemption, as traced in Scripture, God creates all things through "his beloved Son" who is the "first born of all creation. . . . For in him all the fullness of God was pleased to dwell . . ." (Colossians 1:13, 15, 19). God fully communicates in and through Christ, whose reality is fully present in the church and in her apostle. Yet Paul is bold to claim, "in my flesh I am completing what is lacking in Christ's afflictions for the sake of his body, that is, the church" (Colossians 1:24). In these passages "fullness" does not preclude "completion" because God's being is not thought of as static perfection, but dynamic and purposeful love that finds its fulfillment in the company of creatures.

Here Edwards faced a dilemma: what "reason" taught him was shaped by the inheritance of patristic councils, informed by medieval theologians under the spell of Aristotle, preserved by Protestant Reformers, and reflected in Enlightenment Deism: that God is immutable and timeless, whose reality is in no way dependent upon anything but "himself" (gender identity was also part of this rational consensus on the divine nature). But what Scripture taught him was that God created out of love, suffered disappointment with humans of his own making, responded dramatically to their prayers, entered history as a man, was glorified in the redemption of believers, poured out his own spirit into creatures, and is awaiting the consummation of joy in the establishment of his kingdom on earth. It is hard to contemplate the drama of "the history of the work of redemption" and remain convinced that God is the disinterested arbiter of human affairs who has supreme regard for himself alone. But that is the task Edwards set himself.

Thus, whatever the relation, Edwards denies that God could benefit from or be enhanced by creatures. Rather we "participate" in God's reality through "a communication of God's infinite knowledge which primarily consists in the knowledge of himself."[20] But if God's self-knowledge is that of eternal perfection, would it not follow, as Eddy later argued, that our knowledge of ourselves would correspond to God's knowledge of us, viz., as perfect reflections of the divine image? Edwards never entertained such implications of his claims. We participate only in "God's own moral excellency," he insists, "which is properly the beauty of the divine nature."[21] God is pleased by our love of him, but since it is only a reflection of his own self-love, our affection adds naught to God.[22] Even though, throughout eternity, believers approach "nearer and nearer to that strictness and perfection of union which there is between the Father and the Son," they never achieve simple equality with God. As the distinctness of divine persons is not lost in their Trinitarian relation, so the integrity of individual believers is not sacrificed in union with the divine. Nevertheless, for Edwards creatures have nothing of value to "add" to God because all their value already comes from God.[23]

Yet, because divine being is the equivalent of "Universal Being," "God and the creature, in this affair of the emanation of divine fullness, are not properly set in opposition";[24] in fact, the more the creature approaches the image of God in the duration of eternity, the closer they converge. "The nearer anything comes to infinite, the nearer it comes to an identity with God. And if any good, as viewed by God, is beheld as infinite, it can't be viewed as a distinct thing from God's own infinite glory."[25] But this hope of apotheosis is eschatological and progressive, beyond the possibility of present experience. In this way Edwards maintains the distinction between God and creature that is essential to both his theology and his piety. The trajectory of his idealism, we might say, approaches final unity as a limit.

By contrast, for Eddy the identity of God and world is original and eternal. Therefore, what for Edwards is the final horizon of the believer's hope is for Eddy a present plain of demonstration. Eddy, by identifying goodness and being, can say that the only reality anything possesses is precisely its correspondence to divine Mind. Edwards also declares that the reality of creatures consists in their reception of "that infinite fullness of good that is in God,"[26] as light from a luminary. But, as always, he adds a cautionary note: "This effulgence or communication is the fullness of all intelligent creatures, who have no fullness of their own."

Thus, the communication of God's fullness to the creature and the creature's love and praise of God "may appear to be entirely distinct things: but if we more closely consider the matter, they will all appear to be one thing. . . . They are all but the emanation of God's glory; or the excellent brightness and fullness of the divinity diffused, overflowing, and as it were enlarged; or in one word, existing *ad extra*."[27] The world is the reflection, but not extension, of divine being.

In this way Edwards avoids saying that creatures contribute anything of value to God, but at the risk of implying that creatures have no reality but God. Since our knowledge of God is God's self-knowledge reflected in us, and our love of God "is God's own love indwelling the will,"[28] whatever virtue we may experience as developing within us is the reflection of eternal infinite divine virtue to which we can add nothing. "Here is both *emanation* and *remanation*. The refulgence shines upon and into the creature, and is reflected back to the luminary. The beams of glory come from God, and are something of God, and refunded back again to their original."[29] Then, at the point of affirming the identity of God and creatures, Edwards introduces, as he did in the first half of the treatise, the notion of endless progression toward unity with God. The saints in heaven will approach *perichoresis* with the Father and Son, but "the particular time will never come when it can be said, the union is now infinitely perfect."[30] This reservation seemed to Emerson a failure of spiritual ambition and to Eddy a denial of the perfection of God's idea of humanity. They therefore insist on a more consistent application of idealism.

III.

Emerson speaks of nature with innocence that we can no longer claim. He could end the introduction to his first book by defining nature as "essences unchanged by man."[31] But even as Emerson wrote, technology was the leading symbol of human progress. Nature, so far from bearing independent witness to divine grandeur, was primarily material for human artifice. Even Emerson sees nature as available without condition as "raw material," finally and fully a reflection of human interest. "More and more, with every thought, does [the human] kingdom stretch over things, until the world becomes, at last, only a realized will,—the double of the man."[32] Let us review the line of thinking that brought Emerson to this remarkable conclusion.

For Emerson the stars awaken reverence, but only as the most impressive of nature's array, for "all natural objects" are capable of influencing the mind through the "poetical sense." He explains that this capacity allows the mind to integrate disparate sensations into, say, a "charming landscape." Thus unified and framed, nature evokes a "wild delight . . . in spite of real sorrows."[33] Emerson assigns primacy to sight as the means of apprehending nature. "In the woods," he writes, "I feel that nothing can befall me in life,—no disgrace, no calamity, (leaving me my eyes,) which nature cannot repair."[34] The parenthetical qualification is crucial: nature cannot repair what is required to experience nature.

But if nature exists only as a composition of vision and imagination, then the notorious metaphor that follows is even more puzzling: "Standing on the bare ground,—my head bathed by the blithe air, and uplifted into infinite space,—all mean egotism vanishes. I become a transparent eye-ball. I am nothing. I see all."[35] But how can the I that is "nothing" also be the I that "sees all"? Or how can an eyeball that is transparent provide a focal point where images may form to be seen? Since every sighting is also a siting—i.e., every visual perception is from a perspective determined by a specific retinal location—an entirely transparent eyeball would be blind. To see all without the discriminate selectivity of a limited perspective would be to see nothing. The eye that sees thus requires the seeing "I."

As Miller warned, however, "to take Emerson literally is often hazardous."[36] Emerson was sufficiently well read in optics to know, as he writes, "The eye is the best of artists."[37] Therefore, the paradox may be intentional, and only intensifies as Emerson moves on to theological ground: "The currents of the Universal

Being circulate through me; I am part or particle of God."[38] One wonders if the metaphor derives from electricity or hydrology. In any case, the phrase "circulating currents" connotes an impersonal, almost mechanical, force of the sort that Franz Anton Mesmer set swirling in his patients. Emerson's language also shifts from the visual to the tactile, and thus from mediated to immediate experience. While we perceive nature at a focal distance, as the object of vision, God enters our awareness directly, as the power that sustains the entire universe, including our individual being.

If nature is the occasion for the immediate awareness of human participation in the divine, however, how does perception of natural phenomena mediate that awareness? Certainly not in any objective way because Emerson recognizes that his delight in any natural scene is in large part a reflection of his interior landscape. "For, nature is not always tricked in holiday attire, but the same scene which yesterday breathed perfume and glittered as for the frolic of the nymphs, is overspread with melancholy today. Nature always wears the colors of the spirit."[39] Emerson may write like an English Romantic, but he read the German Idealists. If the mind shapes our perception of the world, then there is no "nature" apart from the composition of the eye and the valuation of the spirit.

Does that mean natural phenomena have no significance in themselves other than "what we consciously give them"? Emerson answers, "The world is emblematic."[40] The relation between emblem and its referent "stands in the will of God," and when the relation is grasped in a moment of wonder, "the universe becomes transparent, and the light of higher laws than its own, shines through it."[41] Yet, for all its transparency, the universe does not cease to exist—just as Emerson, transformed into a transparent eyeball, did not cease to see. The phenomenal world reveals its origin in the mind. "There seems to be a necessity in spirit to manifest itself in material forms; and day and night, river and storm, beast and bird, acid and alkali, preëxist in necessary Ideas in the mind of God. . . . A Fact is the end or last issue of spirit."[42] Given the benevolence of God,

Emerson finds it no surprise that the issue of divine ideas serves human interests. Nature's dice, he asserts, "are always loaded," with each roll producing benefits.[43] At this point he finds neither threat nor enchantment in nature, only unconditional utility: "It offers all its kingdoms to man as the raw material which he may mould into what is useful,"[44] including moral direction. Nature reflects to us the dictates of conscience, even sounding in our ears an "echo of the Ten Commandments"; therefore, "is nature always the ally of Religion."[45] But her allegiance is not to one alone; nature begets meaning with many lovers.

It is exactly at this point that Emerson found the cosmic visions of Emanuel Swedenborg too restricting because of their expression in Christian language. For Emerson "each individual symbol plays innumerable parts, as each particle of matter circulates in turn through every system."[46] Thus his reading of nature drew from the symbolic resources of a wide range of traditions. "In the transmission of the heavenly waters," Emerson proclaimed, "every hose fits every hydrant."[47] Despite his Christian bias, however, Swedenborg grasped the essential point: that the natural world of objects is a creation by, and reflection of, the spiritual world of subjects. Swedenborg advances on the Platonic view of nature as a shadow of eternal realities and on the Christian doctrine that the world is an artifact of divine will. In both those views human beings are still subject to restricting forces of nature that are indifferent to our needs and desires. In both views we are also dependent on revelation for knowledge and grace for salvation.

Emerson detects beneath Swedenborg's ornate categories the heavy hand of the God of Lutheran piety: "The vice of Swedenborg's mind is its theologic determination."[48] The tight system of correspondences between the divine, the human, and the natural left no room for individual identity or freedom. Swedenborg failed because he attached himself "to the Christian symbol, instead of to the moral sentiment, which carries innumerable christianities, humanities, divinities, in its bosom."[49] Nature instructs us through analogies that transcend narrow religious interests. Swedenborg did manage to rise far enough above his Lutheran grounding to see the general truth that the human spirit creates its own world from the perspective determined by its moral character: "All things in the universe arrange themselves to each person anew, according to his ruling love.... Everyone makes his own house and state."[50]

The power to turn the universe by one's "ruling love" would seem to issue from vaulting confidence; but Emerson has another, darker, source of his belief that reality is a spiritual construction. In the sprawling 1844 essay on "Experience" Emerson laments our customary state of mental lethargy in which even displays of grief are theatrical. Reflecting upon the death of his son, Emerson judges his own mourning to be counterfeit.

> The only thing grief has taught me, is to know how shallow it is.... Well, souls never touch their objects. An innavigable sea washes with silent waves between us and the things we aim at and converse with. Grief too will make us idealists. In the death of my son, now more than two years ago, I seem to have lost a beautiful estate,—no more.[51]

Why does grief make us idealists? Because the heart-breaking loss of a son is experienced as only the loss of "a beautiful estate,—no more." We all recognize that, after forfeiting property and wealth, all that is left is memory: the reality of what was lost is the idea of it, now quickly fading because it corresponds to nothing in "real" nature. Fields, house, gold, and son—all fall away, leaving "no scar" as if their loss had never inflicted a wound in the soul. Is the impermanent character of grief the most intimate evidence that there is no reality but what we sustain by mental effort? If so, then is there not good reason to accept the truth of idealism and celebrate the liberating fact that appearance is not reality, and specifically that death is an illusion? (That is the moral Mary Baker Eddy would have drawn from such experience.)

Emerson realizes that perception is shaped by temperament and interest, so that "Nature and books belong to the eyes that see them. It depends on the mood of the man, whether he shall see the sunset or the fine poem."[52] But he distrusts temperament as the regulator of experience because he is convinced that it is a deceptive mediator. Further, Emerson cannot abandon the conviction that there is a reality to be contacted behind the veil of temperament: a reality that is more than the reductive materialism of physicians can acknowledge. For their "so-called sciences" constrain the individual in "the chain of physical necessity," as does the phrenologist who adapts his conversation to the shape of his interlocutor's head.

But the promptings of the mind and heart call us out of the "sty of sensualism" toward absolute truth and goodness. Only glimpses are possible because we require change and variety, yet the transitory particulars of experience cannot satisfy our longing to restore the original whole. In his later essay on nature Emerson writes, "There is in woods and waters a certain enticement and flattery, together with a failure to yield a present satisfaction. This disappointment is felt in every landscape."[53] As a result, we are aware of the irony of aesthetic perception: insofar as we view nature with the poet's eye we see only the reflection of the poet: "Nature is elsewhere."[54] Nature, that is, as the endless recombination of ideas in the mind of God: "The divine circulations never rest nor linger. Nature is the incarnation of a thought, and turns to a thought again, as ice becomes water and gas. The world is mind precipitated, and the volatile essence is forever escaping again in the state of free thought."[55]

How, then, should we live in a universe that is as mercurial as vapor? With appreciation for each particular individual we are thrown against, seeking to do "broad justice where we are, by whomsoever we deal with, accepting our actual companions and circumstances, however humble or odious, as the mystic officials to whom the universe has delegated its whole pleasure for us."[56] Thus Emerson advises a life of moderation and enjoyment of common experiences, insulated by a robust conscience, because "Nature, as we know her, is no saint."[57] Thus, the conviction that life is an illusion should not prevent one from hearing the evangel: "God's darling! heed thy private dream. . . ." Grant to the reductive skeptics that your persistent idealism appears to them a defect: "Thou art sick, but shalt not be worse, and the universe, which holds thee dear, shall be the better."[58] Emerson's assurances derive from his conviction that our experience is composed of a series of vanishing moments, so any enduring achievement must be "by the grace of God."[59]

Here we are close to the heart of Emerson's piety. He dismisses the ancient solution to the dilemma of continuity through time, viz., to enthrone Chance as divinity, because it cannot account for the remarkable development—he is even prepared to call the improbability a "miracle"—of the human embryo. From the premise that we experience time as a discontinuous series of present moments—such that "Life has no memory"—Emerson concludes that the unity of bodily parts and consciousness that constitutes an individual must be due to an integrative power not intrinsic to life itself. "Underneath the inharmonious and trivial particulars, is a musical perfection, the Ideal journeying always with us, the heaven without rent or seam."[60] Once again, Emerson smuggles a metaphysical claim into a metaphor. Is the Ideal a form, like chord structure in the key of D minor, or a design, like the melodic theme of a composition? To speak more directly, does the Ideal provide the possibility or the actuality of the order we experience in the world? Emerson's deistic preference seems to be for the former; but his poet's "love of the new beauty" discovered in each fresh illumination seems aroused by more specific direction, calling for a purposive agency in the Ideal.

In any case he is clear that the Ideal is discovered, as one comes upon a mountain range in the West, and not created by the mind. It is the constant ground of our existence: "that in us which changes not . . . ineffable cause, which every fine genius has essayed to represent by some emphatic symbol. . . . In our more correct writing, we give to this generalization the name of Being. . . ."[61] Emerson does not use the term in its traditional sense to refer to what is immutable, but as the universal power that propels us into an indeterminate future. He cites approvingly Mencius's description of it as "vast-flowing vigor." Carried on its oceanic energy, "Our life seems not present, so much as prospective," called to higher aspiration by "Being" that in its dynamic influence Emerson calls "the Ideal." "Thus journeys the mighty Ideal before us; it never was known to fall into the rear. No man ever came to an experience which was satiating, but his good is tidings of a better. Onward and onward!"[62]

It is hard to keep a good idealist down, so an essay that begins with reflection on grief ends in buoyant praise of progress. But the metaphysical basis is the same for both attitudes: our experience of reality is shaped by the contour of our own spirits. "Thus inevitably does the universe wear our color, and every object fall successively into the subject itself."[63] Yet Emerson is ambivalent about the capacity of our subjectivity to provide the coherence and direction of the whole of being. He confesses that his mind cannot alone account for all he experiences and that his character does not merit all the benefits he receives. Cast into a world not entirely of his own making, and inspired to creative advance by ideals that transcend his imagination, Emerson knows himself to be a creature of an encompassing grace his essay can name only partially. "I am a fragment, and this is a fragment of me."[64]

In the final chapter in *Nature* on "Idealism"[65] Emerson noted that he has a "child's love" of nature, yet insists that a cultured view of the world is idealist, teaching that the Supreme Being creates nature "through us." In fact, our capacity to grasp absolute ideals, such as Truth and Justice, makes each of us "the creator in the finite." This expansive thought leads Emerson to a conclusion that Eddy would have found entirely reasonable: "[This view] animates me to create my own world through the purification of my soul."[66] Such a world, one assumes, would be free of those aspects of nature, such as sickness, injury, and death, which do not correspond to the objects of contemplation that pure Spirit would delight to watch. That Emerson did not succeed in creating for himself the perfect world, however, Eddy confirmed firsthand:

> Emmerson [sic] went out as a poor specimen of progress. Six months before his death I conversed with him and he babbled like an idiot. The only coherent point he made was that a man wears out, and his brains decay and it is wicked to believe otherwise. He has written good and wise things. But it is simply absurd . . . to take up ethics that lose science at least every other step.[67]

For Eddy, Emerson got only as far as knowing how to live well in the world, but that is far short of the knowledge that allows one to overcome the world. While still young, however, Emerson saw ahead utopian transformation of nature. What has been accomplished so far, he wrote, by the application of mere understanding is a harbinger of the astounding effects achieved by "Reason's momentary grasp of the sceptre" of sovereignty over natural forces. We can expect not only miracles, as in antique times, but also abolition of slavery, religious ecstasies, the wonders of Animal Magnetism, and self-healing.[68]

For Emerson, as much as for Edwards and Eddy, his time was the dawn of redemption: the transfiguration of nature by the unifying imagination of the poet and, he might have added, the grasping dream of the entrepreneur. "Nature is not fixed but fluid. Spirit alters, moulds, makes it."[69] Therefore, Emerson concludes with a metaphysical ambition that could be fulfilled only if idealism were true, "Build, therefore, your own world."[70] It remained for Eddy to extend this claim to the confidence that we already are in the spiritual world, perfected in the Mind of God. Hers was a line of reflection begun 150 years earlier in a student residence in New Haven.

IV.

In his notes *Of Being*, begun while he was at Yale, the young Edwards reflected on the sort of problem that still keeps college students up late at night: Is it possible that there could be nothing at all? For Edwards, even to hold such a thought in our minds "we must think of the same that the sleeping Rocks Dream of and not till then shall we Get a Compleat idea of nothing...."[71] Edwards insists, "A state of Absolute nothing is a state of Absolute Contradiction" because *nothing* cannot be located, yet everything that *is* exists in space. Therefore, "space is necessary, eternal, infinite, & Omnipresent, but I had as Good speak Plain, I have already said as much as that Space is God...." He then extends the concept of space to correspond to the divine being: "all the space there is without ye Bounds of the Creation, all the space there was before the Creation, is God himself...." While everything else might not exist, Edwards writes, "there is no such thing as nothing with Respect to Entity or being absolutely Considered...."

So far, Edwards might be developing a sophomoric version of the ontological argument, but the next step carries him into metaphysical idealism: "... yea it is Really impossible it should be that Any thing should be and nothing know it then you'll say if it be so it is because nothing has Any existence any where else but in Consciousness...." He offers a thought experiment:

> Let us suppose for illustration this impossibility that all the Spirits in the Universe to be for a time to be Deprived of their Consciousness, and Gods Consciousness at the same time to be intermitted. I say the Universe for that time would cease to be of it self and not only as we speak because the almighty Could not attend to Uphold the world but because God knew nothing of it ...

Edwards next invites us to imagine a world in which entropy has achieved final triumph, a universe without light and completely at rest. In such a world no resistance could be exerted and thus there could be no solidity, extension, magnitude, proportion, "nor body nor spirit." Edwards asks, "what then [is] to become of the Universe Certainly it exists no where but in the Divine mind. . . ." Finally, the corollary that makes the daring identification of spirit and substance:

> Corollary. It follows from hence that that those beings which have knowledge and Consciousness are the Only Proper and Real And substantial beings, inasmuch as the being of other things is Only by these. from hence we may see the Gross mistake of those who think material things the most substantial beings and spirits more like a shadow, whereas spirits Only Are Properly Substance.

For all his celebration of the spiritual basis of the natural world, Emerson never went that far. But Mary Baker Eddy did, and further, with enthusiasm.

Eddy's central work, *Science and Health with Key to the Scriptures,* was in continuous revision from 1875 to 1906 because, as she explained, "[s]piritual ideas unfold as we advance."[72] The final edition is her definitive statement of "divine metaphysics" and the practical power of healing that flows from its proper understanding.[73] The text is of such importance for her that she ordained the book, along with the Bible, as the only "pastor" of Christian Science churches, requiring that Sunday worship consist of no other comment on biblical readings but passages from *Science and Health*. Further, she regarded her text, written under divine inspiration, as the messianic word, the fulfillment of Jesus' promise to send "another comforter" to his disciples after his ascension. "This Comforter," Eddy wrote, "I understand to be Divine Science."[74]

The book is composed in such a way that the central themes of Eddy's teaching recur in every chapter. For the obsessively linear reader the repetition can be trying, but the text does not function in Christian Science study and practice as a continuous narrative, much less a discursive argument—but as an occasion for the meditative grasp of her metaphysics as a whole and the practical experience of one's participation in divine Mind. "All that really exists is the divine Mind and its idea, and in this Mind the entire being is found harmonious and eternal."[75] In the process of reading and re-reading the language Eddy perfected over a quarter century, Christian Scientists are not adding discrete items of knowledge to their mental inventory; they are seeking an illumination of consciousness by "the revelation of divine Science."[76] Their aim is to conform their minds to the perfect idea of the human in the mind of God, the idea that constitutes one's true being. It is not sufficient to exercise the will to believe in God, one must engage in the discipline of understanding what God knows.[77] The goal is "that man shall have no other spirit or mind but God, eternal good, and that all men shall have one Mind." From unity of thought will issue unity of good, bringing "health, holiness, and life eternal," end to war, and universal love.

The parallels to Edwards' "Notes on the Mind" are unmistakable. Edwards wrote, "the very substance of the body itself . . . is nothing but the Divine power, or rather the Constant Exertion of it."[78] While he claimed, "the world is therefore an ideal one,"[79] Edwards is quick to add, "when we say that the World, i.e. the material Universe, exists no where but in the mind, we . . . must be exceedingly careful." For he does not want to deny

> that things are where they seem to be. For the principles we lay down, if they are narrowly looked into, do not infer that. Nor will it be found, that they at all make void Natural Philosophy, or the science of the Causes or Reasons of corporeal changes; For to find out the reasons of things, in Natural Philosophy, is only to find out the proportion of God's acting. And the case is the same, as to such proportions, whether we suppose the World, only mental, in our sense or no.[80]

Thus for Edwards metaphysical idealism does not invalidate scientific study of the world because God's ideas are expressed in perceptible events that are ordered "according to his mind, and his ideas." It is only when we join with other minds which are "made in his image, and are emanations from him," that we realize our common "excellency" is our love of God's "Infinite mutual Love of Himself." Thus, "all that is the perfection of Spirits may be resolved into that which is God's perfection, which is Love."[81] For Edwards "true virtue" is a *spiritual* perfection, not one that could be exhibited in the body. Eddy sees no reason why perfection cannot be fully "demonstrated" in the phenomenal world that is, they both agree, a manifestation of divine mind.

In itself, Eddy insists, matter is not intelligent and so cannot communicate pain. Edwards also held "that Colours are not really in the things, no more than Pain is in a needle; but strictly no where else but in the mind."[82] For Eddy whatever pain one experiences is the result of the belief that one is suffering. "Mortal mind alone sentences itself," she declared.[83] One of the principles of Christian Science practice, accordingly, is to avoid talking of disease because the language can become self-fulfilling prophecy.[84] By establishing a taboo on talk about sickness, Eddy seeks to break its power on the human imagination and replace the illusions of "mortal mind" with divine ideas. The following directions are exemplary of her therapy:

> You say a boil is painful; but that is impossible, for matter without mind is not painful. The boil simply manifests, through inflammation and swelling, a belief in pain, and this belief is called a boil. Now administer mentally to your patient a high attenuation of truth, and it will soon cure the boil. The fact that pain cannot exist where there is no mortal mind to feel it is a proof that this so-called mind makes its own pain—that is, its own *belief* in pain.[85]

What is not rendered into language cannot become an object of consciousness; it must therefore remain "unreal." But as we all know, what is forbidden often becomes fascinating; and if it cannot be spoken in public, it will be dreamed in private. What does not take form in words may spring forth, snarling, in images. But Eddy teaches, "It breaks the dream of disease to understand that sickness is formed by the human mind, neither by matter nor by the divine Mind."[86]

It is as urgent for Eddy as it was for Edwards; however, to distinguish idealism from pantheism: Jesus "laid the axe of Science at the root of material knowledge, that it might be ready to cut down the false doctrine of pantheism,—that God, or Life, is in or of matter."[87] She defines pantheism as "a belief in the intelligence of matter,—a belief which Science overthrows" and then adds the practical counsel: "We must abandon pharmaceutics, and take up ontology,—'the science of real being.'"[88] For Eddy the view that matter had the power to produce effects on the mind was pantheism, "and carries within itself the seeds of all error."[89]

For Edwards the error of pantheism lay in blurring the line between God and world by elevating the fallen creation to divine status. For Eddy the danger lies in reducing God to materiality and subjecting humans who are expressions of God's idea to the conditions of mortality. Thus, she resisted pantheism with a consistent monism: "If [God] is All, He can have no consciousness of anything unlike Himself; because, if He is omnipresent, there can be nothing outside of Himself."[90] Eddy applies with metaphysical rigor Edwards' insistence that God aims at nothing in the creation of the world that is not already present in the divine fullness. If our knowledge participates in God's self-knowledge, if our virtue flows from the divine Spirit within, if our joy is a reflection of the eternal happiness of the Triune God—as Edwards taught[91]—then why should our bodies not also correspond to the divine idea of perfect health?

Eddy frequently points to the fact that "the Scriptures are full of accounts of the triumph of Spirit, Mind, over matter."[92] Particularly the miracles of Jesus "annulled the laws of matter, showing them to be laws of mortal mind, not of

God."[93] While Edwards and Emerson looked for changes in spiritual and moral realms, Eddy rejects the implicit dualism and demands changes in the physical world as well, following the logic of monism. From the same classic theism Edwards said "reason teaches," she argues that divine immutability means that creatures' defects could not register on God's consciousness for, as his actions are eternal, so are his thoughts. Since both are perfect, from eternity God could have no other consciousness of humans than their perfection. "What is in eternal Mind must be reflected in man, Mind's image."[94] Starting with a belief in divine sovereignty as strong as that of any Puritan—and as convinced that God employed no material means in creation as any defender of *creatio ex nihilo*—Eddy asks the obvious question: how could divine spirit bring forth from itself a world entirely opposite to itself? Either God is material or the world is spiritual. Since the former is unthinkable, the latter is necessarily true.[95] It follows, then, that if God were absent, "the universe would disappear"[96]—a conclusion the youthful Edwards had also reached and on similar grounds.

For Eddy the sheer dependence of the world upon God is the supreme example of the truth that every thing is the creation of mind, thus "everything is as real as you make it, and no more so."[97] Edwards would have recoiled at attributing to humans the power to create and Emerson would have embraced her statement for the wrong reason. For Eddy was no humanist and did not share the Transcendentalists' enthusiasm for the saving power of human thought.[98] Rather, she taught our perception must advance toward the "apprehension of its own nothingness" in that loss of self that is the only hope of saving the self. She ends her brief work, *Unity of Good,* with a hymn that Edwards might have been tempted to join in singing: "This is the mystery of godliness—that God, good, is never absent, and there is none beside good."[99]

The image of God freely extending his presence into the being of the world that Edwards drew in his last treatises is reflected in Emerson's writings on nature—but in an attenuated impersonal form able to slip easily into any number of religious costumes but unable to evoke either the dreadful shudder of spiritual rebirth or the ecstatic joy of personal communion. Emerson provides a thoroughly immanent, and weakly inspiring, deity. In Eddy, God regains personal qualities, prayer becomes ecstatic participation in the divine nature, and the entire natural world including the human body becomes pliable to ideal thoughts. In her "divine metaphysics," the trajectory of Edwards' idealism came to rest in a consistent monism and an ambitious practice of spiritual and physical perfection. Eddy's conclusions follow from a notion of divine immutability that Edwards defended to the last—even as he recognized its theological and devotional limits.

DAVID L. WEDDLE received the B.R.E. from Grace Bible College (Grand Rapids, Mich.); the A.B. from Hope College (Holland, Mich.); and both the M.A. and Ph.D. from Harvard University. He is professor of religion at Colorado College (Colorado Springs, Colo.). Among his many, wide-ranging publications are papers on Edwards, law, Jehovah's Witnesses and Christian Science.

NOTES

[1] R. G. Collingwood, *The Idea of Nature* (New York: Oxford University Press, 1960), 177.

[2] For a detailed tracing of the intellectual sources of Edwards' philosophical thought and a discussion of his modification of John Locke's empiricism, see Wallace E. Anderson, editor's introduction to *Works of Jonathan Edwards*, vol. 6, *Scientific and Philosophical Writings* (New Haven: Yale University Press, 1980), 52–136.

[3] Perry Miller, *Errand into the Wilderness* (New York: Harper Torchbook, 1964), 185. The essay was originally published under the title "From Edwards to Emerson," in the *New England Quarterly* (December 1940).

[4] Ibid., 203.

[5] Mary Baker Eddy, *Science and Health with Key to the Scriptures*, 1875 edition (Boston: First Church of Christ Scientist, 1971), 113.

[6] See *Images or Shadows of Divine Things*, ed. Perry Miller (New Haven: Yale University Press, 1948). A few of the entries in Edwards' "book of emblems" are included in *A Jonathan Edwards Reader*, ed. John E. Smith, et al. (New Haven: Yale University Press, 1995), 16–21.

[7] *Errand into the Wilderness*, 185.

[8] Ibid., 191.

[9] *Errand into the Wilderness*, 192. Miller understands that the objections were not all theoretical in nature. For along with doctrines that encouraged belief in inward communication and divine immanence, Puritan theology upheld "an ideal of social conformity, of law and order, of regulation and control." And nothing is more notoriously unrestrained than mystic visions and private revelations.

[10] Ibid., 194.

[11] Claude Lévi-Strauss, *The Savage Mind* (Chicago: University of Chicago Press, 1966), 220.

[12] *Errand into the Wilderness*, 187.

[13] *Errand into the Wilderness*, 196.

[14] *The Works of Jonathan Edwards*, vol. 8: *Ethical Writings* (New Haven: Yale University Press, 1989), 639. Emphasis added. What Edwards means by "holiness" is made clear by the biblical reference. In that text holiness is the result of a mature moral response to the "discipline" of trials.

[15] Ibid., 640.

[16] *Dissertation I. Concerning the End for Which God Created the World* in *The Works of Jonathan Edwards*, vol. 8, *Ethical Writings*, 420.

[17] Ibid., 422.

[18] Ibid., 432f.

[19] Ibid., 439.

[20] *Concerning the End for Which God Created the World*, 441.

[21] Ibid., 442.

[22] Ibid., 446.

[23] Ibid., 447; ". . . nor do any of these things argue any dependence in God on the creature for happiness." Ibid., 448. ". . . God is absolutely independent of us; that we have nothing of our own, no stock from whence we can give to God; and that no part of his happiness originates from man."

[24] Ibid., 458.

[25] Ibid., 459.

[26] Ibid., 521.

[27] *Concerning the End for Which God Created the World*, 527.

[28] Ibid., 531, n. 7. Paul Ramsey's phrase here captures the thesis of Edwards' *Treatise on Religious Affections*.

[29] Ibid., 531.

[30] Ibid., 536.

[31] Ralph Waldo Emerson, *Nature,* original edition, 1836 (Boston: Beacon Press, 1985), introduction by Jaroslav Pelikan, 7.

[32] *Nature,* 51.

[33] Ibid., 11.

[34] Ibid., 13.

[35] Ibid., 13.

[36] *Errand into the Wilderness,* 188.

[37] *Nature,* 19f. "By the mutual action of its structure and of the laws of light, perspective is produced, which integrates every mass of objects, of what character soever, into a well colored and shaded globe, so that where the particular objects are mean and unaffecting, the landscape which they compose, is round and symmetrical."

[38] Ibid., 13.

[39] Ibid., 14.

[40] Ibid., 41.

[41] *Nature,* 43.

[42] Ibid., 43f.

[43] Ibid., 49.

[44] Ibid., 51.

[45] Ibid., 51, 52.

[46] *Representative Men: Seven Lectures* (Philadelphia: David McKay, 1892), 124f.

[47] Ibid., 125.

[48] *Representative Men,* 139.

[49] Ibid., 139.

[50] Ibid., 128f.

[51] "Experience," *Essays: Second Series* (1844) in *The Collected Works of Ralph Waldo Emerson,* vol. 3 (Cambridge: Belknap Press, 1983), 29.

[52] Ibid., 30.

[53] "Nature," *Essays: Second Series,* 111.

[54] Ibid., 111.

[55] Ibid., 113.

[56] "Experience," 35.

[57] Ibid., 37.

[58] Ibid., 38.

[59] Ibid., 40.

[60] "Experience," 41.

[61] Ibid., 42.

[62] "Experience," 43.

[63] Ibid., 45.

[64] Ibid., 47.

[65] Catherine Albanese argues that Emerson's essay cleverly obscures a fundamental contradiction between two views of nature: as embodiment of divine Spirit to be embraced and as illusion to be escaped. Albanese sees Emerson moving away from his initial expression of ecstatic harmony with nature to an instrumental mastery of nature, opening the door to both wilderness preservation and mind cure. The pivot for the turn in his reflection, she believes, is the chapter on

Idealism. See *Nature Religion in America: From the Algonkian Indians to the New Age* (Chicago: University of Chicago Press, 1990), 80–87.

[66] *Nature*, 80.

[67] I am indebted to Susan Cobb for this citation from a letter written by Eddy, dated February 28, 1888 (Accession Document: LO8486 in the Mary Baker Library for the Betterment of Humanity, Boston, MA).

[68] *Nature*, 90.

[69] Ibid., 93.

[70] Ibid., 94.

[71] There is a modernized edition of these notes in *The Works of Jonathan Edwards*, vol. 6, *Scientific and Philosophical Writings*, ed. Wallace E. Anderson (New Haven: Yale University Press, 1980). I prefer to use the version in the older anthology, edited by Clarence H. Faust and Thomas H. Johnson, *Jonathan Edwards: Representative Selections* (New York: Hill & Wang, 1962) because its arbitrary capitalization and spare punctuation retain the integrity of the original manuscript. It makes a difference, as Jennifer Bernstein argues in her paper, "Experiencing Edwards: Sentences as Thought Experiments." For example, the run-on first sentence in *Of Being* is an intentional rhetorical device to draw the reader into the experience of mental confusion created by the idea of absolute nothing. Quotations in this paragraph and the next are from Faust and Johnson, 18–23.

[72] *Science and Health with Key to the Scriptures* (Boston: The First Church of Christ Scientist, 1971), 361.

[73] *Science and Health*, 330.

[74] Ibid., 55. For a detailed examination of these themes, see David L. Weddle, "The Christian Science Textbook: An Analysis of the Religious Authority of *Science and Health* by Mary Baker Eddy," *Harvard Theological Review* 84:3 (July 1991), 273–297.

[75] *Science and Health*, 151.

[76] Ibid., 330.

[77] *Science and Health*, 339. "The basis of all health, sinlessness, and immortality is the great fact that God is the only Mind; and this Mind must be not merely believed, but it must be understood."

[78] *Jonathan Edwards: Representative Selections*, 27.

[79] Ibid., 28.

[80] Ibid., 28f.

[81] *Jonathan Edwards: Representative Selections*, 36.

[82] Ibid., 27. Eddy also cites an "astronomer" who writes that "physicists" recently concur that "color is in *us*, not **in the rose**...." in *Rudimental Divine Science*, 1891 (Boston: The First Church of Christ Scientist, 1973), 6.

[83] *Science and Health*, 391.

[84] Ibid., 396.

[85] Ibid., 153.

[86] Ibid., 396.

[87] Ibid., 27. She devotes an 1898 essay to the topic "Christian Science versus Pantheism," arguing that if material things were invested with life and intelligence they would be "god-like." But such an attribution is tantamount to "idolatry" (*Miscellaneous Writings and Prose Works*, 1925).

[88] *Science and Health*, 129.

[89] Ibid., 294.

[90] *Unity of Good*, 1887 (Boston: The First Church of Christ Scientist, 1973), 3.

[91] Edwards developed the notion that the indwelling Spirit becomes a fountain of virtue within the believer in *Religious Affections,* a copy of which Eddy marked throughout. For this reference I am indebted to Lesley Pitts, manager of the archives at the Mary Baker Eddy Library for the Betterment of Humanity in Boston, MA.

[92] *Science and Health,* 139.

[93] *Unity of Good,* 11.

[94] Ibid., 14. For Eddy the Calvinist claim that God foreknew humans as fallen—even if such knowledge was atemporal—introduced sin into the mind and, therefore, being of God. If God knew sin, he would be "infinite sinner." Since God sees only his own glory, Eddy argues he cannot know evil—and only what God knows is real because infinite knowledge is necessarily foreknowledge which is one with foreordination. Here Eddy pushes the logic of divine timelessness in a way that usually ends in a demand for theodicy, but she moves in quite another direction: since all that God can know is good, then good is all he foreknows; therefore, good is all that can exist. It follows as a corollary that evil does not exist and that is why God does not know it.

[95] "Here comes in the summary of the whole matter, wherewith we started: that God is All, and God is Spirit; therefore there is nothing but Spirit; and consequently there is no matter" (ibid., 34).

[96] *Unity of Good,* 60.

[97] Ibid., 8.

[98] Robert Peel locates Eddy between the abstract optimism of the Transcendentalists and the hope of technological utopia of the Pragmatists in his still unsurpassed study, *Christian Science: Its Encounter with American Culture* (New York: Holt, Rinehart and Winston, 1958).

[99] *Unity of Good,* 62.

Edwards—Thoreau—Dillard: Reading/Writing Nature and the Awakened/Awakening Self

Michael G. Ditmore

Adapting the spirit (if neither the spirituality nor the communication genius) of Samuel F. B. Morse, I should like to begin, mid-stream and unnaturally, by telegraphing the following query: "What hath Perry Miller wrought?" The question may seem far afield from the subject of Jonathan Edwards and nature writing, and, to adumbrate some of my later discussion, Henry David Thoreau might acidly note that it may be we, like Maine and Texas, have nothing of consequence to telegraph to one another (albeit we dearly love to talk). But my question specifically concerns the methodology—loosely speaking—Miller employed in his seminal 1940 *New England Quarterly* article, "From Edwards to Emerson," reprinted in *Errand into the Wilderness* (1956), wherein Miller modeled a means for mapping intellectual lineages radically different from documentary "source studies" of direct transmission of influence. Miller's article, whatever its detractors had to say, has itself been so influential that it would be difficult to calculate the number of articles and chapters that in one way or another have undertaken Miller's basic formula "from X to Y."

Both the formula and the concept, however, are far older than Miller himself; indeed, they might well be understood as a secular, scholastic adaptation of the kind of typological exegesis the Puritans Miller studied were so adept at. Thus, it would be interesting to trace a way "from Jonathan Edwards to Miller" himself, and, if that does not seem too obvious, that would not be quite so odd as it sounds, not just because of Miller's book and articles on Edwards, and not just because of Miller's editorial position on the Yale edition of Edwards' works, but because Miller's methodology in this article is in some way—and I stress in *some way*—connected with the one Edwards text Miller actually edited (and which he titled): *Images or Shadows of Divine Things* (1948). That collection of unpublished material represented Edwards' attempt at what might be called "natural" typology, as opposed to the biblical variety Edwards undertook in "Types of the Messiah." A similar hermeneutic approach to some extent grounds both forms, but Miller, I presume, was drawn to the more freewheeling natural than the biblical form. In his introduction Miller reflects his knowledge of both strands of exegesis.

But however fascinating it may be, natural typology obviates historicism, and so it is the scriptural format that would be more appropriate for an historian. Thus, the rhetorical construction of Miller's essay title, "From Edwards to Emerson," suggests indebtedness to the historical or biblical aspect of typological exegesis, which is the maneuver whereby an interpreter connects two seemingly disparate incidents or figures, separated by historical distance, in terms of an underlying prophetic, adumbrative unity that can be witnessed (with the help of the Holy Spirit, because of human fallibility) only in hindsight. As Miller explains in the introduction to *Images*, biblical typology gave the "promise of delivering a unified meaning for history. If the types could be finally deciphered, history would be no longer a haphazard series of events but the steady accomplishment of a purpose" (7).[1] With a small amount of revision ("purpose" could be reworded with the more neutral "coherence"), those sentences adequately describe much of Miller's own project, especially in the Edwards-to-Emerson essay, whereby he imparted a sense of unity to a sequence that might otherwise appear haphazard. Or rather, perhaps a bit more to Miller's chagrin, we might work from Cotton Mather to Miller, on the grounds that Mather in his filiopiety set precedent by rerouting the types from biblical *figurae* to the political, human *figurae* of the first-generation founders of New England while always maintaining a spiritual-intellectual inheritance. Miller does not quite follow that path, to be sure. But it would not be difficult to understand Miller's methodology as a secular appropriation and reapplication of biblical typology as Edwards (and Mather) understood it for the purpose of human intellectual understanding. More to the point, Miller's adaptation aimed to bring out the unifying, underlying Americanness of seemingly disparate opposites like Edwards and Emerson—and himself—and then you and me.

My own methodology here, inspired by Miller, aims to collapse differently both strands of Edwards' typology: on one hand, to trace in brief a kind of ironic, continualistic historical nexus from Edwards to Henry David Thoreau to Annie Dillard while, on the other hand, attending to how each of these three authors employed a kind of isolationist natural typology almost omnipresent in American cultural history and writing. Put differently, and to confuse matters further: I aim to describe a partial historical typology of a persistent American natural typology.

To summarize the nature and practice of typology, Edwards' employment of typology took one or two lines, each of which had a long history before he undertook them: perhaps the more familiar, and circumscribed one, takes the more obviously historical route of connecting Old and New Testaments under a single, subtle narrative trajectory, a tradition extending well before Edwards; the other is closer to what may be termed spiritualized natural allegory, which is a matter of contemplating the present natural environment (with little regard for historical motion) as a divine symbology for the regenerate. In this sense, the difference between the two corresponds nicely to the traditional distinction between two divinely composed Books, that of Nature (or the Creatures) and that of the Bible, coordinate and fully consistent with one another; although, from a certain orthodox perspective, the latter is more trustworthy for the fallen intellect.[2] In this regard, as interpreters of nature both Edwards and Emerson fit within a much larger and longer tradition of what we might call natural exegesis. This tradition may be seen, for instance, in the earlier craze for emblems and emblem books throughout western Europe in the sixteenth and seventeenth centuries, which in turn dovetails with the devotional disciplines of meditation and contemplation (and other acts of personal piety) during the same period. These strands are perhaps most clearly represented in the writings of the Bishop Joseph Hall and in the verse emblems of Frances Quarles (the illustrations from some of which, for some reason, grace the frontispieces of various of the Yale volumes of Edwards' works). The exactness of Edwards' familiarity with either tradition is beyond my knowledge, although their broad influences are not difficult to trace in his typological writings.

Unlike natural typology, scriptural typology no longer seems to be practiced much, even in more conservative theological circles, partly because it is not an exegetical technique that admits much of innovation (it presumes rather a closed text and becomes almost a catechistical affair of memorization rather than an area for creative development) and, because of "higher criticism," the connections will now strike many exegetes as extraordinarily strained and captious. (Or rather, scriptural typology remains closed unless the exegete presumes to include later figures as further types of some sort.) Miller's typological methodology bears reconsideration because something like it, if not its exact model, is always present any time we try to "get from" an author/subject "to" another when there is no viable connection to be made between the two except the interpretive will of the critic. Needless to say, Miller imposed limits on himself. And, too, it is the case that the exercise can easily devolve into an intellectual parlor game, something on the order of "six degrees of separation," "if you were on a sinking ship and could take only ten books," etc. Depending on the skill, knowledge, and ingenuity of the critic, it is not hard to imagine how one might get "from" anyone (including Edwards) "to" virtually anyone else more or less successfully; and, after all, getting oneself "to" and "from" (or "to and fro," to echo a particular biblical text) has been described as the especial pursuit of a particular eternal being.

We might ask, conversely, which figures can we *not* get "to" "from" Edwards—which might seem like an impossibly long list—or would it? Considered purely as an intellectual exercise, could we get from Edwards to, say, William S. Burroughs? Malcolm X? Alice Walker? Thomas Pynchon? Jay Leno? Britney Spears? William S. Bennett? Well, I hope not, too, but . . . One of the main values of such exercises is to expose the conventionally obvious as strained, and what seems preposterously strained as merely subtle. Even for all the attendant problems, there is value as a mere pedagogical exercise for awakening critical thought.[3] Finally, I would argue that "from-to-ing" is always an inescapable and even useful habit of mind, but one that cannot be disciplined no matter how much it may also be disputed and eventually left to a matter of relativized "taste." And in these postmodern times in which we live, we might nowadays reverse and diversify the chronological arrow (from Emerson to Edwards—and back again!) or render it into a Mobius loop (from Edwards to Edwards).

But please note that in my title I left out those two essential phrases in Miller's title: "from" and "to." I don't know whether or not I find them "totalizing," yet I feel that current scholarship forbids me to think otherwise, so in their place I have inserted mere indifferent dashes to imply something of the random, provisional nature of the selection of authors: Edwards—Thoreau—Annie Dillard.[4] When I first read Miller's article, I thought it a stroke of genius to "get from" Edwards "to" Emerson, neither of whom I much understood nor much cared to understand at the time. But Miller helped me see something of a paradigmatic scene in American literature, one that is not repeated everywhere but is repeated often enough to feel intuitively familiar, and with relations throughout world literature/culture. It has a triadic structure: What does (1) the lone individual in experiencing/considering (2) nature claim to understand about (3) the transcendent/immanent character of divinity/spirituality (the transhuman, in short)? Emerson, of course, was central because in the strangely mistitled *Nature* (1836) (I would argue it should have been titled Spirit, but that would hardly have sold in the same way) he theorized this paradigm in as clear a manner as he could and then went on to solve it (which is to say that the solution lay in how he designed the problem).

I do not know that the paradigm is necessarily, exceptionally, or essentially "American," although the American variety seems to have a certain denuded quality. This is best indicated when we attempt to connect American nature writing with European varieties through the generic term "pastoral"; in its European setting, pastorals typically involve swains or weeping damsels or nymphs or fantastic creatures and emblems as part of the physical landscape.[5] Poems as different as Spenser's *The Faerie Queen* and Wordsworth's great ode, *Intimations of Immortality* (which must have exercised influence in some way on Emerson's thought), might be adduced as relevant examples. Considered in this way, much of American nature writing can be seen as un- or even anti-pastoral. When, for instance, Thoreau recounts his voyage in *A Week,* as often as not—or rather, more often than not—he rarely interacts at all but responds to other human beings he and his brother encounter along the way as unwelcome intruders and/or as objects for virulently negative reaction. Similarly, Thoreau's New England wilderness in *Walden,* such as it was, is utterly shorn of fable and fantasy—no aberrant prodigies or *lusus naturae* to speak of, and it is a lone mosquito in the morning that must stand for Achilles.

It would seem to have been difficult for the European mind really to conceive utter isolation before the invention of America, although figures such as Petrarch and Francis of Assisi might serve. At least this helps me to understand more readily one of the odder moments in the early exploration of the Americas detailed in Alvar Nunez Cabeza de Vaca's narrative (or *Relacion*). Cabeza de Vaca was one of four survivors of the miserably executed Narvaez expedition of some 300 men that in 1527 explored the Gulf of Mexico coastal area from present-day Florida to Texas. Narvaez foolishly decided to split the party ashore from the ships, and the expedition members soon became separated from one another. As a result, many men died from hunger, exposure, etc. Cabeza de Vaca and his companions wound up walking from the western coast of Florida as far as New Mexico before encountering other Spaniards—eight years after landing in Florida. One of the most fascinating episodes in his narrative recounts how he, naked and hungry, became separated from his companions and from all human contact for five days:

> As I went looking for [my companions] that night I became lost, and it pleased God that I found a tree burning and survived the cold of that night by its fire; and in the morning, I searched for them and traveled in this manner for five days, always with my fire and load of firewood; for if the fire were to go out in a place where there was no wood (and in many places there was none), I would have something with which to make new firebrands and would not be left without a fire, for I had no other protection against the cold, being naked as the day I was born. . . .
>
> During all this time I had not a bite to eat, nor did I find anything that could be eaten; as my feet were bare the blood ran from them freely. And God had mercy on me, for during all this time there was no wind from the north, for otherwise there was no way in which I could have survived. . . . (69)[6]

Although Cabeza de Vaca does not much dilate on this scene, it would not require a great stretch of the imagination to fit it within an American paradigm that would include writings as diverse as William Shakespeare's depiction of Caliban in *The Tempest* or Daniel Defoe's *Robinson Crusoe* or William Bradford's account of the arrival of the Pilgrims at Cape Cod or with Thomas Morton's depiction of the same "desolate and hideous wilderness" as a Canaan flowing with milk and honey for English adventurers or with Henry David Thoreau's project for self-sufficiency at Walden—or any number of similar enterprises and experiences throughout (or about) American history. One might note that for all its adaptations, this paradigmatic scene has a certain tough, ineradicable weedy quality that continues to flourish regardless of drought or herbicide, and it would require only a small dose of ingenuity to trace its emergence in someone so seemingly different as, say, Henry Adams. Such scenes can even help us to understand those authors who in some way stand in opposition to it (Frederick Douglass crouching in the cornfields, disoriented and afraid to return to his master, for instance).

The scene partakes especially nicely of the Emersonian visionary paradigm outlined in the first chapter of *Nature,* even though Cabeza de Vaca seemed less than uplifted at the oneness he experienced. And, as Roderick Nash points out in *Wilderness and the American Mind,* the American response to the wilderness has often been one of threat rather than invitation. In a rather different scene, we find Crèvecoeur's James the Farmer enjoying a leisurely and "enlightened" stroll out in nature, noting flora and fauna, when he witnesses one of the most grotesque sights recorded in American literature—the details of which I will not rehearse presently—and recoils in irrational horror.[7] A somewhat more recent version might be James Dickey's *Deliverance,* which belies the idea that the Southern conception of the wilderness was more benign than "howling."

More paradigmatically, we might go to John Filson's 1784 account of Daniel Boone's experiences in settling in Kentucky. Reflecting on his first foray into the "howling wilderness" with a companion, Boone said, "Nature was here a series of wonders, and a fund of delight. Here she displayed her ingenuity and industry in a variety of flowers and fruits, beautifully colored, elegantly shaped, and charmingly flavoured; and we were diverted with innumerable animals presenting themselves perpetually to our view" (213). Shortly afterward, they were taken captive by Indians but escaped within a week. Boone's companion was later killed, leaving just himself and his brother, to whom Boone observed, "You see now how little nature requires to be satisfied. Felicity, the companion of content, is rather found in our own breasts than in the enjoyment of external things: and I firmly believe it requires but a little philosophy to make a man happy in whatsoever state he is" (214). He and his brother began to work on creating a settlement until late spring when his brother went for supplies, leaving Boone entirely to his own devices. At first, things did not go well.

> . . . on the first day of May, 1770, my brother returned home to the settlement by himself, for a new recruit of horses and ammunition, leaving me by myself, without bread, salt or sugar, without company of my fellow creatures, or even a horse or dog. I confess I never before was under greater necessity of exercising philosophy and fortitude. A few days I passed uncomfortably. The idea of a beloved wife and family, and their anxiety upon the account of my absence and exposed situation, made sensible impressions on my heart. A thousand dreadful apprehensions presented themselves to my view, and has undoubtedly disposed me to melancholy, if further indulged.
>
> One day I undertook a tour through the country, and the diversity and beauties of nature I met with in this charming season, expelled every gloomy and vexatious thought. Just at the close of day the gentle gales retired, and left the place to the disposal of a profound calm. Not a breeze shook the most tremulous leaf. I had gained the summit of a commanding ridge, and, looking round with astonishing delight, beheld the ample plains, the beauteous tracts below. On the other hand, I surveyed the famous river Ohio that rolled in silent dignity, marking the western boundary of Kentucke with inconceivable grandeur. At a vast distance I beheld the mountains lift their venerable brows, and penetrate the clouds. All things were still. . . .

This situation lasted several days. Boone notes that he could have given in to fear and anxiety; instead he concludes:

Thus was I surrounded with plenty in the midst of want. I was happy in the midst of dangers and inconveniences. In such diversity it was impossible I should be disposed to melancholy. No populous city, with all the varieties of commerce and stately structures, could afford so much pleasure to my mind, as the beauties of nature I found here. (215)[8]

Much the same could be said of the writings of John Muir; or we could turn to multiple vestiges in popular culture. This might help account for the enormous popularity of Kevin Costner's 1990 Oscar-winning *Dances with Wolves,* which I would argue was not just *about* another American loner trying to discover himself in the solitude of the wilderness but was equally an opportunity *for* urbanized audiences darkly, comfortably, and temporarily to fantasize through large-screen cinematography of their own solitary treks in such wildernesses. Surely that is the appeal also of the dozens and dozens of SUV commercials that promise our own comfortable wilderness experience.

It seems that wherever, and whenever, we go in America, we are never far from natural revelation.

I. Edwards and Excellency

It is well-nigh superfluous to note the high unlikelihood that Edwards will ever enter the pantheon of American nature writers, especially as it morphs into environmental writing and, now, "eco"-variations (ecoliterature, ecocriticism, ecotheology, etc.), except in the slimmest, dustiest, most marginalized, most antiquated way—or perhaps even as object of scorn and ridicule. And I suspect Edwards would rightly be happy with that. Consider, for instance, his one specific foray into what we might aptly call "nature writing," with "The 'Spider' Letter" at about age twenty. This brief work reflects a more than decent aptitude for close observation; how differently matters might have turned out had he persisted in that line rather than the pulpit. But it is not the preciseness of the observation that fascinates so much as the corollaries Edwards draws from his observations. First, he notes "the wisdom of the Creator" in designing the spider and providing the means for its "wonderful" operation. But not stopping there, he next notes "the exuberant goodness of the Creator, who hath ... provided ... for the pleasure and recreation of all sorts of creatures, even the insects." But then Edwards digresses in a macabre turn to assert that

> the chief end of this faculty that is given them is not their recreation but their destruction, because their destruction is unavoidably the constant effect of it; and we find nothing that is the continual effect of nature but what is the end of the means by which it is brought to pass: but it is impossible but that the greatest part of the spiders upon the land should every year be swept into the ocean. (167)

Talk about being in the hands of an angry God! Edwards dilates further:

> Hence [there] is reason to admire at the wisdom of the Creator, and to be convinced that it is exercised about such little things in this wonderful contrivance of annually carrying off and burying *the corruption and nauseousness of the air,* of which flying insects are little collections, in the bottom of the ocean where it will do no harm; and especially the strange way of bringing this about in spiders, which are collections of these collections, their food being flying insects, flies being the poison of the air, and spiders are the poison of flies collected together. (168, emphasis added)

Characterizing spiders as "corruption" and "nauseousness" would not likely lend itself to praise from naturalists.[9]

Attention to nature per se rarely occupied Edwards in his writing. But of course I am not really concerned so much with nature (or naturalistic) writing per se but rather with the paradigm of the isolated individual in nature who meditates to attain epiphanic insight. The Edwardsean Ur-text, I suppose, would be found in his "Personal Narrative" (buttressed by *Miscellanies* 1069), but I should like to begin with an earlier, related text, viz., *A Faithful Narrative,* in part because of its widespread popularity in Edwards' own time.

I have sometimes encountered highly abridged versions of the *Faithful Narrative* in literature anthologies, wherein the portions retained reflect mainly those aspects that will strike postmodern sensibilities as morbid or extreme. It therefore becomes easy to dismiss Edwards' depiction of the conversion process as a bizarre obsession with guilt and sin and mind control, but Edwards very carefully arranged the narrative to illustrate what might be termed the benefits of conversion, which are not merely a relief from guilt or a vapid celebration of groupthink. Instead, mature converts experienced what Edwards liked to call "the excellency" of Christ, an aesthetic experience that included a regenerated and intense sense of the beauty of the natural environment:

> Many, while their minds have been filled with spiritual delights, have as it were forgot their food; their bodily appetite has failed, while their minds have been entertained with meat to eat that others knew not of [John 4:32]. The light and comfort which some of them enjoy, gives a new relish to their common blessings, and causes all things about 'em to appear as it were beautiful, sweet and pleasant to them: all things abroad, the sun, moon and stars, the clouds and sky, the heavens and earth, appear as it were with a cast of divine glory and sweetness upon them. The sweetest joy that these good people among us express, is not that which consists in a sense of the safety of their own state, and that now they are out of danger of hell; frequently, in times of their highest

spiritual entertainment, this seems to be as it were forgotten. The supreme attention of their mind is the glorious excellencies of God and Christ, which they have in view; not but that there is very often a ravishing sense of God's love accompanying a sense of his excellency, and they rejoice in a sense of the faithfulness of God's promises, as they respect the future eternal enjoyment of God. (183)

Readers familiar with Edwards' "Personal Narrative" will immediately recognize echoes in this passage. But I would note that these converts do not appear to turn toward nature with any didactic interest at all, i.e., to discern God's providence or eschatological fulfillment. Rather, their regenerated experience of nature is one of sweetness and delight, of pure aesthetic pleasure, of beholding divinity in a way that—I infer—cannot be done, first, cooperatively or, second, by beholding human beings. Something of this hint is carried out in his account of the notable conversion of Abigail Hutchinson later in *A Faithful Narrative*:

She often expressed a sense of the glory of God appearing in the trees, and growth of the fields, and other works of God's hands. She told her sister that lived near the heart of the town, that she once thought it a pleasant thing to live in the middle of the town, but now, says she, "I think it much more pleasant to sit and see the wind blowing the trees, and to behold what God has made." (195)

Here, too, the convert Hutchinson experiences a "sense" and engages in "beholding," in a plain natural environment without social companionship. In both these instances, it is not just that converts have a different sense of nature, but also that natural beauty and divine promises become inextricably mingled, perhaps in the spirit of entry 64 of Edwards' work on natural types:

> Hills and mountains are types of heaven, and often made use of as such in Scripture. These are difficultly ascended. To ascend them, one must go against the natural tendency of the flesh that must be contradicted in all the ascent, in every step of it, and the ascent is attended with labor, sweat and weariness, and there are commonly many hideous rocks in the way. 'Tis a great deal easier descending into valleys.
>
> This is a representation of the difficulty, labor and self-denial of the way to heaven; and how agreeable it is to the inclination of the flesh to descend into hell. At the bottom of valleys, especially deep valleys, there is water—either a lake or other water. But water . . . commonly signifies misery, especially that which is occasioned by the wrath of God. So in hell is a lake or gulf of misery and wrath. (72)

Perhaps in the spirit of that entry—but here Edwards has devoted significant intellectual effort to interpreting hills and mountains as types of heavens, whereas Hutchinson and the unnamed converts of *A Faithful Narrative* seem to have been merely experiencing glory and beauty.[10]

The "sense of the heart" Edwards had so carefully delineated in "A Divine and Supernatural Light" (1734), and the consequences for rehabilitating reason, is especially apropos. This light, he asserts,

> not only removes the hindrances of reason, but positively helps reason. It makes even the speculative notions the more lively. It engages the attention of the mind, with the more fixedness and intenseness to that kind of objects; which causes it to have a clearer view of them, and enables it more clearly to see their mutual relations, and occasions it to take more notice of them. The ideas themselves that otherwise are dim, and obscure, are by this means impressed with the greater strength, and have a light cast upon them; so that the mind can better judge of them.

> As he that beholds the objects on the face of the earth, when the light of the sun is cast upon them, is under greater advantage to discern them in their true forms, and mutual relations, than he that sees them in a dim starlight or twilight.
>
> The mind having a sensibleness of the excellency of divine objects, dwells upon them with delight; and the powers of the soul are more awakened, and enlivened to employ themselves in the contemplation of them, and exert themselves more fully and much more to purpose. The beauty and sweetness of the objects draws on the faculties, and draws forth their exercises: so that reason itself is under far greater advantages for its proper and free exercises, and to attain its proper end, free of darkness and delusion. (415)[11]

But it should be noted that Edwards tends to think here in highly private and internalized terms, of the isolated individual who comes to this regenerate experience largely in isolation, somewhat like Kierkegaard's "knight of faith." I would first note that Edwards not only had an easy time thinking in terms of utter isolation, but I am not certain he often thought otherwise. Part of what contributed to his keen logical powers was his ability to sliver arguments to their most atomized specifics, and he often applies that same ability rhetorically to his audience. In "Sinners in the Hands of an Angry God," for instance, Edwards aims to arouse his audience by eliciting their utter solitude from one another—a la Shirley Jackson's "The Lottery": only one in the audience might be damned; we don't know his thoughts or where he sits; but he could be next to *you*, or could in fact BE you—and he carries this to the point of atomizing common, daily experience into the barest molecular constituents of narrative instants (you went to bed last night, you slept, you got up this morning, you got ready for church, you came here, you are sitting here right now), at any of which God could release the miserable reprobate into hell. When Edwards reminds the unconverted that

God "is under no obligation," he is saying that there is no covenant agreement, that each individual is utterly isolated not just from God but also from others. The only way to lose such isolation is through conversion, wherein the solitary individual is not so much brought into fellowship with others but in which he (or she) attains a relationship with only one other figure, God.

Similarly, one of the more difficult aspects of the "Personal Narrative" for modern readers is Edwards' own self-abstraction; for instance, Edwards intimates not in the slightest about his wife and children; one might have wanted to know what his father looked like, or his mother, or one of his ten sisters. Instead, Edwards maintains a severely strict focus on the experience of the spirit utterly and almost thoroughly abstracted from social contact. And this aspect is all the more remarkable because Edwards seems always to have insisted on the importance of church membership; perhaps his own tendency to isolation explains why. It is in the "Personal Narrative"—unpublished in his lifetime, the provenance of which remains obscure—that the practice (but not the theory) of Edwardsean contemplation is most amply described. Although Edwards alludes to the prayer booth he had constructed "in a swamp, in a very secret and retired place" and hints at "particular secret places of [his] own in the woods" (282), much of the early narrative represents Edwards as bookish and confined to his room. Where exactly was he when he had his momentous experience in reading 1 Tim. 1:17? He does not specify, but a chamber of some kind seems likelier than under a tree. Yet when he contemplatively envisions the excellency of Christ, he does so through biblically coded poetic metaphor that prompts him into nature:

> And found, from time to time, an inward sweetness, that used, as it were, to carry me away in my contemplations; in what I know not how to express otherwise, than by a calm, sweet abstraction of soul from all the concerns o[f] this world; and a kind of vision, or fixed ideas and imaginations, of being alone in the mountains, or some solitary

wilderness, far from all mankind, sweetly conversing with Christ, and wrapt and swallowed up in God. (793)

Not that Edwards *literally* is in a natural landscape, far from society, but rather that his fantasy of that setting—"of being alone in the mountains, or some solitary wilderness"—provides the best mental analogy for his desire.[12] This becomes a recurrent and paradigmatic scene for Edwards' devotional practice reflected in "Personal Narrative." It reappears in the metaphor of the "little white flower" that images the "soul of a true Christian" (796). And it undergirds two lengthier passages absolutely central for understanding Edwards at all. The first passage concerns the post-conversion difference he experienced, much like the converts in *Faithful Narrative*.

The appearance of everything was altered: there seemed to be, as it were, a calm, sweet cast, or appearance of divine glory, in almost everything. God's excellency, his wisdom, his purity and love, seemed to appear in everything; in the sun, moon and stars; in the clouds, and blue sky; in the grass, flowers, trees; in the water, and all nature; which used greatly to fix my mind. I often used to sit and view the moon, for a long time; and so in the daytime, spent much time in viewing the clouds and sky, to behold the sweet glory of God in these things: in the meantime, singing forth with a low voice, my contemplations of the Creator and Redeemer. And scarce anything, among all the works of nature, was so sweet to me as thunder and lightning. Formerly, nothing had been so terrible to me. I used to be a person uncommonly terrified with thunder: and it used to strike me with terror, when I saw a thunderstorm rising. But now, on the contrary, it rejoiced me. I felt God at the first appearance of a thunderstorm. And used to take the opportunity at such times, to fix myself to view the clouds, and see the lightnings play, and hear

> the majestic and awful voice of God's thunder: which oftentimes was exceeding entertaining, leading me to sweet contemplations of my great and glorious God. (793–94)

Here Edwards *is* literally in the natural landscape, almost as a proto-Romantic attracted not just to the serenity but also to the turbulent fury and volatile power of nature as a medium for "the sweet glory of God." To be sure, it is rather an abstract, generalized landscape, without detail or significant feature. There are mere "grass, flowers, trees," but not particular species nor in particular locations. But in a later passage, Edwards does offer specifics, not of the landscape but of when he had such near mystical experiences and how long they lasted:

> Once, as I rid out into the woods for my health, *anno* 1737; and having lit from my horse in a retired place, as my manner commonly has been, to walk for divine contemplation and prayer; I had a view, that for me was extraordinary, of the glory of the Son of God; as mediator between God and man; and his wonderful, great, full, pure and sweet grace and love, and meek and gentle condescension. This grace, that appeared to me so calm and sweet, appeared great above the heavens. The person of Christ appeared ineffably excellent, with an excellency great enough to swallow up all thought and conception. Which continued, as near as I can judge, about an hour; which kept me, the bigger part of the time, in a flood of tears and weeping aloud. (801)[13]

The posthumous publication of "Personal Narrative" suggests Edwards' reticence in publicizing his personal spiritual experience, even though it clearly accords with the very popular *Faithful Narrative*. I have been less concerned here with the theory undergirding Edwards' view—*The End for Which God Created the World* would be key, along with "A Divine and Supernatural Light" and key portions of

Religious Affections—than with its practice and with the picture it suggests of the devotional practices of Edwardsean converts, who neither retreated to monastic cells nor always joined themselves together in the sweet communion of church fellowship but rather turned to wandering in the woods, gazing at the heavens, marveling at thunderstorms, all to deepen their sweetly sensible experience of the excellency and glory of God. And, as Edwards notes, they did so both literally and imaginatively. Perhaps the great question for us is why this procedure seems so familiar and comfortable instead of novel, strange, and off-track. In short, why does this expression of spirituality seem so very natural?

II. Thoreau and Reticence

In looking back on "From Edwards to Emerson" with crystalline hindsight, Miller began by noting that "[t]here can be no doubt that Jonathan Edwards would have abhorred from the bottom of his soul every proposition Ralph Waldo Emerson blandly put forth in the manifesto of 1836, *Nature*" (184).[14] That, of course, actually boosted Miller's own ingenuity in the essay, but unfortunately, I doubt . . . somewhat. Not that the two men would not have sharply parted company in the end, and perhaps well before. But first of all, I find nothing "bland" in Emerson's *Nature*. Secondly, I am not convinced that Edwards' undoubted rejection would have been quite so extreme. Miller thought that Edwards would have recognized in Emerson "an inevitable outcome of that degenerate 'Arminianism'" (184), known in the 1830s as Unitarianism; rather, I would say that Edwards would have immediately understood Emerson as a kind of philosophically abstruse Quaker, or a latter-day antinomian, and a serious threat precisely because Emerson's "transparent eyeball" hewed so closely to his own experiences with the one significant difference that the irremovable dividing wall between mortal and divinity is dissolved in Emerson, or, rather, is rendered transparent.[15] (To Miller's credit, that is precisely what he argues in the body of the 1940 essay.) That is to say that

Edwards and Emerson shared enough radio frequency as to at least understand the ground of their differences, and I believe they also would have maintained a mutual respect as ministers despite their differences.

Those who followed in Emerson's wake, such as Henry David Thoreau and Walt Whitman, are entirely a different matter, as they rarely acknowledged the sources of Emerson's anxieties but had the luxury of proceeding as though, via Emerson, the anxieties had been dispensed with. Whitman's "open communion" policy described in what became section 19 of "Song of Myself" or his pretense of being Christ crucified in 38, just to describe the more salient points, would have been simply beyond the pale for Edwards, who would have at least known how to respond to Emerson's conscientious decision not to observe the Lord's Supper. That is not even to touch on Whitman's overt alogicality, free verse, or graphic sexual descriptions. It is possible Edwards would have stopped at the title page as soon as he got a glimpse of Whitman's "one of the roughs" pose. Or that is to say, getting from Edwards to Whitman is either unimaginable or thoroughly uninteresting for me, even as a study in virtually absolute self-canceling contrasts (and even though Whitman's approach to nature as symbol also partakes of the emblematic method). It *can* be done, I suppose, but why bother?

Thoreau also seems more an obstacle than otherwise but of a milder variety. One might say that Edwards would have responded to Thoreau's Sunday sermonizing in *A Week* with severe contempt and disdain, but I am inclined to think that the normally staid, level-headed Edwards would have further lost his self-control for once and tossed the book in the fire, after having thoroughly stomped and shredded it. It would not have been worth a considered response. Had he known any of the children of his parish to have been passing a copy around, the "bad book" affair would have paled in comparison. Nursing manuals and Arminians are one thing, but Thoreau?

That may seem a bit extreme to say for Edwards, especially because Thoreau seems so tame alongside, say, Whitman. But Edwards still would have been able to identify Thoreau, and that recognizable proximity is precisely what would have irritated and outraged. Consider the Sunday morning passage from *A Week:*

> I trust that some may be as near and dear to Buddha, or to Christ, or Swedenborg, who are without the pale of their churches. It is necessary not to be Christian to appreciate the beauty and significance of the life of Christ. I know that some will have hard thoughts of me, when they hear their Christ named beside my Buddha, yet I am sure that I am willing they should love their Christ more than my Buddha, for the love is the main thing, and I like him too. (55)

Appreciating the "beauty and significance of the life of Christ" without being a Christian—I think Thoreau meant a nominal, church-going professor—would, I think, be a sure sign of the "natural man" as Edwards described him, the man capable of flawless morality—and yet surely damned for all eternity. Thoreau, I think, would have represented for Edwards the essence of relativistic pagan pantheism. Or Thoreau again, in one of his glib jibes responding to the "miracles controversy": "there is no infidelity, now-a-days, so great as that which prays, and keeps the Sabbath, and rebuilds the churches" (62). Edwards might have concurred, were those churches filled with Arminians, but the tone of correctness and nostalgia absent in Thoreau would have been noxious to him. In the face of a corrupted church, Thoreau simply abandons the project that Edwards would have used to launch yet another awakening. At the same time, Edwards would surely have appreciated some of Thoreau's stinging criticism, such as that of how New Englanders treated the New Testament: "I know of no book that has so few readers. There is none so truly strange, and heretical, and unpopular" (59). I am unsure whether Thoreau really believed that, but that he felt it necessary to be superior to his neighbors on all accounts is undeniable.[16]

Perhaps more pointedly, consider Thoreau's statement on "Spring" in *Walden:* "In a pleasant spring morning all men's sins are forgiven. Such a day is a truce to vice. While such a sun holds out to burn, the vilest sinner may return" (573). Could any statement have more fully epitomized pagan pantheism for Edwards—and helped to explain its great danger? Edwards would have fully appreciated the regenerative possibilities in common grace, but surely he would have reminded us that Thoreau takes the sun—and the air and the earth itself—entirely too much for granted.

Furthermore, Thoreau's lavish attention to concrete physical detail, and even to historical accounts of the landscape, is vastly different from Edwards. Edwards' descriptions of the natural landscape are close to empty stereotypes, whereas Thoreau more carefully brings out the landscape front and center for the reader's own experience.

Much of this, and much more, goes without saying. And yet, perhaps we ought to dig deeper. As Mason Lowance put it:

> Like Taylor and Edwards, Thoreau has employed the imagery of nature to explore abstract principles, which he believes to be eternally verifiable. Unlike his Puritan predecessors, Thoreau perceived in nature the full expression of spirit rather than a 'symbol of spirit,' and in this way, the transcendental mode closely approximates the epistemological discourses of Edwards, whose elect perception received impressions of divine grace through natural sources of revelation as well as from Scripture. (291)

The difference may be subtle, but it is all too crucial. Or again, Perry Miller, this time from a late essay, "Thoreau in the Context of International Romanticism." Drawing on two seemingly contradictory passages in Thoreau's first published essay, "Natural History of Massachusetts" (1842), Miller calls attention to a passage wherein Thoreau says that in walking in the woods he found that his "most delicate experience is typified there." Miller picks up on the odd usage of "typifies" and observes,

> If at one and the same time nature is closely inspected in microscopic detail and yet through the ancient system of typology makes experience intelligible, then Thoreau will have solved the Romantic riddle, have mastered the destructive Romantic irony. Seen in such a context, his life was an unrelenting exertion to hold this precarious stance. (177)[17]

Thoreau may have been wrangling with European Romantics like Wordsworth, but he did so by adapting the tools and resources of his New England Puritan predecessors to his environment.

As true as this is, it is also difficult to pinpoint and substantiate. That is in part, I think, because Thoreau was such a meticulous literary craftsman; considered merely as a matter of style, Edwards' jottings on natural typology would have bothered Thoreau because of their abstract, rigid, highly formulaic character. One always more or less knows the ending of an Edwards meditation on a type; Edwards' style has a solid deductive tone, as though he always knew precisely how a thought would end. But Thoreau's style is more exploratory, more languorous, and open-ended—so open-ended that it is not always clear that there *is* an end. It is easy and tempting to assume an overly simplistic method in *Walden,* which would be that Thoreau meticulously scrutinizes some natural scene, incident, or habit and then extracts from it some pithy moral, but the more one looks for such passages the rarer they seem to become, somewhat like the loon he chased on the lake. Instead, Thoreau seems to have had to wait.

> It would seem as if the very language of our parlors would lose all its nerve and degenerate into *parlaver* wholly, our lives pass at such

remoteness from its symbols, and its metaphors and tropes are necessarily so far fetched, through slides and dumb-waiters, as it were; in other words, the parlor is so far from the kitchen and workshop. The dinner even is only the parable of a dinner, commonly. As if only the savage dwelt near enough to Nature and Truth to borrow a trope from them. How can the scholar, who dwells away in the North West Territory or the Isle of Man, tell what is parliamentary in the kitchen? (517)

Both Thoreau's style and approach are summarized plainly and pithily in the concluding paragraph of "The Natural History of Massachusetts": "We must look a long time before we can see" (29). Before one sees, of course, one may devote considerable time to talking, or writing, for that is part of the process of looking. This matches nicely with a statement earlier in the same paragraph: "Let us not underrate the value of a fact; it will one day flower into a truth" (28). It is that attention to minute fact and detail that makes Thoreau such a favorite with naturalists and environmentalists, but it is the "flowering" of such facts that I find interesting—and which takes a considerably long amount of time to emerge in *Walden*. And then, what kind of "truth" is it? Thoreau, unlike Edwards, would claim a fully inductive method, in which he has no formative idea what bud will emerge at the temporal end of a fact in its organic architecture, but "Natural History" provides an invaluable clue that this truth may not be an expressible idea at all but a stance, a way of being, something akin to the Edwardsean perception of excellency: "When I detect a beauty in any of the recesses of nature, I am reminded, by the serene and retired spirit in which it requires to be contemplated, of the inexpressible privacy of a life,—how silent and unambitious it is. The beauty there is in mosses must be considered from the holiest, quietest nook" (4). Privacy, silence, unambitiousness, beauty—are these not the very qualities Thoreau himself aspired to? If so, then insofar as Thoreau conceived of nature as type and/or emblem, it was not as a metaphor that, upon reflection, revealed something else but as a revelation of himself in the present.[18]

Here, too, we find one of the stranger, more difficult connections—or disconnections—between Emerson and Thoreau, between each other and even within themselves. In *Nature,* Emerson *does* conceive of every mental datum as emblematic, which in turn means that *this* single, entire datum (nature *in toto*) is also emblematic; thought is filled with nothing but metaphors as a medium for Spirit, and that matrix in turn is itself metaphorical. But at the outset of the essay, Emerson carefully delineates his philosophical understanding of nature not as the rocks, hills, trees, etc. but as "all that is separate from us . . . both nature and art, all other and my own body" (8). In practice, Emerson tends not to observe the philosophical distinction so precisely; Thoreau, on the other hand, hardly ever seems to allow such a distinction in the first place, preferring instead to lavish extraordinary attention on concrete, physical detail in and for itself. Thus, it is not until relatively late in *Walden*—in fact, in the penultimate chapter titled "Spring," which deals most obviously with regeneration—that he finally touches more expansively on questions of abstract meaning in nature stemming from his two-year residency at Walden. He does so by adapting older "book of nature" terminology.

> Thus it seemed that this one hillside illustrated the principle of all the operations of Nature. The Maker of this earth but patented a leaf. What Champollion will decipher this hieroglyphic for us, that we may turn over a new leaf at last? This phenomenon is more exhilarating to me than the luxuriance and fertility of vineyards. True, it is somewhat excrementitious in its character, and there is no end to the heaps of liver lights and bowels, as if the globe were turned wrong side outward; but this suggests at least Nature has some bowels, and there again is mother

of humanity. This is the frost coming out of the ground; this is spring. It precedes the green and flowery spring, as mythology precedes regular poetry. I know of nothing more purgative of winter fumes and indigestions. It convinces me that Earth is still in her swaddling clothes, and stretches forth baby fingers on every side. Fresh curls spring from the baldest brow. There is nothing inorganic. These foliaceous heaps lie along the bank like slag of a furnace, showing that Nature is "in full blast" within. The earth is not a mere fragment of a dead history, stratum upon stratum like the leaves of a book, to be studied by geologists and antiquaries chiefly, but living poetry like the leaves of a tree, which precede flowers and fruit,—not a fossil earth, but a living earth; compared with whose great central life all animal and vegetable life is merely parasitic. Its throes will heave our exuviae from their graves. You may melt your metals and cast them into the most beautiful moulds you can; they will never excite me like the forms which this molten earth flows out into. And not only it, but the institutions upon it, are plastic like clay in the hands of the potter. (568)

To get at this differently, consider Emerson's pronouncement in the second paragraph of *Nature,* wherein he also saw nature as hieroglyphic: "Undoubtedly we have no questions to ask which are unanswerable. We must trust the perfection of the creation so far, as to believe that whatever curiosity the order of things has awakened in our minds, the order of things can satisfy" (7). Emerson further insists nature/spirit itself is ethical and didactic; it always purposes to teach us moral lessons, if we will be attendant (which is yet another summation of Edwardsean natural typology).[19] Thoreau, again from "Spring," sees nature very differently: "At the same time that we are earnest to explore and learn all things, we require that all things be mysterious and unexplorable, that land and sea be infinitely wild, unsurveyed and unfathomed by us because unfathomable . . .

We need to witness our own limits transgressed, and some life pasturing freely where we never wander" (575). The wildness and mystery Thoreau insists on, most memorably emblemized by his encounter with the solitary loon on Walden pond, is an affront to Emerson's optimistic doctrine that the universe is fully orderly except for the curable "ruin or the blank . . . in our own eye" (*Nature* 47), that we need only apply ourselves to reading the hieroglyphic to understand that the answer is veiled but co-existent with the problem. The opacity that Emerson believed could be rendered transparent is Thoreau's mystery and wildness of nature, so that Thoreau was content and even determined to leave such inexplicable hieroglyphs undisturbed. Merely tracing the facticity of their contours could be quite enough without bothering to claim that one could unlock their meaning or see through them to Spirit. That is not, of course, to suggest that Thoreau was any less of an optimist than Emerson, but it helps us to understand how differently their optimisms operated. To Emerson's cosmic faith in the totality of meaning, Thoreau finds meaning in a kind of antisocial, atemporal (or ahistorical) experience of perfection, exemplified in the parable of the artist of Kouroo in the conclusion to *Walden*.

Unlike Emerson, or Edwards, therefore, Thoreau more rarely moves to deliver the moral tag we might expect from his patient exploration of natural circumstances. The chapter on "Winter Animals" in *Walden* is a good example. It is a beautifully crafted chapter, but it is not necessarily much of a contribution to natural science, nor does it offer a philosophical summation. Its value lies in the sense that it convincingly imparts of what it would it mean to live in enough solitude, and with enough informed attentiveness, that one could observe and identify and enjoy not only the realities of nature but could indulge oneself in creating prose-formed poetic music of the same.

> For sounds in winter nights, and often in winter days, I heard the forlorn but melodious note of a hooting owl indefinitely far; such a sound as the

frozen earth would yield if struck with a suitable plectrum, the very *lingua vernacula* of Walden Wood, and quite familiar to me at last, though I never saw the bird while it was making it. I seldom opened my door in a winter evening without hearing it; *Hoo hoo hoo, hoorer hoo* sounded sonorously, and the first three syllables accented somewhat like *how der do;* or sometimes *hoo hoo* only. One night in the beginning of winter, before the pond froze over, about nine o'clock, I was startled by the loud honking of a goose, and, stepping to the door, heard the sound of their wings like a tempest in the woods as they flew low over my house. They passed over the pond toward Fair Haven, seemingly deterred from settling by my light, their commodore honking all the while with a regular beat. Suddenly an unmistakable cat-owl from very near me, with the most harsh and tremendous voice I ever heard from any inhabitant of the woods, responded at regular intervals to the goose, as if determined to expose and disgrace this intruder from Hudson's Bay by exhibiting a greater compass and volume of voice in a native, and boo-hoo him out of Concord horizon. What do you mean by alarming the citadel at this time of night consecrated to me? Do you think I am ever caught napping at such an hour, and that I have not got lungs and a larynx as well as yourself? *Boo-hoo, boo-hoo, boo-hoo!* It was one of the most thrilling discords I ever heard. And yet, if you had a discriminating ear, there were in it the elements of a concord such as these plains never saw nor heard. (539)

With some trimming and revision, that is not terribly far from Wallace Stevens and his various hullabaloos, I would say; and the concord-in-discord is mightily suggestive of something profoundly below the surface of the details recorded. It is, like so many paragraphs and even entire pages of *Walden,* entirely lovely, both for the details and for the delight in the telling; it even bears some of the wildness and mystery of the very nature Thoreau so closely observed. But if one—say, a severe typologist—were to insist, what does it *mean*? where does it take us? what is the (dare we say) moral or the application?, I think I would be baffled, perhaps consternated. Why ask? Here Thoreau is rendering an array of wild facts, is engaged in the process of merely and patiently looking; perhaps whatever he saw in this looking was finally incommunicable or perhaps inexpressible. Or, more probably, what he saw did not issue in some kind of abstract codification about behavior—what he saw was the very wildness and solitude he came so much to celebrate and live out in his own life. Note the reticence of the various soundmakers: he never caught the hoot owl in the act of hooting; the geese are perhaps closer, but the cat-owl's location is not uncovered. Perhaps the distance *is* the implicit moral, since it certainly fits Thoreau's own stance.

That is not to say that Thoreau does not occasionally give us some sense of the human meaning to be derived from nature. He can say, for instance, that owls "represent the stark twilight and unsatisfied thoughts which all have" (422). But I am not sure I find that an entirely satisfactory "meaning." It reads, instead, as though Thoreau follows the emblematic formula but turns the ending on its head. And certainly, his *tour de force* account of the great ant war, symbolically balanced with his stalking of the loon, represent his brilliance as a transcendental—if satirical—emblematist, although even there he trusts his reader to supply the moral should the need arise.

Thoreau's greatest anxiety, to employ the terminology of Harold Bloom, was his strong, defensive sense of belatedness, which appears, first, in his frequent denials of the priority of Homer and the heroic ages (or what-have-you) and, second, in his repeated desire to be as early as possible, even ad absurdum. These two strains (along with the imperative to simplify) tend to coalesce in Thoreau, or at least they reside nearby: "To anticipate, not the sunrise and dawn merely, but, if possible, Nature herself!" (336). This leads to one of the subtler metaphysical admissions in all of Thoreau:

> Near the end of March, 1845, I borrowed an axe and went down to the woods by Walden nearest to where I intended to build my house, and began to cut down some tall arrowy white pines, still in their youth, for timber. *It is difficult to begin without borrowing,* but perhaps it is the most generous course thus to permit your fellow-men to have an interest in your enterprise. The owner of the axe, as he released his hold on it, said that it was the apple of his eye; but I returned it sharper than I received it. (354–55, emphasis added)

Rhetorically, Thoreau always had a clever way of snatching victory from the jaws of defeat. Absolute originality is impossible (unless one can attain self-conception), but one can hope to improve the belated situation and simultaneously dismiss one's cloddish neighbors. Edwards, in contrast, appears to have been singularly unruffled by such anxiety, which is why he can loom so large as a great writer/thinker to us, and why Thoreau can seem a bit more approachable.

Thoreau's is a world more carefully detailed in particulars and fine points, an awareness of statistics, minutiae, etc. But it is equally, and perhaps more importantly, a book about consciousness itself. In the chapter on "Solitude," Thoreau writes:

> With thinking we may be beside ourselves in a sane sense. By a conscious effort of the mind we can stand aloof from actions and their consequences; and all things, good and bad, go by us like a torrent. We are not wholly involved in Nature. I may be either the driftwood in the stream, or Indra in the sky looking down on it. I *may* be affected by a theatrical exhibition; on the other hand, I *may not* be affected by an actual event which appears to concern me much more. I only know myself as a human entity; the scene, so to speak, of thoughts and affections; and am sensible of a certain doubleness by which I can stand as remote from

myself as from another. However intense my experience, I am conscious of the presence and criticism of a part of me, which, as it were, is not a part of me, but spectator, sharing no experience, but taking note of it; and that is no more I than it is you. (429)

Such doubleness might be the very blockage that would prevent the transparency of the Emersonian eyeball, but more than "Nature itself" it is the very subject of *Walden*—it is, in fact, the lesson Thoreau aims to impart: how each of us, in our independent way, can attain that self-consciousness. For Thoreau, that could be done only by putting society aside and to spend time in isolation at Walden. And in the midst of this, Thoreau, for all his reserve and reticence, gets as close as he ever does to an Edwardsean brush with deity:

I have occasional visits in the long winter evenings, when the snow falls fast and the wind howls in the wood, from an old settler and original proprietor, who is reported to have dug Walden Pond, and stoned it, and fringed it with pine woods; who tells me stories of old time and of new eternity; and between us we manage to pass a cheerful evening with social mirth and pleasant views of things, even without apples or cider,—a most wise and humorous friend, whom I love much, who keeps himself more secret than ever did Goffe or Whalley; and though he is thought to be dead, none can show where he is buried. An elderly dame, too, dwells in my neighborhood, invisible to most persons, in whose odorous herb garden I love to stroll sometimes, gathering simples and listening to her fables; for she has a genius of unequalled fertility, and her memory runs back farther than mythology, and she can tell me the original of every fable, and on what fact every one is founded, for the incidents occurred when she was young. A ruddy and lusty old dame, who delights in all weathers and seasons, and is likely to outlive all her children yet. (431–2)

It is no wonder that Thoreau, in a rare theological admission, can assert that "God is alone" (431), a statement not so much of unbridled anthropomorphism but, more exactly, of Thoreaumorphism in projecting his need for solitude on the divinity.

As with any great book, *Walden* is many kinds of books in one binding. For instance, it really is an eloquently practical book about self-sufficient housekeeping and farming, although it is shorter than one would like on specifics (buy this, do that) and illustrated diagrams; and it also turns out to be a satire and a book of wit and wisdom. It is also autobiographical narrative. It is one man's attempt to remind his neighbors at once how little and far removed they are from nature. It is certainly an important model for naturalists of all stripes. But chiefly, it is about awakening and remaining awake, about stirring both the consciousness and the conscience. That Thoreau found an ideal setting for doing so in a fairly secluded "natural" setting may be accident or coincidence, but it has turned out that, in the American mind, consciousness and conscientiousness seem to demand just such a setting.

III. Dillard and Indeterminate Wonder

One of the more striking aspects, conspicuous by various absences, of Thoreau's *Walden* is the humdrum, routine calmness of Walden Pond in the years 1845–1847. To be sure, the ice breaks up dramatically, and there are statistical variations to be recorded in the thawing, and there is even a major ant war; but apparently there were no cataclysmic upheavals or catastrophic disasters, hardly so much as the kind of thunderstorm Edwards so much delighted in—perhaps Edwards would have been disappointed or even bored. Or perhaps there were such storms, but Thoreau ignored them in his more scientific pursuit of the gradual and general rather than the unique and specific; perhaps he ducked back into Concord at the first sign of tumultuous weather. At any rate, the lack of thunder in *Walden* robs us as readers of a specific point of comparison.

That is not quite the case with Annie Dillard's Pulitzer prize-winning *Pilgrim at Tinker Creek* (1974), a late twentieth-century classic in American nature writing.[20] Dillard's book seems almost to have been designed to invite endless comparisons to *Walden* as literary forebear. Its voice is solitary; its wide-ranging allusiveness—even bookishness—reflects its author's intellectual record and background (especially her grounding in Thoreau); it recounts a year spent in close observation of the natural landscape; it attains to a kind of wisdom; it has a dazzling, delightful prose style. Unlike Thoreau, however, Dillard is entirely reticent about her living circumstances, how she sustained herself, how she spent her days and nights, and that is so because her purpose—which is also a little hazy—was not exactly that of Thoreau (i.e., testing his solitary self-sufficiency for whether it might help to reveal the value of life, while writing *A Week on the Concord and Merrimack Rivers* and spending a night in the pokey). Thoreau is never far from a satirical jibe at his fellow New Englanders, but Dillard seems to be entirely uninterested in such matters. Dillard's readers have noted also that throughout most of the book she describes herself very much like Thoreau, in solitude and in nature, with one significant exception. The ninth chapter recounts a summer flood, so that Dillard is forced to consider not only an extraordinary natural force but also some of her neighbors near Tinker Creek who have to contend with the consequent beauties and dangers of nature in its extraordinary aspects.

Undoubtedly, Dillard's prose—with its odd contortions of tense and perspective to impart a sense of familiar intimacy—deserves more analysis than it is possible to undertake here. She frames her account of the flood, for instance, as something that happened "just this time last year," although as a reader I had no idea what is/was "this" year, much less what was "last year." To enliven the account, she begins in the following way: "That morning I'm standing at my kitchen window." Narratively considered, the tense is difficult to unravel, as past is transformed into present; colloquially speaking, this is how people tell stories, to render the immediacy of a past experience, to give a sense of one's consciousness just as an occurrence or a reflection happened. That is a key to understanding Dillard's entire approach, here and elsewhere, for, somewhat like Thoreau, she is deeply concerned about consciousness and about being awake (the book opens and closes significantly/symbolically with her memory of being awakened by an old tom cat's nightly rambles). Her descriptions thus turn to brief catalogues of metaphor (in a single sentence, the flood is "like somebody else's creek" and "like a blacksnake"); evocative descriptive terms loaded with strong Anglo-Saxon wording and alliterative, rhyming sound effects (example: "It smashes under the bridge like a fist, but there is no end to its force; it hurtles down as far as I can see till it lurches round the bend, filling the valley, flattening, mashing, pushed, wider and faster, till it fills my brain"); and basic, semi-scientific, semi-loopy observations (she explains that flood water packed with clay "looks worse than other muddy waters, because the particles of clay . . . spread out and cloud the water so that you can't see light through even an inch of it in a drinking glass": who would be collecting such floodwaters into a drinking glass?) (151–52).

Flooding, brought on by Hurricane Agnes, caused significant damage in Maryland, Pennsylvania, and New York, but not so much at Tinker Creek although it threatened the community, including the bridge near her residence. In gazing at the waters near the bridge, Dillard finds herself feeling "dizzy, drawn, mauled" because the extreme disturbance of the accepted natural landscape has disoriented her: "All the familiar land looks as though it were not solid and real at all, but painted on a scroll like a backdrop, and that unrolled scroll has been shaken, so that earth sways and the air roars" (153). Her somewhat childish imagination is unleashed so that she "expect[s] to see anything at all," including John Paul Jones or "Amelia Earhart waving gaily from the cockpit of her floating Lockheed" or the

Franklin expedition (154). She questions, "What do animals do in these floods?" and after thoughtful pondering concludes, "I don't know" (155). At the conclusion of the chapter, she recounts "a final flood story" from a house that was flooded and survived. The story comes secondhand from someone who had visited the family showing off a giant mushroom, which Dillard imagines "wrinkled, black, and big as a dinner plate, erupting overnight mysteriously in the Bings' living room"—i.e., a large mushroom grew in the house, a result of the floodwaters. But then she swiftly corrects herself, admitting "the story as I had fixed it in my mind proved to be only partly true," since the mushroom "had grown outside, under a sycamore, on high ground that the flood hadn't touched. So the flood had nothing to do with it." Still, unable to waste something so precious as a fantastic story, she writes, "But it's still a good story, and I like to think that the flood left them a gift, a consolation prize, so that for years to come they will be finding edible mushrooms here and there about the house, dinner on the bookshelf, hors d'oeuvres in the piano. It would have been nice" (160).

One might well ask: then what is/was the point? What is the point of recounting a "partly true" story but then indulging one's fancy just because "it's still a good story"? Should a "good story" predominate over reality? But why not just present the "good story" without bothering to inject the verisimilitude of telling us that it is "only partly true"? For me, the pleasant effect of a good story is ruined by any admission that it *is* a story or if the teller metanarratively chooses to tell me how the story is contrived. Foregrounding the joints and bolts of artifice suggests that an altogether different story predominates.[21] For all the similarities between Thoreau and Dillard, something has happened between them, something abstract and metaphorical (or antimetaphorical) but as devastating as the flood at Tinker Creek. That something is knowingly identified in *Pilgrim at Tinker Creek* as having occurred in 1927 with Werner Heisenberg's promulgation of the Principle of Indeterminacy. Dillard's summation of the principle is not particularly precise or even persuasive, but the conclusion is apt: "physicists are saying that they cannot study nature per se, but only their own investigation of nature. And I can only see bluegills within my own blue shadow, from which they immediately flee" (205). The applicability of this principle to ordinary observation, and even to most microscopic/telescopic observation, is, I think, questionable, but the principle itself has become emblematic, if you will, of postmodernity. One consequence, the one that Dillard elaborates in *Pilgrim,* is that, having to abandon certain knowledge of things apart from us (Emersonian nature in its most philosophical consideration), and to the extent that we seek certainty, we are thrown back to our consciousness, which, oddly, most usually turns out to be a consciousness *of* something (such as, again to resort to Emerson, "a certain number of congruent sensations" or "the same appearances . . . inscribed in the constant faith of man" [32]). Thus, one would be drastically mistaken to assert that *Pilgrim at Tinker Creek* is about nature; more correctly, it is about the process of Dillard's consciousness under the aegis of an artfully polished prose composition; even more correctly, I suppose, I could not accurately go so far: there is no "it" that is not a particle of *my* own consciousness. But for Dillard, telling us a story that is only "partly true" but then indulging her fancy, or telling us how "dizzy" she felt at the flood, or her admitting she does not know what happens to animals during a flood—all these bits and pieces, and their syntagmatic connectedness, reflect not "reality" in an external way but the pure internality of her perceptions and conceptions. Thus, the flood she witnessed is emblematic of the flood of consciousness itself.

But "what is the difference," Emerson ideally asked as a way out of the tempting trap of epistemological solipsism, whether reality subsists or simply is painted on the consciousness? (32) Perhaps that solved the matter once and for all for Thoreau, who might have seen time as a mere illusion but not material reality; at least, Thoreau had an ardent desire to

> settle . . . and work and wedge our feet downward through the mud and slush of opinion, and prejudice, and tradition, and delusion, and

> appearance . . . till we come to a hard bottom and rocks in place, which we can call *reality,* and say, This is, and no mistake; and then begin, having a *point d'appui,* below freshet and frost and fire, a place where you might found a wall or a state, or set a lamp-post safely, or perhaps a gauge, not a Nilometer, but a Realometer . . . (*Walden* 400)

Thoreau, it would appear, assumed such a reality apart from individual fantasy/desire, a reality that had been encumbered and encrusted with social distortion. But to suggest to Thoreau that that very *reality* ultimately is no more than a projection of individual fantasy/desire (as Dillard's turn to Heisenberg suggests) might have been genuinely shocking—and disgusting.

But Edwards, I think, would have been delighted, for idealist epistemology was a territory he knew quite well. Unlike Thoreau, Edwards had no reason to take reality for granted, since he understood it as sustained at every instant by God, who, in His aesthetic sublimity and divine sovereignty, does whatever He pleases. And Edwards, more than Thoreau, would have sympathized—I think—with Dillard's repeated symptoms of dizziness in the face of the complexities of the natural world. It is not unusual to lose your sense of balance (not your balance, but your sense of it) as you ponder what holds it all together.

I think it fair to say that Dillard does not consistently adhere to the Principle of Indeterminacy throughout her narrative—although it is questionable how one can really deviate from it—insofar as she, like Emerson, assumes she can reflect on her observations drawn from a source not of herself. And insofar as she does do so, *Pilgrim* is largely in the genre known as theodicy (a subject which hardly ruffled Edwards), prompted by the first extended observation she mentions of nature, involving a frog and a bug.

> . . . At last I knelt on the island's winter killed grass, lost, dumbstruck, staring at the frog in the creek just four feet away. He was a very small

frog with wide, dull eyes. And just as I looked at him, he slowly crumpled and began to sag. The spirit vanished from his eyes as if snuffed. His skin emptied and drooped; his very skull seemed to collapse like a kicked tent. He was shrinking before my eyes like a deflating football. I watched the taut, glistening skin on his shoulders ruck, and rumple, and fall. Soon, part of his skin, formless as a pricked balloon, lay in floating folds like bright scum on top of the water: it was a monstrous and terrifying thing. I gaped bewildered, appalled. An oval shadow hung in the water behind the drained frog; then the shadow glided away. The frog skin started to sink. (7–8)

In the succeeding paragraph, she explains more carefully and plainly the odd and disturbing event that she has witnessed: "The frog I saw was being sucked by a giant water bug" (8). Undoubtedly, something in this "monstrous and terrifying" scene is hardly far from Edwards' balloon spiders joyfully swinging their way to their own mass destruction, but with significant differences. One is that Edwards registers nothing of his emotional response to his investigation of the spiders (although his language is somewhat loaded with connotation), but Dillard gives us both the process by which she made her discovery as well her reaction to it. And unsurprisingly, Dillard follows this account with a musing about God's purposes and intent:

That it's rough out there and chancy is no surprise. Every live thing is a survivor on a kind of extended emergency bivouac. But at the same time we are also created. In the Koran, Allah asks, "The heaven and the earth and all in between, thinkest thou I made them *in jest*?" It's a good question. What do we think of the created universe, spanning an unthinkable void with an unthinkable profusion of forms? Or what do we think of nothingness, those sickening reaches of time in either direction?

> If the giant water bug was not made in jest, was it then made in earnest? Pascal uses a nice term to describe the notion of the creator's, once having called forth the universe, turning his back to it: *Deus Absconditus*. Is this what we think happened? Was the sense of it there, and God absconded with it, ate it, like a wolf who disappears round the edge of the house with the Thanksgiving turkey? "God is subtle," Einstein said, "but not malicious." Again, Einstein said that "nature conceals her mystery by means of her essential grandeur, not by her cunning." It could be that God has not absconded but spread, to a fabric of spirit and sense so grand and subtle, so powerful in a new way, that we can only feel blindly of its hem. In making the thick darkness a swaddling band for the sea, God "set bars and doors" and said, "Hitherto shalt thou come, but no further." But have we come even that far? Have we rowed out to the thick darkness, or are we all playing pinochle in the bottom of the boat?
>
> Cruelty is a mystery, and the waste of pain. But if we describe a world to compass these things, a world that is a long, brute game, then we bump against another mystery: the inrush of power and light, the canary that sings on the skull. Unless all ages and races of men have been deluded by the same mass hypnotist (who?), there seems to be such a thing as beauty, a grace wholly gratuitous. (9)

Unlike Edwards, Dillard is not an exacting, rigorous logician; her thought processes are more associative and allusive, less controlled. Moreover, Dillard rarely attains closure or finality with her questions, but she *is* asking the questions that beg asking, and her questions proceed from close encounters with the everyday world (as she says of the frog incident, "This event is quite common in warm fresh water" [9]). Unlike Thoreau, Dillard never seems content merely to render a fact or a detail and wait. That is to say, that for all ideological differences, Dillard has adopted a recognizably typological or emblematic frame of mind: close analysis of an object or incident prompts questions about larger spiritual significance, even if she cannot quite attain closure. That she is rarely able to provide a solid account of the spiritual significance is symptomatic of the postmodern approach to emblematic procedure. In fact, Dillard goes beyond, to indicate that something inexplicable—and delightful—escapes analysis and explanation: "beauty, a grace wholly gratuitous," something akin to Thoreauvian wildness. That, for her, is as bizarre as a frog's innards being sucked out by a giant water bug and is emblemized by the flight of a mockingbird. And then, in a sublime moment, both the horror of the frog/bug and the beauty of the mockingbird are combined inextricably:

> Another time I saw another wonder: sharks off the Atlantic coast of Florida. There is a way a wave rises above the ocean horizon, a triangular wedge against the sky. If you stand where the ocean breaks on a shallow beach, you see the raised water in a wave is translucent, shot with lights. One late afternoon at low tide a hundred big sharks passed the beach near the mouth of a tidal river in a feeding frenzy. As each green wave rose from the churning water, it illuminated within itself the six- or eight-foot-long bodies of twisting sharks. The sharks disappeared as each wave rolled towards me; then a new wave would swell above the horizon, containing in it, like scorpions in amber, sharks that roiled and heaved. The sight held awesome wonders: power and beauty, grace tangled in a rapture with violence. (10)

Attentive Edwards readers may pick up on echoes of the paradoxing rhetoric of "Personal Narrative," although prompted by a more pacific object:

> ... I walked abroad alone, in a solitary place in my father's pasture, for contemplation. And as I was walking there, and looked up on the sky and clouds; there came into my mind, a sweet sense of the glorious majesty and grace of God, that I know not how to express. I seemed to see them both in a sweet conjunction: majesty and meekness joined together: it was a sweet and gentle, and holy majesty; and also a majestic meekness; an awful sweetness; a high, and great, and holy gentleness. (793)

For Dillard, what then ought we do? Ironically, over and over again she suggests that answers, one way or another, are not *the* answer. Immediately after describing the frenzied sharks, she notes: "We don't know what's going on here" (10) and then, "We don't know" if there is an underlying order or cause, or how to explain it, but, "We must somehow take a wider view, look at the whole landscape, really see it, and describe what's going on here. Then we can at least wail the right question into the swaddling band of darkness, or, if it comes to that, choir the proper praise" (11). In reflecting on the mockingbird's flight, she notes: "The answer must be, I think, that beauty and grace are performed whether or not we will or sense them. The least we can do is try to be there" (10).

To use Edwardsean terminology, we must have a "sense" of these things, a true experience that blossoms into sweetness. Dillard's *Pilgrim at Tinker Creek* is largely a jumbled record of such solitary and wondrous scenes of "being there," with associated questions and reflections. To "be there," one must achieve Thoreauvian awakeness, which is more than a matter of rolling out of bed. Thinking of the ephemerality of natural appearances, Dillard notes: "These disappearances stun me into stillness and concentration; they say of nature that it conceals with a grand nonchalance, and they say of vision that it is a deliberate gift, the revelation of a dancer who for my eyes only flings away her seven veils" (18). Elsewhere: "The secret of seeing is, then, the pearl of great price. . . . But although the pearl may be found, it may not be sought. The literature of illumination reveals this above all: although it comes to those who wait for it, it is always, even to the most practiced and adept, a gift and a total surprise. . . . I cannot cause the light; the most I can do is try to put myself in the path of its beam" (35). Or to put it yet again in somewhat Edwardsean terms, "Experiencing the present purely is being emptied and hollow; you catch grace as a man fills his cup under a waterfall" (82).

Although Dillard invokes Thoreau often, and just as often has been compared to him, more properly the source—once again—is Emerson and his "transparent eyeball," since that is the very experience she yearns for, without perhaps quite attaining; and *mutatis mutandi,* that links her back to Edwards sensing divinity in the thunderstorm. Undeniably, Edwards could have found much to object to, such as Dillard's extravagant waste of language, the book's undisciplined and repetitive "poetic" logic, etc. And if Dillard's subtle allusions to Judeo-Christian belief render her somewhat closer in spirit to Edwards, that very closeness might well have prompted a coolness or harshness because of its soft syncretism. But surely Edwards would have appreciated very much the scientific orientation of her observations; moreover, he certainly would have warmed to her fascination with the creepy ickiness of nature; and he might have understood quite well her final conclusion about the Creator's personality: "You have finally understood that you are dealing with a maniac" (275).

V. Conclusion

It is finally perhaps not so strange that the strain of natural typology has had such durability, and even permanence, in American cultural life, but it is rather remarkable that it should have attained, in its various guises and manifestations, such an ever-renewable popularity. It is difficult to imagine its disappearance in any conceivable future, even a digitally manipulated postmodern one. The point of *Walden* was only to remind each and everyone that "you can do it, too," although strong and valiant natures rarely need such reminding; the rest of us, however, sometimes seem restless without reading about someone else not necessarily doing it for us but at least exhibiting to us someone else's joy and wonder at its being done at all—that is, someone truly awake and in awe before the most ordinary (and sometimes extraordinary) of natural spectacles, probing for meaning and inspiration. It is not a little remarkable, too, that Jonathan Edwards, slightly unnoticed, should be found at the very core of this paradigm. Indeed, it is entirely fitting to close this essay with a last look at an essay Edwards composed in 1726, toward the end of his tutorship at Yale.

"Beauty of the World" is, in my estimation, one of the most moving, stunning, breathtaking, and rapturous of Edwards' writings and of all eighteenth-century— perhaps *all*—American literature. On the one hand, it expresses an Enlightenment-era absolute confidence in the divine order of physical creation, "surpassing the art of man" and shadowing forth "spiritual beauties" that are "infinitely the greatest" and which co-exist in a "complicated . . . harmony and proportion." For example, "How much a resemblance is there of every grace in the fields covered with plants and flowers, when the sun shines serenely and undisturbedly upon them." Some beauties, he asserts, we can understand and explain; others are beyond explication and simply must be indulged so that, finally, "the more complex a beauty is, the more hidden is it" (and vice versa). True, we may subject even such hidden beauty to rational speculation: "mere light is pleasing to the mind" *perhaps* because "either that light, or our organ of seeing, is so contrived that an harmonious motion is excited in the animal spirits and propagated to the brain." This reduces Edwards to a rare epistemological synaesthesia, wherein light dissolves into music: "each sort of rays play a distinct tune to the soul, besides those lovely mixtures that are found in nature—those beauties, how lovely, in the green of the face of earth, in all manners of colors in flowers, the color of the skies, and lovely tinctures of the morning and evening." And then Edwards offers a corollary, contradistinct from those for the flying spider:

> Hence the reason why almost all men, and those that seem to be very miserable, love life: because they cannot bear to lose the sight of such a beautiful and lovely world—the ideas, that every moment whilst we live have a beauty that we take not distinct notice of, but bring a pleasure that, when we come to the trial, we had rather live in much pain and misery than lose. (306)[22]

That, ultimately, is the last word in American natural typology: the rousing of the pleasurable perception of beauty in the natural world that transcends otherwise unbearable pain and misery, even among those most miserable.

MICHAEL G. DITMORE received the B.A from Austin College (Sherman, Tex.), and both the M.A. and Ph.D. from the University of Texas (Austin). He is professor of English at Seaver College in Pepperdine University (California). His academic interests include American history and literature, and religion and literature, areas in which he has widely published.

NOTES

[1] Perry Miller, ed., *Images or Shadows of Divine Things* by Jonathan Edwards (New Haven: Yale UP, 1948).

[2] See especially Mason I. Lowance, Jr., *The Language of Canaan: Metaphor and Symbol in New England from the Puritans to the Transcendentalists* (Cambridge: Harvard UP, 1980), chap. 10 passim, important especially as a correction of Miller's introduction to *Images*. Edwards is something of a rarity in Christian thought for his effort at practicing both types of typology, although not simultaneously. Commenting on Edwards' Miscellany 1069 (known as also *Types of the Messiah*)—the introduction of which is the key text for understanding this form of natural exegesis—Lowance notes that Edwards "consciously applied the nomenclature of orthodox typology to the allegorical correspondence" between natural things and spiritual meanings (256). I would add only that the floodgates in some sense had already been opened in the early seventeenth century with Hall, Quarles, et al.; moreover, the first publication of Hall's meditational writings predates that of the first of the English typologists, William Guild, by over a decade.

[3] When I first approach Edwards in the classroom, I sometimes ask my students how Edwards (and his contemporary Benjamin Franklin) might have lined up during the Antinomian Controversy a century earlier. The knee-jerk response is sensible enough: In the voice of many a Hawthorne narrator, my students will intone how John Winthrop typifies the backwards, narrow, repressive religious orthodoxy; Anne Hutchinson championed innovation and rebellion and independence and toleration and all the other cherished American values; and who else was more determinedly orthodox in religion than Edwards, and who more inventive, rebellious, independent, etc., than Franklin? But just a little below the surface, we discover just how close Edwards was to Hutchinson (which was why he was always touchy on the subject, and which also helps to explain exactly the connection Charles Chauncy drew between the Antinomian Controversy and the Great Awakening in his preface to *Seasonable Thoughts*)—it requires little maneuvering at all to get from "immediate revelation" to a "sense of the heart"—whereas Franklin, pretty much like Winthrop, trashed revelation altogether in the move for something like a social covenant above that of the individual. True, we can find the connections crossed and reversed and confounded in other layers. And where would this result in our own age? Strangely enough, if you like, it is the Democratic party—that bastion of cutting-edge liberal belief—that, like Winthrop, still insists on the importance of individuals sacrificing for Big Government, whereas it is the Republicans who harp on individual initiative. Is that to say, if we could magically transport Winthrop and Hutchinson to 2006, could we predict their vote? Well, no. Winthrop would surely be a Republican after all, and Hutchinson—ever the unpredictable—would take up either with the Libertarians or Greens (the Republicans would be far too "establishment").

[4] I would point out that I once taught a class titled "Edwards to Emerson to Stevens," which I liked because it reminded me of Franklin P. Adams' 1910 "Baseball's Sad Lexicon" on the double play ability of the Chicago Cubs infield, "Tinker to Evers to Chance." But also, it allowed me to extend the possibilities. The course readings both ante- and post-dated the trio I highlighted, beginning with Anne Bradstreet and concluding with Patiann Rogers.

[5] A more fitting precedent then might be the literature of saintly hermits, the desert monks such as Antony, who have exercised fascination for more recent writers such as Kathleen Norris; Dillard also alludes to them. A certain strain of American nature writing—the kind I am concerned with here—might be seen as a conflation of pastoral, monastic hagiography, and autobiographical essay.

[6] Alvar Nunez Cabeza de Vaca, *Castaways,* ed. Enrique Pupo-Walker, trans. Frances M. Lopez-Morillas (Berkeley: University of California Press, 1993).

[7] It is fair to note that the kind of "strain" or "tradition" I am enumerating would operate rather differently under the African experience of Americas, as Crèvecoeur's text indicates. An especially pertinent text is Frederick Douglass' slave narrative, published in Thoreau's first year

at Walden (around the very time that he spent his infamous night in jail). Aside from the Maryland bay sails, one of the most tormented moments in the narrative comes as he makes his way back and therefore finds himself fairly much alone in nature. Solitude seems to torment Douglass, and he expresses resentment that he was forced to it through distrust.

[8] John Filson, *The Adventures of Col. Daniel Boon* in *American Lives: An Anthology of Autobiographical Writing*, ed. Robert F. Sayre (Madison: University of Wisconsin Press, 1994).

[9] Jonathan Edwards, *Scientific and Philosophical Writings*, ed. Wallace E. Anderson, *The Works of Jonathan Edwards*, vol. 6 (New Haven: Yale UP, 1980).

[10] Jonathan Edwards, *A Faithful Narrative* in *The Great Awakening*, ed. C. C. Goen, *The Works of Jonathan Edwards*, vol. 4 (New Haven: Yale UP, 1972).

[11] Jonathan Edwards, "A Divine and Supernatural Light" in *Sermons and Discourses, 1730–1733*, ed. Mark Valeri, *The Works of Jonathan Edwards*, vol. 17 (New Haven: Yale UP, 1999).

[12] For an enlargement, see Edwards' pleading for the intense imaginative experiences of some converts in *The Distinguishing Marks* (in *The Great Awakening*, see n. 10): "Such is our nature that we can't think of things invisible, without a degree of imagination. I dare appeal to any man, of the greatest powers of mind, whether or no he is able to fix his thoughts on God or Christ, or the things of another world, without imaginary ideas attending his meditations? And the more engaged the mind is, and the more intense the contemplation and affection, still the more lively and strong will the imaginary idea ordinarily be; especially when the contemplation and affection of the mind is attended with anything of surprise.... It appears to me manifest in many instances I have been acquainted with, that God has really made use of this faculty to truly divine purposes; especially in some that are more ignorant: God seems to condescend to their circumstances, and deal with them as babes; as of old he instructed his church while in a state of ignorance and minority by types and outward representations" (236). Put differently, mental thought is doomed to metaphor, but to that I would add therefore that the particular metaphors become highly illustrative. That in his "Personal Narrative" Edwards describes his imagination as turned away from civilization and toward a "solitary wilderness" is very telling.

[13] Jonathan Edwards, "Personal Narrative" in *Letters and Personal Writings*, ed. George S. Claghorn, *The Works of Jonathan Edwards*, vol. 16 (New Haven: Yale UP, 1998).

[14] Perry Miller, "From Edwards to Emerson," *New England Quarterly* 13 (1940): 589–617, rpt. in *Errand into the Wilderness* (Cambridge: Belknap-Harvard UP, 1956).

[15] To the various passages from Edwards' "Personal Narrative" noted above, I would add that Edwards expressed a frequent concern for attaining "emptiness" so as to be filled by God, suggesting that his union with the divine was neither as complete nor as easily attainable as Emerson's eyeball description suggests.

[16] Henry David Thoreau, *A Week on the Concord and Merrimack Rivers/Walden; or, Life in the Woods/Cape Cod*, ed. Robert F. Sayre (New York: Library of America, 1985). Unless otherwise noted, all Thoreau references are to this edition.

[17] Perry Miller, "Thoreau in the Context of International Romanticism" *New England Quarterly* 34 (1961): 147–59, rpt. in *Nature's Nation* (Cambridge: Belknap-Harvard UP, 1967).

[18] Henry David Thoreau, "Natural History of Massachusetts" in *The Natural History Essays*, ed. Robert Sattelmeyer (Salt Lake City: Peregrine Smith, 1980).

[19] Ralph Waldo Emerson, *Nature* in *Essays and Lectures*, ed. Joel Porte (New York: Library of America, 1983).

[20] Annie Dillard, *Pilgrim at Tinker Creek* (N.p.: Perennial Classics-HarperPerennial, 1999).

[21] See Dillard's *Living by Fiction* (New York: Perennial-Harper & Row, 1988) for her effort at delineating an aesthetic theory of fictive meaning.

[22] Jonathan Edwards, *Typological Writings*, ed. Wallace E. Anderson, Mason I. Lowance, Jr. and David H. Watters in *The Works of Jonathan Edwards*, vol. 11 (New Haven: Yale UP, 1993).

PART IV

EDWARDS & AMERICAN PHILOSOPHY

Experience as Religious Discovery in Edwards & Peirce

Roger Ward

A new interest in spirituality has taken hold in many different forms in current American culture. Against the expectations of most forecasters, conservative expressions of Christianity are thriving along with nature spiritualism and world religions. As philosophers seek to understand and deal with the "problems of men [and women]" it is natural that we investigate this phenomenon and work out its connections to our American philosophical heritage.

One avenue of connection is Jonathan Edwards who is recognized as the voice of the Great Awakening—one of America's most spiritually defining experiences. Edwards survives almost exclusively in our tradition by reputation from "Sinners in the Hands of an Angry God." His association with the revival through sermons like "Sinners" and others covers over his extensive critical writings on the revival. Edwards is no religious enthusiast. Rather, he is an American thinker whose appropriation and development of religious experience is unique and challenging. He outstrips his contemporaries, making his thought difficult to evaluate, since useful comparisons are hard to find. Charles Sanders Peirce may be the one thinker enough like Edwards to warrant comparison. In his introduction to Edwards' *Religious Affections,* John Smith aligns Peirce's and Edwards' views of traditional religious belief as implying "a separation between the self and the item of belief, whereas religion defines the very being of the self."[1] Michael Raposa points out that Edwards and Peirce both use the category of practice as a source of validating conclusions concerning the self and God,[2] and Sang Lee appropriates Peirce's anti-Cartesian metaphysics to interpret Edwards' novel "relational ontology."[3] These instances of reading Edwards and Peirce together are significant for understanding the religious dimensions of experience in the American tradition.

H. R. Neibuhr, in his epochal book *Christ and Culture,* makes a conscious turn from the traditional dialectic of grace and nature to examine grace and culture. Culture, for Neibuhr, is whatever manmade structure is brought to bear on the natural state, and it is in this realm that the effect of Christ on our world can be fruitfully described.[4] Peirce and Edwards agree fundamentally with Neibuhr's approach. Both argue that if God is real and influential the resultant character or growth of human products must be sufficient to describe and identify the objective character of God. But they differ from Neibuhr in their generality of scope. Peirce and Edwards do not so much gauge the effect of religious objects already defined; they train their attention on the emergence of these objects from experience. Their dialectic is discovery and God. This discovery is apparent only as a structure, an architectonic found within experience that connects human nature and inquiry in its most general form to the content of God. Illuminating Peirce's and Edwards' architectonic of experience as a religious discovery is the primary focus of this essay.

Edwards treats the emergence of divine character in the person or soul in his *Treatise Concerning Religious Affections.* His argument is relatively simple: if God is real and active in the lives of individuals, their affections, the "more vigorous exercises of the intellect and the will," must reflect this influence. Edwards develops a normative account of the "rules" that individuals can follow to discern whether the origin of their affections is divine or not. In the process of discerning these rules, Edwards gives a holistic account of an individual discovering God. Aesthetically, the soul is touched with the love of divine beauty. Cognitively, the person's faculty of reason is informed with a "new simple idea" by which it perceives God (or the absence of God). Morally, the soul develops a desire to attain universal obedience to the law of God. And most importantly, the soul is converted by the objective character of Christ revealed in scripture, so that the soul finds this same character in itself.

Edwards is peculiar because, on the one hand, the transcendence and divinity of scripture and Christ appear to depend on a kind of inferential warrant that follows the appearance of religious affections. The continuity and coherence of the signs of religious affection give this claim its authority. On the other hand, the signs are the manifestation in human action of a supernatural character that judges human hearts rather than being judged by them. In both cases, however, the result is a satisfaction and conviction percolating through the person's faculties of reasoning and willing that Christ is of God and that the soul is indwelled with Christ. I will focus on the structured character of the signs of affection as a description of experience coming to reflective rest in the objects of God and the soul.[5]

Peirce also develops an architectonic of experience, with the conclusion that the reality of God is the highest-order hypothesis possible. Commentators like Mary Mahowald and Michael Raposa suggest that God is an object of Peirce's thought from his earliest essays, and I agree.[6] My effort here will be to show that his general architectonic of discovery is connected directly to the conclusion of God, even though he does not articulate it this way. I will focus on his 1868 essay, "Some Consequences of Four Incapacities Claimed for Man." This essay reflects a schema that Peirce fleshes out during his career. The consequence of this framework of thought is a longing for an object, not a singular term, but an object that can sustain inquiry, the apparent yet vague conclusion of all reasoning and experience. This object must be independent of "the vagaries of me and you" (*CP* 5.311), an insight which Peirce expresses in terms of personal negation and communal trust.[7] That God is the satisfying object for thought and the practice of inquiry summarizes Peirce's argument. Our focus here, however, is on the framework that conditions this conclusion.

The upshot of Edwards' and Peirce's architectonics is a kind of discovery that leads inquirers to a conclusion regarding the objective character of God, self, and the community. In the exposition to follow, I will illuminate these structures of thought and describe the kind of conclusions possible from them. Placing Peirce and Edwards together in this treatment is intended to expand our ability to describe experience as religious discovery in the American tradition. But this focus on discovery and its object is an implicit challenge to naturalism and forms of spirituality that reject traditional objects of religion out of hand as limiting or flawed. The architectonics of Peirce and Edwards are an affirmation of the natural discovery of transcendent conclusions and the imputation of religious worth to those conclusions. The naturalism of religious experience in Edwards and Peirce cannot be separated from the character of the objects that orient their thought. I hope that exposing this dialectic of natural discovery and the kind of object which grounds it will give American thinkers a more substantial platform for evaluating religious claims from experience.

Peirce and the Consequences of Inquiry

Understanding the significance of inquiry for Peirce is difficult. The reason it is difficult is that inquiry is the principle that orders the various aspects of his philosophy, weaving them together into an ordered investigation. Although this investigation remains vague, it does provide the ground for demonstrating completely self-controlled thought. And all inquiry stems from experience. As Peirce says, thought is rudely interrupted by the external world: "I call such forcible modification of our ways of thinking the influence of the world of fact or *experience*" (*CP* 1.321). Peirce expands on the interruptive quality of experience in the cognition essays. Cognitive awareness results only from a change in the thing. Awareness comes from meeting the face of resistance. Experience is the beginning of inquiry because it is the brute fact that thought's construction of the world is in error. Peirce embraces this state of negation in "Some Consequences of Four Incapacities Claimed for Man" and makes it a structural touchstone. This negation solidifies most clearly into his rejection of the self, not a rejection of the idea of the self, but a doubt that there could ever be satisfactory content to the self; as Peirce eloquently says, man apart from his fellows "is only a negation. This is man: / proud man, / Most ignorant of what he's most assured, / His glassy essence" (*CP* 5.317). Peirce's existential and metaphysical puzzle is how this particular negation can be overcome by the process and conclusions of inquiry without denying its reality.

Peirce begins "Some Consequences" with a backward glance at "Four Incapacities Claimed for Man." In that essay, Peirce turns the results of Cartesian philosophy directly back on itself. As Peirce notes regarding the failure of Descartes' skepticism, "there are things which it does not occur to us can be questioned. Hence this initial skepticism will be a mere self deception, and not real doubt; and no one who follows the Cartesian method will ever be satisfied until he has formally recovered all those beliefs which in form he has given up" (*CP* 5.265). And the condition of that philosophy is worse than the first. To avoid self-deception Peirce suggests that only genuine doubt and negation can succeed in showing what thought is not and so provide a proper opening or beginning for inquiry. In order to achieve a non-self-deceptive holistic denial, Peirce introduces an architectonic of comprehensive negation framed by four denials: "(1) We have no power of Introspection, but all knowledge of the internal world is derived by hypothetical reasoning from our knowledge of external facts. (2) We have no power of Intuition, but every act of cognition is determined logically by previous cognition. (3) We have no power of thinking without signs. (4) We have no conception of the absolutely incognizable" (*CP* 5.265). The fruit of Cartesian philosophy is the articulation of these particular denials that form a structure of limits to thought. The Cartesian desire to deny the limits of thought made those very limits manifest, and this is why it serves as a proper beginning for scientific inquiry.

The transition to Peirce's positive statement follows directly from this frame of negation. "These propositions," he says, "cannot be regarded as certain; and, in order to bring them to a further test, it is now proposed to trace them out to their consequences" (*CP* 5.265). Peirce suggests earlier that "modern science and modern logic require us to stand upon a very different platform from this [Cartesian platform]" (*CP* 5.264). The nature of this test is the driving question in Peirce studies. Is the test one of adequacy for practice, of avoiding static forms (ultimate fallibility), or one of comprehensive metaphysical description? The result of that debate is still undecided, but it is not necessary to unearth Peirce's plan in this essay.

> What is essential for the structure of Peirce's inquiry is that the character of negation not be dropped from the process of inquiry already started. Let me say this another way. The four negations above constitute the body of Peirce's essay. And since he begins by positing nothing but the difference between experience and thought, his inquiry must continue within that frame or else it deviates from its origin. If inquiry is to react to the external world, it must at all costs avoid the tendency to take provisional answers without continuing to subject them to possible negation. Inquiry is not a principle, but a kind of expansion possible within a framework of denials, trustworthy in its conclusions as long as it holds its responsiveness to potential negation in its very fiber. The architectonic of inquiry is the holding of negation together with the continuity of developing reason where the absence of each particular negation gives the object or problematic that requires the next "consequence."

This moving principle is clear in the transitions that Peirce employs between consequences 1 and 2, 2 and 3, and 3 and 4. For instance, the first "supposition" is that we have no power of introspection but that all that "passes within us" is a hypothesis necessary to explain the "external world." The second proposition, that we have no power of intuition, means that cognition arises by a continuous process, and this is a hypothetical platform for the further inquiry into the form of this process. The hypothetical character of inquiry, stated in the initial rejection of introspection, is in this way carried forward—so that propositions 2, 3, and 4 are the justifying extensions that support this beginning hypothesis—as that which "explains the fact" of the rejection of Cartesian dependence on introspection. The third proposition expands on the second. That all thought must be of a general type and be hypothetical is the problem solved by the hypothesis that all thinking is in signs, which is not a private process or dependent on "obscure premises."

The most critical transition for the larger purpose of my essay here involves the transition from proposition 3 to 4. Here we find Peirce returning to the problem of an object. "Now a sign has," Peirce says, "as such, three references: first, it is a sign to some thought which interprets it; second, it is a sign for some object to which in that thought it is equivalent; third, it is a sign, in some respect or quality, which brings it into connection with its object" (*CP* 5.283). That an object is necessary for this sign system to obtain follows from Peirce's earlier claim that all thought, even fallacies, are representative of valid forms of thinking. The question Peirce faces is what stabilizes these fallacies? What prevents solipsism even in this system? Only an object, an interruption, but one that does not undermine the continuity of thought. Thought of an object must yield a subsequent thought and an infinitely receding origin in thought—but still it must be an equivalent to "what is" enough to show the error of fallacies of hypothetical thought. Peirce makes a crucial transition at this point:

> But it is plain that the knowledge that one thought is similar to or in any way truly representative of another, cannot be derived from immediate perception, but must be an hypothesis (unquestionably fully justifiable by facts), and that therefore the formation of such a representing thought must be dependent upon a real and effective force behind consciousness, and not merely upon a mental comparison. (CP 5.288)

So to ground thinking in signs, Peirce needs a "real and effective force behind consciousness," which translates into an equivalent of an object. But this object cannot be derived from introspection, intuition, or any obscure premises.

This last point puzzles Peirce. To know this effective force would mean that we have an immediate conception of it, which is impossible according to his theory of thought. And to know it as a feeling is to have it "left inexplicable, but only something we cannot reflectively know" (CP 5.289), marking an end to inquiry. Here, Peirce turns his attention to the self, which would demonstrate such an effective force in real terms. As Colapietro points out, the self is the labyrinthine term in Peirce's metaphysics and probably the most significant. Reason is *self*-controlled thought, and if the self is a problem, then there is no hope of genuine reason, of finding "what is" in light of our (in)capacities.[8] The self in Peirce is similar to Leibniz's image of the laws of nature, having no definite final articulation but manifesting a principle of orientation dependent on an origin outside the system of continuity.[9] Peirce attempts to mediate this puzzle of the origin of the self by expanding the concept of an object that is both present/absent in inquiry, what Peirce calls a vague, and absent/present conclusion of the community's inquiry. The self reflects this ambiguity. The self is a necessary character in relation to the discovery of the community, but it is also possibly an error to be overcome.

Even at this early point in his career, the inquiry into self and community looms in Peirce like a mountain he has to traverse and on which his thinking will be exposed to its ultimate test. What could stabilize inquiry into a discernable whole is not a modern "factum" but an object that explains the communal movement toward self-control, a discovery that responds to the opening denials of "Some Consequences" without eliminating them. The desire for this content in Peirce's structure of inquiry is the reason I disagree with Skagestad that the motivation of Peirce's inquiry is fallibilism. For Peirce, fallibilism is only a preventative appropriate in active discovery. A conclusive object is not an impossibility for Peirce, but it would necessarily outstrip any other "object," particularly the self, and fallibilism is the only way the ultimate temptation of an objective self can be avoided. The motivation of Peirce's inquiry is more accurately connected to the last denial in "Some Consequences," "that we have no conception of the absolutely incognizable." This is a demand for the kind of inquiry that is infinitely propelled to render this hypothetical account of inquiry justified by fact; it demands that such an object would in fact only be the result of the complete orientation of semiotic thinking, bringing inquiry to rest in an infinitely continuing discovery of the principle of orientation which it manifests. Peirce makes the character of the orientation of inquiry a prominent theme in his "Law of Mind," discovering there the personal God he more explicitly describes in his 1908 "The Neglected Argument for the Reality of God," the "real and effective force behind consciousness," the beautiful idea that orients the three universes of experience.[10]

Experience is ultimately continuous with the discovery of God for Peirce. He does not wear his religion on his sleeve, but neither does he deny traditional forms of religious discovery. Manuscript evidence suggests that Peirce was ready to make a clear articulation of his idea of God which is consistent with traditional language of Christianity,[11] and he even records his experience of responding to the invitation of the Lord to take communion.[12] Peirce does despise theoretical religion, but only for the way it limits inquiry by resolving into forms that demand authoritative privilege and claiming immunity from continuing discovery. For Peirce, religious discovery is the proper end of the interruption of experience.

Edwards and the Structure of Conversion

Few American writers have matched Jonathan Edwards' rhetorical achievements or his significance for the development of American theology and philosophy. One reason for Edwards' continuing significance is that he chose his subjects well. In his *Treatise Concerning Religious Affections: In Three Parts*, he responds to questions that arose from the Great Awakening of 1735–1742.13 *Religious Affections* is a complex book because it treats a unique event in American history and because it marks a shift in Edwards' intention. His earlier work on the revival intended to extend that revival, but in this work, he intends to bring these religious experiences to order, to make sense out of religious conversion (*RA* 98).

One way to phrase the problematic of the *Affections* is to ask after the objective experiential ground of religious conversion. What could validate the claim that this experience is a result of an encounter with God? The pastoral aspect of this book revolves around Edwards' conviction that "it be plain that Christ has given rules to all Christians, to enable 'em to judge of professors of religion," although it is not God's intention to "give us any rules, by which we may certainly know, who of our fellow professors are his, and to make a clear separation between sheep and goats" (*RA* 193). Edwards' task in the *Affections* is to give a description of these rules.

Part One of the *Affections* makes the scriptural claim that religion consists in affections, that are, "the more vigorous and sensible movements of the will and the intellect." Part Two articulates what are not convincing signs of religious affections. Here Edwards documents his distrust of "enthusiasm." Enthusiasm is not truly religious because its object is not real. This negation is significant, and Edwards stands firm that any discernment of the gracious affections includes discerning those that are not.[14] There is a possibility of error in religious experience, and describing this error is necessary to describe real religious experience. Part Three contains "What are Signs of a Truly Gracious and Holy Affection" where Edwards articulates twelve signs of gracious affection.

The twelve signs of gracious affection have been a real puzzle. Edwards gives no indication why there are twelve or if there is a structure to them. Even commentators as familiar with Edwards as John Smith puzzle over the arrangement of these signs. Smith notes that Edwards rejects formalism, for reasons we will see in a moment, but he points out that several of the signs, 1, 4, and 7, are "more basic than the others" since they describe the spirit's activity on the soul (*RA* 24). I think this is correct, and that we should also include sign 10 here. But contrary to Smith, I think there is a structure to the signs that incorporates both Edwards' rejection of a fixed order of revelation or conversion and his desire for a plain setting out of the rules that can guide us to discern whether the soul has been graciously affected.

Let me take a moment to talk about Edwards' use of "sign" since his structuring of religious experience is given in these terms and since we have already said something about Peirce's account. Edwards uses "sign" in a way close to its conventional use, such as we might discuss the signs of a change in weather when clouds increase or the temperature drops. Signs include both public and sensory qualities, but also a pattern or history of interpretation. In this way, Peirce and Edwards walk similar terrain. Both also claim that a sign must have an object. It must be a sign of something substantial. Sang Hyun Lee develops this connection between Peirce and Edwards, but I think he reads a bit too much of Peirce's realism of "would-be's" into Edwards' account, for reasons I will give in a moment. Suffice it to say that for Edwards there is no way we can have signs without a substantial object. He is not concerned about the kind of reality entailed so much as he is about the ability to distinguish genuine affections from spurious ones. Here, Peirce and Edwards diverge, since Edwards uses signs almost exclusively as the way of determining genuineness of a character, and Peirce's semiotic is the ubiquitous state of sign dependency for all thought.

When Edwards does talk about signs as an indication of genuineness, he is talking about the realness of a character, the habitual disposition that Lee is concerned with. Edwards says, "the degree of religion is rather to be judged by the fixedness and strength of habit that is exercised in affection, whereby holy affection is habitual: and the strength of that habit is not always in proportion to outward effects and manifestations. . . . No light of understanding is good which don't produce holy affection in the heart: no habit or principle in the heart is good, which has no exercise; and no external fruit is good, which don't proceed from such exercises" (*RA* 118–119). This statement matches Peircean realism except that for Edwards the character can be securely described, "[f]or the rules in themselves are certain and infallible, and every saint has, or has had those things in himself, which are sure evidences of grace; for every, even the least act of grace is so" (RA 194). The substantial character of the soul comes not from a determination about the affections themselves, but only by virtue of the security of the signs and what they mean, which is given to us by God in scriptural revelation. "I know of no directions or counsels which Christ ever delivered more plainly," Edwards says, "than the rules he has given us, to guide us in our judging of others' sincerity; viz. that we should judge of the tree chiefly by the fruit" (*RA* 185).

Edwards' attention is on the signs that are the distinguishing characters between genuine religious affections and natural or spurious affections: "'Tis by the mixture of counterfeit religion with true, not discerned and distinguished, that the devil has had his greatest advantage against the cause and kingdom of Christ" (*RA* 86). This is especially the case if trust is placed in an order of experiences, as the Puritans had formulated. Edwards remarks, "The nature of divine things is harder for the devil to imitate than their order. He can't *exactly* imitate divine operations in their nature, though his counterfeits be very much like them in external appearance; but he can exactly imitate their order" (*RA* 159). The signs, by unerringly manifesting the character of the affections, reveal the motivating object behind those affections. Thus, they are the key to securing the saint's knowledge of his or her state of grace, but also for protecting and purifying the work of the church in furthering Christ's kingdom.

With this emphasis on signs in Edwards' work, it is surprising that he does not give his readers more of an indication about what structure his presentation of them follows. I think a little of the puzzle can be resolved if we consider a structural key from a sermon Edwards preached and published in 1734, "A Divine and Supernatural Light." This sermon closes with four "considerations to influence and lead to this light":

First. "This is the most excellent and divine wisdom, that any creature is capable of," that exceeds "the greatest speculative understanding in divinity, without grace." This knowledge has the most noble object that is, or can be, which is "the divine glory, and excellency of God, and Christ."

Second. This knowledge is peculiarly "sweet and joyful. This light gives a view of those things that are immensely the most exquisitely beautiful, and capable of delighting the eye of the understanding."

Third. This light "effectually influences the inclination, and changes the nature of the soul." This change "assimilates the nature to the divine nature," namely the glory that is beheld in Christ. The effect of this assimilation is a "saving close with Christ."

Fourth. "This light, and this only, has its fruit in an universal holiness of life." This obedience does not arise from a notional or speculative understanding, but from the influence that "reaches the bottom of the heart."[15]

These considerations are significant for Edwards' signs of affection. Each consideration is a heading for three signs of the twelve. So, for instance, the third consideration above, the change of inclination, is developed by signs 7, 8, 9, that (7) gracious affections are attended with a change of nature, (8) that this change differs from a false change in that gracious affections "tend to" the spirit and temper of Jesus Christ, and (9) that they yield a softening of the heart and Christian tenderness of spirit (*RA* 340, 344, 357).

Let me make two points about this suggestion regarding structure. This structure gives the signs of affection a four-fold outline, meaning that Edwards assesses the influence of a divine object on human experience under the general heading of aesthetic attraction to God, a cognitive assent that transcends speculative reason, the conviction of the truth of Christ and the Bible, and practical moral living governed by "holy rules." I cannot develop these here, but these four categories appear to be a compendium of the most visible influences on human affections. They also represent the most complete image of the soul in Edwards' work.

The second point is that Edwards includes equally general negations within this treatment. These negations form an objective absence of content that must be overcome by discovery while at the same time the tendency of the soul to stop discovery prematurely is acknowledged and resisted. For example, the difficulty of understanding the "moral excellency of divine things" (sign 3) becomes the impetus for the examination of a "divine spiritual taste, which in its whole nature is diverse from any former kinds of sensation of the mind" (*RA* 259), which leads Edwards to examine the understanding in signs 4, 5 and 6. The "sense of the heart" (sign 4) is the access to describing the transcendent character of understanding and its excellence (sign 5), but lest this discovery lead to an end of inquiry, Edwards points to the awareness that the sense of the heart is without a proper object in sign 6:

> The soul of a saint, by having something of God opened to sight, is convinced of much more than is seen. There is something that is seen, that is wonderful; and that sight brings with it a strong conviction of something vastly beyond, that is not immediately seen. So that the soul, at the same time, is astonished at its ignorance, and that it knows so little, as well as that it loves so little. The soul, in a spiritual view, is convinced of infinitely more in the object, yet beyond sight; so it is convinced in the capacity of the soul, of knowing vastly more, if clouds and darkness were but removed. (*RA* 324)

The discovery of this object and the soul that desires it propels Edwards to discuss conversion to Christ. Making something like an abductive inference, Edwards claims that only divine power is sufficient to transform and not merely restrain the soul, working "a complete change of nature" which does not erase individuality but gives individuals real substance. Edwards is convinced that only Christ is such an infinitely extending object that demonstrates power to alter the very nature of the soul. Edwards reflects on this power: "The soul is deeply affected by these discoveries and so affected as to be transformed" (*RA* 340). And this discovery is continuous; "as it is with spiritual discoveries and affections given at first conversion, so it is in all illuminations and affections of that kind, that persons are the subjects of afterwards; they are all transforming . . . and they still reach the bottom of the heart, and affect and alter the very nature of the soul" (*RA* 343).

The character of the signs of affection is the significant moment in Edwards' study. One characteristic is the overcoming of cognitive absence through discovery, but this discovery entails the real limit of experience. This means that Edwards' discovery is not only an intellectual approach to God and the soul, but one that incorporates the will and emotions as well. The distinctness of the discovery of God is only possible in light of the same kind of perception that separates the sweetness of honey from the taste of honey itself. The experience of God cannot be accounted for by description. The structure Edwards describes relates to the perception of a unique content within the "things whatsoever the mind of men is subject to, . . . a beauty that is seen, and goodness that is tasted" (*RA* 282).

Edwards' structured account of the signs of affection illuminates an experience that is already a fact, or as a minimum, reveals what present experience is *not* by comparison. In other writings, such as his sermons, he intends to provoke the awareness of one's affections through a dramatic portrayal of the soul's condition. But even this provocation depends on the appeal to experiences—not to create experience so much as to interpret it. Experience is the opening for the kind of discovery that leads to an awareness of the soul's demand for a sufficient object. For Edwards, this sufficiency depends on an appropriation of the Christian tradition to the peculiar needs arising in the person's understanding. This experiential demand opens up into the continuous discovery of the "infinite dignity of the person of Christ, and the boundless length and breadth, and depth and height, of the love of Christ to sinners" (*RA* 324).

Religious Discovery

Peirce's and Edwards' accounts of the discovery possible in experience bear a strong resemblance. They both reflect an overcoming of the absence of knowledge or self-control with an intellectual/moral content that stands as an object in our tradition or our thought. They differ over the role of the community. For Peirce, there is no discovery of God separate from the inquiry of the community, and the perception of a "real and effective force in consciousness" that is more than what can be shown in any individual—the religious—must be a scientific discovery. For Edwards, religious discovery is almost exclusively individual in significance and ground, except that the soul searches for satisfaction in objects of faith that are traditionally held. The result of this search can only be perceived in a demonstration of this satisfaction through communal action. There is no substantial demonstration of this discovery apart from communal living, and the object that stabilizes the soul is the community property of the tradition that preserves and proclaims the Christ of the gospel.

Religious discovery for both Edwards and Peirce is the ultimate significance or *telos* of experience. For them both, this discovery is only meaningful in consideration of its object. I have attempted to dwell in the thought of these thinkers long enough to indicate what kind of object they both discover and the architectonic of that discovery. By doubling the structure of discovery, I have attempted to make a further claim that the American tradition cannot be properly characterized without taking account of the need to extend beyond individual content or emotionally satisfying accounts of spirituality to engage in a structural discovery of the meaning of experience.

ROGER A. WARD received the B.S. from Pennsylvania State University (University Park); the M.Div. from Southwestern Baptist Theological Seminary (Fort Worth, Tex.); the M.A. from Baylor University (Waco, Tex.); and the Ph.D. from Pennsylvania State University (University Park). He is associate professor of philosophy at Georgetown College (Georgetown, Ky.). His scholarly interests focus on such classic American philosophers as Edwards, Peirce, and Dewey, and on Baptist church history and applied ethics. Among his major publications is *Conversion in American Philosophy: Exploring the Practice of Transformation*.

NOTES

[1] Jonathan Edwards, *The Works of Jonathan Edwards: Religious Affections*, vol. 2, ed. John Smith (New Haven: Yale University Press, 1959), 34.

[2] Michael Raposa, "Jonathan Edwards' Twelfth Sign," *International Philosophical Quarterly* 33, no. 2 (1993): 153–162.

[3] Sang Hyun Lee, *The Philosophical Theology of Jonathan Edwards* (Princeton, NJ: Princeton University Press, 1988), 46.

[4] H. Richard Neibuhr, *Christ and Culture* (Middletown, CT: Wesleyan UP, 1951), 39.

[5] William J. Wainwright, *Reason and the Heart* (Ithaca, NY: Cornell University Press, 1995), 43ff. Wainwright uses Edwards' affections as the ground for an argument about the natural discovery of supernatural truths. My difficulty with Wainwright is that the form of Edwards' discovery is explained without the particular focus on the content of that discovery.

[6] Mary Mahowald, "Peirce's Concepts of God and Religion," *Transactions of the Charles S. Peirce Society*, vol. 12 (Fall 1976): 367–377. Michael Raposa, *Peirce's Philosophy of Religion* (Bloomington, IN: Indiana University Press, 1989). See also John Smith, "Religion and Theology in Peirce," *Studies in the Philosophy of C. S. Peirce*, ed. Philip Wren (Cambridge, MA: Harvard University Press, 1952); C. F. Delaney, "Peirce on the Hypothesis of God," *Transactions of the Charles S. Peirce Society*, vol. 28, no. 4 (Fall 1992): 725–739; and Doug Anderson, "Peirce's God of Theory and Practice," *Revista Portuguesa de Filosofia*, vol. 51, no. 1 (Jan–Mar 1995): 167–178.

[7] Parenthetical references are to the *Collected Papers of C. S. Peirce*, ed. Hartshorne and Weiss (Cambridge, MA: Harvard University Press, 1934).

[8] Vincent Colapietro, *Peirce's Approach to the Self* (Albany, NY: SUNY Press, 1989).

[9] The continuity of natural laws and divine character leads Leibniz to claim "each soul knows the infinite—knows all but confusedly." G. W. F. Leibniz, "Principles of Nature and Grace, Based on Reason," *Philosophical Essays*, ed. Garber & Ariew (Indianapolis & Cambridge: Hackett, 1989), 211.

[10] See Douglas Anderson, *Strands of System* (Indianapolis: Purdue University Press, 1995), 150.

[11] Manuscript letter to Professor Keyser, May 14, 1908. "The other volume I want to write would give my views on the whole idea of Christianity [unreadable] so far as it relates to Jesus. While totally full on the religious side it would argue metaphysics generally and that I do not think it possible to go before the public with."

[12] In 1897, Peirce wrote a letter to Reverend John W. Brown, rector of St. Thomas Episcopal Church in New York City, in which he describes a religious experience of being "called by the Master" to communion. Reflecting on this experience, he describes his "work for the church" as his own particular task. Clearly, this work has to do with his philosophy and his logic. The letter is found in the Max Fisch Collection at the Peirce Edition Project, Indiana University and Purdue University at Indianapolis.

[13] Subsequent references to *Religious Affections* will be parenthetically shown in the text.

[14] "What I aim at now, is to show the nature and signs of the gracious operations of God's spirit, by which they are to be distinguished from all things whatsoever that the minds of men are subjects of, which are not of a saving nature." *Religious Affections*, 89.

[15] Jonathan Edwards, "A Divine and Supernatural Light," *A Jonathan Edwards Reader*, ed. Smith, Stout, Minkema (New Haven: Yale University Press, 1995), 123–4.

Jonathan Edwards as Proto-Pragmatist and John Dewey as Post-Theological Calvinist

Stuart Rosenbaum

I come to this conference with what I might characterize as a "sense of the heart," a sense that Jonathan Edwards was more than a person of his time, more than an Enlightenment Calvinist who was trying to hold in coherence his scientific and his theological worlds. And I admit that this sense is inspired by Perry Miller's treatment of Edwards in his 1949 biography;[1] this sense finds further confirmation in recent work by Douglas Anderson.[2] I realize that Miller's exposition is controversial, but having encountered some other treatments of Edwards, I remain impressed by Miller's conception of Edwards. The sense of the heart I bring is a diffuse one, one I can try to identify only by standards that are disreputable in many areas of philosophy: by techniques of association many may be inclined to think fallacious. Nevertheless, such techniques are all that are available to me, and I find them interesting and at least worth conversation.

Begin with the idea of grace, and start out on what looks to be completely neutral—it may even appear irrelevant—ground. Elie Wiesel's book, *Night,* is a description of his experiences as a young Polish Jew during the horror of the 1940s holocaust that enveloped all of European Jewry. Though Wiesel's story is well known, his crushing, God-extinguishing experiences have become rare in our American part of the world. Not rare for us, however, are theological puzzles, admittedly lacking in psychological power, but of the sort that defeated Wiesel's faith. The response of the Christian, Francois Mauriac, to Wiesel's story, which is printed as the foreword to Wiesel's book, is relevant:

> And I, who believe that God is love, what answer could I give my young questioner . . . ? What did I say to him? Did I speak of that other Jew, his brother, who may have resembled him—the Crucified, whose Cross has conquered the world? Did I affirm that the stumbling block to his faith was the cornerstone of mine, and that the conformity between the Cross and the suffering of men was in my eyes the key to that impenetrable mystery whereon the faith of his childhood had perished? . . . We do not know the worth of one single drop of blood, one single tear. All is grace. If the Eternal is the Eternal, the last word for each one of us belongs to Him. This is what I should have told this Jewish child. But I could only embrace him, weeping.[3]

Mauriac's acknowledgement that all is grace is his honest Christian response to the Jewish child for whom God no longer existed. For Jonathan Edwards, too, the inscrutability of Divine grace was essential in his thought about God. Edwards could have had no more theologically substantial a response to Wiesel's experience than did Mauriac. Edwards' work centered on finding a theological way to think about himself, and about all of humanity, in social, cultural, and natural contexts that were no more consonant with natural human hopes than were the more contemporary contexts of Wiesel and Mauriac. Even though one's enemies in Edwards' world did not have the military power of the twentieth century, the uncertainties of daily life were enormous. (All of Edwards' children survived to adulthood, an almost unheard of happenstance in the early eighteenth century; only two of Cotton Mather's fifteen children survived to adulthood.)

Given Edwards' commitments to Lockean empiricism and Newtonian naturalism, his steadfastness in seeking to elaborate a theological account of grace coherent with that empiricism and naturalism is quite natural. The empiricist passivity of individuals in their cognition of the world parallels their powerlessness in the hands of God,[4] and the deterministic Newtonian physics supports well Edwards' refusal of Arminian heresies in whatever guise they might present themselves. Not only the uncertain benevolence of the natural world that supported life in the early eighteenth century, but also the dominant intellectual tendencies of his age supported in Edwards' thought an idea of grace recognizably similar to the one to which Francois Mauriac had recourse in the twentieth century. Mauriac's words, "all is grace," would have suited Edwards.

Edwards' intellectual problem, or if you prefer, his theological or philosophical problem, was to find a place for divine grace in his scientific world. His solution to this problem was to locate divine grace in the particular habits of the elect, in their distinctive ways of being in the natural world and in their communities. The elect were those whose characters were infused with religious affections, those who understood that Christ was the telos of history and who lived that understanding, those whom God infused with his own modes of perception and understanding.[5] Although this conception of divine grace indeed cohered with Edwards' scientific world, it presented grave epistemological problems for earnest Calvinists, of whom none was more earnest than Edwards. Who were the elect? Who evidenced genuine religious affections? Who lived their understanding of Christ as the *telos* of history? These problems Edwards apparently struggled with all of his life. Anderson puts Edwards' dilemma this way:

> [W]e may reveal through our beliefs and actions the traits of salvation, but we cannot *know* that we are saved; at best we become hermeneuts of the religious affections.[6]

These particular epistemological problems are, by contrast with the typical epistemological problems of seventeenth- and eighteenth-century philosophy, distinctive in the American intellectual context. Their distinctiveness is largely a function of their focus on the affections, the habits, and the character of individuals who are seeking to make sense of their own lives and their own communities.

Who among us is elect? Who among us has religious affections? These questions find no answers—indeed, they are not even asked—in the work of any of the prominent rationalists or empiricists of the seventeenth or eighteenth centuries. For those traditional epistemologists, the being of God, and God's relationship to the world, are the only epistemological questions. For Edwards, the being of God and God's relationship to the world are, relatively speaking, settled issues; urgent for him is the issue of individual relationships to God and how one may discern the quality of those relationships.

Edwards' concern with the epistemology of individual relationships to God signals his significance for American pragmatism; it signals the primary respect in which he is a "proto-pragmatist." How does Edwards' epistemology of individuality signal this significance? Hold that question and cut to John Dewey.

Richard Rorty and Alan Ryan have recently praised Dewey's 1892 essay, "Christianity and Democracy." Let me quote from Rorty the passages he singles out for attention:

> It must have seemed strange to the University of Michigan's Christian Students Association to be told, in 1892, that "God is essentially and only the self-revealing" and that "the revelation is complete only as men come to realize him."
>
> Dewey spelled out what he meant by going on to say, "Had Jesus Christ made an absolute, detailed and explicit statement upon all the facts of life, that statement would not have had meaning—it would have not been revelation—until men began to realize in their own action the truth that he declared—until they themselves began to live it."[7]

Rorty's way of seeing Dewey's 1892 perspective on Christianity is perhaps distinguishable from, but is recognizably similar to, that of Jonathan Edwards' response to his own epistemological problem about individual relationships to God:

One can detect the meaning of Jesus Christ for individuals only to the extent that they begin to live that meaning in their lives, and such meaning exists at all for individuals only to the extent that they live that meaning in their relationships and in their communities. Dewey is appealing to the test of practice. An idea, a value, or an ideal has traction in an individual life only to the extent that an individual lives that idea, value, or ideal in ways that concretely acknowledge or manifest that idea, value, or ideal. John Dewey's 1892 test of the meaningfulness of Christianity to any individual is whether that individual's practice, habits, and character conform to Christianity's historical exemplar, Jesus Christ. In the words of Bruce Kuklick, explicating Jonathan Edwards' account of grace,

> God related to individuals through human experience, and he became, through Christ, the reason for behavior. For the elect, Christ, the personal wisdom of God, was the telos of history.[8]

Edwards' epistemological focus on individuality, on the need to discern "gracious affections," commitments to specific concretely exemplified Christian ideals of habit and character, signals his proto-pragmatism. Dewey's 1892 commitment to testing individual character in habit and action signals his pragmatism (or perhaps only his own proto-pragmatism, if we take seriously the effort by many scholars to divide Dewey into an earlier idealistic period and a later pragmatic period). In any case, Dewey's later, and more systematic treatment of these same issues reveals his own full-blown pragmatism.

In his later work, Dewey abandons earlier efforts to hold together some remnant of creedal Christianity with his commitments to science and democracy. Instead, Dewey seeks to practice his understanding of Christianity, meaning that, for Dewey, Christianity "morphs" into democracy. But to say that Christianity metamorphoses into democracy is not to say that it mutates into democracy. A mutation is a change in which something essential or significant is left behind;

a metamorphosis is a change in which nothing essential or significant is left behind. Dewey's democracy is as filled with Dewey's Christianity of practice as his Christianity is filled with his democracy. Democracy, in Dewey's conception of it, is Christianity in practice; it is the systematic practice of Christianity in our moral, political, social, and cultural worlds. Nothing is left behind. Or is it?

Before trying to answer this question, let us take a quick look at Dewey's democracy in order to see how it signifies his Christianity. The 1939 talk on the occasion of his eightieth birthday, published as "Creative Democracy, the Task Before Us," shows us Dewey's large understanding of democracy:

> Democracy is a way of life controlled by a working faith in the possibilities of human nature. Belief in the Common Man is a familiar article in the democratic creed. That belief is without basis and significance save as it means faith in the potentialities of human nature as that nature is exhibited in every human being irrespective of race, color, sex, birth and family, or material or cultural wealth. This faith may be enacted in statutes, but it is only on paper unless it is put in force in the attitudes which human beings display to one another in all the incidents and relations of daily life. . . . The democratic faith in human equality is belief that every human being, independent of the quantity or range of his personal endowment, has the right to equal opportunity with every other person for development of whatever gifts he has.[9]

The faith in human nature of which Dewey speaks must be "put in force in the attitudes which human beings display to one another in all the incidents and relations of daily life." The test of whether one has "the democratic faith" is the test of practice: what are the attitudes one displays toward one's fellows? One believes that "every human being . . . has the right to equal opportunity with every other person for development of whatever gifts he has" only if one has, or cultivates in oneself and seeks to inculcate in others, habits and dispositions of behavior toward others that support this democratic faith. The essential issue for Dewey in the question of democratic faith is the test of practice. What does one do? What is one disposed to do? What does one seek to encourage in others? At this point in his thought, Dewey is unwaveringly committed to the Peircean, pragmatic understanding of belief as habit of action. Faith of any kind has become a matter of practice, of habit, tendency, and disposition.

The question of whether this democratic faith Dewey expresses so eloquently and forcefully is identical with, or approximates, Christian faith is the question of whether Dewey's commitment to Christianity has metamorphosed into his commitment to democracy, an interesting and important question that I believe should be answered in the affirmative. Here, however, I do not pursue that issue, for our central focus at this point is on Edwards as a proto-pragmatist.

Returning to Edwards, I note that the defining question of his *Religious Affections* is the question how to identify recipients of grace. For Edwards, the only clue we have in our efforts to answer this question is the practice of those recipients, their habits, tendencies, and dispositions to behave in gracious ways. Here is Kuklick's account:

> For Edwards, Christian practice evidenced gracious affections. But such practice was not simply behavioral change. It was impossible to know certainly if someone had received grace. The sinful heart might always deceive. Sinners might not be just hypocrites but also self-deceivers. Nonetheless, the saved would act differently, and in describing this grace-infused behavior Edwards most clearly collapsed the distinction between reflection and sensation, between inner and outer, affection and understanding, mind and the world.[10]

In his emphasis on practice, following Kuklick's account closely, Edwards "collapsed the distinction between reflection and sensation, between inner and outer, affection and understanding, mind and the world." I do not think there is a tremendous gap, if indeed there is any gap at all, between collapsing these distinctions and thinking of belief or faith as a matter of how one is in the world, or as a matter of habit, disposition, and tendency to behave in specific ways in one's world. The apparent gap between the Calvinist and the pragmatist on the issue of what it means to be a person in the world, to have a certain kind of faith and to have certain beliefs, has now become very narrow indeed. The test of grace, of belief, of faith, is the test of practice, in Edwards as well as in Dewey. Edwards' turn toward practice in addressing his personal epistemological questions is a turn similar to the one made again and again in the American context in the centuries following him.[11] Admittedly, later thinkers became more intentionally concrete and practical in their reaction against the theoretical issues of epistemology and metaphysics that dominated the European intellectual scene. Peirce, James, and Dewey took on the Europeans very aggressively, and they were rewarded with equally aggressive reactions against their thought. Nevertheless, in Edwards' distinctive turn toward practice as a cornerstone of his thought, one does see the makings of an incipient pragmatism, a proto-pragmatism.

Recall now in conclusion the question whether Dewey left something behind when his Christianity metamorphosed into his democracy. Here again, I think we can read Dewey as a systematic purveyor of the Calvinism distinctively expressed by Edwards, though admittedly in Dewey that Calvinism has become distinctively a-theological. But the a-theological Calvinistic democracy into which Dewey's Christianity metamorphosed gives evidence of a fuller flowering of Edwards' ideas of God's sovereignty and grace.

What might Dewey have left behind when his Christianity metamorphosed into his democracy? The natural answer to this question is that he left behind the specifically Christian supernaturalism that appears in all the standard creeds of the Church—in the Apostle's Creed, in the Nicene Creed, and in the Confession of Dort to which Edwards subscribed. That Dewey left behind the supernaturalism of the Christian metaphysical tradition is not in question. He did. The question is whether his leaving it behind was a leaving behind of something in some sense "essential."

I think Dewey's leaving behind Christian supernaturalism may be seen as a symptom of two possibly unique characteristics of Dewey's religious perspective. The first characteristic is that Dewey takes more seriously than any previous thinker the idea that practice is the "bottom line" in understanding personal commitments. The fullness of Dewey's commitment to understanding humanity in terms of organic habit, tendency, and disposition is one that leaves behind any fragment of hiddenness of personality or character; no longer may we think of ourselves or of others as hidden behind veils or guises that conceal our real selves. Our real selves are what we do, or more modestly, our real selves are what we tend to do, are disposed to do, or what we habitually do; our real selves are a matter of our organic practices that make us who we are in the worlds we inhabit. The souls or minds of seventeenth- and eighteenth-century philosophy have disappeared and no longer provide any theological or philosophical solace for those who might be worried about their eternal destinies. Ontology can no longer posture as a source of comfort to the fully human creatures of God's natural world. Dewey's commitment to practice is, in this respect, simply a more systematic recourse to the same idea of practice that finds expression in Edwards' *Religious Affections:* "By their fruits ye shall know them."

The second unique characteristic of Dewey's religious perspective is that his God has become, conceptually speaking, a God of practice. "The Unity of all Ideal Ends" is Dewey's characterization of God in *A Common Faith*. As mysterious as Dewey's account of God is to those accustomed to thinking of God as "The Being than which no Greater can be Conceived," it nonetheless has the virtue of pointing toward the significance of human practice for the religious life. The point of the religious life, for Dewey, is to live toward God, and his very concept of God expresses that point. The Anselmian formulation is no better than a distraction from that understanding of the point of the religious life, for it mires one in epistemological and ontological conundrums. But Dewey, as much as Edwards, sees that the whole point of the religious life, of the Christian life, is Christian practice or taking Christ as the *telos* of one's life. Dewey's embrace of the deep morality of democracy is his taking of Christ as the *telos* of life.

Although the concept of God changes in Dewey's account, the sovereignty of God remains. Christian practice, the practice that sees Christ as the *telos* of life, is strongly preserved in Dewey's democracy and in his concept of God. Finally, Dewey would embrace, as wholeheartedly as would Edwards, Francois Mauriac's words: "All is grace. If the eternal is the eternal, the last word for each one of us belongs to him."

STUART E. ROSENBAUM received the B.A. from Baylor University (Waco, Tex.), the M.A. from the University of Nebraska, and the Ph.D. from Brown University. He is professor of philosophy at Baylor University. He has published widely on various issues in social and applied ethics and pragmatism, one of his central interests. He has recently completed a monograph, *The Reflective Life: An Introduction to Pragmatic Moral Thought*.

NOTES

[1] Perry Miller, *Jonathan Edwards* (New York: William Sloane Associates, 1949).

[2] See Douglas Anderson, "Awakening in the Everyday: Experiencing the Religious in the American Philosophical Tradition," in *Pragmatism and Religion,* ed. Stuart Rosenbaum (Urbana: University of Illinois, 2003), 143–152.

[3] Elie Wiesel, *Night* (New York: Bantam Books, 1960), foreword, x.

[4] But see Bruce Kuklick, *A History of Philosophy in America, 1720–2000* (Oxford: Oxford University Press, 2001), 18. Kuklick says that Edwards "emended Locke to give the mind constructive powers."

[5] Kuklick, 18.

[6] Anderson, 143.

[7] Richard Rorty, "Pragmatism as Romantic Polytheism," in *Pragmatism and Religion,* ed. Stuart Rosenbaum (Urbana: University of Illinois Press, 2003), 122.

[8] Kuklick, 19.

[9] Reprinted in Rosenbaum, *Pragmatism and Religion,* 91–96. See p. 93.

[10] Kuklick, 19.

[11] See for example the essay by Perry Miller, "From Edwards to Emerson," in his *Errand into the Wilderness* (Cambridge: Harvard University Press, 1956), 184–203.

PART V

EDWARDS IN HIS CONTEXT

Bishop Butler and Jonathan Edwards

David White

1. Parallel Lives.—Joseph Butler and Jonathan Edwards had parallel lives:

1692 BUTLER born	1703 EDWARDS born
1715–1718 BUTLER at Oriel College	1716–1722 EDWARDS at Yale
1719–1726 BUTLER preacher at the Rolls Chapel	1722 EDWARDS begins pastoral work
1726–1738 BUTLER rector of Stanhope	1726–1750 EDWARDS pastor in Northampton
1738–1750 BUTLER bishop of Bristol	
1750–1752 BUTLER bishop of Durham	1751-1758 EDWARDS at Stockbridge
1752 BUTLER dies at Bath	1758 EDWARDS dies at Princeton

2. Praiseworthy Pair.—Butler and Edwards are of comparable importance (the highest), but they are far less often praised as a pair than individually. The following passage is exceptional:

> The writers to whom Dr. Taylor was most indebted, and whose principles he sought to apply, to complete, and in some cases to correct, were Bishop Butler and Jonathan Edwards. Bishop Butler suggested the principles and the course of argument concerning the benevolence and equity of God's government, which were matured by him into a more exact system, and carried only to their legitimate conclusions. President Edwards was often in his hands, and the careful reader of these volumes

will see the relation of many of the discussions to the teachings of that prince of New England divines, and to the whole current of what is called New England theology. The works of all the New England divines were the familiar hand-books of his reading. He was also entirely at home with the writers on natural theology, for which the English church in other times was so distinguished. From all of these authors, and the bold and energetic workings of his own mind, he reasoned out the system of principles and conclusions which is found in these volumes.[1]

3. Undervalued Men.—Appreciation of Butler and Edwards is blocked by selective, stereotyped reading.

4. Pastors.—Butler and Edwards were primarily pastors and should be evaluated on the basis of pastoral effect in the early eighteenth century, throughout the nineteenth century, and now. Pastoral philosophy is the same as any philosophy in its various appeals to reason, to experience, and to authoritative testimony. Pastoral philosophy differs from academic philosophy in that it is motivated in the first instance by specifically religious concerns and that it is successful or unsuccessful in the last instance depending on its religious effects.

5. Systems of Divinity.—Butler and Edwards should both be studied as complete systems of divinity, but also as complementary, especially today. (A) "System" needs to be understood here in the sense in which it was used by Butler and by Edwards, with reference to many parts working together to achieve a single purpose. (B) Perhaps the most obvious contrast between Butler and Edwards is that, compared with Edwards, Butler wrote almost nothing. Edwards left many pages of unpublished material; Butler had all his papers destroyed at his death. Edwards wrote about his life and worked hard to be well known as a writer. Butler actively discouraged biographers and published only in direct relation to his pastoral duties or his quest for ecclesiastical advancement. He neither engaged in controversy nor answered critics. Great as they are, these differences seem to have had little effect on the study of Butler and Edwards, especially during the nineteenth century. (C) The best explanation for why Edwards says so little about Butler explicitly is simply that prior to the late eighteenth century there was relatively little discussion of Butler by anyone.

6. Common Project.—Butler and Edwards were engaged in a common project: to marshal high-order intelligence in opposition to a (perceived) state of irreligion. Iain H. Murray compares Butler and Edwards on exactly this point, saying that the supposedly modern worldview is not all that recent but was well known to Butler and Edwards and formed the context in which they worked.[2]

7. Eighteenth-century Scene.—The early eighteenth-century scene in philosophical Christian divinity can be reconstructed by looking at Newton, Clarke, Berkeley, Hume, Wesley, and Edwards together with the principal deists (e.g., Chubb, Tindal, Toland, Collins) and the moralists cited by Hume: Locke, Shaftesbury, Mandeville, Hutcheson, and Butler. (A) The principle of unity running through Unitarian, deistic, skeptical, evangelical, and rationalist thought was the desire to discover a religion that could be practiced whole-heartedly in the present state of the world by those who took religion (and human life as a whole) seriously. (B) These writers also showed a keen interest in establishing a theory of human nature that derived primarily from experience.

8. Self-love & Benevolence.—For Butler, the fundamental insight of Christian ethics is that self-love (concern for our own happiness) and benevolence (concern for the happiness of others) are not in essential conflict (they may incidentally conflict, just as any two principles of action may conflict), and that people generally need to give more regard to their own true good just as much as they need to be more concerned for the good of others. The need is not to develop a theory that will pass muster with professional philosophers, but rather to bring people (all, or as many as will listen) to see (A) wherein their true self-interest and happiness lies and (B) themselves as part of a story, i.e., a progressive system, that can ultimately be resolved into a single purpose. As Edwards says, "in pure love to others (i.e., love not arising from self-love) there's a union of the heart with others; a kind of enlargement of the mind, whereby it so extends itself as to take others into a man's self: and therefore it implies a disposition to feel, to desire, and to act as though others were one with ourselves. So, self-love implies an inclination to feel and act as one with ourselves: which naturally renders a sensible inconsistence with ourselves, and self-opposition, in what we ourselves choose and do, to be uneasy to the mind. . . ."[3]

9. Human Ignorance.—A main theme of Butler's *Analogy of Religion* (1736) is clearly stated by Edwards: "If God will give us a revelation from heaven of the very truth concerning his own nature and acts, counsels and ways, and of the spiritual and invisible world, 'tis unreasonable to expect any other, than that there should be many things in such a revelation that should be utterly beyond our understanding, and seem impossible" (*Miscellanies,* no. 583, 18:118). In Butler's work, this appeal to the extent of human ignorance is used repeatedly not only to answer objections to scripture as revelation but also to reply to the problem of natural and moral evil in a world governed by God. Butler makes the related point that far more important than what we believe about redemption is whether we feel redeemed and act accordingly.

10. Deism.—Edwards says little about Butler explicitly, but his lack of comment is important as evidence regarding Butler's role in the deistic controversy. For more than a century now, Butler has been presented in histories of philosophy as having "defeated the deists." It is often said that he was so successful at defeating the deists that there is no longer any need to study his writings; their work is done. The reason Edwards does not associate Butler with criticism of the deists is that for the entire eighteenth century no one associated Butler particularly with replies to deism.

11. Anglicanism.—(A) Butler is often described as one of the great Anglican divines, but in such an expression, the force of "Anglican" is the same as the force of "New England" in calling Edwards one of the great New England divines. The point is essentially geographical and to some extent temporal but not at all doctrinal. (B) If there is a substantive meaning to "Anglican," the word refers to those writers who defended the rights of the English Church against the Church in Rome. They argued that the Church in England ought to be the Church of England. Butler and Edwards held similar opinions regarding the pope, and the issue of whether there ought to be a Church of England had been settled by Butler's time. Hence, for example, More and Cross date the period of Anglicanism as from 1594 to 1691, i.e., ending the year before Butler was born. (C) Obviously, Butler and Edwards disagreed somewhat regarding the manner of worship, but we need to remember that Butler was born into a Presbyterian family and only converted to the Church of England after arguing to his family and the elders that the reasons for separation from the Church of England were not sufficiently strong to warrant his giving up a career in the ministry. Butler did not see a good career prospect among the dissenters. So, we might say that both Butler and Edwards determined early in life that they wanted nothing more than to be ministers and have a career in the Church and that both acted in such a way as to best pursue that goal. (D) There is no denying, however, a very significant difference regarding an American episcopate. Butler argued for a bishop in the colonies who would have no political but only spiritual authority. There were many who denied any such distinction was possible. Edwards went further. Edwards had a religious objection to the spread of Anglican missions in the colonies.

12. Enthusiasm.—Many people associate Jonathan Edwards with the methods of George Whitefield and John Wesley, and they think of Butler as opposed to such "emotionalism." There are many problems with this view. (A) Those who subscribe to this view usually ignore Butler's sermons on the love of God in which he states explicitly that fear of extreme enthusiasm ought not to drive us to the opposite extreme. (B) The record of Butler's dealings with Whitefield and Wesley is very inadequate and has only recently been transcribed properly. Butler's main point against Wesley was that Wesley, as a priest in the Church of England, needed permission from him (the bishop of Bristol) to preach in the diocese of Bristol. Wesley denied that Butler had any such authority. Obviously, none of this debate had any application to Edwards. (C) Some have also claimed that Butler's remark about "whole nations going mad" was a reference to the Methodists, but there is no proof one way or the other as to whom Butler was talking about and no proof that Edwards would have disagreed regarding the phenomenon in question.

13. Future Life.—Butler and Edwards both stress the reality of punishment in a future life. Both attribute the punishments to God, and both recognize that many people find such preaching distasteful. The essential difference is that for Butler God acts through the normal "course and constitution of nature." Butler argues that just as vice is naturally punished by bad consequences in this world, so we ought to expect vice will continue to be punished in the next world. Edwards sees the punishments as particular acts of God, wholly justified, certainly, but not merely acting in accord with the laws of nature. This disagreement seems like a good one for the theologically inclined student to ponder.

14. Miracles.—An analogous point can be made regarding miracles. Which view is more theologically correct and why: Butler's claim that what we call miracles are actually not violations of natural law but just the operation of laws of nature entirely unknown to us, or Edwards' view that miracles are interventions by God? The practical effect of miracles was essentially the same for both.[4]

15. Free Will.—The term "Arminian" is not generally used with regard to Butler, but he certainly seems opposed to what he would call "the doctrine of necessity." Yet, Butler never tries to disprove necessity or predestination. His main argument is that even one who is convinced of the doctrine of necessity will have a hard time living by it, since, even for such a person, the subjective feeling of being free and of one's deliberations and decisions being relevant is unshakable.

16. Scripture.—Butler understood the Christian scriptures to be the revealed word of God, and he considered it the duty of every Christian to make a regular practice of "searching the scriptures." It is important to stress that Butler did not elevate reason above the scripture any more than he reduced religion to morality. Rather, Butler placed scripture in the category of testimony, a form of evidence that has long been recognized as potentially very strong but also potentially very weak. Butler tries to show that scripture holds up well when considered as testimony. He was a creationist. He took seriously the claim that all that exists was created by God. Therefore, when Butler looks at human nature, he asks how human nature fits into God's world, what its purpose might be. And he asks the same question with regard to physical nature and of reason. Butler asks how reason might best be put to use given the assumption that God is sovereign and that it is by virtue of God that we have reason. He comes to the conclusion that reason ought to be used to form judgments, just as the eyes are used for seeing and legs for walking. For Butler, not to use reason in this way would be to deny God's manifest purpose. How fruitful is it to argue this point as an issue in theology? Might it not be more important just to search the scriptures for whatever reason? Edwards reads scripture in almost exactly the same way. So for example, in considering the question of whether Moses wrote the first five books of the Bible, Edwards answers yes, and gives many reasons in support of that claim, but in dealing with the account of Moses' death, reason tells him that those few passages must be by another hand. Like Butler, Edwards is willing to debate, with regard to a particular passage, whether it is astonishing but true or whether it needs a more plausible interpretation.

17. Slavery.—Edwards was a slave owner and raised no objection to the institution of slavery. Butler seems to have had no issue with the slave trade in Bristol while he was bishop there. In his only recorded statement on slavery, Butler argues mainly for the importance of recognizing slaves as children of God. Edwards' view seems essentially the same. This was an enlightened opinion for the time, however regrettable it appears with hindsight. Certainly Butler's inability to see a problem with the institution of slavery puts stress on his claims about the universality and reliability of conscience.

18. Ecclesiastical Ceremonies.—Edwards argued that once one accepted the extra-biblical ceremonies of the Church of England, one might as well accept those of the Church of Rome. Butler, of course, would not agree, but Butler's expressed sympathy for images, set prayers, and other forms of "external" religion was enough to provoke charges that he had converted to the Roman Church, and John Henry Newman cited the argument of Butler's *Analogy* as instrumental in his conversion to Rome.

19. Pragmatism.—The sense of the presence of God is crucial for both Butler and Edwards. Butler was something of the perfect pragmatist in religion. Theological study had the same instrumental role as religious objects and practices. If such study brought one more into the sense of the presence of God, about which all words fail, then it is to be commended. Attempts to gain knowledge of divine truths beyond the minimum needed to lead a life of virtue and piety are a waste of time both because such knowledge is not available to us but also because even if it were available it would be irrelevant to what is our proper business in this world. For Edwards, of course, even attempts to gain knowledge needed for a life of virtue are a waste of time, but Edwards remains a pragmatist, with a close affinity to the Dewey of *Art as Experience*,[5] with his following Locke, as did Butler, in understanding knowledge as human action.

20. Communication.—Butler and Edwards seem similar with regard to government of the tongue, both in expressed opinions and in practice, but Butler was also careful not to leave behind any unnecessary writings.

DAVID E. WHITE received the B.A. from Colgate University, and both the M.A. and Ph.D. from Cornell University. He is associate professor of philosophy at St. John Fisher College (Rochester, New York). He has written articles on Bertrand Russell, Dora Black, George Orwell, John Locke, and David Hume in the second edition of the *Encyclopedia of Unbelief* (forthcoming). He is the editor of a new edition of the works of Joseph Butler for the University of Rochester Press.

NOTES

[1] Noah Porter in his introduction to Nathaniel Taylor, *Lectures on the Moral Government of God* (New York: Clark, Austin & Smith, 1859).

[2] Iain H. Murray, *Jonathan Edwards: A New Biography* (Carlisle, PA: Banner of Truth, 1987), xxiv.

[3] *True Virtue* in Jonathan Edwards, *Ethical Writings* (New Haven: Yale University Press, 1989), 589, and *Notebooks* (New Haven: Yale University Press, 2003), 315f.

[4] See "Controversies" Notebook, (New Haven: Yale University Press, 2003), 297ff., for Edwards' objection.

[5] John Dewey, *Art as Experience* (New York: Minton, Balch & Company, 1934).

Doing Metaethics with Kant and Edwards

Charles Don Keyes

This essay is a dialogue among the essentialist ethical concepts of Jonathan Edwards' *The Nature of True Virtue* (*NTV*), Immanuel Kant's *Foundations of the Metaphysics of Morals* (*FMM*), and my *Brain Mystery Light and Dark: The Rhythm and Harmony of Consciousness* (*BMLD*). Kant's ethical philosophy, I argue, mediates between Edwards' and my own.

Metaethics asks what makes right acts right, according to Veatch.[1] Metaethical essentialism claims that there is at least one ethical truth that cannot be reduced to private or cultural opinion. This article continues the defense of metaphysical essentialism found in *BMLD*, in light of both Kant's and Edwards' positions. My view in that book is the kind of non-eliminative naturalism which holds that mental states are brain events and also recognizes the reality of the spiritual dimension of human life. This spiritual dimension is expressed in aesthetics, ethics, and religion, all of which elude simply materialistic or naturalistic eliminative explanations. Thus, I call my position "spiritual materialism" and argue that it is compatible with belief in a universal ethical truth. Below, I examine potential objections to my metaethical position, which arise in dialogue with Edwards, as well as Kant, and propose hypothetical revisions of my position as a result of this examination. This procedure has the further advantage of bringing Edwards into the orbit of contemporary moral philosophy.

It is worth noting at the onset that Edwards, Kant, and I are all theists; however, as the following shows, the metaethical essentialist core of all three positions can be stated independently of whether God exists. I believe that such non-theological defenses of ethical essentialism constitute an important critique of the malignant relativisms of our time.

I. The Connection between Kant and Edwards

Kant's ethics is based upon duty and decisions, while Edwards, like Aristotle, bases ethics on virtue and dispositions of character. In the following subsection of this paper, I consider how the basically different orientations of Kant and Edwards find expression in terms of their discussions of beauty, good will, and freedom. I then proceed to consider their respective views of the value of ethical actions in terms of their more general views about the worth of human beings.

Beauty, Good Will, and Freedom

The aesthetics of beauty is integral to the ethics of both philosophers, to Kant's duty (and decisions) and to Edwards' virtue (and dispositions of the character). Edwards writes in *NTV*: "Whatever controversies and variety of opinions there are about the nature of virtue ... all excepting some skeptics ... mean by it something beautiful." Furthermore, virtue is "the beauty of those qualities and acts of the mind that are of a moral nature."[2] Virtue is benevolence, and this true virtue is beautiful. It is the kind of love that is both universal in its extent and proportional to each individual being's degree of worth.

In his *Critique of Judgment,* Kant claims that beauty is a symbol of the morally good because it "gives pleasure with the claim for the agreement of everybody else." Beauty postulates this "in others as a duty,"[3] and thus Kant's ethics has at least a superficial resemblance to Edwards' ethical views.

Edwards holds that a good will is a benevolent will, namely, one disposed to virtue. According to Kant, however, a good will is one rationally capable of acting according to duty. He argues in *FMM* that "reason is given to us as a practical faculty, i.e., one which is meant to have an influence on the will . . . because reason, which recognizes its highest practical vocation in the establishment of a good will, is capable only of a contentment of its own kind."[4] Furthermore, "The good will is not good because of what it effects or accomplishes or because of its adequacy to achieve some proposed end; it is good only because of its willing, i.e., it is good of itself."[5]

Good will, like beauty, is a common element in the respective philosophies of Edwards and Kant, despite their contrasting interest in virtue and duty. For Edwards, ethical actions come from virtuous characters, whereas for Kant, all human beings have the capacity to act ethically, i.e., according to duty, because all human beings possess the freedom to act in accordance with reason's dictates. Thus, the greatest difference between the two ethicists can be located with respect to their views on free will.

Edwards argues that our choices are not free. Richard Hall says that Edwards' position means "even the good or benevolent will is causally determined. We are 'free' only in the sense that we are able to act on our choices or volitions (which are determined for us), and not free if we are unable."[6] Our measure of freedom is our ability to act upon the choices that have been determined for us. Only in this sense is the will free; otherwise, for Edwards, the will depends upon causality.

By contrast, Kant's *Critique of Practical Reason* holds that freedom is independent from causality, and it is the property of an intelligent being. Furthermore, "Such independence [of the will from the "law of natural appearances . . . the law of causality"] is called *freedom* in the strictest, i.e., transcendental, sense. Therefore, a will to which only the legislative form of the maxim can serve as a law is a free will."[7]

Thus, we are able to see that for Kant, virtue or character is not a necessary condition for ethical action. On the contrary, all humans possess the freedom to act ethically, i.e., in accordance with duty as prescribed by practical reason.

Kant holds that the categorical imperative is possible because we have free choice. We must act only on what we will to be categorical imperatives, giving our rational consent to acts that we would will to be universal. Kant states that individuals should act in such a way "that the maxim of your will could always hold at the same time as a principle establishing universal law."[8]

For Edwards, something resembling Kant's principle of universality is possible even in the absence of free choice. He argues that "each action must respect the interest of others":

> Every being that has understanding and will, necessarily loves happiness . . . if he be consistent with himself . . . he must approve of those inclinations whereby beings desire the happiness of being in general, and must be against a disposition to the misery of being in general: because otherwise he would approve of opposition to his own happiness . . . it would tend to universal misery . . . he that loves a tendency to universal misery, in effect loves a tendency to his own misery.[9]

Similarly, for Edwards, to be virtuous *is* to be rational, though it is still doubtful that Edwards attributes this rational virtue to all human subjects.

Still, we can see that, in some sense, both philosophers base right actions on consistency and universalizability. Edwards' universalizability is, as Hall says, similar to that which underlies Kant's categorical imperative "even though he would reject the principle of universalized ability *underlying* Kant's imperative."[10] This is because Edwards' position is virtue based and so limited to those subjects possessing virtue.

The core of Edwards' metaethics is thus as follows: Our moral value comes from our capacities for understanding and our will. We are worthy of respect because of our intelligence and benevolence:

> When I speak of an intelligent being ... benevolently disposed to being in general, I thereby mean intelligent being in general. Not inanimate things, or beings that have no perception or will; ... the degree of amiableness of true virtue primarily consisting in ... a benevolent propensity of heart to being in general, is not in the simple proportion of the degree of benevolent affection seen, but in a proportion compounded of the greatness of the benevolent being, or the degree of being and the degree of benevolence. One who loves being in general, will necessarily value good will to being in general.[11]

This is the recognition of one being by another, a recognition, I argue, that essentially entails Being as such. In light of this, consider the metaethical core of Kant's position: we have dignity because we are free to act according to the categorical imperative. Thus, human beings are valuable because we are rationally capable of being the type of universal legislator that the categorical imperative requires:

> Thus if there is to be a supreme practical principle and a categorical imperative for the human will, it must be one that forms an objective principle of the will ... which is necessarily an end for everyone because it is an end in itself. ... The ground of this principle is: every rational nature exists as an end in itself. ... The practical imperative, therefore, is the following: Act so that you treat humanity, whether in your own person or in that of another, always as an end and never as a means only.[12]

For Kant, freedom to perform the categorical imperative bestows dignity upon human beings. Freedom, in turn, depends upon reason and the good will.

II. Keyes' Naturalistic Recasting of Kant

I reformulate Kant's metaethical core into a biological model independent of the question of freedom, which in one respect makes my position closer to Edwards. I argue that we are biologically capable of virtue and of acting according to duty. My analysis, however, focuses on our capability of experiencing and acting in accordance with beneficence and tolerance, while I further emphasize our capacity for formulating metaphysical ideas. Neurobiologist Paul D. MacLean and his interpreters (like Steve Peterson)[13] give scientific evidence to identify how the brain produces these three types of behavior, i.e., the beneficent, tolerant, and metaphysical. I argue that our brain's ability to produce beneficent thought, feeling, and ideas of essences validates our life, i.e., the life of human beings as such. As a result, we are worthy of respect as ends, not merely means; this is, moreover, Kant's conclusion, though I am suggesting a justification for it that differs in significant respects from his own.

Contrary to popular opinion, survival of the fittest does not sanction cruelty. Paul D. MacLean's triune brain hypothesis challenges this mistaken concept, arguing that the present human forebrain retains the earlier structures of the evolutionary past. The result is a biologically trinitarian model of three structures functioning *in unity:* ancient reptilian structures surviving in our basal ganglia are the source of traits like territoriality, power, and ritual; paleomammalian limbic structures contribute emotion, including a sense of parental responsibility for offspring; and neomammalian structures produce rational thought in human beings. Their most recent development is the prefrontal lobes, source of our ability to think about the future.

The medial dorsal nucleus links the same prefrontal lobes with the limbic structures that generate parental responsibility. As a result, MacLean finds that "a parental concern for the young generalizes to other members of the species, a psychological development that amounts to an evolution from a sense of responsibility to what we call conscience."[14] Tracing conscience and related altruistic thoughts, feelings, and actions to their biological origins does not eliminate them. On the contrary, discovering their roots in the brain/mind unity supports their reality.

Light at Midnight: Metaphysical Ideas, Tolerance, and Beneficence

Aesthetic, religious, and ethical experiences have power to heal the wounds of negative experiences. The last chapter of *BMLD* on ethical foundations (meta-ethics) defends essentialism against what Robert M. Veatch rightly calls the "cynicism" at the heart of many types of current relativism, i.e., what I call "the malignant relativisms of our time" above. I argue that life is essentially worthy of respect because it is capable of at least three types of valuation: metaphysical ideas, tolerance, and beneficence.

Our biological capability of attributing ultimate importance to the spiritual dimension of life proves our worth because the self-transcendence it produces incorporates us into a larger reality. Elsewhere, I argue for the belief that God exists, though here, as in *BMLD*, I claim that "Even *if* God does not exist in reality and all religious symbols are brain products and nothing more, the fact that we are biologically capable of attributing ultimate importance to them attests to our essential value."[15] To say this another way, even if Platonic ideas like the Good do not exist, having the sublime illusion that they do would justify the illusionist. This is to say that the human brain's ability to have such illusions makes it worthy of respect. For example, if free will were an illusion, believing in it would still give a value to illusionists that they would not possess otherwise. In other words, such illusions have existential worth, and consequently the brain's capability of producing these ideas renders its possessor valuable. Even if autonomy and wrestling with decisions were illusory, I argue that the existence of such processes in nature and our consciousness of them are what matters. Furthermore, what causes them is irrelevant.

"Tolerance of difference," I argue, "also validates the valuer." In *BMLD*, I define tolerance as "a type of behavior that bestows latitude and allows the other to be."[16] It validates the self by valuing the other. For example, in medical ethics, respect for the patient's autonomy to make decisions seems to spring from tolerance. In sexual interaction, tolerance requires consent. Rape, the supreme denial of tolerance and beneficence, is the supreme violation of the sexual ethical absolute.

As I explain above, MacLean's hypothesis that the link between the prefrontal lobes and certain limbic structures generates conscience argues that beneficence is real. The entire species and even life itself becomes the object of beneficence.

My metaethical theory, stated above, builds on MacLean's hypothesis that beneficence is real. I argue that life is worthy of respect, our fellow creature's and our own, because our biological constitution makes us capable of beneficent thoughts, feeling, and actions. As I have already suggested, this is a naturalistic justification of Kant's conclusion that human beings must be treated as ends in themselves and not mere means. His categorical imperative requires us to be universal legislators of moral laws and not to make exceptions for ourselves. Even if human beings fail to act in this way, they are capable of doing so and we must treat them accordingly. Kant's *FMM* states in a text already cited that one must "act so that you treat humanity, whether in your own person or in that of another, always as an end and never as a means only."

Respect for life does not depend upon whether specific individuals do what they ought but upon the fact that the species as such is capable of it. In light of this, we may conclude that mentally retarded people, those in comas, the physically handicapped, and infants have worth insofar as they are members of the species. MacLean's defense of the reality of beneficence and my essentialist metaethical theory challenge the cynical relativistic devaluation of life. Both arguments remain strictly within the limits of spiritually enlightened naturalism.

III. Two Objections to Keyes' Position

Edwards' Hierarchy of Existence and the Problem of Maleficent Actions

First, contrary to the foregoing, it could be argued that the capability of valuation is not an adequate reason for attributing essential value to anyone. Potentiality is insufficient; a person must actually be engaged in valuation to be essentially valuable.

Second, if acts that bestow value (whether the capability of them or actually doing them) make humanity essentially valuable, then it follows that maleficent actions and violations of the categorical imperative would make humanity essentially worthless.

Edwards represents the first objection to my position well. He argues that beneficent capability alone does not bestow worth upon an individual. Furthermore, he claims that the amount of respect something deserves depends on its intelligence and its will's disposition: "No affections towards particular persons or beings are of the nature of true virtue, but such as arise from a generally benevolent temper, or from that habit or frame of mind, wherein consists a disposition to love being in general."[17] The benevolent act has to be habitual, just as Aristotle notes that one swallow does not make a spring.

Furthermore, Edwards holds that there are "degrees of existence" and these seem to constitute a hierarchy of worth. There is

> "proportion to the degree of existence," because one being may have more existence than another, as he may be greater than another. That which is great has more existence, and is further from nothing, than that which is little. One being may have every thing positive belonging to it, or every thing which goes to its positive existence (in opposition to defect) in a higher degree than another; or a greater capacity and power, greater understanding, every faculty and every positive quality in a

higher degree. An archangel must be supposed to have more existence, and to be every way further removed from nonentity, than a worm.[18]

Edwards' metaethical core includes proportionality of worth. This contrasts with Kant's position and mine, which are non-proportional. In what follows, I argue that these two positions—proportionality of worth and non-proportionality—are both true and can be held as parts of a more general and coherent ethical theory. In the following section, I shall develop the sense in which these positions can be simultaneously held.

IV. Edwards and Keyes in Dialogue

Edwards has caused me to revise my position with respect to the first objection and to seek a new kind of clarification about the second. Below, in the two subsections that constitute this part of the paper, I discuss how this revision and clarification, respectively, develop.

First Objection to My Position

My dialogue with Edwards has two effects at the same time. It is making me attempt (a) to revise my metaethical core to include the truth of proportionality and (b) to find a way to read Edwards that will include the truth of non-proportionality. The result should be a higher truth, one that, as Hegel claims, preserves the truths that it sublates.[19] To do both, I propose understanding Edwards' hierarchy of existence as a nascent model for biological evolution. On the one hand, such a model would differentiate degrees of intelligence and benevolence (or their absence), giving at least some limited validity to the first objection. Whether our actions are good or evil has some effect on our value, or, more specifically, on the value we place on ourselves. On the other hand, Edwards' hierarchy of existence designates a continuous whole. Membership in the larger scale bestows worth on individuals in that scale even if they are less virtuous and therefore less worthy than other individuals. The worm, although lower in the scale than more evolutionarily advanced species, still has a place on the same scale. Respect for life does not depend upon whether specific individuals are beneficent, attribute importance to ideas, or tolerate differences, but upon the fact that beneficence, for instance, is an act of life as a whole, not merely an act of individuals either on their own or collectively. It is an aspect of its evolutionary history and belongs to life's genetic connections and processes. Beneficence is both potential and, sometimes, also actual in parts of the biological whole.

The higher validates the lower in yet another sense through social responsibility. It bestows value upon everything in the scale because each part is qualitatively implicated in the whole. As J. S. Mill says, for instance, fulfilling the need of one applies to all.[20] Therefore, good in the part validates the whole. The healing act cannot eliminate all suffering and untimely death, but as MacLean writes, "In the words of T. S. Eliot, we might imagine that 'The whole world is our hospital,' and we might continue with Howard Sackler's comment that 'somehow to intervene, even briefly, between our fellow creatures and their suffering or death, is our most authentic answer to the question of our humanity.'"[21] MacLean's statement suggests that specific beneficent acts are ultimately important even if they are statistically insignificant. We cannot alleviate all pain on earth, but affirming the value of a particular fellow creature by intervening on its behalf has infinite value.

Second Objection to My Position

For Kant, the capability of violating the categorical imperative attests to our worth. As Hall says, "the shadow side of moral worth,"[22] specifically, the sense of remorse, illustrates this.

The second objection is less directly related to Edwards' thought than the first, but at least touches on it. Edwards' hierarchy of being has some relation to it, since any location in the hierarchy makes it part of the whole. Furthermore, the objection that maleficent actions and disobedience of the categorical imperative make humanity worthy of contempt resonates with Edwards' remark that anyone who deliberately dissents against another being (and so, by extension, Being as such) offends rationality. For Edwards, Being is in some sense the good, a harmonious network of relations. Evil disrupts that network and is therefore dependent on the whole, while detracting from it. The good is an impulse or drive toward order, while evil's destructiveness depends upon the good that it negates. In this sense, good and evil are not symmetrical, since good is seen to be the more fundamental of the two.

On December 21, 2003, I asked Hall if he could develop the meaning of the concepts just mentioned. This question stemmed from my attempt to argue that an object made up of many parts gets its validity from its best part. He offered the following intuitive illustration:

> Imagine the abysmal darkness of a prairie or some other vast area of space at night when neither moon nor stars are visible. Suddenly one small light appears, and it rebukes the darkness. Now picture the same place in broad daylight. A dark spot, even many dark spots, do not rebuke the light. A little good would have power over the whole even if the whole were otherwise dark, and not vice versa.[23]

This intuitive illustration of the asymmetrical nature of good and evil is aesthetically significant because it suggests that the appearance of goodness, i.e., ethical acts, has the power to give worth to situations that would otherwise be evaluated in an exclusively negative way.

V. Conclusion

Edwards' impassioned intellect is essential to contemporary metaethical concepts because his belief in virtue is infused with the aesthetics of beauty, and that might be the primordial source of our care for life.

Acknowledgements

As a newcomer to the study of Edwards' philosophy, I talked with Richard Hall extensively about the content of the texts pertinent to my essay. Some of the information in the foregoing manuscript has been mediated through those discussions. I am also grateful to Hall for his editorial criticisms of preliminary drafts of this paper.

Substantial amounts of my 1999 essay cited below have been incorporated into the foregoing manuscript by permission of La Roche College, and its publication, *Sensibilities*.[24]

I especially want to thank David Hoinski and Michael Rudar, graduate assistants at Duquesne University, both of whom have given valuable contributions editing this manuscript.

CHARLES DON KEYES received the B.A. from the University of Oklahoma; the B.D. and S.T.M. from Seabury-Western (Evanston, Ill.); the M.A and Th.D. from the University of Toronto; and the Ph.D. from Duquesne University (Pittsburgh, Pa.), where he is Professor of Philosophy. He is currently doing research in biomedical ethics and the brain/mind problem. He focuses on the relation between neurobiological monism and foundational ethics, aesthetics, and religious symbols. His major publications are *Brain Mystery Light and Dark: The Rhythm and Harmony of Consciousness; New Harvest: Transplanting Body Parts and Reaping the Benefits;* and *Foundations for an Ethic of Dignity: A Study in the Degradation of the Good.*

NOTES

[1] Robert M. Veatch, *Case Studies in Medical Ethics* (Cambridge, MA & London: Harvard University Press, 1977), 2.
[2] Jonathan Edwards, *The Nature of True Virtue,* foreword by William K. Frankena (Ann Arbor, MI: The University of Michigan Press, 1960 [1765]), 1.
[3] Immanuel Kant, *Critique of Judgment,* trans. Norman Smith (New York: St. Martin's Press, 1968 [1790]), 198–99.
[4] Immanuel Kant, *Foundations of the Metaphysics of Morals,* trans. Lewis Beck, ed. R. Wolff (Indianapolis, IN: Bobbs-Merrill, 1969 [1785]), 12–13.
[5] Ibid., 10.
[6] Richard Hall, written correspondence and conversations, unpublished, 2003, 1.
[7] Immanuel Kant, *Critique of Practical Reason,* trans. Lewis Beck (Indianapolis, IN: Bobbs-Merrill, 1956 [1788]), 28.
[8] Ibid., 30.
[9] Edwards, *The Nature of True Virtue,* 101–02.
[10] Hall, written correspondence and conversations, 1.
[11] Edwards, *The Nature of True Virtue,* 11–12.
[12] Kant, *Foundations of the Metaphysics of Morals,* 47.
[13] Steven Peterson, "The psychobiology of hypostatizing," *Micropolitics* 2, no. 4 (1983): 423–51; "Human ethology and political hierarchy: is democracy feasible?" Paper prepared for presentation at conference on biology and the prospects for democracy, Villa Vigoni, Menaggio, Italy, 24–26 November 1988.
[14] Paul MacLean, *The Triune Brain in Evolution* (New York: Plenum, 1990), 562.
[15] Charles Don Keyes, *Brain Mystique Light and Dark: The Rhythm and Harmony of Consciousness* (London and New York: Routledge, 1999a), 124.
[16] Ibid., 130.
[17] Edwards, *The Nature of True Virtue,* 5.
[18] Ibid., 9.
[19] G. W. F. Hegel, *Hegel's Science of Logic,* trans. A. V. Miller, foreword J. N. Findlay (New York: Humanities Press, 1969 [1816]).
[20] J. S. Mill, *Utilitarianism* (Indianapolis, IN: Hackett, 2001 [1861]).
[21] Paul MacLean, "Obtaining knowledge of the subjective brain ('epistemics')," in *So Human a Brain: Knowledge and Values in the Neurosciences,* ed. Anne Harrington (Boston, MA: Birkhäuser, 1992), 70.
[22] Hall, written correspondence and conversations, 2.
[23] Hall, 2.
[24] Charles Don Keyes, "Medical ethical meditation on *Brain Mystery Light and Dark: The Rhythm and Harmony of Consciousness,*" *Sensibilities,* Spring 1999, vol. 2, no. 2. 1999b.

PART VI

EDWARDS & THEOLOGY

Satan and his *Maleficium* in the Thought of Jonathan Edwards

Scott D. Seay

Introduction

On Sunday morning, June 1, 1735, Jonathan Edwards' uncle, Joseph Hawley, cut his own throat and died. One of Northampton's leading citizens had committed suicide at the height of the religious revival, and this was unintelligible to most people of the region, especially to supporters of the Awakening. Edwards regarded him as "a gentlemen of more than common understanding, and strict morals, religious in his behavior," but recognized that inwardly he was tormented by "[concern] about the state of his soul." Finally, as Edwards explained, discouragement and melancholy simply overpowered his uncle, and he ended his life.[1] Two days after the suicide, in a letter to Benjamin Colman (1673–1747), Edwards attributed Hawley's suicide to the "great rage" of Satan at the "extraordinary breaking forth of the work of God."[2] In the mind of Edwards, the primordial, cosmic battle of the Devil and his angels against the agents of God had played itself out in his parish, indeed in the very life of one of his parishioners.

Edwards' explanation of the Hawley suicide was not simply a desperate attempt to make sense of a devastating pastoral and personal crisis. To the contrary, Edwards actually believed in Satan and in his ability to affect the lives of individuals and broader events of history. This might come as a surprise to some, because most historians of late seventeenth- and early eighteenth-century Anglo-American culture have grown accustomed to speaking of a "decline of the demonic" during this period, at least among the educated and influential.[3] This "declension thesis" is not without merit. The art and literature of the period, especially that of John Milton (1608–1674), "mythologized" Satan and his activity, treating them more as literary devices to be manipulated according to human fancy than as malevolent, real-world forces.[4] More importantly, the debacle of the Salem witchcraft trials, reaching its nadir in 1692, and the English Enlightenment critique of the "enchanted world" from the 1670s onward snuffed out belief in Satan and demonic activity altogether in the minds of some on both sides of the Atlantic.[5] But Edwards is not one of them. To be sure, Satan and his *maleficium* prove to be potent themes in Edwards' writings as he attempts to interpret individual religious experience and broader events of history.

The descriptive essay that follows synthesizes references scattered throughout the writings of Jonathan Edwards in an effort to discern what he believed about Satan and demonic activity. This study assumes that what we discern in Edwards' writings is a transformation of (not a decline in) traditional Puritan beliefs about Satan. Edwards' demonology is as vigorous as that of his Puritan forbears, but he simply reformulated it in light of Lockean epistemology and continued ecclesio-political tensions between Puritan and non-Puritan parties in both England and America.[6] This study begins to pin down what Edwards believed about Satan and demonic activity, leaving the question of Edwards' place in the history of late early modern Anglo-American demonology to future research.

What *did* Edwards believe about Satan and demonic activity? He believed that Satan and his angels are real, albeit supernatural entities. They neither have nor can take on corporeal existence. Impelled by jealousy toward humanity, Satan and his angels pridefully rebelled against God, and God expelled them from heaven as a result. In an effort to exact revenge against God, Satan and his angels restlessly work for humanity's downfall and continued misery to tarnish the glory of God in the created world. Satan and his angels have the power—insofar as God allows them—to influence the religious experience of individuals and thereby to misdirect and pervert the redemptive work of God in the world. Despite the pervasive and destructive influence of Satan and his demons in the world, God providentially secures Satan's defeat in dramatic reversals of Satan's *maleficium*. Indeed, these repeated instances of Satan's defeat in the world foreshadowed his eschatological punishment in hell.

Thus, Edwards' interpretation of the Hawley suicide could not be more representative of his overall beliefs about Satan and his activity. Because the Spirit of God already was withdrawing from Northampton and the revival was winding down, Satan was allowed to rage once again against the people of the region. Precisely by taking advantage of Hawley's "distemper" and "melancholy," Satan drove him to those despairing thoughts about the state of his soul. And Satan encouraged suicidal tendencies in Hawley and others of the region "as if somebody had spoke to 'em, 'Cut your own throat, now is a good opportunity: *now*, NOW!'"[7] Yet, Satan's *maleficium* in the life of an individual also represented a turning point in the broader work of God in the revival.[8] The Hawley suicide was sensible proof to Edwards that the revival was over: not that Satan had triumphed over God's work in Northampton, but that the momentum in Satan's primordial struggle against God again had shifted back in Satan's direction.

Satan, Devils, and the Damned

From at least two generations of Puritan religiosity, Edwards inherited a surprising flexibility in the way in which he uses terminology for the demonic.[9] Like his Puritan predecessors, Edwards applied the words "devil" and "devils" with equal force to Satan himself, the angels who do his bidding, and the men and women whose souls are under demonic influence. In fact, at times readers of Edwards have to use particular care in determining precisely which dimension of the demonic alliance Edwards means. Nevertheless, Edwards in many instances relies on other vocabulary to distinguish between them. Satan is most often "Lucifer," the "old serpent," "Beelzebub," and "the Dragon," reflecting Edwards' reliance on biblical terminology.[10] In addition to the more general "devils," Edwards most often refers to the angels who do Satan's bidding simply as "fallen angels." And finally, men and women who are under demonic influence, in addition to being called "devils," are called simply "the damned," or "the wicked."[11]

As his starting point for understanding who Satan is, Edwards interprets Revelation 12:7–9 quite literally. The text reads:

> And there was war in heaven: Michael and his angels fought against the dragon; and the dragon fought and his angels, and prevailed not; neither was their place found any more in heaven. And the great dragon was cast out, that old serpent, called the Devil, and Satan, which deceiveth the whole world: he was cast out into the earth, and his angels were cast out with him. (KJV)

There really was a war in heaven, in which Satan and those angels whom he could convince to join him fought against the archangel Michael and the angels loyal to God. The rebellion occasioned God's judgment: Satan and the rebel angels were cast from heaven to the earth. Following Milton's lead, Edwards takes considerable poetic license in elaborating this basic narrative into a rich mythology of the demonic.[12]

For Edwards, *pride* probably motivated Satan and some of the angels to rebel against God. Time and again, Edwards refers to some angels' unwillingness to serve a lower creature (i.e., humanity) despite God's command for them to do so. Serving humanity would be according to these angels "degradation and misery,"[13] and Satan thought it a "great debasing of him."[14] Particularly galling to these angels was God's decree that one of these humans, Jesus Christ, would have a relationship to God qualitatively different from that of all other created beings. "It seems to me," Edwards wrote:

that the temptation of the angels, which occasioned their rebellion, was, that when . . . God declared his decree that one of that human nature should be his son, his best beloved, his greatest favourite, and should be united to his eternal Son, and that he should be their Head and King, that they should be given to him, and should worship him, and be his servants, attendants and ministers.[15]

That a human being, an inferior creation, should be exalted in this way was intolerable to Satan and like-minded angels. The angels' "appetite for their own honor" overcame their "holy dispositions" and caused them to resist the decree of God.[16]

But there are some logical problems occasioned by Edwards' poetic license. After all, the incarnation and exaltation of Jesus Christ were unnecessary until humanity fell, but Edwards assumed that this pride motivated the fall of Satan and his angels when "God was about to create man, or had first created him."[17] To the extent that Edwards even tried to explain this apparent logical inconsistency, he predictably relied on the providence and sovereignty of God. Knowing beforehand that humanity would fall, God set in motion "preparation for the work of redemption"[18] through Christ even though Satan and his angels did not know particularly how it was to be, "God having only in general revealed it to them."[19] Elsewhere, Edwards dismissed the problem of chronology altogether: whether the establishment of God's redemptive plan in Christ "was without the fall predestinated as some suppose, or upon supposition of the fall, as others . . ." seemed immaterial to him.[20] Moreover, Edwards completely sidestepped the issue of Satan's initial motivation to incite rebellion. For Edwards, all sin was the direct result of temptation. But, "seeing [Satan] had no tempter," Edwards can only say unconvincingly that "'tis probable that some extraordinary manifestation of God's sovereignty was his temptation."[21] Unlike Milton's, Edwards' poetic license took him only so far.

Therefore, it is important to note that Edwards was at best tentative in his description of the angels' fall. He apparently knew that he is elaborating without direct support from Scripture, and often appealed to "some leading divines" in support of his arguments.[22]

If the motivation for the angels' rebellion could be stated with only relative certainty, the actual mechanics were more certain to Edwards: Satan emerged very clearly in Edwards' writings as the instigator of the war in heaven. Unquestionably, the chief reason for Satan's influence over those angels who would follow him was the angelic hierarchy intrinsic to the created order. In speaking of Satan before his fall, Edwards called him "the chief of all the angels, or greatest in natural capacity, strength, and wisdom, and highest in honor and dignity, the brightest of all those stars of heaven. . . ."[23] Moreover, Satan was "God's chief servant, and the grand minister of his providence, and the top of the creation. . . ."[24] Because of Satan's status among the angelic host before his fall, Edwards was certain that the rebellious initiative had lain with Satan and no one else: as an archangel, Satan "conceived rebellion against the Almighty and drew away a vast company of the heavenly hosts with him."[25]

God's punishment of Satan and this vast company of rebel angels took two forms in Edwards' thought. First, as Revelation 12:9 asserts, Satan and the fallen angels were cast from heaven to earth, where they continue to build a kingdom in opposition to God's. Satan remains the leader of the pack, for he "restlessly endeavors to set himself up in this world, and maintain his dominion here, and to oppose God. . . ." With the other devils as "his servants, his wretched slaves," Satan "seeks to reign as god of this world, and affects to be worshipped as God."[26] But in what sense is this "independent kingdom of themselves" a *punishment* for Satan and the fallen angels? In short, Edwards argued that opposition to God was its own punishment. Indeed, by their continued rebellion, Satan and his angels are perfect slaves to the pride and ambition that reign over them.[27] God had given them over to that same disposition which they exercised when they fell, and by that means makes them forever a procuring of their own misery. And this is a misery they are plunged into as a punishment for their first rebellion.[28]

The restless work of Satan and his angels meets continual "confusion,"[29] "disappointment and vexation."[30] Satan's efforts are persistently thwarted, because no matter how highly evil exalts itself in the world, Jesus Christ is always exalted above it in the work of redemption.[31] In short, Satan and his angels are fighting a losing battle, and they know it.

But according to Edwards, this temporal disappointment and vexation will pale in comparison with the eschatological punishment that awaits Satan, devils, and the damned.[32] In fact, mere anticipation of this "future state of perfect misery" inspires a hellish fear in Satan and his angels that torments them even at the present.[33] They have good reason to be afraid; hell is a "world of misery," a "lake of burning brimstone" and a "dreadful pit of the glowing flames of the wrath of God."[34] Moreover, in a kind of providential irony, it is Jesus Christ to whom judgment of the devils has been committed:

> how remarkably will [Satan] be mortified at the last day, when he shall be judged by a man, by one of the race, yea one that is as it were all the redeemed. [Devils] must be brought in chains to have their judgment and condemnation before his throne, [he] being united personally to the Deity then sitting on his throne, judging those fallen angels with all his assessors with him in his throne, judging of those angels that thought to have had such a good sport of their destruction.[35]

What makes this scene so ironic is Edwards' conviction that Jesus Christ actually *replaced* Satan as the anointed one to whom judgment would be committed.[36] Satan fell because his pride prevented him from serving a lower creation; yet, by virtue of his humiliation (which was directly proportional to Satan's pride), Jesus Christ was exalted into the place of the fallen archangel, attaining a status that Satan attempted to usurp by force.[37] To make matters even worse for the devils, those elect against whom the devils strove in their work in the world join Jesus Christ in their judgment. Humanity, then, and Jesus Christ in particular, emerge in the eyes of Satan and his angels as both the *reason* and the *instrument* of the punishment for their fall.

As if the fires of hell and the bitter irony were not punishment enough for them, Satan, his angels, and the damned in hell will realize that their eternal misery will only "double the ardor" of the elect angels and humanity in heaven.[38] Moreover, in hell, Satan and his angels will finally realize the magnitude of their sin; their "spiteful rebellion and direct malicious war against God" was an unforgivable sin against the Holy Spirit.[39] They suffer in the realization that they never had an opportunity for a Savior. And finally, the devils in hell are "like spiders shut up together": because they cannot catch flies, they devour one another.[40] In short, hatred will be perfected in hell, just as love is perfected in heaven.[41]

Satan's *Maleficium*

But this rich mythology of Satan, devils, and the damned composed barely half of the story of Edwardsean demonology. Edwards appeared equally concerned throughout his writings about the *work* of Satan, his *maleficium,* and how to discern it in individual religious experience. The external, spectral evidence for Satan's work which captured the imaginations of at least two generations of Puritan witch-hunters found no place in the writings of Edwards. Rather, Edwards took a turn inward, into the interior life of the human imagination, to find compelling evidence of Satan's work. Yet the work of Satan can also be discerned in the contours of broader historical events. Indeed, all history for Edwards consisted of God's redeeming work in creation, whose chief aim is bringing glory to God. But

Satan aims to rob God of the glory by repeatedly thwarting that redeeming work however he can. In both arenas of Satan's work—in the human imagination and in the events of history—Edwards saw the primordial conflict between Satan and God repeated, with the fate of humanity hanging in the balance.

"The imagination or phantasy," Edwards wrote, "is the devil's grand lurking place, the very nest of foul and delusive spirits."[42] However the later Romantic traditions in America may have evaluated Edwards' claim, there is no denying that he took a dim view of the imagination as a source for spiritual understanding. As Edwards made sense of the human mind, the will and the understanding are rational faculties, and in some sense generally operate independently of the body. Indeed, the ideas of the will and the understanding are *sui generis*. The imagination, on the other hand, is a non-rational faculty somehow intricately dependent on the body as its source of ideas. The imagination often uncritically accepts whatever external ideas are presented to and mediated through the body's "animal spirits." Without being held in check by the understanding and the will—which according to Edwards is unlikely—the imagination lays the human mind bare to whatever ideas are presented to it.[43]

The Edwardsean Satan knew this, and regularly took full advantage of the human imagination. In fact, Edwards went so far as to say that *only* by the imagination does Satan have access to the soul of any person. Satan cannot "excite any thought or produce any effect in the soul of man" except by his crafty and subtle influence on the human imagination. Even though every human has an imagination, Edwards argued that certain kinds of people are relatively more susceptible to the influences of Satan. For example, "common people" were easily bewitched by a "glittering show of high religion" without realizing that Satan has transformed himself into an angel of light.[44] And, like Hawley, "persons that are under the disease of melancholy" were often visibly and remarkably subject to the suggestions and temptations of Satan.[45] But is it important to remember that, for Edwards, no one was exempt from temptation by Satan, not even Christ himself.

Among Christians Satan enjoyed particular advantages in making impressions upon the imagination, because he can adulterate truly gracious experiences and spiritual discoveries with what Edwards calls "counterfeit religion." In fact, Edwards claims that

> 'Tis by the mixture of counterfeit religion with true, not discerned and distinguished, that the devil has had his greatest advantage against the cause and kingdom of Christ, all along, hitherto.[46]

Nearly all forms of counterfeit religion are products of Satan's impressions on the human imagination.[47]

For example, the pernicious notion of "immediate revelation" arises when individuals imagine themselves to have direct, unmediated communication with God which grants them unique spiritual understanding or allows them to predict the future. But such communication, as divine in origin as it may seem, in reality come from Satan's impressions on the human imagination; they are "imaginary revelation[s]" excited by external ideas suggested by Satan. Edwards cites the followers of Thomas Muntzer (1489?–1525) and Caspar Schwenkfeld (1489–1561) among the "many sects of the enthusiasts that swarmed in the world after the Reformation," and concludes that their claim to immediate revelation was a delusion of Satan.[48] The threat of such delusional, counterfeit religion was very real:

> By such a notion [immediate revelation] . . . Satan would have opportunity . . . to set up himself as the guide and oracle of God's people, and to have his word regarded as their infallible rule, and so to lead 'em where he would, and to introduce what he pleased, and soon to bring the Bible into neglect and contempt.[49]

This subordination of the Scripture to alleged immediate revelation often led to other erroneous practices of religion. Rather than "declaring one's faith in Scripture expressions," candidates for ministry were required to submit to creeds and confessions of faith, which Edwards calls "the chief engines that Satan has made use of to tear the church of God into pieces."[50] Indeed, Satan's primary purpose in impressing Christian imaginations with so-called immediate revelation is to "draw [them] off from the Word of God."[51]

But Satan's interest in impressing human imaginations went beyond his desire to delude individuals. Satan was keenly aware that the delusion and sin of individual persons grow until they infect larger groups of people and influence broadly felt events of God's redemptive history. Edwards likens the delusion and sin inspired by Satan to a crocodile. Though a crocodile is born of an egg no larger than that of a goose, it grows incessantly until the time it dies, and may reach a length of thirty cubits. So it is with the delusion and sin of individual persons; it

> is comparatively easily crushed in the egg, taken in its beginning; but if left alone, what head does it get, how great and strong, terrible and destructive does it become, and hard to kill, and grows as long as it lives.[52]

The point of Edwards' typology is apparent enough. The Satanic delusions and sins of individuals, if recognized as such early on, are easily stamped out. But once those delusions and sins infect "towns, countries and empires, and the world of mankind," Edwards says, they are highly destructive and hard to be destroyed.[53]

The growth of papal power between the fifth and sixteenth century was a sterling example of this dynamic according to Edwards. Roman Catholicism, Edwards asserted, "seems to be the masterpiece of all the contrivances of the devil against the kingdom of Christ," and has as its end to "turn the ministry of the Christian Church into a ministry of the devil."[54] Yet Roman Catholicism was built solely upon the sum total of each pope's delusion and pretensions to power. The pope began as a minister of the congregation at Rome, but with the complicity of the temporal rulers equally deluded by Satan, popes gradually assumed more and more power for themselves. The logical end, as Edwards saw it, was the pope's demonic claim to be the vicar of Christ on earth, tantamount to claiming the same power that Christ would have if he were still on earth. For Edwards, this power belongs only to God; the papal claim was thus motivated by the same pride and ambition that occasioned the rebellion of Satan and his fall from heaven. Moreover, with its power, the papal-satanic alliance has led countless numbers of people throughout history into the greatest sins of Reformed theology: idolatry and ignorance of Scripture.[55]

Nevertheless, Edwards' Satanic crocodile was growing closer to home, too. Indeed, in Edwards' day Satan had spoiled the "paradisaic [sic] state of the church of God in New England" with an intractable theological controversy over religious affections. On the one hand, Satan had deluded some New Englanders into believing that "manifold fair shows" and "glistening appearances" of high religion were evidence that God had savingly wrought upon them.[56] In truth, according to Edwards, such counterfeit religious experiences are an abomination to God and have dire soteriological consequences:

> By this means [Satan] deceives great multitudes about the state of their souls; making them think they are something, when they are nothing; and so eternally undoes 'em: and not only so, but establishes many, in a strong confidence of their eminent holiness, who are in God's sight, some of the vilest of hypocrites.[57]

In one sense, Edwards sympathizes with those led astray by false affections; Satan's counterfeit comes very close to the real thing. Satan often brings texts of Scripture to the mind, lending credibility to his imaginative delusions;[58] Satan often inspired (counterfeit) love and humility, mimicking the Christian virtues and graces of highest repute;[59] and Satan even counterfeited the order of the saving operations of the Spirit of God which are preparatory to conversion.[60]

On the other hand, others in New England had grown to reject religious affections altogether because of the extremism of some.[61] Here again, Satan is at work persuading them "that all affections and sensible emotions of the mind in things of religion . . . are to be avoided, and carefully guarded against, as things of a pernicious tendency."[62] The soteriological consequences of this delusion are equally dire according to Edwards:

> This [Satan] knows is the way to bring all religion to a mere lifeless formality, and effectually shut out the power of godliness, and every thing which is spiritual, and to have all true Christianity turned out of doors.[63]

Indeed, the "prevailing prejudice against religious affections" is evidence for spiritual death, according to Edwards. By such prejudice, Satan intends

> to harden the hearts of sinners, and damp the graces of many of the saints, and stunt the life and power of religion, and preclude the effect of ordinances, and hold us down in a state of dullness and apathy, and undoubtedly causes many persons greatly to offend God, in entertaining mean and low thoughts of the extraordinary work he has lately wrought in this land.[64]

Thus, both in the excesses of experiential religion and in the denial of its importance, Satan impresses the imaginations of individuals, and then allows their delusion and sin to grow into prevailing attitudes which thwart the redeeming work of God in the world. In all such cases of Satan's *maleficium,* he aims to rob God of glory and to bring ruinous misery upon humanity.

As confidently as Edwards describes Satan's work in the imagination of postlapsarian humans and in expanding individual delusion into ruinous historical trends, he is surprisingly reticent about Satan's role in humanity's initial fall. In fact, in his treatise on original sin Edwards does not mention Satan, even in passages where mention of Satan is ordinarily anticipated.[65] When he addresses Satan's role in the Fall of humanity, Edwards speaks only in surprising generalities. By his subtle temptations, Satan "procured the fall of our first parents, and so brought about the ruin of the whole race."[66] Satan successfully tempted Adam and Eve because he "deceitfully and lyingly told them that they should be as gods."[67] Edwards does not skirt around the issue of moral agency in dealing with Satan and postlapsarian humanity. Though Satan may impress the imaginations of fallen human beings, *they* bear responsibility for the resulting beliefs and actions. In the Fall of Adam and Eve, however, Edwards appears to avoid making a firm commitment one way or the other regarding moral agency and the work of Satan. In short, the degree of Satan's responsibility for the initial Fall relative to that of Adam and Eve remains an open question for Edwards.[68]

Satan's purpose in procuring the Fall is far more clear to Edwards. By rebelling against God and introducing sin and misery into the world, Satan sought to "rob God of [the] glory"[69] expressed in the created order, especially in humanity. "Satan rose up against God," Edwards wrote,

> endeavoring to frustrate his design in the creation of this lower world, to destroy his workmanship here, and to wrest the government of this lower world out of his hands, and usurp the throne himself, and set himself up as God of this world instead of the God that made it. And to these ends he introduced sin into the world, had made man God's enemy, he

brought guilt on man and brought death into the world, and brought the most extreme and dreadful misery into the world.[70]

But Satan's end in tempting humanity was equally directed at humanity itself in destroying its pristine happiness and holiness. Indeed, humanity's Edenic happiness especially inspired in Satan an overpowering jealousy and a desire to see humanity fall:

> That man who was of earthly original should be advanced to such honors, when he who was originally of a so much more noble nature should be cast down to such disgrace, his pride could not bear. How then would Satan triumph when he had brought him down![71]

In a certain sense, the Fall of Adam and Eve recapitulated the fall of Satan himself: the temptation itself was similar in both cases: Satan "aimed at nothing else but to fool man out of his happiness, and make him his own slave and vassal, with a blinded expectation of being like a god."

Nevertheless, what Satan intended to accomplish in procuring the Fall and what actually came about are two very different matters according to Edwards. In tempting humanity with the imaginative promise of being like a god, Satan ironically became a prophet of the incarnation and of salvation itself:

> But little did Satan think that God would turn it so, as to make man's fall an occasion of God's becoming a man; and so an occasion of our nature being advanced to a state of closer union with God.[72]

Moreover, such a providential reversal could only be considered a "defeat" of Satan if the degree of redemptive happiness and holiness of God's elect *exceeded* the degree of lapsarian misery which Satan introduced by the Fall.[73] Elsewhere,

Edwards asserts that the degree of happiness among redeemed humanity also exceeds the happiness of prelapsarian humanity in its Edenic paradise.[74]

God's providential reversal of Satan's *maleficium,* one instance of which has been described, emerges as one of the most prominent themes of Edwards' demonology. Other examples are equally compelling. Although God prepared the Jewish world to receive the doctrine of satisfactory sacrifice by commanding animal sacrifice, Satan deluded Gentiles into the practice of human sacrifice. Yet God providentially combined both practices in the crucifixion, thereby facilitating an understanding of the atonement by both Jews and Gentiles.[75] Satan contrived to increase the learning of the Roman Empire in an effort to snuff out Christianity. Yet God made use of the apologists like Justin Martyr and Tertullian to ply that great learning in defense of Christianity.[76] Although many other instances of Satan's defeat could be cited, the point is made. In all instances of this defeat, Satan intended to thwart God's redemptive work in history but painfully discovered that his *maleficium* only facilitated that redemptive work.

Conclusion

One thing is certain following this provisional survey of Edwards' demonology: it is impossible to speak in absolute terms about a "decline of the demonic" among the educated and influential by the turn of the eighteenth century in Anglo-American culture. If any absolute statement of the "declension thesis" can be maintained, it must be done with the exclusion of Edwards' writings as aberrant, or at least unrepresentative of his age. It is more likely that the writings of Edwards reflect a transformation of belief in the demonic, and this transformation deserves fuller contextualization.

Edwards' own demonology, however, deserves closer scrutiny before the task of contextualizing it should be undertaken. For one thing, it is not at all clear from internal evidence why Edwards veers away from his rhetoric of Satan in some of his treatises, while the rich mythology of Satan and his *maleficium* dominates others. In particular, the absence of Satan in Edwards' *Freedom of the Will* (1754) and *Original Sin* (1758) is particularly baffling. It is not the case that these later treatises simply witnessed in Edwards' own theology a "decline of the demonic"; sermons, notes on scripture, and miscellanies dating from the same period make full use of Edwards' typical rhetoric about Satan and the demonic. The respective audiences of these writings may in part account for the absence of Satan in Edwards' more philosophical treatises. But at best this is a provisional, impressionistic conclusion. More research is needed, then, to assess the reasons for Satan's peculiar absence in certain of Edwards' treatises.

Also, closer scrutiny should be applied to Edwards' handling of Satan's *maleficium* and human moral agency, especially as he understands the initial Fall of humanity. This issue, to be sure, was the hobgoblin of Reformed theologians and churchmen throughout the seventeenth and into the eighteenth century. But in the end, it appears that Edwards is no closer than his Puritan forbears to solving the dilemma of human moral agency and Satan's temptation in the Fall. This failure on Edwards' part dampens his argument in *Original Sin* and leaves him wide open to the Arminian critics whom he aims at answering. If Edwards represents the last great assertion of traditional belief in human depravity, he certainly fails to explain adequately the origin of that depravity, at least relative to Satan's *maleficium*.

Finally, given Edwards' obvious interest in the apocalyptic, more research is needed to connect adequately his interpretation of Revelation to his understanding of Satan and his *maleficium*. One sub-theme of the present study has suggested that Edwards sees the primordial conflict between Satan and God—narrated in Revelation 12:7–9—recapitulated in the religious experience of individuals and in broader events of God's redemptive activity in the world. But this assertion is only the starting point for drawing such a connection between Edwards' exegesis of Revelation and his demonology. Indeed, this point might be broadened to include

Edwards' exegesis generally and its connection to his demonology. On what Scriptural evidence other than Revelation does Edwards draw in making sense of Satan and his *maleficium*? To what degree does his poetic license take him beyond the texts of Scripture into the realm of artistic speculation? In other words, is Edwards' demonology firmly grounded in sound exegesis, or is it a second-order reflection of a religiosity more influenced by Milton than by Scripture after all?

SCOTT SEAY holds the B.A. from Wabash College (Crawfordsville, Ind.); the M.A. from the University of Chicago Divinity School; the M.Div. from Christian Theological Seminary (Indianapolis, Ind.); and the M.A. and Ph.D. from Vanderbilt University. He is assistant professor of church history at Christian Theological Seminary. His research interests encompass American religious history and modern European church history, the relationship between Christian faith and social problems, and the relationship between religion and politics. His publications include over forty entries in reference works on American religion.

NOTES

[1] Jonathan Edwards, *Faithful Narrative of the Surprising Work of God,* vol. 4 of *The Works of Jonathan Edwards,* ed. Harry Stout (New Haven: Yale University Press, 1972), 206. After this initial citation, references to the Yale Edition of Edwards' works will be made simply as *Works* (Yale), followed by a volume and page number.

[2] "Letter to Benjamin Colman," *Works* (Yale), 4:110.

[3] See, for example, Michael Winship's *Seers of God: Puritan Providentialism in the Restoration and Early Enlightenment* (Baltimore: Johns Hopkins University Press, 1996). See esp. chap. 7.

[4] Jeffrey Burton Russell makes this point in his *Mephistopheles: The Devil in the Modern World* (Ithaca: Cornell University Press, 1986), 95–127. The influence of Milton's poetry on the religious imagination of Anglo-American culture in the seventeenth and eighteenth centuries has been the subject of studies too numerous to mention here. Some of the more important of these studies, however, include George Sensabaugh, *Milton in Early America* (Princeton: Princeton University Press, 1964); K. P. Van Anglen, *The New England Milton: Literary Reception and Cultural Authority in the Early Republic* (University Park, PA: University of Pennsylvania Press, 1992); and John Mulryan, *"Through a Glass Darkly": Milton's Reinvention of the Mythological Tradition* (Pittsburgh: Duquense University Press, 1996).

[5] See Russell, pp. 78–79 and Winship, p. 128.

[6] An important study which makes a similar claim about the transformation of attitudes toward witchcraft in England between 1650 and 1750 has recently been published. See Ian Bostridge, *Witchcraft and Its Transformations c.1650–c.1750* (Oxford: Clarendon Press, 1997). Bostridge emphasizes the ecclesio-political situation as decisive in the transformation. With regard to Edwards (and perhaps even the English thinkers of Bostridge's study), Lockean epistemology cannot be ignored as an influence.

[7] *Faithful Narrative, Works* (Yale), 4:206–207. Edwards' words "as if" should not be missed. Edwards is not claiming that Satan actually *spoke* to Hawley, but that Satan made it *seem* as though *someone* had. For Edwards, this is characteristic both of Satan's subtlety and his cruelty in making impressions on the human imagination, explored below.

[8] Granted, Patricia Tracy has drawn attention to the possibility that Edwards adjusted the chronology of events in his *Faithful Narrative* to make the Hawley suicide the turning point in the revival. See Patricia Tracy, *Jonathan Edwards, Pastor: Religion and Society in Eighteenth-Century Northampton* (New York: Hill and Wang, 1980), 116–117.

[9] Richard Godbeer emphasizes this flexibility in his summary of Puritan sermonic literature generally between about 1640 and 1700. See his *The Devil's Dominion: Magic and Religion in Early New England* (New York: Cambridge University Press, 1992), 87.

[10] In "Miscellany 936," Edwards ticks off a list of all the names for Satan that he has found in the Scripture, "which are never found in the plural number." Most of the ones listed, however, are rarely used elsewhere in his writings. The names for Satan listed above are the ones that Edwards regularly uses as synonyms for "Satan." See *The Works of Jonathan Edwards,* vol. 2, (Carlisle, PA: Banner of Truth Trust, 1976), 608. After this initial citation, all references to the Banner of Truth Edition will be given as *Works* (BT), followed by a volume and page number.

[11] In this instance, Edwards seems to part company with his Puritan forbears, whose vocabulary for human recruits of Satan is much more picturesque. See Godbeer, p. 88.

[12] Sensabaugh alludes to Milton's influence on Edwards by saying simply that the latter "thought highly" of the former. Edwards apparently spoke in some place about the "inimitable excellencies" of Milton's work, but Sensabaugh provides no reference. Sensabaugh presents more evidence for Milton's influence on two people close to Edwards: Benjamin Colman and Joseph Bellamy. See Sensabaugh, pp. 43–52, esp. p. 49.

[13] "Miscellany 438," *Works* (Yale), 13:487.
[14] "Miscellany 320," *Works* (Yale), 13:401.
[15] "Miscellany 320," *Works* (Yale), 13:401.
[16] "Miscellany 438," *Works* (Yale), 12:487.
[17] "Miscellany 320," *Works* (Yale), 13:401.
[18] "Miscellany 833," *Works* (BT), 2:608.
[19] "Miscellany 438," *Works* (Yale), 13:487.
[20] "Miscellany 1261," *Works* (BT), 2:611.
[21] "Miscellany 290," *Works* (Yale), 13:382–383.
[22] In "Miscellany 1057," Edwards mentions specifically Charles Owen (d. 1746) and John Glas (1695–1773). And, in "Miscellany 1261," Edwards mentions Girolami Zanchi (1516–1590), whom he accounts as "one of the best protestant writers" and Fransisco de Suarez (1548–1617), "the best of the schoolmen." Finally, in "Miscellany 1266," Edwards mentions Thomas Goodwin (1600–1680) in support of his position. See *Works* (BT), 2:611. It is interesting to note the homiletical use that Edwards made of this theme of demonic pride. For example, in his treatise *Some Thoughts*, Edwards argued that spiritual pride is the main door through which Satan has access to the hearts of the religious. In fact, pride is the sin that makes human beings most like Satan, that is, makes them devils. See *Works* (Yale), 4:414–417. Occasionally, Edwards makes polemical use of the same theme. For example, in "Miscellany 340," the same pride that caused the apostasy of Satan also prevented the pope (the "antichrist") and the Roman curia from being true servants of God. See *Works* (Yale), 13:415.
[23] "Miscellany 936," *Works* (BT), 2:608.
[24] "Miscellany 936," *Works* (BT), 609.
[25] "Miscellany 320," *Works* (Yale), 13:402. The double entendre of Edwards' word "conceived" is intriguing. Satan's rebellion is a conception both in the intellectual sense and in the sense that rebellion is the "offspring" of Satan.
[26] "Miscellany 936," *Works* (BT), 2:610.
[27] "Miscellany 1261," *Works* (BT), 2:611.
[28] "Miscellany 258," *Works* (Yale), 13:366.
[29] "Miscellany 258," *Works* (Yale), 13:367.
[30] "Miscellany 936," *Works* (BT), 2:610.
[31] Edwards develops this theme at length in a lecture-sermon entitled "Christ Exalted: Jesus Christ Gloriously Exalted Above All Evil in the Work of Redemption." See Works (BT), 2:213–217.
[32] Edwards' notion of the eschatological fate of the damned cannot be pursued at length here. But it is worth noting that, in reference to Satan's endless misery in hell, Edwards makes the following supposition: "As the devil's ministers, servants, and instruments, of the angelic nature, those who are called the devil's angels, shall have their part with him; for the like reason we may suppose, his servants and instruments of the human nature, will also share with him." See "Miscellaneous Remarks," chap. 2, par. 28 in *Works* (BT), 2:523. Yet, Edwards argues that there is a qualitative difference between Satan and the damned which should not be missed. Although wicked men are the children of the devil, the devil 1) is proportionally more wicked; 2) has a greater habit of sin; and most importantly, 3) is not subject to restraining grace as wicked men often are. See "Miscellany 433," *Works* (Yale), 13:482, n. 2.
[33] "Miscellany 435," *Works* (Yale), 13:483–484.
[34] "Sinners in the Hands of an Angry God," in Harry S. Stout, et al., ed., *A Jonathan Edwards Reader* (New Haven: Yale University Press, 1995), 95.
[35] "Miscellany 298," *Works* (Yale), 13:385–386. This theme of providential irony is explored in some length below.

[36] The Ezekiel passage speaks of the king of Tyre as an anointed cherub. Because Edwards understands the king of Tyre as a "type of devil," he concludes that prelapsarian Satan was the Messiah, or Christ, as he was anointed. See "Miscellany 936," *Works* (BT), 2:608–609.

[37] Edwards frequently alludes to the contrast between Satan's pride and Christ's humility as if the latter recapitulated the former. See, for example, "Miscellany 941," *Works* (BT), 2:606.

[38] "Miscellany 279," in Harry S. Stout, ed., *A Jonathan Edwards Reader*, 42. In two treatises published posthumously, Edwards develops a related theme: the conviction that the "torments of the wicked in hell" will not be an "occasion for grief to the saints in heaven." Rather, the saints in heaven will rejoice at the justice, power, and majesty of God, while praising him for the grace and love that God bestows upon them. See "The End of the Wicked Contemplated by the Righteous," *Works* (BT), 2:207–212.

[39] "Miscellany 296," *Works* (Yale), 13:385.

[40] "Images of Divine Things, no. 107," *Works* (Yale), 11:107.

[41] "Miscellany 232," *Works* (Yale), 13:350. Edwards' theology of hell deserves far more attention than it can be given here. But the references provided are sufficient to give the reader a basic impression of how hell functions in the punishment of Satan and the fallen angels.

[42] *Works* (Yale), 2:288.

[43] In a bewildering passage, Edwards attempts to make this clear relative to his fourth of the distinguishing signs of gracious affections. And, as editor John Smith notes, in his ideas about the imagination Edwards relied heavily on Anthony Burgess (d. 1664). See *Works* (Yale), 2:288–289.

[44] *Works* (Yale), 2:287–288.

[45] *Works* (Yale), 2:289.

[46] *Works* (Yale), 2:86.

[47] Discerning counterfeit religion from the true is unquestionably the central theme of Edwards' Awakening apologetics and deserves far more attention than it can be given in this study. In assessing the person and work of Satan in Edwards' theology, we must confine our attention to descriptions of so-called counterfeit religion where Satan and his work figure prominently according to Edwards.

[48] *Works* (Yale), 2:286–287.

[49] *Works* (Yale), 4:432. See Carter Lindberg, *The European Reformations* (Oxford: Blackwell, 1996), 143–158 for an excellent, succinct narrative of Munzter's personal religious experience and his leadership of the Christian community at Munster.

[50] "Miscellany 17," *Works* (Yale), 13:209. Edwards' appeal to "conscience" and "liberty" in religious belief, not to mention the broader theme of anti-creedalism, sounds amazingly like the rhetoric that would emerge in the so-called Second Great Awakening. See Nathan Hatch, *The Democratization of American Christianity* (New Haven: Yale, 1989), esp. chap. 2.

[51] *Works* (Yale), 2:309.

[52] "Images of Divine Things, no. 177," *Works* (Yale), 11:118.

[53] Ibid.

[54] *Works* (Yale), 9:411.

[55] *Works* (Yale), 9:412–414.

[56] *Works* (Yale), 2:88. Though he mentions no one by name, Edwards undoubtedly has in mind James Davenport (1716–1757), New England's most infamous enthusiast of the Great Awakening Era. For a succinct account of his bizarre activities, see Sydney Ahlstrom, *A Religious History of the American People* (New Haven: Yale, 1972), 285–286. See also Winthrop Hudson and John Corrigan, *Religion in America*, 5th ed. (New York: Macmillan, 1987), 74.

[57] *Works* (Yale), 2:88.

[58] *Works* (Yale), 2:144–145.

[59] *Works* (Yale), 2:146.
[60] *Works* (Yale), 2:158–159.
[61] The anti-revival, anti-affection faction in New England was led by Charles Chauncy (1705–1787). Chauncy's *Seasonable Thoughts on the State of Religion in New England* (1743) is a point-by-point refutation of Edwards' *Some Thoughts* (1742). Chauncy denounced revivalism and experiential religion as a resurgence of antinomianism. See Ahlstrom, pp. 302–303, and Corrigan and Hudson, pp. 74–75.
[62] *Works* (Yale), 2:120.
[63] *Works* (Yale), 2:120.
[64] *Works* (Yale), 2:121.
[65] In answering Dr. Taylor's contention that Adam could not sin without a sinful inclination, Edwards comes close to mentioning Satan, but in a footnote, he says that Taylor is right, but that the sinful inclination was "begotten in him by the delusion and error he was led into . . ." See *Works* (Yale), 3:228–229, n. 6.
[66] "Christ Exalted," *Works* (BT), 2:213.
[67] *Works* (Yale), 9:500.
[68] Edwards apparently struggled with the relationship between his convictions about moral agency and those about Satan's work in the world. It is interesting to note that passages in which Edwards contemplates free will and moral agency in the Fall of Adam and Eve, mention of Satan is noticeably absent. See, e.g., Miscellanies 291, 501, and 436 in *Works* (Yale), vol. 13. Godbeer suggests that the ambiguity of Puritan teaching on the "allocation of responsibility for human sin" inadvertently encouraged some to rely on "rival supernatural agency," i.e., magic and witchcraft. See Godbeer, p. 85. Edwards may forcefully state his position on the moral agency of postlapsarian humanity, but he appears no closer than his Puritan forbears to answering the question of human moral agency and Satan's work in the initial Fall of humanity.
[69] "Miscellany 344," *Works* (Yale), 13:417.
[70] *Works* (Yale), 13:123.
[71] "Some Wonderful Circumstances of the Overthrow of Satan," *Works* (BT), 2:152.
[72] "The Wisdom of God Displayed in the way of Salvation," *Works* (BT), 2:152.
[73] Edwards develops this point at length in "Miscellany 158." His point can be illustrated almost mathematically: if lapsarian misery > redemptive happiness, then Satan is not defeated; if lapsarian misery = redemptive happiness, Satan is frustrated in part; if lapsarian misery < redemptive happiness, then Satan is "wholly disappointed of all his aim." Of course, Edwards favors this last formula. See *Works* (Yale), 13:308.
[74] "Miscellany 344," *Works* (Yale), 13:417. This motif of the *felix culpa,* which finds artistic expression in Milton's poetry, finds theological articulation in Edwards.
[75] "Miscellany 307," *Works* (Yale), 13:391–392.
[76] *Works* (Yale), 9:390–392.

Jonathan Edwards' Trinitarian Theology in the Context of the Early-Enlightenment Deist Controversy

Steve Studebaker

Contemporary trinitarian theologians have increasingly turned to Jonathan Edwards' (1703–1758) Trinitarianism as a resource for constructing social models of the Trinity. Included in this appropriation is the judgment that the social elements of his trinitarian thought result from his reaction to and rejection of the emphasis on divine oneness and simplicity in the Western, Reformed, and Puritan trinitarian traditions.[1] Although the early-Enlightenment trinitarian controversies are not ignored they are not taken as the decisive factors that shaped his Trinitarianism.[2] Yet when read in its context, Edwards' trinitarian theology bears important similarities with that of those who sought to defend the traditional doctrine amidst its early-Enlightenment critics. The common features among Edwards' trinitarian theology and that of other traditional trinitarians suggest that these controversies were not incidental, but central to his trinitarian writings.

The trinitarian controversies took place on several fronts and involved various personages. On the most basic level, the orthodox debates were with the non-trinitarians and other trinitarians. The former group included Deists and Socinians—also called Unitarians—and Arians. In this respect, the trinitarian controversy was part of the larger Deist controversy. The trinitarian controversies also included debates that ranged among theologians who accepted the validity of the doctrine of the Trinity but disagreed on the proper explanation of the traditional doctrine so as to avoid the pitfalls of tritheism and Sabellianism.[3] For example, Athanasian trinitarians Robert South (1634–1716) and William Sherlock

(1641?–1707) disputed over the proper theological formulation of the Trinity, yet they fought in common cause against the Socinians—i.e., Sabellians, Arians, and Semi-Arians.[4]

Here I specifically focus on Edwards' response to Deist criticisms that relate to the Trinity. I highlight two of his apologetic strategies for the Trinity, both of which endeavor to give a rational foundation for the doctrine. On the one hand, he defended the Trinity against the Deists by rationally arguing that the goodness of God necessarily implies a trinitarian God and negates the monist God of Deism. On the other hand, he used the *prisca theologia* to demonstrate the presence of the doctrine of the Trinity in non-Christian religions and thereby to show that the Trinity is not a specious doctrine of mystery and revelation. When Edwards' apologetics for the Trinity are placed in their historical-theological context, it can be seen that he did not formulate his trinitarian theology to correct an emphasis on divine unity in Western, Reformed scholastic, and Reformed Puritan Trinitarianism, but that he penned his trinitarian theology as a conscious participant in what scholars of the early-Enlightenment call the Trinitarian Controversy and the critique of Deism.

The Apologetic Context of Edwards' Trinitarianism

Deism and the Scandal of Particularity

In Miscellany 96, Edwards wrote "it appears that there must be more than a unity in infinite and eternal essence, otherwise the goodness of God can have no perfect exercise."[5] Edwards proceeds to argue that only the trinitarian concept of God fulfills the requisite for the divine communication or exercise of goodness. What is the historical-theological context for this claim? Why does he make this argument? Who are the unidentified opponents? In other words, why does Edwards defend the goodness of God by way of trinitarian argument? I maintain that his reference to the goodness of God to defend the Trinity presupposes a critical polemic. The polemical opponents behind this miscellany are Deists who criticized of the traditional Christian theory of soteriological exclusivism. Miscellany 96 is a continuation of the argument of Miscellany 94 where Edwards declared, "it is within the reach of naked reason to perceive certainly that there are three distinct in God."[6] Miscellany 94 illustrates the reasonableness of the Trinity with the mental analogy of mind, idea, and love. Miscellany 96 further demonstrates the reasonableness of the Trinity by arguing for its necessity from the rational principle of God's goodness. However, before detailing Edwards' defense of the rationality of the Trinity, I briefly reconstruct the Deist criticisms of traditional Christian theology that render Edwards' comments apposite.

A central Deist criticism of the traditional Christian view of God and Christian doctrines can be described as the *scandal of particularity*.[7] Particularity refers to the teaching that salvation is dependent on explicit faith in and devotion to Christ. The *scandal* is that the majority of human beings throughout history, through no fault of their own, were without sufficient means of redemption because they possessed no knowledge of Christ. The limitation of the means of salvation to a relatively brief period of the world's history and to a relatively small number of people seemed contrary to the goodness of God. Aside from the intuitive immorality of soteriological particularism, reports in the travel literature of the period revealed that many of the cultures outside of Christendom were not the domains of a supposed barbarism but sophisticated and virtuous cultures; the Chinese were a favorite example among Deists.[8] According to the Deists, the virtuousness of these non-Christian cultures seriously questioned the necessity of Christian revelation for the present and future life.[9]

At root, the scandal of particularity is a charge that the traditional Christian teaching that Christ is the exclusive savior is unjust. The charge of injustice rests on the moral principle that a person is culpable only for that which he/she can or cannot perform.[10] Applied to religion, this principle means that those without access to knowledge of Christ cannot be condemned for not living in devotion to him because they have no means to do so. Put positively, justice demands that the means of salvation are equally and universally available to all people in all times.[11]

The scandal of particularity included the two interrelated issues of revelation or the necessity of revealed religion for salvation and predestination. From the Deist standpoint, both of these notions implied a capricious deity because people are arbitrarily consigned to either salvation or perdition. The necessity of revelation implied arbitrariness because a very low percentage of people in the history of the world received it by accident of birthplace. Prior to Christ, revelation was restricted to the Jewish people. After Christ, revealed religion was largely confined to the Mediterranean and Europe.[12] In light of its limited reach, Charles Blount (1654–1693) concluded that revelation is unnecessary. In contrast, he argued that God gave all people reason, as a universal constitutive component of human nature, to discern the dictates of natural religion.[13] Thus for the Deists, if revealed religion is necessary for salvation, God knowingly and willingly left the vast majority of human beings without the necessary means to attain salvation. Deists insisted that such a notion controverts the goodness and mercy of God.[14]

Predestination impugned the goodness of God because it teaches that God determines the eternal fate of individuals without any reference to their moral behavior. The criticism that predestination is immoral was not new with the Deists. Arminius (1560–1609), in the early-seventeenth century, and the Cambridge Platonists, in the mid- to late-seventeenth century, expressed moral umbrage toward the Reformed version of this doctrine.[15] Lord Herbert of Cherbury (1583–1648), the father of English Deism, voiced the problematic with revelation and predestination:

> How could I believe that a just God could take pleasure in the eternal punishment of those to whom he had never afforded a method of

salvation, and whom he necessarily foresaw as being damned absolutely, with no possibility of escape? I could not understand that people could call that God Greatest and Best who had created men only to condemn them without their knowledge and against their will.[16]

For Herbert and other Deists, the necessity of revelation for salvation and eternal predestination to salvation or condemnation are immoral and undermine the justice and goodness of God.[17] In light of the scandal of particularity, Edwards turned to the Trinity to defend the goodness of the God of traditional Reformed theology and to argue that the Deist concept of God contradicts the rational concept of the goodness of God.

The Trinity and the Goodness of God: A Trinitarian Apologetic

For Edwards, the doctrine of the Trinity provided an indirect response to the Deist charge that the traditional God and doctrines of Christianity were immoral. It is indirect because rather than deal directly with the scandal of particularity, Edwards countered with an attack on the God of Deism. He argued that the Deist God could not meet the requirements of infinite goodness and that only the Christian trinitarian God meets these conditions.

The foundation of his criticism of the God of Deism and defense of the Trinity is his theory of the communicative nature of goodness. Edwards believed that goodness requires the communication of happiness to another.[18] The communication of happiness that constitutes goodness is love. Since God is infinite, God's communication of happiness or love must be infinite. An infinite communication of happiness requires an object of infinite goodness; otherwise, the object is not commensurate with the quality of the communication. Only God is infinitely able to communicate happiness and provide an infinite object suitable for an infinite communication of happiness.[19] Edwards concluded, therefore, that the communicative nature of goodness requires a plurality within the Godhead.[20]

Edwards maintained that God conceived as a solitary infinite mind cannot meet the criterion of infinite goodness because it does not allow for the genuine communication of goodness or love. The monad simply delights in itself. The monad, as the object of love, does not personally receive and return love, as a person receives and returns love from and to another person. Communication requires at least two giving and receiving subjects. In the Godhead, the subjects must be two infinite subjects giving and receiving love.[21] However, if God is a solitary monad, a genuine communication is impossible because the object of the communication of love—i.e., the Unitarian/Deist God—is not a subject communicating love to another person. The object of love is *personally* identical with the communicator of love.[22] This form of love is enclosed and oriented to the self and not to another. The self-love of the Deist God is selfish and, therefore, not good.

In contrast, Edwards' theology of the Trinity portrays a genuine communication of love between two infinite subjectivities. He used the Augustinian mutual love model to articulate the trinitarian communication of love. The Father and the Son infinitely and mutually love each other. The trinitarian God is truly good by virtue of this mutual love that meets the requirement of the communicative nature of goodness.[23] Furthermore, his apologetic indicates that the fulcrum of the debate between Deists and Reformed theologians was over their relative conceptions of the goodness of God.[24] The Deists charged that the God of Reformed theology was immoral. Edwards did not respond directly by giving an account of how and why the necessity of revelation and predestination is consistent with God's goodness but rather skirted the issue and argued that the Deist notion of God is inconsistent with a rational theory of divine goodness.

Significant regarding Edwards' argument and its historical context is that he did not begin with Scripture and revealed religion, but with reason and natural religion to demonstrate the doctrine of the Trinity. He argued from the commonly accepted principle of the goodness of God. He showed that the Trinity is not an obtuse product of metaphysical flights of fancy or an inscrutable mystery but the necessary postulate for belief in the goodness of God that can be demonstrated on the very terms of the rational religion of the early Enlightenment—reason.[25]

In addition, Edwards shared this strategy of criticizing the Deists with Andrew Michael Ramsay (1686–1743).[26] Edwards wrote Miscellany 96, in which he outlined his argument that the goodness of God requires a plurality within the Godhead, between January and February of 1724.[27] Twenty-six years later, when he read excerpts from Ramsay's *The Philosophical Principles of Natural and Revealed Religion* (1748–1749) in the March 1751 issue of the *Monthly Review*, his delight must have been great, for he discovered that Ramsay employed a very similar trinitarian strategy to refute the Deist concept of God and defend the trinitarian notion.[28]

The parallels between Edwards' and Ramsay's formulations of the Trinity and trinitarian apologetic against the Deist concept of God are striking.[29] Like Edwards, Ramsay argued that the God of Deism does not meet the criterion of moral goodness. In contrast, the Christian doctrine of the Trinity allows for divine goodness because it accommodates the communicative nature of goodness. Infinite goodness requires the infinite exercise of love to an object worthy of infinite love. Only the divine nature is worthy of an infinite act of love. Moreover, since love is communicative, the immanent love of the Godhead must be between two persons giving and receiving love to one another. Also like Edwards, Ramsay portrays the Father as the divine mind conceiving and the Son as the idea conceived. The Father and Son, therefore, are two subjects that infinitely love each other. The personal identity of the Holy Spirit is the mutual love of the Father and the Son.[30]

No source connection can be drawn in either direction between Edwards and Ramsay. Ramsay's writings did not influence Edwards' basic trinitarian concepts because Edwards wrote Miscellanies 96 and 94 between January and February of 1724, which was twenty-four years prior to the publication of Ramsay's *The Philosophical Principles of Natural and Revealed Religion* (1748–49).[31] Ramsay could not have relied on Edwards because Edwards' trinitarian writings and miscellanies on the Trinity were not published during Edwards' or Ramsay's lifetimes. The similarity between their terms and concepts suggests that they both tapped a common vein of polemical interaction with Deism. However, in my readings of early-Enlightenment trinitarian texts, I have not discovered this argumentation outside of Ramsay and Edwards.

Edwards, the Trinity, and the *"Prisca Theologia":* An Apology for the Trinity
Edwards also participated in countering the Deist criticism that the revealed doctrine of the Trinity is irrational and, therefore, inconsistent with rational natural religion. Natural religion is the belief that the source of religious belief and practice is reason and not revelation. It also tends toward practical moral principles and avoids metaphysical constructions.[32] Concomitant with the Deist emphasis on reason in natural religion was their rejection of theological mystery. Deists discarded doctrines such as the Trinity and the Incarnation as hopeless contradictions to the rational religion of nature and of little use to a person's practical religious-moral life.[33] Along with mystery, they rejected the necessity of revelation, which they generally saw as the source of theological mysteries. They believed that God created all human beings with a rational capacity to deduce the necessary principles of religion. Revelation was superfluous. Moreover, the insistence by the orthodox on the necessity of revelation again raised the scandal of particularity. As Blount reasoned, what is necessary for eternal life must be universally given, and since revelation is not universally given, it is not necessary for the religious life.[34] Travel literature, bringing stories of the moral virtue of non-Christian cultures, seemed to support the Deist claim that revelation was unnecessary for the religious life.

However, traditional Christians did not stand idle as the Deists penned their invective against revelation and its doctrines.

The Trinity and the *"Prisca Theologia"*

Christian scholars from the Patristic era through the Renaissance and the early-Modern period used the *prisca theologia*—i.e., ancient theology—to account for the similarities between Christian theology and the philosophical and theological ideas of classical antiquity.[35] In mid-seventeenth century England, Cambridge Platonists, such as Henry More, Joseph Glanvill, and Ralph Cudworth, employed the *prisca theologia* to counter the scandal of particularity. They used the ancient theology to show that Christian doctrines were revealed to the ancient philosophers and thus were not confined to the environs of western Europe.[36] For example, while Ralph Cudworth traced the origin of idolatry to the Egyptians, he also argued that they possessed a deposit of true religion.[37] He taught that the doctrine of the Trinity was included among this original "theology of divine tradition or revelation" given to the Egyptians by Moses and by them passed on to thinkers like Orpheus, Pythagoras, and Plato.[38]

Early-Enlightenment Christian apologists used the *prisca theologia* to counter Deists' claims that natural religion was the product of reason alone, that natural religion obviates the necessity of revelation, and that doctrines such as the Trinity, Incarnation, and mediatory work of Christ were unnecessary obscurities. Contrary to the Deists, they argued that the principles of natural religion are not natural at all, but derive from the original deposit of revelation—i.e., *prisca theologia*—given to ancient cultures. According to *prisca theologia*, all ancient cultures were recipients of revelation. The common moral teachings and theological ideas found in the world religions are the vestiges of an original deposit of revelation. Defenders of traditional Christianity most often attributed the source of this original revelation to the ancient philosophers' communication with Moses and the ancient Israelites in Egypt, Noah's sons Shem and Japheth, or to one of the antediluvian figures such as Enoch and Adam.[39] Christian advocates of the *prisca theologia* taught that the theological and religious divergences from Christianity in the non-Christian cultures were the result of a tendency toward religious degeneration.[40] Thus, the *prisca theologia* was an apologetic to the Deist claim that revelation is superfluous. Rather than unnecessary, revelation was the primeval source of the so-called natural religion.[41]

Edwards and the *"Prisca Theologia"*

In concert with early-Enlightenment apologists for revelation, Edwards adopted the *prisca theologia* to counter the Deist claim that revelation is needless for piety.[42] His use of the prisca *theologia* is largely confined to the miscellanies. Additionally, many of these are transcriptions from other texts with little of his comment as to their utility. The task then is to determine why he made these transcriptions. I suggest that they provide insight into the current of thought that Edwards found a convincing retort to Deist arguments against the necessity of revelation. Gerald R. McDermott points out that the sources that Edwards used for his understanding of many of these ancient religious thinkers were errant.[43] Nevertheless, these miscellanies reveal that Edwards proactively engaged a leading criticism of Deism using, what was in his time, the latest intellectual resources.

Edwards used the *prisca theologia* for three apologetic tasks. The first two relate to defending the notion of revelation against the Deist view of natural religion. Based on the *prisca theologia*, Edwards argued the ancient philosophers such as Aristotle, Plato, and Cicero acknowledged the necessity of revelation.[44] His transcriptions and notes on the *prisca theologia* document the presence and source of the teachings of natural and revealed religion in non-Christian religious traditions. He often cited doctrines in non-Christian religions that were typically categorized by Deists under natural religion. These included the unity of God, immortality of the soul, future rewards and punishment, moral conscience, and the Noahic deluge.[45] His transcriptions show traditional revealed doctrines present in non-Christian traditions, namely, the Trinity, the necessity of a messiah and mediator, original sin, an Edenic paradise, and eschatological judgment.[46]

The presence of teachings in non-Christian religions typically attributed to revelation and mysteries in Christianity suggests the universality of revelation. These common religious teachings were vestiges of an ancient religious tradition imbedded in the cultures of the world. This ancient tradition derived from contact with Noah, Moses, or the ancient Israelites.[47] Edwards credits much of the learning of Aristotle, Plato, Plutarch, and Porphyry to contact with the ancient Israelites.[48] The important point is that Edwards attributed the presence of these religious notions in non-Christian religious traditions to an original revelation given to these peoples or to contact with someone in the lineage of the ancient Israelites who transmitted revealed religion to them. Moreover, these echoes of Christian mysteries in the ancient philosophers contradicted the Deists' claims that doctrinal mysteries and revelation are irrational. For instance, if the revered Greek philosopher Plato taught the concept of a mediator between God and human beings, then it is certainly not irrational for Christians to teach that Christ is the mediator.[49]

Finally, Edwards drew on the *prisca theologia* to defend the doctrine of the Trinity. He transcribed several citations in the *Miscellanies* that show the presence of trinitarian ideas in non-Christian religions.[50] His transcriptions focus on remnants of the Trinity in Greek and Chinese thought. According to the writers on which he relied and the passages he quoted from these sources, ancient Greek thought contained ideas commensurate with the Christian theology of the Father, the Son, and the Holy Spirit.[51] In Edwards' theological traditions, the Father is the first person of the Godhead and as such is self-subsistent, the divine person who is not from another divine person. Similarly, Greek thinkers discussed the first principle that is self-existent. The first principle—common in Edwards' trinitarian traditions—is the infinite power and supreme cause of all things. Theologians also described the Son as eternally begotten from the Father by an intellectual act of the divine understanding. So, the Son is the image, Word, or idea of the Father. The Greeks posited a second hypostasis in the divinity begotten from the first. They described the second hypostasis in terms of the idea, word, reason (Logos), and exemplar of the first divine principle. Christian theologians represented the Holy Spirit as the Godhead's immanent act of love; the Augustinian depiction of the Spirit as the mutual love of the Father and the Son was especially common. The Greeks similarly described the third divine principle as love and the active power of the deity.[52] On several occasions, Edwards cites the Greek practice of referring to the divine triad as the "Father, the Word or Mind, and the Universal Spirit or Soul."[53] These citations indicate that Edwards found strong echoes of the mutual love model of the Trinity in the teachings of the Greeks.

In Miscellany 1181, Edwards copied a section from Ramsay's *Philosophical Principles of Natural and Revealed Religion* that depicts trinitarian notions in ancient Chinese religious thought.[54] According to the Chinese sacred texts, collectively titled King, and its commentators, God is triune. The triunity of the Chinese deity rests on the distinct names and commensurate characteristics that they applied to God.[55] First, God is named *Chang-Ti*.[56] Chang-Ti refers to God as self-existent, simple, omnipresent, and the source of all motion and action. The attributes of Chang-Ti correspond with the Christian notion of the Father. Second, God is called *Tao*. Tao signifies eternal reason, truth, and law. Like Chang-Ti, Tao is omnipresent and infinite. The description of Tao in terms of reason and truth invites association with the Christian doctrine of the Son. Although the transcription does not identify a correlate for the Holy Spirit in the books of *King,* it does note that the book *Tonchu* teaches that the oneness that produces all else is in fact a triunity. The "self-existent unity produces necessarily a second; the first and second by their union produce a third; in fine, these three produce all."[57] Moreover, the philosopher Laotsee speaks of God in trinitarian language. He calls the self-existent source of all being *Hi*. The source of all knowledge is called *Yi*. The omnipresence of the deity that animates all life is *Ouel*. Liyong, a Chinese commentator, says that Hi, Yi, and Ouel are a triplicity that is one. The correspondence that Ramsay drew, and presumably also Edwards, between the Chinese teachings and the Christian doctrine of the Trinity is clear. Hi corresponds with the Father, Yi with the Son, and Ouel with the Holy Spirit.[58] Recalling Edwards' Augustinian mutual love model of the Trinity, it is easy to suppose that he saw instant rapport between his trinitarian model and the notions of the Chinese as presented by Ramsay.

Although Edwards did not fully develop an apologetic use of the *prisca theologia*, I conclude on the basis of these transcriptions and positive uses of the *prisca theologia* in other areas that it incipiently played an important role in his emerging defense of the Trinity.[59] The Deists routinely ridiculed the Trinity as irrational because it derives from revelation and not from natural religion.[60] Edwards' transcriptions of trinitarian teachings in Greek and Chinese religious and philosophical literature suggest that he saw these as an antidote to Deist criticisms. I interpret the transcriptions of the *prisca theologia* that show affinity between the Christian doctrine of the Trinity and ancient Greek and Chinese religious thought as part of Edwards' broader polemic against the Deists such as his other anti-Deist writings contained in the *Miscellanies* and more familiar texts written to defend the Calvinist doctrines of freedom of the will and original sin.[61]

Conclusion

Edwards' trinitarian writings reflect a robust interaction with the polemical issues over the Trinity in the early-Enlightenment Deist controversy on two levels. Based on the rational principle of the goodness of God, Edwards argued that God must be triune. The monad of Deism is inconsistent with rational religion, whereas the Christian doctrine of the Trinity is consistent with the rational notion of divine goodness because the community of three divine persons allows for the infinite communication of love necessary for infinite goodness. Edwards also utilized the common apologetic method of the *prisca theologia* to defend the rationality of revelation and the Trinity. The presence of trinitarian notions in non-Christian religious traditions supported the universal distribution of revelation in general and the reasonableness of the doctrine of the Trinity in particular. Thus, the triune God of Christianity is just because it is universally revealed and reasonable because it is universally recognized as triune. Finally, in regard to the idea that Edwards was an incipient social trinitarian, Edwards used the Augustinian mutual love model in both of his polemical interactions with the Deists. This is problematic for the view that presents Edwards as a proto-social trinitarian reacting against the alleged overemphasis on divine unity in the Western trinitarian tradition. It is so because few if any social trinitarians consider the Augustinian mutual love model a social model of the Trinity.

STEVEN M. STUDEBAKER earned the B.A. from Northwest College (Kirkland, Wash.); the M.A. from Trinity Evangelical Divinity School (Deerfield, Ill.); and the Ph.D. from Marquette University (Milwaukee, Wisc.). He is assistant professor of systematic and historical theology in McMaster Divinity College at McMaster University (Hamilton, Ontario). His publications include studies of Edwards, Pentecostalism, and ecumenicism.

NOTES

[1] Amy Plantinga Pauw's work is the most significant of these interpreters: see her "'Heaven is a World of Love': Edwards on Heaven and the Trinity," *Calvin Theological Journal* 30 (1995): 392–401; "The Future of Reformed Theology: Some Lessons from Jonathan Edwards," in *Toward the Future of Reformed Theology: Tasks, Topics, Traditions*, ed. David Willis and Michael Welker (Grand Rapids: Eerdmans, 1999), 456–69; *"The Supreme Harmony of All": The Trinitarian Theology of Jonathan Edwards* (Grand Rapids: Eerdmans, 2002); and "The Supreme Harmony of All: Jonathan Edwards and the Trinity" (Ph.D. diss., Yale University, 1990).

Building on Plantinga Pauw's work, William J. Danaher Jr. also argues that Edwards used the social model of the Trinity to complement the psychological analogy. Danaher's is perhaps the most nuanced interpretation of Edwards' "social" model vis-à-vis its relationship to the Western trinitarian traditions; see *The Trinitarian Ethics of Jonathan Edwards*, Columbia Series in Reformed Theology (Louisville: Westminster John Knox, 2004), 69–94.

Also see, Steven H. Daniel, "Postmodern Concepts of God and Edwards' Trinitarian Ontology," in *Edwards in Our Time: Jonathan Edwards and the Shaping of American Religion*, ed. Sang Hyun Lee and Allen C. Guelzo (Grand Rapids: Eerdmans, 1999), 49 and 54; Michael Jinkins, "'The Being of Beings': Jonathan Edwards' Understanding of God as Reflected in His Final Treatises," *Scottish Journal of Theology* 46 (1993): 181–83; Krister Sairsingh, "Jonathan Edwards and the Idea of Divine Glory: His Foundational Trinitarianism and Its Ecclesial Import" (Ph.D. diss., Harvard University, 1986), 69–73 and 144–51; and Rachel S. Stahle, "The Trinitarian Spirit of Jonathan Edwards' Theology" (Ph.D. diss., Boston University, 1999).

[2] E.g., Plantinga Pauw, *The Supreme Harmony of All*, 22–32.

[3] Modern literature on the early-Enlightenment trinitarian controversies includes William S. Babcock, "A Changing of the Christian God: The Doctrine of the Trinity in the Seventeenth Century," *Interpretation* 45 (1991): 133–46; Robert T. Carroll, *The Common Sense Philosophy of Religion of Bishop Edward Stillingfleet, 1635–1699*, International Archives of the History of Ideas 77 (The Hague: Martinus Nijhoff, 1975), 86–101; James P. Ferguson, *An Eighteenth Century Heretic: Dr. Samuel Clarke* (Kineton: Roundwood, 1976); and Martin Greig, "The Reasonableness of Christianity? Gilbert Burnet and the Trinitarian Controversy of the 1690s," *Journal of Ecclesiastical History* 44 (1993): 631–51.

Also see, Robert T. Holtby, *Daniel Waterland 1683–1740: A Study in Eighteenth-Century Orthodoxy* (Carlisle: Charles Thurman and Sons, 1966), 12–49; John Marshall, "Locke, Socinianism, 'Socinianism,' and Unitarianism," in *English Philosophy in the Age of Locke*, ed. M. A. Stewart, Oxford Studies in the History of Philosophy 3 (Oxford: Clarendon, 2000), 111–82; and Thomas C. Pfizenmaier, *The Trinitarian Theology of Dr. Samuel Clarke (1675–1729): Context, Sources, and Controversy*, Studies in the History of Christian Thought 75, ed. Heiko O. Oberman (New York: Brill, 1997).

Additionally, see John Redwood, *Reason, Ridicule and Religion: The Age of Enlightenment in England, 1660–1750* (Cambridge: Harvard University Press, 1976), 156–72; G. A. J. Rogers, *Locke's Enlightenment: Aspects of the Origin, Nature, and Impact of his Philosophy*, Europaea Memoria: Studien und Texte zur Geschichte der europäischen Ideen 3 (New York: Georg Olms, 1998), 143–56; Udo Thiel, "The Trinity and Human Personal Identity," in *English Philosophy in the Age of Locke*, ed. M. A. Stewart, Oxford Studies in the History of Philosophy 3 (Oxford: Clarendon, 2000), 217–43; Gary Wedeking, "Locke on Personal Identity and the Trinity Controversy of the 1690s," *Dialogue* 29 (1990): 163–88; and Maurice Wiles, *Archetypal Heresy: Arianism through the Centuries* (Oxford: Clarendon, 1996), 63–134.

⁴ My use of "Athanasian" refers to the widespread theory in the early Enlightenment that *homoousios* means one numerical substance. The use of the term here does not assume this is the actual doctrine of Athanasius or Nicaea, but only that those in this period who believed that *homoousios* means one numerical substance believed that they were following the doctrine taught by Athanasius.

⁵ *The Works of Jonathan Edwards,* gen. ed. Harry S. Stout, vol. 13, *The "Miscellanies" (Entry Nos. a–z, aa–zz, 1–500),* ed. Thomas A. Schafer (New Haven: Yale University Press, 1994), 96 (13:263).

⁶ Edwards, *Miscellanies,* 94 (13:257).

⁷ I borrow this term and learned of its importance for Edwards and the early Enlightenment from Gerald R. McDermott's excellent study on Edwards' philosophical-theology of world religions (McDermott, *Jonathan Edwards Confronts the Gods: Christian Theology, Enlightenment Religion, and Non-Christian Faiths* [New York: Oxford University Press, 2000], 17–33). The scandal of particularity was one criticism that the Deists used within their broader political and social agendas. I focus on the scandal of particularity and its implication of a capricious deity because it is the issue that Edwards indirectly responded to with the doctrine of the Trinity.

⁸ Frank E. Manuel, *The Eighteenth Century Confronts the Gods* (Cambridge: Harvard University Press, 1959), 58–61 and Arnold H. Rowbotham, *Missionary and Mandarin: The Jesuits at the Court of China* (Berkeley: University of California Press, 1942), 247–54.

⁹ Leslie Stephen, *History of English Thought in the Eighteenth Century,* 2 vols., 3rd ed. (1902; reprint, New York: G. P. Putnam's Sons, 1927), 1:81–82.

¹⁰ Anthony Collins, *A Discourse of Free-Thinking, occasion'd by the Rise and Growth of a Sect call'd Free-Thinkers,* The Philosophy of John Locke 2, ed. Peter A. Schouls (1713; reprint, New York: Garland, 1984), 37; and Matthew Tindal, *Christianity as Old as the Creation,* ed. and intro. Günter Gawlick (1730; reprint, Stuttgart-Bad, Cannstatt: Friedrich Frommann, 1967), 250 and 374–75.

¹¹ Bruce Marshall, *Christology in Conflict: The Identity of a Savior in Rahner and Barth* (New York: Basil Blackwell, 1987), 1–3.

¹² Deists maintained that the benevolence of God requires the universal distribution of the means of proper religion. Moreover, religious truth and precepts must be ahistorical. Christianity, which links true religion with the historical person and life of Christ, conflicts with the universal benevolence and ahistorical nature of true religion (Peter Byrne, *Natural Religion and the Nature of Religion: The Legacy of Deism,* Routledge Religious Studies, ed. Stewart Sutherland [New York: Routledge, 1989], 52–61).

¹³ Charles Blount, *The Oracles of Reason,* in *The Miscellaneous Works of Charles Blount, Esq.* (London, 1695), 1–4 and 197–98. While sometimes characterized as a cad and crass plagiarizer of Hobbes, Spinoza, and other influential thinkers, John Redwood argues that Blount, despite his unoriginality, is important to the rise of Deism and Free Thought in the early-Enlightenment. Blount's anti-clericalism, rejection of revelation and miracles, emphasis on religion as morality, and advocacy of toleration kindled the wider and more public promotion of these themes by the Deists later in the seventeenth century (Redwood, "Charles Blount [1654–93], Deism, and English Free Thought," *Journal of the History of Ideas* 35 [1974]: 490–98).

Natural religion is the concept that all necessary theological and religious knowledge is ascertainable by human reason. In the Christian traditions, it was common to distinguish between natural theology and revealed theology. Natural theology encompasses knowledge of God the creator. It is true, but partial and tentative. For example, the unity and oneness of God is a doctrine of natural theology. Knowledge of God the savior and doctrines such as the Trinity derive only from revelation. In effect, natural religion assumes that unaided human reason is sufficient for religious knowledge and revelation is unnecessary (Byrne, *Natural Religion and the Nature of Religion,* 1–4).

[14] For examples of this argumentation, see Tindal, *Christianity as Old as the Creation*, 196, 250, 374–75, 401, and 409; Collins, *A Discourse of Free-Thinking*, 37–38; and John Toland, *Christianity not Mysterious* (1696; reprint, Stuttgart-Bad Cannstatt: Friedrich Frommann, 1964), 133–34.

[15] *The Works of Arminius: The London Edition*, 3 vols., trans. James Nichols and William Nichols (vol. 1 1825, vol. 2 1828, vol. 3 1875; reprint with an intro. by Carl Bangs, Grand Rapids: Baker, 1996), 1:630 and 2:715–16; and for the Cambridge Platonists' criticism, see Frederick C. Beiser, *The Sovereignty of Reason: The Defense of Rationality in the Early English Enlightenment* (Princeton: Princeton University Press, 1996), 146–47.

[16] Herbert of Cherbury, *Pagan Religion: A Translation of "De religione gentilium,"* ed. John A. Butler, Dovehouse Studies in Literature 5; Medieval and Renaissance Texts and Studies 152 (Binghamton, NY: Carleton, 1996), 53–54. Herbert also criticized predestination in *Lord Herbert of Cherbury's "De religione laici,"* ed. and trans. Harold R. Hutcheson, Yale Studies in English 98 (New Haven: Yale University Press, 1944), 119.

[17] According to J. A. I. Champion, the thesis of the *Antient Religion of the Gentiles* (English translation of *De religione gentilium*) is that a just God cannot countenance the eternal destruction of those who have no means of remedy (Champion, *The Pillars of Priestcraft Shaken: The Church of England and Its Enemies, 1660–1730*, Cambridge Studies in Early Modern British History, ed. Anthony Fletcher [New York: Cambridge University Press, 1992], 140–41).

[18] Edwards, *Miscellanies*, 87 (13:251–52), 97 (13:264), and 104 (13:272).

[19] Ibid., 117 (13:283–84).

[20] Ibid., 96 (13:263).

[21] *The Works of Jonathan Edwards*, gen. ed. John E. Smith, vol. 8, *Ethical Writings*, ed. Paul Ramsey (New Haven: Yale University Press, 1989), 377.

[22] In trinitarian theology, the plurality is personal and not essential. That is, by criticizing the Deist Unitarian theory of God, Edwards is not teaching a plurality of discrete divine substances, but the necessity of a plurality of persons within the divine nature.

[23] Edwards, *Miscellanies*, 96 (13:263–64).

[24] McDermott, *Jonathan Edwards Confronts the Gods*, 17–19.

[25] Miscellany 94 clearly shows that Edwards directly engaged critical challenges to the doctrine of the Trinity (Edwards, *Miscellanies*, 94 [13:256–57]). Moreover, his comments such as "I think that it is within the reach of *naked reason* to perceive certainly that there are three distinct in God . . . [and] I think it really evident from the *light of reason* that there are these three distinct in God" explicitly reveal his concern to demonstrate the reasonableness of the Trinity (emphasis added; Edwards, *Miscellanies*, 94 [13:257 and 262]).

[26] Ramsay was born at Ayr in 1686 to a family of low social standing. His father was a strict Calvinist, while his mother was an Anglican, who taught her son from an early age the odiousness of the Calvinist doctrine of predestination. In his later teens and early twenties, Ramsay embraced liberal Scottish mysticism and skepticism. In 1710, he left England, traveled to Holland, eventually arriving in Cambrai to visit Fénelon, who converted him to Catholicism. From 1716 until his death in 1743, he lived mainly in Paris earning his way by writing and tutoring children of the nobility. Ramsay is best known for his texts *Les voyages de Cyrus, avec un discours sur la mythologie* (1727)—translated into English under the title, *The Travels of Cyrus* (1727)—and *The Philosophical Principles of Natural and Revealed Religion* (1748).

[27] For dating Miscellany 96, see "Table 2," in *Miscellanies*, vol. 13.

[28] In Miscellanies 1180 and 1181, Edwards copied segments of *The Philosophical Principles* quoted in the *Monthly Review* (1751): 341. The topic of the quotations is the presence of Christian theological principles in non-Christian religions; see *The Works of Jonathan Edwards*, gen. ed. Harry S. Stout, vol. 23, *The "Miscellanies" (Entry Nos. 1153–1360)*, ed. Douglas A. Sweeney

(New Haven: Yale University Press, 2004), 23:95–104. Subsequently, Edwards obtained a copy of *The Philosophical Principles* attested by his lengthy quotations from it in *Miscellanies* 1252 (23:184), 1253 (23:184–88), and 1254 (23:188–90).

[29] Although unlike Edwards, Ramsay abhorred Reformed theories of predestination; see G. D. Henderson, *Chevalier Ramsay* (London: Thomas Nelson and Sons, 1952), 13 and 216.

[30] Andrew M. Ramsay, *The Philosophical Principles of Natural and Revealed Religion*, 2 vols. (Glasgow: Robert and Andrew Foulis, 1748–49), 1:81–90. Ramsay, more clearly and strongly than Edwards, defines the divine persons as "distinct agents," "self-conscious agents," and "intelligent beings" (Ramsay, *Philosophical Principles*, 1:88–89). Nevertheless, he clarifies that the Trinity is not three divine minds consisting of three separate substances, but that the divine persons have the same self-consciousness. Here, and like Edwards, Ramsay is caught in the inconsistency of his conceptions. He thinks of God as an infinite mind. The analogy of the human mind—i.e., mind, idea, and love—gives the impression that the divine persons are merely modes of an intellect. Yet, he wants to understand the divine persons in the Cartesian sense of centers of consciousness and action without its implication of three substances and tritheism (Ramsay, *Philosophical Principles*, 1:90–91 and 97).

[31] For the dating of Edwards' Miscellanies 94 and 96, see Schafer, "Table 2," in *Miscellanies*, vol. 13.

[32] Lord Cherbury's five principles of natural religion are a case in point (Edward, Lord Herbert of Cherbury, *De Veritate*, trans. Meyrick H. Carré, University of Bristol Studies 6 [Bristol: J. W. Arrowsmith, 1937], 289–307).

[33] For criticism of the Trinity and the portrayal of religion as essentially a moral affair, see Blount, *Oracles of Reason* and *Great is Diana of the Ephesians* in *The Miscellaneous Works of Charles Blount*, 100–101, 198, and 3; and Tindal, *Christianity as Old as the Creation*, 206. The vacuity of the Trinity for the Christian religious life is also lamented by modern theologians, but in contrast to the Enlightenment critics they do not call for its abandonment but its revitalization in Christian theology (e.g., Babcock, "A Changing of the Christian God," 133–35; Robert Jenson, *The Triune Identity: God according to the Gospel* [Philadelphia: Fortress, 1982], ix; Catherine Mowry LaCugna, *God for Us: The Trinity and Christian Life* [New York: HarperCollins, 1991], ix; and Karl Rahner, *The Trinity*, trans. Joseph Donceel, intro. Catherine Mowry LaCugna [New York: Crossroad, 1998], 10–11).

[34] Blount, *Oracles of Reason*, in *The Miscellaneous Works of Charles Blount*, 198–99.

[35] The most thorough presentation of the *prisca theologia* is D. P. Walker, *The Ancient Theology: Studies in Christian Platonism from the Fifteenth to the Eighteenth Century* (London: Duckworth, 1972). Patristic apologists used the *prisca theologia* to show that one could adhere to Neo-Platonism and Christianity and that eminent non-Christian philosophers received their insights from the ancient Israelites. In the Renaissance and into the early-seventeenth century, Christian theologians also sought to demonstrate with the *prisca theologia* the compatibility of Neo-Platonism with Christianity (Walker, *The Ancient Theology*, 2). The principal texts for the ancient theology were the *Hermetica*, *Orphica*, and the *Sibylline Oracles* and they were thought to predate the Christian era. However, practitioners of textual criticism in the seventeenth century increasingly exposed these alleged ancient texts as forgeries drafted in the second through fourth centuries. For instance, in 1614 Isaac Casaubon refuted the antiquity of the *Hermetica* by showing that it was written in the Christian era (Anthony Grafton, "Protestant versus Prophet: Isaac Casaubon on Hermes Trismegistus," *Journal of the Warburg and Courtauld Institutes* 46 [1986]: 78–93; Peter Harrison, *'Religion' and the Religions in the English Enlightenment* [New York: Cambridge University Press, 1990], 132; and Walker, *The Ancient Theology*, 10–21). However, not wanting to lose the apologetic value of the ancient theology, adherents developed counter criticisms to the text-critical conclusions (e.g., Ralph Cudworth, *The True Intellectual System of the Universe*, 3 vols., trans. John Harrison [1678; London: Thomas Tegg, 1845], 1.4.18 [1:540–43]).

[36] Harrison, *'Religion' and the Religions in the English Enlightenment*, 133–36.

[37] Cudworth, *True Intellectual System of the Universe* 1.4.18 (1:518–19 and 531).

[38] Ibid., 1.4.36 (2:312–13). Mention of Cudworth's use of the ancient theology for apologetic purposes is important to the study of Edwards' use of it because Edwards copied sections from Cudworth's *True Intellectual System* that show Aristotle's and Plato's belief in the unity of God (Edwards, *Miscellanies*, 1343 [23:380–81]). However, Edwards also often used Theophilus Gale's *The Court of the Gentiles, or a Discourse Touching the Original of Humane Literature* (5 parts, 1669–1678), which, contrary to Cudworth, argued that all true religions derive from the ancient Hebrews and that religious concepts found in the other ancient religious traditions are flawed and misleading. For instance, while Gale noted that the Greek philosophers propounded a theory of the Trinity, he insisted that it was corrupt and unsalutary (Gale, *The Court of the Gentiles*, 3:48–49). For a comparison of Cudworth's and Gale's use of the *prisca theologia* and evaluation of Plato, see Sarah Hutton, "The Neoplatonic Roots of Arianism: Ralph Cudworth and Theophilus Gale," in *Socinianism and Its Role in the Culture of the Sixteenth to Eighteenth Centuries*, ed. Lech Szczucki (Warsaw- Łódź : PWN-Polish Scientific Publisher, 1983), 139–45.

[39] Walker, *The Ancient Theology*, 1–2 and 12. For example, Duhalde states as commonplace the opinion that the Chinese received their religious and political ideas from a son of Noah who traveled into Asia after the Flood (Jean Baptiste Duhalde, *The General History of China. Containing a Geographical, Historical, Chronological, Political, and Physical Description of the Empire of China, Chinese-Tartary, Corea, and Thibet. Including an Exact and Particular Account of their Customs, Manners, Ceremonies, Religion, Arts, and Sciences*, 4 vols., 3rd ed. [1735; trans. from the French anon., London: J. Watts, 1741], 3:15–16). Duhalde's text was a popular source book for many of the Enlightenment thinkers desiring to emphasize the virtuousness of Chinese culture (Rowbotham, *Missionary and Mandarin*, 256–57 and 264). The theory that some of the religious ideas of the Chinese were the result of contact with ancient Jews was set forth earlier by Jesuit missionary Matteo Ricci in the late-sixteenth century (Ricci, *China in the Sixteenth Century: The Journals of Matthew Ricci: 1583–1610*, trans. Louis J. Gallagher [1942; reprint, New York: Random House, 1953], 106–14).

[40] Orthodox theologians attributed the degeneration to original sin (McDermott, *Jonathan Edwards Confronts the Gods*, 96–97).

[41] McDermott, *Jonathan Edwards Confronts the Gods*, 94.

[42] Gerald McDermott's text is indispensable for Edwards' use of the *prisca theologia* (McDermott, *Jonathan Edwards Confronts the Gods*, 87–109).

[43] McDermott, *Jonathan Edwards Confronts the Gods*, 187–89.

[44] *The Works of Jonathan Edwards*, gen. ed. Harry S. Stout, vol. 20, *The "Miscellanies" (Entry Nos. 833–1152)*, ed. Amy Plantinga Pauw (New Haven: Yale University Press, 2002), 953 (20:222–24), 959 (20:239–40), 977 (20:287–88), and 978 (20:288).

[45] Edwards, *Miscellanies*, 953 (20:222–26), 954 (20:226–27), 975 (20:278–80), 978 (20:288–91) and *Miscellanies*, 1268 (23:214).

[46] Edwards, *Miscellanies*, 953 (20:222–26), 955 (20:227–29), 970 (20:253–54), 971 (20:254), 992 (20:321–23), 1017 (20:349), 1018 (20:350), 1073 (20:456–58), and 1075a (20:459) and *Miscellanies*, 1181 (23:95–104), 1236 (23:171), and 1244 (23:176–77).

[47] Edwards, *Miscellanies*, 350 (13:424); *Miscellanies*, 953 (20:222–24), 954 (20:226), 959 (20:239–40), 963 (20:247), 969 (20:251–53), and 973 (20:275–77); and *Miscellanies*, 1236 (23:171) and 1255 (23:190–91). Miscellany 953 is a transcription from Theophilus Gale's *The Court of the Gentiles* (edition used by Edwards: 2 vols. [London: vol. 1, 1672 and vol. 2, 1677]) and his commentary in support of the *prisca theologia*. Theophilus Gale, a frequent source of the *prisca theologia* for Edwards, taught that Plato received his learning from the Jews, but also that this deposit of revelation was corrupted and of no soteriological value (Gale, *The Court of the Gentiles* [5 parts, London: 1669–1678], 1:4 and 3:48–49).

[48] Edwards, *Miscellanies*, 969 (20:251–53).

[49] Edwards, *Miscellanies*, 971 (20:254).

[50] Edwards drew from several sources to document the presence of trinitarian ideas in non-Christian religious traditions. He cited from Isaac Barrow's *The Works of the Learned Isaac Barrow* . . . (1683–1687) because he was famous for citations from the Greek philosophers. Edwards drew numerous passages from Theophilus Gale's *The Court of the Gentiles* (1669–1678). Edwards also cited Hugo Grotius' *De veritate religionis Christianae* (1627), which was an apologetic text to prepare sailors for contact with non-Christian religious thought and practices. He likely used Simon Patrick's translation of *De veritate* (1680) as it is listed in no. 218 of the reading "Catalogue" ("Jonathan Edwards' Reading 'Catalogue' with Notes and Indexes," ed. L. Brian Sullivan, *The Works of Jonathan Edwards* Office, Yale Divinity School, New Haven, CT.). He copied passages from Michael Ramsay's *The Philosophical Principles of Natural and Revealed Religion* (1748) from the March 1751 edition of the *Monthly Review*, pp. 340–48, and later from Ramsay's text itself. For Ramsay's use of the *prisca theologia*, see Henderson, *Chevalier Ramsay*, 117–29 and Walker, *The Ancient Theology*, 240–63. He also cited from Philip Skelton, *Opiomaches: or, Deism Revealed* (1749); Richard Kidder, *A Demonstration of the Messias* (2nd ed., 1726); and Jacques Basnage, *History of the Jews, from Jesus Christ to the Present Time* (1708).

[51] The Greek thinkers mentioned are Marcilius Ficinus, Parmenides, Plato, Plotinus, Porphyry, the Pythagoreans, and Sanchoniathon (Edwards, *Miscellanies*, 955 [20:227–29], 970 [20:253–54], and 992 [20:321–23]).

[52] Edwards ascribes these teachings to Greek thinkers in *Miscellanies*, 955 (20:227–29), 970 (20:253–54), and 992 (20:321–23).

[53] Edwards, *Miscellanies*, 970 (20:253–54) and 992 (20:321–23).

[54] He copied the citation of Ramsay from the *Monthly Review* of April 1751. Ramsay adopted the *prisca theologia* to demonstrate the rationality of the Christian faith in light of Deist criticisms. The second volume of *The Philosophical Principles of Natural and Revealed Religion* is devoted to showing the presence of vestiges of revealed religion in the non-Christian world religions (Ramsay, *Philosophical Principles*, 2:iii–vi; and Henderson, *Chevalier Ramsay*, 218–26).

[55] Note that the Protestant practice of associating these Chinese terms with the Christian notion of God began with Jesuit missionaries, particularly Matteo Ricci, in the fifteenth and sixteenth centuries (C. W. Allan, *Jesuits at the Court of Peking: Studies in Chinese History and Civilization*, ed. Joseph En-pao Wang [Arlington, V.I.: University Publications of America, 1975], 163; and Rowbotham, *Missionary and Mandarin*, 128–29).

[56] Duhalde records that the Chinese worshipped Chang-Ti or Tien as the supreme being of the universe (Duhalde, *General History of China*, 3:16–21 and 27). Note also that Ramsay used Duhalde to understand Chinese religious ideas (Ramsay, *Philosophical Principles*, 2:179 and 409; and Henderson, *Chevalier Ramsay*, 219–20).

[57] Edwards, *Miscellanies*, 1181 (23:98). In Miscellany 1236, Edwards cited a passage from Philip Skelton's *Opiomaches: or, Deism Revealed* that also ascribed this teaching to Lao Kiun (*Miscellanies*, 23:171). Duhalde recorded that Lao Kiun, leader of a Chinese religious group, taught that "Tao, or reason, hath produced one, one hath produced two, two have produced three, and three have produced all things" (Duhalde, *General History of China*, 3:30). Three scenarios account for the similarity between Skelton and Duhalde. First, Skelton transcribed the teaching ascribed to Lao Kiun in *Deism Revealed* (1751) from the English translation of Duhalde, which appeared in 1741. Second, Duhalde and Skelton shared a common source. Third, Skelton copied it from another text, such as Ramsay's *The Philosophical Principles of Natural and Revealed Religion* (1748), which in turn relied on Duhalde or another text recording the teaching of Lao Kiun.

[58] Edwards, *Miscellanies*, 1181 (23:95–99).

[59] For Edwards' earlier use of the *prisca theologia,* see *Miscellanies,* 350 (13:424).

[60] E.g., Tindal, *Christianity as Old as the Creation,* 206; and Toland, *Christianity not Mysterious,* 25.

[61] Edwards wrote numerous miscellanies under the heading "Christian Religion" that interact with various Deist challenges to traditional Christian doctrines, such as revelation, the necessity of a mediator, miracles, and theological mystery. For Edwards' anti-Deist miscellanies, see *Miscellanies,* 125b (13:288–89), 127 (13:291), 128 (13:291–92), 129 (13:292), 131 (13:293), 132 (13:294), 197 (13:336), 204 (13:339–40), 249 (13:361–62), 266 (13:372), 283 (13:380), 382 (13:451); *The Works of Jonathan Edwards,* gen. ed. Harry S. Stout, vol. 18, *The "Miscellanies" (Entry Nos. 501–832),* ed. Ava Chamberlain (New Haven: Yale University Press, 2000), 514 (18:57–58), 544 (18:89–90), 583 (18:118–19), 596 (18:130–31), and 652 (18:192–93); *Miscellanies,* 953 (20:222–26); and *Miscellanies,* 1169 (23:87–88), 1170 (23:88), 1234 (23:167–68), 1239 (23:175), and 1340 (23:359–376), which is an extended essay on the viability of revelation in light of Tindal's *Christianity as Old as the Creation.* Also see, *The Works of Jonathan Edwards,* gen. ed. Perry Miller, vol. 1, *Freedom of the Will,* ed. Paul Ramsey (New Haven: Yale University Press, 1957) and *The Works of Jonathan Edwards,* gen. ed. John E. Smith, vol. 3, *Original Sin,* ed. Clyde A. Holbrook (New Haven: Yale University Press, 1970).

PART VII

MISCELLANEOUS THEMES IN EDWARDS

Jonathan Edwards, Children, and Young People: Less of Earth and More of Heaven

Charles Pierce

In his recent biography of Jonathan Edwards, George M. Marsden points out that to Edwards' contemporaries "what sort of person Edwards appeared to be depended largely on how fully one shared his vision."[1] In a similar vein, Edwards' views on children and young people can be viewed sympathetically or unsympathetically depending on how one imaginatively reconstructs Jonathan Edwards' relationship with children and young people. Edwards' views of children and youths coincide closely with traditional Puritan/Calvinist views of children as naturally evil but capable of redemption. Throughout his life, Jonathan Edwards was deeply concerned with the spiritual growth of children and young adults.

In Calvinistic thought there is no smooth evolution from childhood to adulthood. Instead, each human life may be seen as divided into two parts: before being saved and after being saved. Unless the child, youth, or adult experiences saving grace and a conversion, he misses the hinge upon which the rest of life and eternal life must open. In every moment before conversion, a child is living in a state of peril: "In Adam's Fall we sinned all"—the rhyme for the letter A in the *New England Primer*—reminds the child from the beginning of his education that he is not in a state of grace.

Much can be learned about Jonathan Edwards' own childhood in his "Personal Narrative" of 1739.[2] At the beginning of this work, Edwards explains that as a nine-year-old child he took great pleasure in building a "booth" in a swamp where he could retreat for prayer (Hopkins 24). At times, he invited a small group of friends to accompany him; thus, one could surmise that he was preparing to be a minister by imitating his father. However, at least some of the time he seems to have traveled to his sanctuary alone or to have traveled to other secret spots in the woods to pray. Leaving aside the argument that the Puritans paid special attention to the biblical injunction to pray in private as well as in public places, one may note Edwards' life-long habit of combining a private meditative and scholarly life with a public life as a minister.[3]

In the "Personal Narrative," Edwards looked into what Yeats called the "foul rag and bone shop of the heart" and decided that as a child he was not yet saved. Building the "booth" was for him an awakening, but an awakening is not the same as conversion. Although Edwards prayed five times a day, he indicates that during these early childhood experiences of worship he was performing a pharisaical ritual. The childish vanities of his worship in the swamp and woods were not pious worship but "much self-righteous pleasure" (Hopkins 24).

It has been generally considered surprising that Timothy Edwards, Jonathan's father, wrote to his wife advising her to "take special care of Jonathan . . . that he doesn't learn to be rude and naught[y] etc. of which you and I have lately discoursed" (qtd. in Marsden 20–21). As the only male child in a household of ten daughters, Jonathan may have been in a fair way to be spoiled, although as an adult he noted that although Timothy Edwards loved all of his children, he did not "favor" them (Marsden 21). Instead, Jonathan Edwards indicates that Timothy fought against the evil inherent in his children and made sure they submitted to the will of God.

In both England and New England, the "breaking" of children's wills is a traditional Puritan theme.[4] As early as 1628, the Puritan John Robinson declared that as a first step to salvation, "children's wills and willfulness [should] be restrained and repressed" (qtd. in Stannard 48).[5] The breaking of wills was designed to save the souls of children, and in general was not a violent act. Most children learned obedience as a habit, and one should not suppose that Puritan children were whipped on a daily basis. Cotton Mather writes in his diary, "The slavish way of Education, carried on with raving and kicking and scourging (in Schools as well as in Families,) 'tis abominable; and a dreadful judgment of God upon the World" (qtd. in Morgan 105).[6] In fact, Puritan parents hoped that a frown or a gentle look of disappointment might keep their children in line.[7]

Samuel Hopkins, Edwards' friend and first biographer, points out that in the Edwards' own household when "they [Jonathan and Sarah] discovered any considerable degree of will and stubbornness, he [Jonathan] would attend to them till he had thoroughly subdued them and brought them to submit" (43). He accomplished this task "with the greatest calmness, and commonly without striking a blow" (43). Hopkins also comments on Sarah Edwards' "excellent way of governing her children" (qtd. in Marsden 321). According to Hopkins, she was "firm and mild and always explained her reasons for disciplining . . . without loud, angry words, or heavy blows" (qtd. in Marsden 251). In short, the Edwards' household seems to have been well-ordered, with well-disciplined children who seldom opposed their parents or quarreled with each other.

In Edwards' theology, there is a vast difference between children and children of God. In later life, Edwards provided a revealing explanation of the biblical verses in which Christ says, "suffer little children to come unto me. . . . Whosoever shall not receive the kingdom of heaven as a little child shall in no wise enter therein" (Luke 18:16–17). He explains that a person becomes a little child in God's sight and governance not because of a young age but because he or she has been born again:

> becoming as a little child is necessary in order to a right receiving the kingdom of heaven, because Christ tells us that unless we receive it as a little child, we cannot enter into it. But however, it don't [*sic*] hence follow, that a man becomes as a little child before his conversion. That is a thing wrought in conversion, as is evident by Matt. 18:3, "Except ye

be converted, and become as little children, ye shall not enter into the kingdom of heaven...." (*Works* 18:116)

In his *Advice to Young Converts,* Edwards explains that the adult Christian remains God's child: "In all your course, walk with God and follow Christ as a little poor helpless child, taking hold of Christ's hand, keeping your eye on the mark of the wounds on his hands and side, whence comes the blood that cleanses you . . ." (*Works* 16:95).[8]

Although children were prone to evil, Edwards believed there was such a thing as a child saint.[9] His most famous anecdote about a saved child deals with Phebe Bartlett. Like oil portraits of many colonial children, Edwards' portrait of Phebe seems somewhat flat and predictable rather than the record of a particular child at a particular moment. Like the children depicted in colonial portraits, Phebe Bartlett possesses a preternaturally adult air.

That Edwards should find similarities between Phebe and himself is hardly surprising. Edwards' account of Phebe points out that, like Edwards, she went to her secret place ("closet") to pray.[10] More important, like Edwards, Phebe was concerned with salvation and feared for those who were not yet saved. She was particularly concerned that her three sisters were not yet saved and might meet death unprepared. She is reported to have exclaimed, "Poor Nabby!" "Poor Eunice!" "Poor Amy!" (*Works* 4:201) and to have shed tears because they were not yet saved.[11]

Edwards' descriptions of child saints do not stand alone, for accounts of the Puritan child saint are numerous.[12] One of the earliest New England accounts of such child saints is found in *A Token for Children. . . . To which is added A Token for the Children of New England* (See Earle 23).[13] The second half of the book, by Cotton Mather, illustrates the characteristics of the New England child saint: "Young babes chide their parents for too infrequent praying, and have ecstasies of delight when they can pray ad infinitum. One child two years old was able . . . to understand the mysteries of Redemption" (qtd. in Earle 250). Phebe Bartlett and other child saints invariably loved their ministers and listened intently to sermons. In *Jonathan Edwards: Religious Tradition and Popular Culture* (1995), Joseph Conforti points out:

> Missionary memoirs usually begin with accounts of their subjects' pious childhoods to impress upon the readers the importance of early religious training. These childhood experiences laid the religious foundations for the missionaries' conversions, which most commonly occurred during early adulthood and which elicited a desire to bring the gospel to non-Christians.[14]

Like Phebe Bartlett, who worried about the salvation of her siblings, Edwards emphasized that children must be prepared for death at any time. His own concern about children's preparation for death is evident in a letter to his son, Jonathan Edwards, Jr.:[15]

> Dear Child: . . . The week before last, on Thursday, David died; whom you knew and used to play with, and who used to live at our House. Whether he was prepared for Death, we don't know. This is a loud call of God to you to prepare for Death. You see that they that are young die, as well as those that are old; David was not very much older than you. Remember what Christ said, that you must be born again, or you never can see the kingdom of God. (qtd. in Ferm 15–16)[16]

According to Edwards, not to warn children was to be negligent—it was as if they were not being told that the ship was about to split on the rocks or that the house they were in was on fire. Thus, it is not surprising that on another occasion while speaking to a group of children, Edwards said, "I know that some of you will die in a little time . . . , some sooner than others. 'Tis not likely that all of you will grow up" (qtd. in Stannard 66). In *The Puritan Way of Death,* David E. Stannard notes:

> If children were frightened, even terrified, by the prospects of life and death conjured up by their parents and ministers, that . . . was a natural and rational response. As more than one Puritan writer has suggested, to fail to be frightened was a sure sign that one was spiritually lost, or stupid or both. (70)

Edwards believed that children and young people should be given assistance along the road to salvation and that they also should have a chance to have their voices heard. He points out that in many cases women and children would not speak out in large groups because of modesty or timidity. However, he says that they should be encouraged to "speak freely" if "the case . . . [is] so extraordinary as fully to warrant it" (*Works* 4:486).

Like other ministers, Edwards was aware that if the church were to survive it would have to attract children and young people. This reality had, of course, been known for a long time. According to N. Ray Hiner, beginning in 1694, Cotton Mather "gave enthusiastic support to those young people who 'met every week to seek the face, and sing the praise, and repeat the word of God. . . .' He campaigned for the formal establishment of young men's associations for this purpose and published a model charter which could be used as a guide for this group" (265).[17] Like Mather, Edwards encouraged young people to create informal religious groups and prayer meetings. Not all youth, however, occupied their spare time by attending such religious meetings; the lure of sensuality seems to have had its place in Edwards' Northampton.

In 1744, a group of young men, not adolescents but acting like adolescents, circulated a book on midwifery that apparently contained diagrams and pictures which the youths felt epitomized the latest in salacious information on the female anatomy. One youth actually paid a large sum for acquisition of the book. Several young men made improper comments to young women about the menstrual cycle and taunted them with off-color remarks.

Eventually, the young men were brought before a church committee that tried to make them repent. Instead, while they were waiting to be examined they skipped out to drink "flip" at the nearest tavern. Referring to church officials, one of the offenders said he would not "worship a wig" and another exclaimed, "I don't care a fart," apparently referring both to the investigation and the church authorities.[18] This so-called bad book incident and its repercussions have been discussed primarily within the context of an increasing tension between secular and religious life in the frontier society of Massachusetts.

But misbehavior of young people was not new in western Massachusetts of the 1740s. In 1717, Edwards' grandfather Solomon Stoddard decried the tendency of the young to gather together at various times, especially on public days and in the evening, to participate in "a great deal of vain worldly proud discourse, and corrupt communication" (qtd. in Hiner 264). In part, Puritans solved the problem of how to use leisure time by advocating that both children and adults remain busy: idle hands were the devil's tools. However, the emphasis on work and godly activities only partly solved the problem of leisure time for Massachusetts youth of the early eighteenth century. While it is difficult to document an increase in "frolicking" and generally bad behavior among youth, it can be documented that more children were being born out of wedlock in the 1740s. It was undoubtedly in the spirit of correction but also of concern that Edwards became involved in the "bad book" incident.

A man of Edwards' temperament would not understand why young men were attracted to forbidden acts when salvation was at stake, and he had been concerned about slipping morality for some time. According to William J. Scheick,[19] even before the "bad book" incident of 1744, Edwards' sermon *Joseph's*

Great Temptation (1738) "indicts negligent parents" (49) and the "liberalizing social trends of early eighteenth-century America" (49–50). At the end of the sermon, Edwards "invited young people who did not agree with his arguments and were unwilling to give up the amusements he had denounced to bring satisfying answers to the arguments he had presented. 'I don't desire,' he said, 'that young People should be abridg'd of any lawful & proper Liberties.'"[20] Notwithstanding this invitation, there is no evidence that the young people involved tried to rebut his case, and Edwards undoubtedly laid himself open to attack by daring to criticize the parents of out-of-control children.

Most Puritans believed that young people were often guilty of the sins of pride and sensuality; both of these sins increased in those who kept bad company. Edwards would have seen the "bad book" as containing all three elements: Sensuality because the young men visualized women pornographically; pride because the young men refused to bend to any kind of discipline; and bad company because the young men reinforced each other's bad behavior. Because Edwards believed that the experiences of children and young people must be channeled in a positive religious direction, he would have been disturbed that the young men involved showed few signs of repentance.

In her recent article "Bad Books and Bad Boys: The Transformation of Gender in Eighteenth-Century Northampton, Massachusetts," Ava Chamberlain[21] suggests that Edwards was defending an earlier view of men and women as helpmates. She suggests that this view was being superseded by a new relationship in which women were more subservient and men were claiming special prerogatives. Marsden partially agrees with Chamberlain, but he also suggests that this emphasis may not be quite accurate in an eighteenth-century context of ecclesiastical and paternal authority. He notes that those accused finally seem to have made no apologies about their sexism but instead apologized for their scandalous behavior to church authorities.[22]

During the "bad book" incident, Edwards seems to have tried to exert the full extent of his authority as minister of the Northampton church. It must have been disappointing to Edwards that the young men involved in the incident were mostly members of the church and had probably been involved as children in the Great Awakening. Also, it must have been particularly troubling to Edwards that the young men implicated considered the book to be "the young folks' Bible." He would have believed that the young men were guilty of sacrilege and an irreverent parody of holiness.

As a spiritual leader, Edwards could not simply ignore the actions of the young men involved because they were replacing his vision of the world, in which spirit and matter existed in some mutual if problematic relationship, with a view that only the material world mattered. As Wilson H. Kimnach points out, "Edwards continually strove to bridge the imaginative gap separating the eternal world of spiritual reality and the Lockean world of sensation in which natural men live."[23] He expected others to do the same.

Edwards did not countenance sin silently. He was concerned with the morals of young people during his entire ministry. The "bad book" incident brought matters to a head, and Samuel Hopkins believed the incident may have ended Edwards' ability to work with children and young people in the congregation (54). Approximately a year later, children and young adults were disrupting church services. Northampton town records report:

> The Town being Sensible of the Irreverent & disorderly behaviour of many of the young people and children in the house of God in the time of publick worship, and at the Same meeting made choice of . . . [a list of four names follows] to inspect the behaviour of the young people & children in time of publick Worship & to prosecute them for their irreverent & disorderly behaviour. . . . (Winslow 229)[24]

Perhaps Edwards himself let a malevolent genie out of the bottle during the Great Awakening. The Great Awakening gave youth more of a say in public matters. In the religious arena, Edwards provided a forum for their thoughts and feelings; that this forum might be translated into leverage in the secular sphere and might result in insolence and disrespect seems not to have crossed his mind.

Throughout both his youth and adult years, Edwards was concerned with children and young people. Principled and strong minded, he did what he thought was right for children and young adults. He was alive to the existence of evil in the world, and his belief that children were "vipers" who were inherently drawn toward sin led him to believe that they must be safeguarded and educated against experiences harmful to the soul. He was undoubtedly patriarchal and thought of himself as the father not only of his genetic children but also of his congregation in Northampton. In his *Farewell Sermon,* as he prepared to give up his Northampton ministry, he indicates a "peculiar concern for the souls of the young people"—his "Dear children, [whom he leaves] . . . in an evil world, that is full of snares and temptations."[25]

To many in the twenty-first century, Edwards' views on childhood and his interactions with youth may seem stiff and unbending. Given his personality, his beliefs, and his upbringing, his interactions with children and youth must have been a mixture of gentleness and authoritarianism. That Edwards was gentle with his own children frequently has been attested; that he was concerned with all children and young people and their problems is evident throughout his career. Marsden even suggests that "six practical steps in seeking salvation" appended to *Sinners in the Hands of an Angry God* may have been designed for small groups of young people to give them practical and kind-spirited advice (224). I think that Edwards himself felt that he mishandled the "bad book" incident—not intentionally or maliciously—but by providing a venue for "acting out" for the young men and by not realizing that he was fueling small-town gossip and creating lasting enmities.

Finally, there may have been very significant slippage between Edwards' official pronouncements and his private actions. Although he was a sometimes authoritarian and dour Calvinist, he was also aware that young people needed to find themselves and needed a voice within the church. As a result of the sympathetic side of his nature, he was kindhearted toward children and young people. In fact, Edwards' contemporaries realized he had some special talent for dealing with young people. It seems appropriate, therefore, that at the end of his life he was about to begin a new career, one in which he would have ministered to young people as president of Princeton.

CHARLES PIERCE earned his B.A. and M.A. both at the University of New Hampshire. His research interests lie in women's studies of the Middle Ages and Renaissance, and all aspects of Colonial New England. He has published reviews for the *Renaissance Quarterly* and articles for the Gayle Publishing Series. He currently teaches at Tidewater Community College, Virginia Beach, Virginia.

NOTES

[1] George M. Marsden, *Jonathan Edwards: A Life* (New Haven: Yale UP, 2003), 254.

[2] Jonathan Edwards, "Personal Narrative"; Samuel Hopkins, *The Life and Character of the Late Reverend Mr. Jonathan Edwards; Jonathan Edwards: A Profile,* ed. David Levin (New York: Hill and Wang, 1969). Personal Narrative has been frequently anthologized and can be found in numerous textbooks and collections. I have used the page numbers from Levin's readily accessible edition of Hopkins' text of the "Narrative." For other quotations from Edwards, I have used the *Works* when I could do so. Jonathan Edwards, *The Works of Jonathan Edwards: The Miscellaneous Works,* vol. 18, ed. Ava Chamberlain (New Haven: Yale UP, 2000); *Letters and Personal Writings,* vol. 16, ed. George S. Cleghorn (New Haven: Yale UP, 1998); *The Great Awakening,* vol. 4, ed. C. C. Goen (New Haven: Yale UP, 1972).

[3] A need for privacy, first visible in Edwards' youthful experiences, seems to have been an organizing force in Edwards' Northampton household. It is commonly recognized that Sarah Edwards often took charge of seeing that the household ran smoothly while Edwards spent much of the day in private concentrating on his sermons and other studies (See Marsden, p. 135). One could argue that his private study was also a sanctuary and that Edwards' massive center desk which was added to on either side became almost a triptych—or at least a symbol of the Trinity. At this desk, alone, Jonathan Edwards spent much of his adult life as he continued a pattern of privacy that he had begun as a child.

[4] Some of the Puritan breaking of the will can be compared to what has sometimes been called "tough love."

[5] David E. Stannard, *The Puritan Way of Death* (New York: Oxford UP, 1979).

[6] Edmund S. Morgan, *The Puritan Family* (New York: Harper & Row, 1966).

[7] John Locke, *Some Thoughts Concerning Education,* ed. John W. and Jean S. Yolton (Oxford: Clarendon Press, 1989). Similar ideas to Jonathan Edwards' ideas on childhood can be found in John Locke's *Some Thoughts on Education.* Locke especially notes the power of disapproval on a parent's face, the importance of subjecting the child's will to the parent's will, and the avoidance of corporal punishment when possible. Edwards' ideas that adults may spoil their children by loving them too much are also found in *Some Thoughts on Education.*

[8] Edwards says in "A Personal Narrative" that "I very often think with sweetness . . . of being a little child, taking hold of Christ, to be led by Him through the wilderness of this world."

[9] For descriptions of the *puer senex* (the wise and old child) see Shulamith Shahar, *Childhood in the Middle Ages* (London: Routledge, 1992), 15.

[10] See especially Matthew 6:6. "But thou, when thou prayest, enter into thy closet . . . pray to thy Father which is in secret."

[11] Edwards reports that when a poor man lost his cow, Phebe attempted to get her father to give the poor man one of his cows. At another time, she repeated over and over again, "Mr. Edwards is come home!" Edwards recounts that, on another occasion, she took plums from a neighbor's tree but was horrified to find this was considered stealing.

[12] Gilbert Tennent's unprinted manuscript account of a young girl's religious awakening seems to have much in common with Edwards' account of the awakening of Phebe (See MX Lesser, *Jonathan Edwards: An Annotated Bibliography, 1979–1993* [Westport, CT: Greenwood Press, 1994], 28).

[13] Alice Morse Earle, *Child Life in Colonial Days* (Stockbridge, MA: Berkshire House Publishers, 1993). (First published in 1899.)

[14] Joseph Conforti, *Jonathan Edwards: Religious Tradition and Popular Culture* (Chapel Hill: UNC Press, 1995), 82.

[15] For similar concerns about young people being prepared for death, see the sermons *Children Ought to Love the Lord Jesus Christ Above All* and *Youth Is Like a Flower That Is Cut Down*, in *Works*, vol. 22.

[16] See editorial comments in *Works*, vol. 8: "Edwards believed that children under the age of fifteen were more likely to convert than the middle-aged or elderly" (168). Robert L. Ferm, *Jonathan Edwards the Younger* (Grand Rapids: Eerdman's Publishing, 1976).

[17] N. Ray Hiner, "Adolescence in Eighteenth-Century America," *History of Childhood Quarterly* 3 (Fall 1975) 253–280.

[18] For more details, see Marsden pp. 292–302 and elsewhere; Patricia A. Tracy, *Jonathan Edwards: Pastor* (New York: Hill and Wang, 1980) 160–164.

[19] William J. Scheick, *The Writings of Jonathan Edwards* (College Station: Texas A&M University Press, 1975).

[20] Ola Elizabeth Winslow, *Jonathan Edwards* (New York: Macmillan, 1941), 149.

[21] Ava Chamberlain, "Bad Books and Bad Boys: The Transformation of Gender in Eighteenth-Century Northampton, Massachusetts," *New England Quarterly* 75 (20:276–285).

[22] Almost nothing in Edwards' published writings refers to the "bad book" experience. However, in his *Farewell Sermon*, Edwards seems to be referring obliquely to the incident in the passage: "I formerly led this church to some measures for the suppressing of vice among our young people, which gave so great offence, and by which I became so obnoxious."

[23] Wilson Kimnach, "Jonathan Edwards' Pursuit of Reality," *Jonathan Edwards and the American Experience*, ed. Nathan O. Hatch and Henry Stout (New York: Oxford UP, 1988), 113.

[24] The subject of disturbances by youth in Puritan churches is an interesting one. In *Puritans at Play*, Bruce C. Daniels says that the disturbances were minimal: "And despite the fact that magistrates occasionally prosecuted people for 'rude and indecent behavior' or for 'laughing in the meeting house,' the service usually lived up to the community's expectations for good conduct. We should not look for anachronistic Tom Sawyer behavior in Puritan boys . . ." (77). A systematic investigation of disturbances in New England town and church records needs to be undertaken. Bruce C. Daniels, *Puritans at Play: Leisure and Recreation in Colonial New England* (New York: St. Martin's Press, 1995).

[25] Harold P. Simonson, *Selected Writings of Jonathan Edwards* (New York: Frederick Ungar Publishing, 1970), 148–149.

Edwards' Contribution to the Missionary Movement of Early Baptists

Michael D. Thompson

Most Protestant missions historians refer to the eighteenth-century Baptist, William Carey, as the "Father of Modern Missions." That title can be questioned; certainly, others predated Carey. The labors of John Eliot and David Brainerd among Native Americans were noteworthy, as were those of the Moravians Henry Plutschau and Bartholomew Ziegenbalg, who worked effectively in India decades before Carey arrived there. It is indisputable, though, that Carey, the little English cobbler, provided both a spark and a model for the "Great Century" of Protestant missions, a period usually dated from 1792 (the year Carey sailed) to the beginning of World War I. His legacy as a linguist, missions strategist, and inspirational figure suggests that his role was a critical one and his reputation well deserved.

Yet in the decades immediately preceding Carey's departure for India, the question was not when or where Baptists would launch their missionary enterprise, but rather if they would do so at all. The sticking point was theology—Calvinism to be exact—and classic differences existed between those who favored aggressive evangelism and those who opposed it.

The early Baptists had grown out of English separatist roots and formed their initial congregations during the first decades of the seventeenth century. They were of two basic theological persuasions. One strain tended toward Arminianism and was therefore identified as the *General* Baptists because of adherence to a general atonement. The other group held to the Calvinistic view of a particular atonement and became known as the *Particular* Baptists. Both groups struggled with questions of identity and with religious persecution, and by the dawning of the new century, both were in decline. The Generals allowed their theology to drift away from orthodoxy, especially in regard to the deity of Christ. The Particulars, on the other hand, maintained their traditional doctrinal moorings, but gradually embraced an interpretation of Calvinism that drained vitality from their faith and brought evangelism to a standstill.

It was that second group, the Particular Baptists, from whom Carey and the missions emphasis eventually emerged. However, the theological difficulties first had to be confronted, and the writings of Jonathan Edwards played a decisive role in the unfolding story.

The staunch Calvinism of the Particulars had protected them from the heresies of the Socinians and Arians, but not from the deadening effects of their own theological system when carried to an extreme. By the first two decades of the eighteenth century, election and predestination became the hallmarks of their faith to the extent that all else was judged in that light. The accompanying insistence on the perseverance of the elect even led some to embrace antinomianism, claiming that all behavior was foreordained and therefore should be excused. As a result, the churches declined in both number and vitality.[1]

Such was a clear departure from the pattern established by their spiritual ancestors. The earlier Particular Baptists had been firm Calvinists but were also aggressively evangelistic and committed to high standards of conduct in their congregations. Now, however, several key pastors and theologians held sway with their hyper-Calvinism, and it yielded what to them seemed to be logical conclusions. If some human beings were not foreordained to eternal salvation, and there was nothing those individuals could do about it, then to offer the gospel to them was at best a waste of time, and at worst an insult to God and divine providence. Therefore, any pointed attempt to call the "lost" to faith and repentance was fundamentally incorrect and should be avoided.

Not everyone within the Particulars' camp, however, found those positions palatable. A group of younger pastors began to look askance at a system which decried the preaching of the gospel to all, recognizing that the sad effects of that narrow position were all too obvious. They began to proclaim from the pulpit and the printed page that the orthodox Calvinism to which they were solidly committed did not preclude evangelism.

One of their number, Andrew Fuller, deserves mention here because he took a leadership role (along with Carey and others) in initiating the Baptist missionary movement and highlighted the instruction and encouragement that he received from the writings of Jonathan Edwards. Though nurtured in the narrow Calvinistic teaching prevalent among some of his prominent Baptist brethren, the young pastor found himself developing troubling doubts about the theology. Besides the influence of personal contacts with other like-minded individuals, it was his reading of several authors, especially Edwards, that led to greater clarity.

Edwards' involvement and leadership in the New England awakening had been amply documented in *A Faithful Narrative of the Surprising Work of God,* published in 1737, and in his later works that reflected upon the awakening and related theological issues. Fuller and others certainly read at least some of those writings, along with *The Life of David Brainerd,* Edwards' edited version of Brainerd's diary and journal, published in 1749, all of which revealed that Edwards' Calvinism differed greatly from that of the hyper-Calvinists who had for decades exercised great influence among Particular Baptists.

In the preface to his 1785 publication, *The Gospel Worthy of All Acceptation,* Fuller described part of the process that led to a change in his thinking regarding the interpretation and application of Calvinism. He maintained that his doubts about the teaching he had received as a young man came from several directions. First, the idea of not preaching to unconverted sinners and calling on them to repent seemed in direct contrast to the examples of Christ, John the Baptist, and the apostles. Further, reading about the labors of Brainerd, John Eliot, and others among the "American Indians" yielded the same conclusion.[2] Finally, on the advice of another young pastor, "he [Fuller] had also read and considered, as well as he was able, President Edwards's *Inquiry into the Freedom of the Will,* with some other performances on the difference between natural and moral inability":

> He found much satisfaction in this distinction; as it appeared to him to carry with it its own evidence—to be clearly and fully contained in the Scriptures—and calculated to disburden the Calvinistic system of a number of calumnies with which its enemies have loaded it, as well as to afford clear and honourable conceptions of the Divine government.[3]

Fuller drew heavily upon this "distinction" of Edwards, with its conclusion that a person's failure to believe in Christ arose not from any natural inability, for that would erase personal responsibility, but rather from moral inability, which fully preserved such responsibility. His study of scripture increasingly confirmed what he read in Edwards, namely that a lack of belief in human beings arose from their hearts:

> They *will not* come to Christ that they may have life; *will not* hearken to the voice of the charmer, charm he never so wisely; *will not* seek after God; and *desire not* the knowledge of his ways.[4]

There was no doubt in Fuller's mind about the validity of the classical doctrine of election. Yet that did not preclude preaching to all and commanding them to repent and believe:

> They that are in the flesh *cannot* please God; but it does not follow that they are not obliged to do so; and this their obligation requires to

be clearly insisted on, that they may be convinced of their sin, and so induced to embrace the gospel remedy.[5]

If any further doubt existed for a reader, Fuller sought to erase it later in the text, concluding from the scriptures that "Unconverted sinners are commanded, exhorted, and invited to believe in Christ for salvation."[6] He could accept no other interpretation.

Preaching the gospel, then, and exhorting people to accept it, were the means of bringing listeners to conversion by pointing out their need for redemption and the divine means of provision. The fact that some would not receive it only pointed out their guilt and the fact that they were morally responsible and therefore blameworthy.

In a corresponding vein, Fuller and others of his persuasion undoubtedly warmed to Edwards' focus on the experiential aspects of conversion and true spirituality. While the New England theologian did not interpret ecclesiology in exactly the same way, his 1746 work, *Religious Affections,* meshed well with the Baptist insistence on a congregation consisting only of those whose baptism testified to genuine conversion and whose subsequent actions supported that testimony.

Thus Fuller and his colleagues found in Edwards' writings a solid theological and philosophical foundation to help combat the beliefs which were stifling so many churches in the Particular camp. *The Gospel Worthy of All Acceptation* was Fuller's classic statement of this evangelical theology, and had a tremendous impact on Baptists of his day:

> It turned Particular Baptists around, brought a new style of preaching, helped stave off the paralysis of hyper-Calvinism, developed a theology of moderate conservatism which made possible the missionary movement

embodied in William Carey, and laid the groundwork for Baptist advance in the nineteenth century.[7]

Converted a few years after Fuller, Carey was ordained as a Baptist minister in 1786. While a pastor, he maintained the cobbler trade to support his family. His diligent study revealed genuine promise as a linguist. That skill, coupled with his hobby of mapmaking, contributed to a growing passion for seeing the gospel spread to unreached areas of the globe. He believed that Christ's commission to the apostles to "teach all nations" was still a mandate for Christians, and during a ministers' meeting in 1787, he suggested that idea as a topic for discussion. One of the older pastors reportedly responded, "Sit down young man. You are an enthusiast! When God pleases to convert the heathen, He will do it without consulting you or me."[8]

Carey was undaunted. In 1792, he published *An Enquiry into the Obligations of Christians to use means for the Conversion of the Heathen*. His thesis was a simple one: since the commission to Christ's apostles was to take the gospel to the ends of the earth and the task was not yet completed, each generation of believers had to personally adopt the challenge and pursue it in the best way possible.[9] He denied any arguments that attempted to restrict the responsibility to those first century Christians, and especially any claim that God would somehow bring the gospel to people who needed it without the utilization of preaching and evangelism.[10] He further rejected the contention from "learned divines" that the time had not yet come for the conversion of the heathen.[11] Quite to the contrary, the situation called "for every possible exertion to introduce the gospel amongst them [the heathen]."[12]

Jonathan Edwards' shadow and importance were again evident. His theological impact on Andrew Fuller certainly influenced Carey, who looked to Fuller as a mentor. Even more important, apparently, were Edwards' efforts in preserving Brainerd's story. Carey twice mentioned the young missionary's labors among the Indians, how he had preached, prayed, and seen an "extraordinary work of conversion."[13]

As with Fuller and others, Carey obviously labored under no illusions that the gospel should not be preached to non-Christians or that they should not be called upon to repent and believe. Quite to the contrary, when the fledgling "Particular Baptist Society for the Propagation of the Gospel among the Heathen" formed in October of 1792, he offered himself as its first missionary and shortly after sailed for India and into the pages of Protestant missions history.

Baptists have continued to the present day to exert aggressive leadership, both as theorists and practitioners, in world missions. The scope of their work has been a broad one, including medical, educational, agricultural, and human rights emphases. The heart of the effort, though, has always been evangelism and church planting—making contact with those of other faiths, or of no faith and calling, to follow Jesus and to align themselves in meaningful fellowship with others who are following Him.

Most of those Baptists locate the roots of this missionary commitment in their reading of scripture and in the examples of post-New Testament individuals who served as effective models. A careful examination, though, of the eighteenth-century setting which birthed their missions movement must include the theological struggles within the ranks of the Particular Baptists in England. Andrew Fuller, William Carey, and others merit attention due to their willingness to wade through what they saw as the quagmire of hyper-Calvinism. Providing a significant light for the path, were the writings of Jonathan Edwards, and his contribution must not be overlooked.

MICHAEL D. THOMPSON received the B.S. from Oklahoma University; the M.Div. from Southwestern Baptist Theological Seminary; and the Ph.D. from Golden Gate Baptist Theological Seminary. He is Phoebe Schertz Young Professor of Religious Studies at Oklahoma State University. He has contributed various articles to denominational periodicals. His academic research focuses on the intersection of Christianity with specific Native American tribes.

NOTES

[1] H. Leon McBeth, *The Baptist Heritage* (Nashville: Broadman Press, 1987), 171–72.
[2] Andrew Fuller, *The Gospel Worthy of All Acceptation* (1785; reprint, Lafayette, IN: Sovereign Grace Publishers, 1961), 10.
[3] Ibid., 10.
[4] Ibid., 10.
[5] Fuller, *The Gospel Worthy of All Acceptation,* 11.
[6] Ibid., 23.
[7] McBeth, *The Baptist Heritage,* 182.
[8] Ibid., 185.
[9] William Carey, *An Enquiry into the Obligations of Christians to use means for the Conversion of the Heathen* (1792; reprint, London: Baptist Missionary Society, 1942), 6.
[10] Carey, *An Enquiry into the Obligations of Christians,* 8.
[11] Ibid., 12.
[12] Ibid., 13.
[13] Ibid., 36.

Edwards as Mystic

Richard A. S. Hall

Jonathan Edwards has long been reputed a mystic and so the spiritual ancestor of subsequent American mystics as diverse as Emerson, Thoreau, Whitman, and Robinson Jeffers. According to Vernon Louis Parrington, "Jonathan Edwards was the last and greatest of the royal line of Puritan mystics. As a young man he felt himself to be living in the very presence of God; he was conscious of the divine life flowing through and around him making him one with the Godhood; and he was filled with yearning for personal union with the divine love in Christ." Parrington understands Edwards' metaphysical idealism, with its affirmation that God alone is the sole substance in the world and that all our ideas of the physical world we receive through sensation are in reality nothing but ideas in the mind of God, as a philosophical justification for his mysticism insofar as it stresses the reality and immediacy of God. However, Parrington concedes that the mystical strain in Edwards' thought, steeped as it is in Neo-Platonism, is at odds with his Calvinism: "But in adhering to the doctrine of predetermined election by the sovereign will of God, Edwards did unconscious violence to the instincts of the mystics, that throughout his earlier speculations—and in much of his later, as well—impelled him to glorify the love of God the Father, and the sweetness of spiritual communion with Him."[1] Frederic I. Carpenter, extending Parrington's judgment, affirms that "Edwards was the first, if not the greatest, of a royal line of modern American mystics," and that "all of Edwards's work was founded on a psychology of mysticism, which was radically different from the theology of Calvinism"—like Parrington, he notes the tension between Edwards' mysticism and his Calvinism. Carpenter locates Edwards' mysticism in his psychology of conversion, especially as it relates to his own conversion as described in his *Personal Narrative* and in the Plotinian emanationism of his late dissertation, *God's End in Creating the World,* where, Carpenter says, Edwards has achieved a "mystic pantheism" and so abandoned Calvinism.[2]

However, other commentators have demurred that claims for Edwards' mysticism have been exaggerated, and have even questioned whether he is a mystic at all. "One had best leave the mantle of 'mysticism' for another wearer than Edwards, for it fits him loosely at best," ripostes Conrad Cherry. Cherry distinguishes between two schools of thought as to Edwards' alleged mysticism. One, represented by such as Parrington and Carpenter, maintains that Edwards, reacting against an intellectually stifling Calvinism whose forms of thought he could not altogether escape, dwelt "on the internal communication of God to the soul" and adhered "to an idea of the mystical absorption of the individual in the absolute," thereby turning Edwards into a closet Transcendentalist. To this interpretation of Edwards, though, Conrad cites Clyde Holbrook and Thomas Schafer to the effect that Edwards always insisted on the distinction between the individual and God since the divine reality stands above and beyond the human and the natural. The soul is always and utterly dependent upon the divine initiative of saving grace in its justification and sanctification, and so the identity of the human individual is never lost in the Godhead. Cherry concludes, "There is in Edwards' thought and own life no manifest attempt to absorb man into the divine in 'mystical' identity."

On the other hand, Douglas J. Elwood represents another school of thought alleging Edwards' mysticism that maintains, in Cherry's words, "there is for Edwards an internal and mystical union of God with the soul."[3] And Michael J. McClymond thinks that such a union may be implied by Edwards' doctrine of illumination: "If there is a mystical dimension to Edwards's teaching on illumination, it lies in his insistence that the divine light not only gives knowledge but also becomes one with the knower and transforms him or her."[4] But union, notes Cherry, does not imply identity: "God in his Spirit communicates himself to the saint, but He joins the saint as the saint's new principle or foundation and not as human-absorbing divinity."[5] And McClymond concurs: "Yet Edwards does not wish to portray the connection of the divine light and the human vision as so intimate that the light is mystically absorbed into human nature, or the human nature into the divine light. . . . A distinction between God and humanity remains at all times, even though the Spirit and the natural human faculties operate conjointly and coordinately in the process of spiritual perception." Moreover, McClymond hears a mystic note sounded in the *Personal Narrative* where Edwards describes his entirely new sense of natural things as effected by his own illumination: "one is struck by Edwards's mundane mysticism, his capacity for seeing God in and through the world of nature."[6]

This dispute over Edwards' mysticism is not the only disagreement that has bedeviled Edwards scholarship. There has long been a dispute, for example, over his conception of God: is he an orthodox theist, or perhaps a panentheist or, worse, a closet pantheist? There have been disputes over whether he was fundamentally a Calvinist or a Neo-Platonist—the two being at odds—and over whether his mind-set is essentially "modern" or "medieval." Part of the fault lies in Edwards himself where discordant philosophical outlooks remain—at least on the face of it—unreconciled. Yet some of the fault can be imputed to commentators who are unclear about the meaning of key terms or fail to appreciate the subtlety of Edwards' thought—and this is the case with the dispute over Edwards' mysticism.

Nowhere do these disputants spell out exactly what it is they mean by "mysticism" so as to determine whether that term correctly characterizes Edwards' thought or not. They are not entirely to blame for this since "mysticism" is a notoriously slippery term. "No word in our language," says William Ralph Inge, "has been employed more loosely than 'Mysticism.'" One reason, no doubt, is that it eludes precise definition. "Even those writers who have made a special study of the subject," Inge continues, "show by their definitions of the word how uncertain is its connotation." In an appendix to his *Christian Mysticism,* where he makes these statements, Inge distinguishes no less than twenty-six distinct definitions of the term.[7]

Nevertheless, those commenting on Edwards' alleged mysticism do seem to presuppose two distinct conceptions of it in their discussions. One, upon which they all agree—whether or not they agree that Edwards is a mystic—is that the mystic believes in the possibility of a complete identity of the soul with God and believes that at times he has actually experienced it. The second conception of mysticism, suggested, for example, by McClymond, is the subject's awareness of a divinity—typically God—in and through nature. What all the above commentators agree upon, and correctly so, is that Edwards neither believed in the possibility of that identity nor did he ever experience it. Edwards was ever at pains to keep the soul and God distinct, however intimately they might interact.

However, Edwards' rejection of any possible identity of the soul with God and his failure to experience it by no means implies that he is not a mystic. Though that identity may represent an extreme form of mysticism, there are other beliefs and experiences, though not involving the perfect union of identity, that nonetheless qualify as mystical in a broader conception of mysticism. I turn now to this broader conception based upon the reflections of John Ellis McTaggart and William James on this subject, which not only do fuller justice to its range and variety but are more consonant with the literature on mysticism. According to this conception, it can be shown that Edwards is indeed a mystic.

Before we continue, though, we should distinguish between two forms of mysticism which I shall informally designate as "psychological" mysticism and "speculative" or "philosophical" mysticism.[8] Psychological mysticism concerns the actual experiences the mystic undergoes that qualifies her as a mystic. If the mystic reflects on her preternatural experiences in order better to understand them and speculates on the basis of them, then mysticism becomes speculative or philosophical. What began as a mystical experience may germinate into a philosophical system that inevitably bears the tincture of the experience engendering it.

William James, in his magisterial psychological study, *The Varieties of Religious Experience,* concentrates on the psychology of mystical experience, and distinguishes four characteristics that qualify a state of consciousness as mystical. Two of them are both necessary and sufficient to render a mental state mystical. One is "ineffability," which means that "it defies expression, that no adequate report of its contents can be given in words." The mystical state to be known must be experienced directly by the subject; it begs description and cannot be communicated verbally to others. At best, it can be hinted at only poetically through the skillful use of metaphors and analogies.

The second essential characteristic of mystical states of consciousness is what James calls their "noetic quality"; that is, they are "states of knowledge," or "states of insight into depths of truth unplumbed by the discursive intellect. They are illuminations, revelations, full of significance and importance, all inarticulate though they remain; and as a rule they carry with them a curious sense of authority for after-time."[9] The subject of a mystical state, then, knows a truth inaccessible to common experience or reason and incommunicable to those to whom it has not been vouchsafed.

James notes that "the range of mystical experience is very wide" with some mystical states of consciousness being more developed, complex and intense than others. This is useful insofar as it enables us to expand further our conception of mysticism. The lowest rung of the mystic ladder is what James identifies as a "sense of deeper significance" possessed by words or things. It may be "that deepened sense of the significance of a maxim or formula which occasionally sweeps over one." James describes the experience this way: "'I've heard that said all my life,' we exclaim, 'but I never realized its full meaning until now.' 'When a fellow monk,' said Luther, 'one day repeated the words of the Creed: "I believe in the forgiveness of sins," I saw the Scripture in an entirely new light; and straightway I felt as if I were born anew. It was as if I had found the door of paradise thrown wide open.'" However, James hastens to add, "this sense of deeper significance is not confined to rational propositions. Single words, and conjunctions of words, effects of light on land and sea, odors and musical sounds, all bring it when the mind is tuned aright."[10] He is here describing the "eureka" experience that is often serendipitous as well.

The second rung on the ladder of mysticism James designates "dreamy state." This occurs when the subject is overwhelmed by the sense that natural phenomena have some deep, occult meaning resisting disclosure. For a description of this state, James cites Charles Kingsley: "'When I walk the fields, I am oppressed now and then with an innate feeling that everything I see has a meaning, if I could but understand it.'"[11] The dreamy state seems to be a more specific form of the sense of deeper significance. The sense of deeper significance may be a better understanding of a previously understood meaning, or simply the sense of something's importance or value, the meaning of which cannot be precisely articulated; whereas in the dreamy state something is felt to be significant insofar as it holds some as yet *undisclosed* meaning.

The highest rung of the mystical ladder is reached when the subject is united with the Absolute, however conceived, and is aware of that union. According to James, "this overcoming of all the usual barriers between the individual and the Absolute is the great mystic achievement. In mystic states we both become one with the Absolute and we become aware of our oneness. This is the everlasting and triumphant mystical tradition, hardly altered by differences of clime or creed."[12]

We turn now from James' account of psychological mysticism to McTaggart's account of philosophical mysticism. McTaggart believes that two characteristics are essential to speculative mysticism so that if one's thought exhibits them, one qualifies as a mystic. One characteristic is the assertion of "a greater unity in the universe than that which is recognized in ordinary experience, or in science." The second is "the affirmation that it is possible to be conscious of this unity in some manner which brings the knower into closer and more direct relation with what is known than can be done in ordinary discursive thought"; moreover, what is known is known "in a manner so direct and immediate that it may be compared to the perception of matter by our senses."[13] In brief, then, the defining characteristics of that experience called "mystical" are "mystic unity" and "mystic intuition." Unity belongs to ontology insofar as it describes the way things are, whereas intuition belongs to epistemology inasmuch it prescribes how that unity is known.

Mystics disagree, however, as to how thoroughgoing this unity is. Some, like Parmenides, believe unity necessarily precludes any form of real differentiation among the parts of a whole or any form of real individuation or difference in the world, these things being at most illusions; others, like Plato, believe unity is indeed compatible with differentiation and individuation. "The unity may be regarded as only one aspect of the universe, and as combined with diversity," remarks McTaggart. "Or it may be said that, in reality, there is no diversity at all, but only unity." The former view,

> while asserting that there is a deeper unity between the parts of the universe than is generally recognized, does not deny that those parts were really different from each other. Indeed, it is possible to hold, with Hegel, that this deeper unity, so far from making them less differentiated than they are commonly supposed to be, actually makes them more differentiated. Hegel maintained . . . that finite existences can only be really individual and differentiated in proportion as they are united between themselves in a close unity. The organs of a human body are contained in closer unity than the stones in a heap, and at the same time those organs

have each a more individual nature, and are more clearly differentiated from one another than the stones of a heap.[14]

We are now ready to look at some of Edwards' writings in light of the above conception of mysticism to see what they suggest about their author's own mysticism. We shall see that they attest to Edwards' being both a psychological and a philosophical mystic. He is a psychological mystic insofar as he describes himself as being endowed with a "new sense" (what James identifies as a sense of the deeper significance of thing). He is a philosophical mystic inasmuch as he later generalizes his new sense as a "new spiritual sense" vouchsafed to anybody to whom God unites himself.

The earliest published record of Edwards' mystical experiences is to be found in his *Personal Narrative,* a short spiritual autobiography dating from around 1739 but recounting events that occurred during his adolescence; it is a calm, critical, and reflective account of what he once experienced at white heat in order to see what light might yet remain. It is precisely these early experiences that struck McClymond and others as evidence of "Edwards's mundane mysticism, his capacity for seeing God in and through the world of nature."

In his narrative, Edwards reports how a text of scripture suddenly gave him a wholly "new sense" of the glory of God. Thus, upon reading I Timothy 1:17, he writes, "As I read the words, there came into my soul, and was as it were diffused through it, a sense of the glory of the Divine Being; a new sense, quite different from anything I ever experienced before. Never any words of Scripture seemed to me as these words did." Afterwards, when reading scripture, he confesses, sometimes the new sense he had of the text would impede the progress of his reading: "I seemed often to see so much light, exhibited by every sentence, and such a refreshing ravishing food communicated, that I could not get along in reading."

Edwards had a new sense not only of God's glory but of another of his attributes as well, namely, God's sovereignty. He had earlier rebelled with "great and violent inward struggles" against it: "My mind had been wont to be full of objections against the doctrine of God's sovereignty," specifically the idea that God had decided from the beginning whom he would damn and whom he would save. It was the sheer arbitrariness and apparent injustice of God's decision that appalled Edwards. But he underwent a sea change with respect to this doctrine that signaled his conversion: "there has been a wonderful alteration in my mind, with respect to the doctrine of God's sovereignty, . . . so that I scarce ever have found so much as the rising of an objection against God's sovereignty." He now not only understood "the justice and reasonableness of it," but he *delighted* in it, savoring its sweetness: "But I have oftentimes since that first conviction, had quite another kind of sense of God's sovereignty, than I had then. I have often since, not only had a conviction, but a *delightful* conviction. The doctrine of God's sovereignty has very often appeared, an exceeding pleasant, bright and sweet doctrine to me." Yet this was not all. He had a new sense of the doctrines of his faith: "I began to have a new kind of apprehensions and ideas of Christ, and the work of redemption, and the glorious way of salvation by him. I had an inward, sweet sense of these things, that at times came into my heart; and my soul was led away in pleasant views and contemplations of them." Most significantly, Edwards' new sense extended to God's excellence or holiness, which he deemed his supreme attribute. "The holiness of God," he relates, "has always appeared to me the most lovely of all his attributes," but now, through his new sense, it appeared "ravishingly lovely" and as "the highest beauty."

Yet, Edwards' new sense of things went beyond biblical texts, divine attributes and Christian doctrines to embrace even the sights and sounds of nature. "The appearance of everything was altered," he rhapsodizes; "there seemed to be, as it were, a calm, sweet cast, or appearance of divine glory, in almost everything. God's excellency, his wisdom, his purity and love, seemed to appear in everything;

in the sun, moon and stars; in the clouds, and blue sky; in the grass, flowers, trees; in the water, and all nature." The most striking alteration in Edwards' perception of nature is found in his changed attitude toward thunderstorms: "I used to be a person uncommonly terrified with thunder: and it used to strike me with terror, when I saw a thunderstorm rising. But now, on the contrary, it rejoiced me. I felt God at the first appearance of a thunderstorm."[15] Before, thunder, like God's sovereignty, appalled him; now he delighted in both.

Edwards' "new sense" is clearly James' "sense of deeper significance." More particularly, Edwards' "new sense, quite different from anything I ever experienced before," which occurred to him when reading scripture such that "never any words of Scripture seemed to me as these words did," illustrates what James meant by "that deepened sense of the significance of a maxim or formula which occasionally sweeps over one." And Edwards' report that "God's excellency, his wisdom, his purity and love, seemed to appear in everything; in the sun, moon and stars; in the clouds, and blue sky; in the grass, flowers, trees; in the water, and all nature" exemplifies James' point that "this sense of deeper significance is not confined to rational propositions" but may extend to things like the "effects of light on land and sea, odors and musical sounds."

For James, though, Edwards' youthful mystical experiences represent only a *quasi-* or *proto-*mystical experience, not a full-fledged mystical state of consciousness—what he calls "cosmic consciousness" and what Freud calls the "oceanic feeling"—since this involves an acute experience of the annihilation of the finite self or its absorption into something infinitely large.[16] But even when he was most ravished by the revelations of his new sense, Edwards never lost his head. It is noteworthy that Edwards' new sense always turns on the intellect, for it involves understanding the real or deeper meaning of something whether of texts, doctrines, natural phenomena, or divine attributes. Cosmic consciousness is the deepest plunge into mystical consciousness, like the plunge taken by a deep-sea diver, whereas the mystical states described by Edwards are more like wading in or swimming on the surface of the ocean of being. It is perhaps because Edwards never takes the deepest plunge that commentators like McClymond and others think he is a mystic only in a qualified sense; however, if James' typology of mystical experience is correct, he nevertheless is a mystic in an important sense.

In his *Personal Narrative,* Edwards simply gives a phenomenology of his new sense of things as he earlier experienced it. But in his *Treatise on Religious Affections,* dating from 1746, he clarifies it through a rigorous philosophical analysis. It is here that he passes from psychological to philosophical mysticism since he works out the implications of his mystic new sense for our knowledge of God. The dispute over Edwards' mysticism has centered on this text, so it behooves us to look at it closely to see what it reveals about Edwards as a speculative mystic in light of the expanded conception of mysticism described above.

In the treatise, Edwards denominates the new sense illustrated in *Personal Narrative* as "a new spiritual sense" analogous to but distinct from the five natural senses—a "sixth" sense, as it were, "a principle of new kind of perception or spiritual sensation, which is in its whole nature different from any former kinds of sensation of the mind as tasting is diverse from any of the other senses." What is uniquely known by this spiritual sense, then, is nothing that can be simulated by the natural understanding: it is not a form of propositional knowledge or anything expressible in language; neither is it an image that can be conjured up by the imagination; nor is it any esoteric meaning that the natural understanding might divine in a text of scripture or some theological doctrine. Rather, it is a direct knowledge of the reality of God's excellence or holiness as it really is: "the beauty of holiness is that thing . . . which is perceived by this spiritual sense, that is so diverse from all that natural men perceive."

This knowledge is not ratiocinative but intuitive. Edwards calls it a special kind of "sensible knowledge" or a "sense of the heart" as opposed to a merely "notional" or "speculative" one.[17] Notional knowledge is simply a theoretical understanding of anything such as that represented by the body of science. Sensible knowledge involves not only having an intellectual intuition but also responding affectively or emotionally in a proper way to that intuition. It is both cognitive and affective inasmuch as it involves the having of a new understanding as well as a new kind of affections like delight and love. Edwards aptly compares these two kinds of knowledge, notional and sensible, to the knowledge of honey. One person, perhaps a chemist or entomologist, has expert knowledge of the chemical composition of honey or the manner of its production, and knows of its sweetness, but has never tasted it. He has a merely notional knowledge of it. But then, there is the person who has actually tasted honey and can attest to its incomparable sweetness—he not only has acquaintance with its sweetness but has taken delight in it—the proper affective response. Similarly, one may know *that* God is holy and fully understand what that means, and indeed be an expert in biblical and philosophical theology, but this person has nothing more than notional knowledge. By contrast, there is the person who has, through the sense of the heart, actually "tasted" of God's excellence or holiness and has taken exquisite pleasure in it. Such a one has sensible knowledge of God, which is the true knowledge of him. Edwards' sense of the heart, therefore, is primarily aesthetic since its proper object is God's attribute of beauty or excellence.

In describing this spiritual sense together with the knowledge it entails, Edwards performs a delicate balancing act. On the one hand, he is at great pains to affirm that it is not in any way derived from, or compounded of, or explicable in terms of our natural faculties. It is a wholly supernatural endowment, the effect of saving grace or of "those gracious influences" which "are entirely above nature, altogether of a different kind from anything that men find within themselves by nature, or only in the exercise of natural principles." It cannot be simulated by our natural minds. On the other hand, he is no less insistent that it is not a new faculty or mental capacity superadded to or substituted for our natural faculties of understanding and will. Rather, it is a new principle or habit operating within and exercised by these faculties, a new and heightened way of knowing and feeling:

"So this new spiritual sense is not a new faculty of understanding, but it is a new foundation laid in the nature of the soul, for a new kind of exercises of the same faculty of understanding." And this foundation is new because it originates from God the Holy Spirit who is "so united to the faculties of the soul, that he becomes there a principle or spring of new nature and life," and as such he "produces those effects wherein he exerts and communicates himself in his own proper nature."[18] Think of this new spiritual sense as something like genius or virtuosic skill on a musical instrument. The genius of a Newton or the keyboard virtuosity of a Bach, though rooted in the human mind and body, is of a quite different order to mere intelligence or talent, though analogous to it.

Clearly, Edwards' new spiritual sense as philosophically formulated in *Religious Affections* bears all the hallmarks of classic mysticism. First, to use James' terminology, it is *noetic* insofar as it is privy to a unique kind of knowledge insofar as it is not notional or discursive but intuitive and sensible, and is not accessible through the exercise of the five natural senses—"the beauty of holiness... is so diverse from all that natural men perceive"—though it is analogous to them. And that knowledge is *ineffable* insofar as it cannot be formulated and expressed propositionally. This new spiritual sense is McTaggart's *mystic intuition*. Second, this spiritual sense presupposes a union between man and God, who is "so united to the faculties of the soul, that he becomes there a principle or spring of new nature and life." This is McTaggart's *mystic union*. However, this divine/human union by no means implies the annihilation of the human self. Indeed, the self remains intact with all its original faculties of understanding and will, except now they function in a wholly new way, operating according to a new habit or disposition—"this new spiritual sense is not a new faculty of understanding, but it is a new foundation laid in the nature of the soul, for a new kind of exercises of the same faculty of understanding." So this mystic union is not one that excludes differentiation and individuation as being incompatible with itself, but fully embraces them; this union in no way implies the identity of the self and God. This insight has not been lost either on Cherry, who remarks that for Edwards, "God in his Spirit communicates himself to the saint, but He joins the saint as the saint's new principle or foundation and not as human-absorbing divinity," or on McClymond, who similarly observes, "Yet Edwards does not wish to portray the connection of the divine light and the human vision as so intimate that the light is mystically absorbed into human nature, or the human nature into the divine light.... A distinction between God and humanity remains at all times, even though the Spirit and the natural human faculties operate conjointly and coordinately in the process of spiritual perception." Thus, the mysticism evident in Edwards' doctrine of the new spiritual sense is one that, in McTaggart's words, "while asserting that there is a deeper unity between the parts of the universe than is generally recognized, does not deny that those parts were really different from each other." In this respect, Edwards' speculative mysticism is like Hegel's.

We are now ready to resolve the dispute over Edwards' mysticism in light of our more nuanced conception of mysticism. To say with Parrington and Carpenter that Edwards, as Cherry puts it, adhered "to an idea of the mystical absorption of the individual in the absolute" is, of course, wrong since Edwards' mysticism unambiguously presupposes a differentiated unity between the human and the divine in his account of the spiritual sense. Yet to say with Cherry that, therefore, "One had best leave the mantle of 'mysticism' for another wearer than Edwards, for it fits him loosely at best," is no less mistaken since he ignores the fact that mysticism need not exclude a differentiated and variegated unity which honors individuality and difference. Thus, though Cherry is correct in concluding that "there is in Edwards' thought and own life no manifest attempt to absorb man into the divine in 'mystical' identity," this makes Edwards no less a mystic. Those who, like Elwood and McClymond, take a position on Edwards' mysticism midway between Parrington and Carpenter on the one hand and Cherry on the other, are correct. Edwards does, as Elwood says, affirm the possibility of "an internal and mystical union [albeit a differentiated one] of God with the soul," and insists, as McClymond asserts, "that the divine light not only gives knowledge but also becomes one [though not identical] with the knower and transforms him or her."

Edwards' speculative mysticism, exemplified in his doctrine of the spiritual sense with its presupposition of a unity, but not identity, of the soul and God is well within the mainstream of Christian orthodoxy with its insistence on a distinction between creature and Creator. The highest stage of religion, and so of religious mysticism, according to Inge, is "the unitive or contemplative life, in which man beholds God face to face, and is joined to Him." However, Inge cautions that this union is never complete such that the human soul becomes perfectly one with God, but it is an ideal relationship that is approached only asymptotically, in the same way that the horizon may be approached but never reached. Thus, "complete union with God is the ideal limit of religion, the attainment of which would be at once its consummation and annihilation. It is in the continual but unending approximation to it that the life of religion subsists."[19] This is exactly Edwards' point. The denial that an absolute identity of the soul with God is possible makes one no less a mystic. All that is required of the mystic is that he aspire toward it and is in the process of getting ever closer to it, while realizing that it is unattainable.

In conclusion, Edwards certainly qualifies as a psychological mystic insofar as he reports having had a "new sense" of things, what James would call a "sense of deeper significance"—a quasi-mysticism. Edwards qualifies no less as a philosophical mystic inasmuch as he reconceived his "new sense" as a "new spiritual sense," which is mystical in two senses: First, it is the organ of a mystic intuition of God's excellence as it really is; thus, this intuition is noetic since it involves a deeper knowledge of the divine nature not vouchsafed to those who lack this spiritual sense; moreover, it is neither discursive nor ratiocinative for what is known is known "in a manner so direct and immediate that it may be compared to the perception of matter by our senses," nor can it be adequately communicated. Second, the possession of this new spiritual sense presupposes a mystic unity, but not identity, between the soul and God—it is a unity allowing a distinction between the soul and God.

There is much more that is mystical in Edwards than those passages in *Personal Narrative* attesting to Edwards' psychological mysticism or those in *Religious Affections* attesting to his philosophical mysticism. Inge remarks that any philosophy inspired by mysticism—as Edwards' certainly is—is typically a species of idealism, thus setting its face against materialism and skepticism. Speculative mysticism holds that, in Inge's words, "the universe is the thought and will of God expressed under the forms of time and space."[20] Reality, or the world as it really is, existing above the vagaries of space and time, is known only to God, and yet may be glimpsed by human beings in moments of mystic intuition. The existence of the world in the mind of God implies a second tenet of speculative mysticism, namely, that everything in the world shadows forth in different degrees the divine nature. Thus, in the words of Scotus Erigena, "'Every visible and invisible creature is a theophany or appearance of God.'"[21] And more recently, in the same vein, Charles Kingsley writes, "The great Mysticism is the belief . . . that all symmetrical natural objects . . . are types of some spiritual truth or existence. . . . Everything seems to be full of God's reflex if we could but see it."[22] R. L. Nettleship seconds this view with his statement, "The true Mysticism is the belief that everything, in being what it is, is symbolic of something more."[23] Finally, a third tenet of speculative mysticism, of course, is monism, or the belief that the world is fundamentally one kind of thing. And this view is typically accompanied by determinism. Inge's profile of mystical philosophy in fact fits Edwards perfectly. The argument for idealism (or more precisely, perhaps, for immaterialism) in Edwards' early essay "The Mind" and the Neo-Platonic emanationism of his late dissertation *Concerning the End for Which God Created the World* powerfully affirm that "the universe is the thought and will of God expressed under the forms of time and space." And certainly, his new sense, as described in *Personal Narrative,* enabled him to see the natural world as "a theophany or appearance of God." This new perception of external nature as theophany is formalized in Edwards' typology in which natural phenomena are interpreted as ciphers in a vast book of nature, a system of spiritual hieroglyphics. Paula M. Cooey characterizes his typology as follows: "Nature, like scripture, is a book of types; nature, like scripture, is divine communication."[24] Edwards would have assented to Emerson's dictum: "Every natural fact is a symbol of some spiritual fact."[25] This alone would be enough to establish Edwards as a mystic; to cite Kingsley again, "The great Mysticism is the belief . . . that all symmetrical natural objects . . . are types of some spiritual truth or existence." Finally, the rigid determinism of Edwards' *Freedom of the Will* as well as his conception of the solidarity of the human race in sin found in his *Original Sin,* presuppose a "block-universe," an uncompromising monism, which, James thought, was the natural tendency of philosophical mysticism: "mystical states in general assert a pretty distinct theoretic drift. It is possible to give the outcome of the majority of them in terms that point in definite philosophical directions. One of these directions is optimism, and the other is monism."[26] Once it is realized that mystic unity does not necessarily mean identity, then the full mystical dimensions of Edwards' thought open up to view. Edwards' philosophy and theology are as suffused with mysticism as Constable's landscapes are suffused with light. Edwards belongs not only in "the royal line of Puritan mystics" but, no less, in the royal line of classic philosophical mystics that includes Parmenides, Plato, Spinoza, Hegel, and F. H. Bradley. Bertrand Russell has said that "the greatest men who have been philosophers have felt the need both of science and of mysticism: the attempt to harmonize the two was what made their life, and what always must, for all its arduous uncertainty, make philosophy, to some minds, a greater thing than either science or religion."[27] This observation applies as much to Edwards, though with the qualification that for him religion, correctly understood, was greater than either science or philosophy.

In light of this, we need to amend Cherry's appraisal. Instead of saying of Edwards that the mantle of mysticism "fits him loosely at best," we should say that it fits him quite comfortably. In the long run, though, determining whether Edwards is a mystic, or what kind of mystic he is, matters less than describing and evaluating the kind of experience he claims to have had of God and the world and ascertaining its epistemological and metaphysical significance. Whether we label that experience as "mystic" in some sense or another is not nearly as important as the experience itself and its import. And the merit of the dispute over Edwards' mysticism is that it forces us to come to a more precise understanding of what Edwards *himself* experienced and what he thought about his experience.

RICHARD A. S. HALL holds the B.A. from Boston University, the M.A. from Dalhousie University (Halifax, Nova Scotia), and the Ph.D. from the University of Toronto. He is assistant professor of philosophy at Fayetteville State University (Fayetteville, N.C.). His research interests lie in the history of modern philosophy, with a particular emphasis on American philosophy, aesthetics, and the philosophy of art, ethics, and religion. His publications include *The Ethical Foundations of Criminal Justice* and *The Neglected Northampton Texts of Jonathan Edwards: Edwards on Society & Politics*.

NOTES

[1] Vernon Louis Parrington, *Main Currents in American Thought: An Interpretation of American Literature from the Beginnings to 1920, Vol. 1: The Colonial Mind, 1620–1800* (New York: Harcourt, Brace and Company, 1927), 152, 156.

[2] Frederic I. Carpenter, "The Radicalism of Jonathan Edwards," *The New England Quarterly* (629–44), 630, 633, 634.

[3] Conrad Cherry, *The Theology of Jonathan Edwards: A Reappraisal* (Gloucester, MA: Peter Smith, 1974), 88, 85, 87.

[4] Michael J. McClymond, *Encounters with God: An Approach to the Theology of Jonathan Edwards* (New York: Oxford University Press, 1998), 19.

[5] Cherry, *Jonathan Edwards*, 87–88.

[6] McClymond, *Encounters with God*, 13, 25.

[7] William Ralph Inge, *Christian Mysticism: Considered in Eight Lectures Delivered Before the University of Oxford*, 4th ed. (London: Methuen & Co. Ltd., 1899), 3:335–348.

[8] I follow Inge in using the term "speculative" as a synonym for "philosophical" in its application to mysticism. See ibid., p. 22.

[9] William James, *The Varieties of Religious Experience: A Study of Human Nature* (New York: The Modern Library, 2002), 414–15.

[10] Ibid., 416–17

[11] Ibid., 419.

[12] James, *The Varieties of Religious Experience*, 457.

[13] John McTaggart Ellis McTaggart, "Mysticism," in *Philosophical Studies*, ed. S. V. Keeling (Bristol, England: Thoemmes Press, 1996), 47. Bertrand Russell also identifies the affirmation of unity as one of four defining characteristics of mysticism: "The second characteristic of mysticism is its belief in unity, and its refusal to admit opposition or division anywhere." From Bertrand Russell, *Mysticism and Logic, and Other Essays* (Totowa, NJ: Barnes & Noble Books, 1981), 15.

[14] McTaggart, "Mysticism," 50–51.

[15] Jonathan Edwards, "Personal Narrative," in *A Jonathan Edwards Reader*, ed. John E. Smith, Harry S. Stout, and Kenneth P. Minkema (New Haven: Yale University Press, 1995), 284, 289, 282, 283, 284, 291, 287, 285.

[16] Interestingly, McTaggart cites these very passages from *Personal Narrative* as an illustration of a fully-fledged theistic mysticism that exemplifies the union of God and man. See McTaggart, "Mysticism," 53.

[17] Jonathan Edwards, *Religious Affections*, ed. John E. Smith (New Haven: Yale University Press, 1959), 205–06, 260, 272.

[18] Edwards, *Religious Affections*, 205, 206, 202, 200, 201.

[19] Inge, *Christian Mysticism*, 12.

[20] Inge, *Christian Mysticism*, 26.

[21] Ibid., 26.

[22] As cited Ibid., 27.

[23] As cited Ibid., 250.

[24] Paula M. Cooey, *Jonathan Edwards on Nature and Destiny: Systematic Analysis* (Lewiston, NY: Edwin Mellen Press, 1985), 117.

[25] Ralph Waldo Emerson, *Selected Essays, Lectures, and Poems*, ed. Robert D. Richardson, Jr. (New York: Bantam Books, 1990), 28.

[26] James, *Varieties*, 453.

[27] Russell, *Mysticism and Logic*, 9.

"Heaven Is a World of Love"

Ronald Story
October 5, 2003

Who was Jonathan Edwards, and why should we, in the twenty-first century, care about him? This is not an easy question because the reputation of the man who filled this pulpit nearly three hundred years ago has changed so dramatically over the years. He may be the most famous resident Northampton has ever had. But he may also be the most complicated.

For some people, Jonathan Edwards is the ultimate Intellectual, someone who spent his life in his study grappling with the most advanced thought of his day in an effort to reconcile it to Scripture. The results—think volumes of brilliant theology—have impressed scholars and theologians ever since. The fact that he did this in a hick frontier town like Northampton and in the teeth of a rising tide of American materialism makes him all the more impressive. A recent biography calls his effort to reconcile the worlds of faith and natural law "breathtaking."

For others, Edwards is the ultimate unyielding Calvinist, with an absolute faith in an all-powerful God, original sin, free and unearned grace, Christ's atonement, and the primacy of Scripture. He fought against the idea that people could work their own salvation through good works or through a feeling of ecstasy. He opposed both cheap revivalism and buying one's way into Heaven, and he was willing to see most of humanity condemned to perdition rather than compromise his faith. One student calls him the "greatest apologist for human depravity in American history."

For still others, Jonathan Edwards is the godfather of American evangelism. He influenced John Wesley and Charles G. Finney, who brought the word of God to millions by imitating the preaching techniques of Edwards, and Edwards influences revivalists to this day, not least because of the lingering power of his extraordinary sermon, "Sinners in the Hands of an Angry God," which warned people of the agonies that awaited them in hell should God not elect to save them. Hellfire revivalists have always loved this one, especially in the South where I grew up.

To Edwards the Intellectual, the Calvinist, and the Evangelist must be added Edwards the Scold, as every biographer stresses. He spent much of his tenure in Northampton criticizing his parishioners for not being spiritual enough or generous enough or respectful enough—or, for that matter, for being anti-church and anti-minister. He scolded young people for lewdness and business people for greed. Back then, of course, ministers were supposed to scold their congregations. The congregations sort of expected it. And you can be sure that Edwards, with his high purpose and strict standards, did not disappoint.

But Edwards was more than just Intellectual, Calvinist, Evangelist, and Scold. He was certainly these. But to stop there is really misleading as to his full nature and the fullness of his mission in Northampton. For example Jonathan Edwards preached less about fire, as in his notorious "Sinners" sermon, than about Light—about *Christ the Light of the World, A Divine and Supernatural Light, False Light and True,* "Light in a Dark World," and the like.

Light is different from fire. Light means sight and insight, brightness and illumination. In Edwards' sermons it suggests something of "sweetness" and rapture, of personal and collective hope rather than anxiety and dread. And it suggests Christ. "That beauteous light with which the world is filled in a clear day is but a lively shadow of His spotless holiness and happiness." The effects of Edwards' "light" preaching could be magical. Here's a sample from an Ordination sermon:

The light of ministers of the gospel will be like the beams of the sun, that do not only convey light, but give life; and converts will be likely to spring up under their ministry, as the grass and the plants of the field under the influences of the sun; and the souls of the saints will be likely to grow, and appear beautiful as the lily and to revive as the corn, and grow as the vine, and their scent to be as the wine of Lebanon; and their light will be like to the light of Christ, which is the light of life.

And not just Light, but also Beauty. Beauty was everywhere in Edwards' thought, preaching, and writing. He found the physical world—woods and fields, rainbows and flowers, the stars at night, thunderclouds by day—beautiful, filled with harmony and proportion. He loved the sweetness of honey, the harmonies of music, the form of a beautiful building or of a beautiful woman. He wrote of "a beautiful body, a lovely proportion, a beautiful harmony of features of face, delightful airs of countenance and voice, and sweet motion and gesture"—all, I believe, with his lovely wife Sarah in mind. He especially loved the beauty of music. He helped bring new hymns to the Connecticut Valley because the "most beautiful" way of expressing a "sweet concord of mind" was through music. He preached on "The Sweet Harmony of Christ" and Christ's "New Song" and taught children to sing as a way to "soften the heart into tenderness" and "harmonize the affections."

But Edwards insisted that "natural beauty only points to higher spiritual excellencies." The beauty of human love was limited compared to that between Christ and his saints, where "new beauties are continually discovered, and where we shall forever increase in beauty ourselves." Good and generous behavior—virtue—was "something beautiful—a kind of beauty or excellence." Virtue was in fact the absolute love of the infinite beauty of God and his works and creatures. General benevolence would arise from seeing and knowing God's infinite beauties, and this would "soften and sweeten the mind." Beauty was the key concept for Edwards on virtue, as it was a constant theme in his life.

Light and Beauty, then. But also, and even more, Charity. No virtue was more important to Edwards than Charity. "They that do good," he preached, "shall be rewarded, whether to their souls or bodies." "He that gives to the poor lends to the Lord." No one claiming to be a Christian should be "backward and straithanded towards his poor brethren." Edwards warned his congregation that kneeling before God is useless except as a sign of inner reverence. But Charity, the Christian's duty to the widow, the fatherless, the stranger and the poor, is always "significant in itself, for it is to do good." Having property, he said, would not help you get to Heaven. The best use of property was to help "the meek, the broken-hearted, the captive, and the imprisoned."

By what measure should we judge Christian behavior? According to Jonathan Edwards, by how many poor there are in a place. Towns had not done enough if there were *any* "objects of Charity suffering in pinching want." Though Christ is not on earth, "yet he has left others to be his receivers; and they are the poor.... Our needy neighbors are God's receivers." Edwards urged his congregation to collect funds for the poor and even urged a "public stock" for them—an early welfare system.

And we should not merely give to the needy, but reach out to them. God's grace, after all, could descend on anybody, low or high: "You that are ... not much accounted of, you see that your judgment of things is not much regarded, your voice is not so much heard as others." Well, do not be dismayed:

Christ himself, when he was upon earth, confined himself to your condition. He did not appear in the world in the circumstances of a man of note, but in the state of the poor and despised. He was of low parentage; his mother was a woman of low degree, her husband Joseph an obscure person.

This was a message designed to appeal, as Edwards hoped it would, to the socially marginal, to youth without family or property, to women—precisely those people that Edwards' evangelical Awakening preaching had helped draw into the churches. Charity, in other words, involved inclusion as well as generosity.

Light. Beauty. Charity. And underlying everything and above all, Love. Whatever his reputation, Jonathan Edwards was a powerful preacher of the gospel of love. The Edwards of love fairly leaps from the pages of one of his greatest works, *Charity and Its Fruits,* a series of sermons based on verses from I Corinthians. In these astonishing sermons, Edwards urged his congregation in their daily lives to imitate Christ. Christ loved everyone, Edwards says, even his enemies. He loved people so much that he felt one with them; he made them a part of "his flesh and his bone." He so loved us all that he gave everything he had and became poor for us and traded ease and honor for suffering and degradation. Christ loved us as he loved the poor, the maimed, the halt, the blind, the empty and needy and vagabond, without ever expecting to be repaid.

And so should we love. Christian love, Edwards preached, is contrary to a selfish spirit. We must consider not only our own circumstances and necessities but those of our neighbors. We must regard not only our own desires but others' desires, too. We should love even those of "hateful dispositions," even the proud, the greedy, the hard, the profane. We should not only help the poor, we should do it lovingly, "with our hand open wide" and with a charitable heart. Christian love will dispose us to mercy towards a neighbor who suffers "affliction or calamity." We will in this way "bear one another's burdens and weep with those that weep." And it is love, said Edwards, that will check and restrain "bitterness and heated spirits." Love will help us "suppress wrath, rage, resentment, revenge, and bitterness"—all the monstrous passion that stir up "hatred, strife, and violence."

Many people know Jonathan Edwards for preaching on the fiery terrors of hell, which he certainly did. But the sermons of *Charity and Its Fruits* allowed him to define hell more precisely. Hell, he argued, is a place where there is no love, a place without friendship or pity or mercy. It is a place deluged not with fire but with wrath and hatred and rage, with pride and strife, with spite, treachery, fickleness, hypocrisy and deceit. This may be the best definition of hell any minister ever offered: Hell is the place without love.

Heaven, by contrast, is a world of perfect love, as Edwards showed in "Heaven Is a World of Love," the overwhelming climax of these sermons on Corinthians. In Heaven, said Edwards, we may love God, Christ, and one another perfectly, without envy or malice or revenge or contempt or selfishness. In Heaven, no one will ever be grieved that they are slighted by those they love. Nor will the joy of Heavenly love be interrupted by jealousy. "Heavenly lovers," in Edwards' words, "will have no doubt of the love of each other. All their expressions of love shall come from the bottom of their hearts."

In Heaven, we shall have no difficulty expressing our love. Our souls "shall not be like a fire pent up but shall be perfectly at liberty, winged with love with no weight tied to the feet to hinder their flight." Nor will there be any wall of separation to prevent the perfect enjoyment of one another's love—neither physical distance, nor want of full acquaintance, nor misunderstanding, nor disunion through difference of temperament or circumstance or opinion or interest. We shall all be united, related to Christ, the Head of the whole society, the spouse, in Edwards' words, of the whole church of saints, which shall be a single family.

And as love seeks to have the beloved for its own, so in Heaven all shall have property in one another. The saints shall be God's, and he theirs. And so with Christ, who bought them with his life and gave himself to them in death. "And the saints shall be one another's." And they shall enjoy each other's love in perfect and undisturbed prosperity, without adversity or grief of spirit, and shall glory in the possession of all things in common. Heaven will be a garden of pleasure, an abode of heavenly lovers where they may have sweet society. "The very light which shines in and fills that world is the light of love," said Edwards. "It is beams of love; for it is the shining of the glory of the Lamb of God, that most wonderful influence of lamblike meekness and love which fills the heavenly Jerusalem with light."

And we will know such perfect love forever, with no fear that such happiness will ever end. "All things," preached Edwards, "shall flourish in an eternal youth. Age will not diminish anyone's beauty or vigor, and there love shall flourish in everyone's breast, as a living spring perpetually springs, or as a flame which never fails. And the holy pleasure shall be as a river which ever runs, and is always clear and full." He concluded:

> O what tranquility there is in such a world as this! Who can express the sweetness of this peace? What a calm is this, what a haven of rest to arrive at after persons have gone through a world of storms and tempests, a world of pride, and selfishness, and envy, and malice, and scorn, and contempt, and contention, and war? What a Canaan of rest!

Jonathan Edwards did not believe that we could find perfection in this world. If hell is hatred and heaven pure love, this world is a mixture. To find true and perfect love, you have to enter Heaven, which will only come through grace. But in the meantime we should try. He ended this magnificent sermon by telling us that "as Heaven is a world of love, so the way to heaven is the way of love. This will prepare you for heaven, and make you ready for an inheritance with the saints in that land of light and love. And if ever you arrive at Heaven, faith and love must be the wings that carry you there."

"Heaven Is a World of Love" is a sermon easily equal in power and brilliance to "Sinners in the Hands of an Angry God." "Sinners" seems to have stolen the day among people who compile anthologies and train evangelists for the sensationalist reason people find pain more riveting than grace. That's a pity because Edwards' "Heaven" is suffused with light and beauty and charity and love—indispensable attributes of the real Jonathan Edwards, whose message we still need to hear today. When we know "Heaven" as well as we know "Sinners," we will be closer to grasping what he meant to his time and ours.

There is a bronze tablet with a bas-relief of Jonathan Edwards on the wall of this meetinghouse [the First Churches]. Unveiled in 1900, the bas-relief catches much of the conventional wisdom about Edwards—the high forehead of the aloof intellectual, the judging eyes of the fearsome preacher, the lofty, bewigged, unapproachable minister. When the congregation comes into the sanctuary for Sunday service, members drift almost always to the left side, away from the formidable visage on the wall. People drift this way for many reasons, including habit. But I suspect they're also resisting, if only subconsciously, the stare of a figure who seems perhaps ready to scold them—as well he might, should he come suddenly to life once more.

But the sculpture is misleading. If you look at the painting on which the sculpture is based, you see an open face and level gaze. There is no smile. The great divines of New England did not smile. Being liked was not a particular virtue in America until quite recently, and certainly not among these men. God did not put them on the earth to be liked. And yet the eyes are youthful, almost tender, the face modest, almost vulnerable.

It's actually the way the bas-relief is lighted from the bottom and the deep cuts the sculptor used to capture the likeness that make the eyes appear dark and lowering and judgmental and the visage stern and lofty. The impression is not exactly wrong. It simply exaggerates certain features at the expense of others, such as the open and inviting right hand at the lower left reaching to touch us. The real Jonathan Edwards is like the wall sculpture. It's the lighting that history has thrown on him that makes him seem so daunting. If you look closely, you see not only the shadowy judging eyes, but also the warm loving hand.

Amen.

RONALD STORY holds the bachelor's degree from the University of Texas (Austin) and graduate degrees from the University of Wisconsin (Madison) and the State University of New York (Stony Brook). He is professor of history (emeritus) at the University of Massachusetts (Amherst). He has published 28 scholarly articles and essays on a broad array of subjects from wartime dissent to Jonathan Edwards. His work has appeared in journals such as the *American Historical Review* and the *Journal of American History*. Among his books are *Generations of Americans: A History of the United States* (St. Martin's, 1976), *Concise Historical Atlas of World War Two: The Geography of Conflict,* and *The Rise of Conservatism in America, 1945–2000: A History with Documents*.

Appendix

THE NORTHAMPTON JONATHAN EDWARDS TERCENTENARY CELEBRATION

Held at The First Churches
&
The Edwards Church,
Northampton, Massachusetts

October 3rd – 5th, 2003

LOCATIONS:

- All academic sessions of the conference will be held in the sanctuary of The First Churches:
    - Address: 129 Main Street, Northapton, MA 01060
    - Phone: (413) 584-9392

- Lunches will be served in the refectory of The First Churches

- Banquet will be served at Hampshire Room South, Union Station, 125A Pleasant Street

- The Concert will be held in the sanctuary of The Edwards Church

- The concluding session and wrap-up will be held in the parlor of The First Churches

Memorial Plaque of Jonathan Edwards unveiled on June 22, 1900
at The First Churches, Northampton

Convenor's Opening Remarks

On the very site where we are now convened, Jonathan Edwards ministered to his congregation for almost a quarter of a century. A memorial to him in the form of a bronze bas relief sculpted by Herbert Adams is mounted on a wall of the sanctuary, part of the fifth meeting house to occupy this site. It was formally unveiled on June 22, 1900 to commemorate the 150th anniversary of his dismissal. This memorial plaque, according to N. H. Gardiner who chaired the committee commissioning it, "represents more than the desire of this church to atone for the past; it represents rather a general sentiment of respect for the illustrious minister who belongs to no single church exclusively, but to the historic Church Universal." To help commemorate the unveiling of the tablet, addresses were made in this room and subsequently published.

We are met this day to commemorate the 300th anniversary of Edwards' birth on October 3rd. In 1900 the scholarship inspired by Edwards was yet in its infancy; today it is fully mature and growing apace. That scholarship has no doubt reflected the tenor of the turbulent times in which it grew. From our vantage, the dawn of the twentieth century was a relatively halcyon time tuned to a high pitch of optimism and confidently looking forward to a century of limitless progress, peace and prosperity – a secular millennium, as it were. But those hopes were dashed by two world wars and multiple genocides on a scale never before seen and scarcely imagined. The twenty-first century has dawned on a scene where nations still rage furiously together and with no end in sight.

The Jeffersons, Franklins, Diderots and other bright philosophes of the Enlightenment would, were they to return, stand aghast and uncomprehending at the barbarities of our age which mock their polite eighteenth-century pieties and nostrums. Edwards, were he to return, would understand only too well, and would see the terrible events of the last century as the inexorable working out of what he had prefigured in the dark depths of his treatise *The Great Christian Doctrine of Original Sin Defended*. It is appropriate that we consider Edwards and the scholarship devoted to him under the aspect of history. He himself aspired to recast theology historically in *A History of the Work of Redemption*, his unfinished *summa*, where he projected "a body of divinity, in a new method, and in the form of a history."

We who are gathered here this morning have the opportunity, in some small way, of helping to set the course of Edwards scholarship in the twenty-first century. As the sesquicentenary of June 1900 serves as a marker for us who observe the tercentenary in October 2003, so may we serve as marker to those who may mark the quadricentenary of Edwards' birth in October 2103. The scholarship that will play itself out against the backdrop of ideas and events in this century will, though perhaps in an indirect way, influence generations of the future. Therefore, one of the purposes of this 2003 celebration is to prepare for that celebration which will take place one hundred years from now.

We hope that you will join us in now establishing a Jonathan Edwards Society to promote ongoing research and publication on America's Spiritual Founding Father. This society shall take responsibility for convening, in 2103, the *Quadricentenary* Celebration of Jonathan Edwards' birth.

- Richard Hall

FRIDAY, OCTOBER 3RD, 2003

All academic sessions of the conference will be held in the sanctuary of The First Churches, 129 Main Street, Northampton, MA 01060

9:00-9:30 a.m. Convocation

Introductions by Convenor: Dr. Richard Hall

Host: The Rev. Peter Ives, Pastor of The First Churches
Chairman of Academic Conference: Dr. Huston Smith
Chairman of Musical Celebration: Dr. Daniel Pinkham

9:30-10:30 a.m.

- "Jonathan Edwards as America's Spiritual Founding Father"
  – *Herbert Richardson*

- "The Mind of Jonathan Edwards: Beyond America"
  – *M. Darrol Bryant*

10:55-11:55 a.m.

- "Jonathan Edwards' Two Views of the Mystical Apprehension of God"
  – *Richard A. S. Hall*

- "How Edwards' Thought Developed"
  – *Virginia Peacock*

12:10-1:10- p.m.

- "Jonathan Edwards: A Context for An Awakening"
  – *Lloyd David Franklin*

- "Satan & His *Maleficium* in Edwards' Thought"
  – *Scott Seay*

1:10-2:20 p.m.   Lunch
Served in the refectory of The First Churches

Friday P.M.

2:20-3:20 p.m..

- "Jonathan Edwards' Trinitarian Theology in the Context of the Early Enlightenment Deist Controversy"
  – *Steven Studebaker*

- "From Edwards to Emerson to Eddy: A Neglected Trajectory of American Idealism"
  – *David Weddle*

3:40-4:40 p.m.

- "Jonathan Edwards & Bishop Butler on Ethics"
  – *David White*

- "Doing Metaethics with Kant & Edwards"
  – *Don Keyes*

5:00-6:00 p.m.

- "Jonathan Edwards & Chauncey Wright on Science"
  – *Richard Robin*

- "In Edwards's 'Room of the Idea': Newton's *Optics* & the Idea of Grace"
  – *Joan Richardson*

7:00 p.m. BANQUET

"Reflections on this Occasion"
-Professor Huston Smith

Banquet will be served at Hampshire Room South, Union Station, 125A Pleasant Street

SATURDAY A.M.

9:00-10:00 a.m.

- "Edwards' Typology"
- *William Sparks*

- "Experiencing Edwards: Sentences as Thought Experiments"
- *Jennifer Bernstein*

10:25-11:25 a.m.

- "Edwards, Thoreau, Dillard: Reading/Writing Nature & The Awakened/Awakening Self"
- *Michael G. Ditmore*

- "One Vast & Ecumenical Holding Company: Edwardsean Millennium Themes in 19th & 20th Century Dystopic Fiction"
- *James Hewitson*

11:45-1:00 p.m.

- "Jonathan Edwards, Children, & Young People: Less of Earth, More of Heaven"
- *Charles Pierce*

- A Proposal to Organize "THE JONATHAN EDWARDS SOCIETY"

1:00-2:20 p.m.   Lunch

Served in the refectory of The First Churches

SATURDAY P.M.

2:20-3:20 p.m.

- "The Architecture of Religious Experience in Edwards and Peirce"
  – *Roger Ward*

- "Jonathan Edwards as Proto-Pragmatists"
  – *Stuart Rosenbaum*

3:40-4:40 p.m.

- "Edwards & Swedenborg"
  – *Devin Zuber*

- "On What There is Resurrected: The Ontological Doctrines of Jonathan Edwards & Alexius Meinong"
  – *Joseph W. Ulatowski*

5:00-6:00 p.m.

- "Jonathan Edwards' Influence on the Baptist Missionary Movement"
  – *Michael Thompson*

- "The Current Crisis in The Episcopal Church U.S.A. in Light of the Mid-Eighteenth-Century Crisis in The Congregational Church of Colonial America "
  – *John Taylor*

(Free for Supper)

8:00 p.m.   CONCERT (at The Edwards Church)

COMMEMORATIVE CONCERT

8:00 p.m. Saturday, October 4th, The Edwards Church

Welcome: The Rev. Dr. Peter Kakos, Pastor, The Edwards Church

I. *The Bow of God's Wrath*
an anthem by David Kidwell
(incorporating music by William Billings, 18th-century composer

II. *Pilgrim's Blues*
trio for violin, piano and cowbell by Keith Dippre*

III. *Parting Words*
a cantata for mixed voices, tenor solo, and string quartet
by Clifton J. Noble, Jr.*

IV. *String Quartet Number Two* - "Conversing with Some One Invisible"
by Daniel Pinkham*

*Premiere Performance

Sunday, October 5

10:00-11:00 a.m.

- Service of Worship
  The Reverend Peter Ives, preaching

11:00-12:00 noon

- Coffee and concluding discussions

Noon-3:00 p.m.

- Trip to Stockbridge to visit Jonathan Edwards' Mission House
  (Please indicate ASAP if you plan to take part so we can provide travel)

CONFEREES

Jennifer Bernstein *(CUNY Graduate Center, New York)*

M. Darrol Bryant *(Renison College, University of Waterloo)*

Michael G. Ditmore *(Pepperdine University, California)*

Lloyd David Franklin *(Church of God Theological Seminary, Tennessee)*

Richard A. S. Hall *(Fayetteville State University, North Carolina)*

James Hewitson *(University of Minnesota, Duluth)*

Peter Ives *(First Churches of Northampton)*

Peter Kakos *(The Edwards Church)*

Don Keyes *(Duquesne University, Pennsylvania)*

Virginia Peacock *(Northern Michigan University)*

Charles Pierce *(Tidewater Junior College, Virginia)*

Herbert Richardson *(Mellen University)*

Joan Richardson *(CUNY Graduate Center, New York)*

Richard Robin *(Mt. Holyoke College, Massachusetts)*

Stuart Rosenbaum *(Baylor University, Texas)*

John Rupnow *(The Edwin Mellen Press)*

Scott Seay *(Ashland University, Ohio)*

Huston Smith *(Thomas J. Watson Professor of Religion & Distinguished Professor of Philosophy Ermeritus, Syracuse University)*

William Sparks *(CUNY Graduate Center, New York)*

Steven Studebaker *(Emmanuel College, Georgia)*

John A. Taylor *(Southern Illinois University, Edwardsville)*

Michael Thompson *(Oklahoma State University)*

Joseph W. Ulatowski *(University of Utah)*

Richard Ward *(Georgetown College, Kentucky)*

David Weddle *(The Colorado College, Colorado)*

David White *(St. John Fisher College, New York)*

Devin Zuber *(CUNY Graduate Center, New York)*

Composers

Keith Dippre (*Methodist College, North Carolina*)

David Kidwell (*The Edwards Church, Holyoke Civic Symphony, Guilford Festival Orchestra*)

Clifton J. Noble, Jr. (*Smith College, Northampton*)

Daniel Pinkham *(New England Conservatory of Music)*

Musicians

Carol Hutter (Viola, Concert Organizer)
Alexa Adams (First Violin)
Romina Kostare (Second Violin)
Ned Smith Selavka (Tenor Solo)
Arthur Cook (Violoncello)
The Edwards Church Choir

This conference is sponsored by
The Edwin Mellen Press and its affiliate, Mellen University.

The Edwin Mellen Press is an international publisher of scholarly books acquired by research libraries throughout the world. The Press publishes specialized research: monographs, bibliographies, concordances, dictionaries, commentaries, translations, critical editions, methodological studies, criticism, conference proceedings, and multi-volume reference sets. The Press publishes approximately 425 new titles a year, over two dozen continuing series, academic journals, and the research generated by several scholarly institutes.
It was established in Canada in 1974, the United States in 1978, and Great Britain in 1987.

The Edwin Mellen Press established Mellen University in 1992. Mellen University is a non-campus-based university which encourages research by independent scholars and by such organizations as The Jonathan Edwards Society.

The Jonathan Edwards Society

Director: Professor Richard Hall
Fayetteville State University,
Fayetteville, NC 28301-4298

University Phone: (910) 672-1088
Email: richardh@Methodist.edu

Notes

The Northampton Jonathan Edwards Tercentenary Celebration

Commemorative Concert

The Edwards Church,
Northampton, Massachusetts

Saturday, October 4, 2003
8:00 P.m.

PROGRAM

Welcome: The Rev. Dr. Peter Kakos, Pastor, The Edwards Church

**I. *The Bow of God's Wrath*
an anthem by David Kidwell
(incorporating music by William Billings, 18th-century composer**

**II. *Pilgrim's Blues*
trio for violin, piano and cowbell by Keith Dippre***

**III. *Parting Words*
a cantata for mixed voices, tenor solo, and string quartet
by Clifton J. Noble, Jr.***

**IV. *String Quartet Number Two* - "Conversing with Some One Invisible"
by Daniel Pinkham***

*Premiere Performance

I. *The Bow of God's Wrath*
an anthem by David Kidwell
(incorporporating music by William Billings, an 18th-century American composer)

TEXT

The bow of God's wrath is bent, and the arrow made ready on the string, and justice bends the arrow at your heart, and strains the bow, and it is nothing but the mere pleasure of God, and that of an angry God, without any promise or obligation at all, that keeps the arrow one moment from being made drunk with your blood. (from "Sinners in the Hands of an Angry God")

Chester - William Billings

Let tyrants shake their iron rod, and slavery clank her galling chains. We fear them not, we trust in God; New England's God forever reigns. Howe and Burgoyne and Clinton too, with Prescot and Cornwall is joined, together plot our overthrow, in one infernal league combined. When God inspired us for the fight, their ranks were broke, their lines were forced, their ships were shattered in our sight, or swiftly driven from our coast. The foe comes on with haughty stride, our troops advance with martial noise, their veterans flee before our youth, and generals yield to beardless boys. What grateful offering shall we bring? What shall we render to the Lord? Loud hallelujahs let us sing, and praise His name on every chord.

David's Lamentation - William Billings

David the king was grieved and moved; he went to his chamber and wept. And as he went, he wept and said, "O my son, would to God I had died for thee, O Absalom my son."

When Jesus Wept - William Billings

When Jesus wept, the falling tear in mercy flowed beyond all bound; when Jesus groaned, a trembling fear seized all the guilty world around.

Easter Anthem - William Billings

The Lord is ris'n indeed! Hallelujah! Now is Christ risen from the dead, and become the first fruits of them that slept. Hallelujah. And did He rise? Hear it, ye nations! Hear it, O ye dead. He rose; He burst the bars of death and triumphed o'er the grave. Then I rose; then first humanity triumphant passed the crystal ports of light and seized eternal youth. Man all immortal, hail. Heaven all lavish of strange gifts to man; Thine's all the glory, man's the boundless bliss.

II. *Pilgrim's Blues*
a trio for violin, piano & cowbell, by Keith Dippre

PROGRAM NOTE

The summer of 1751 must have been excruciating for Jonathan Edwards. He had been ousted from his Northampton pulpit a year earlier and was now to undertake a journey that surely must have been filled with anguish and foreboding. He was going to laboriously transition his wife and eleven children to Stockbridge, Massachusetts and adopt the lifestyle of a wilderness missionary. What kinds of thoughts, even mental tortures, did this man experience on the road from Northampton to Stockbridge? Was he praying, panicking, attempting some kind of soothing mental diversion, or beseeching God for heavenly guidance? I suspect he experienced all of these, but in the end, bowed to a kind of severe, yet necessary spiritual refinement. *Pilgrim's Blues* is a sonic representation of the journey from Northampton to Stockbridge. The cowbell serves as a kind of cruel timekeeper, striping the inexorable steps of Edwards towards his new assignment. Towards the end of the piece there is an air of triumph and resolution, metaphorically pointing to Edward's great literary and theological accomplishments while residing on the frontier. —*Keith Dippre*

III. *Parting Words*
a cantata for mixed voices, tenor solo, and string quartet by Clifton J. Noble, Jr.

Parting Words was written in response to a commission in celebration of the tercentenary of minister Jonathan Edwards. The text is a gathering of excerpts from Edwards' farewell sermon to his Northampton congregation and bible verses cited therein, Isaac Watts' hymn "Our God, Our Help in Ages Past," and the traditional spiritual "Steal Away."

"Parting Words" is scored for mixed choir, tenor solo, and string quartet. Its three sections, titled "Now," "Then," and "Benediction," follow Edwards' sermon as he outlines for the members of his congregation his vision of their present and future, and concludes with a prayer for their judgment.

The tune "St. Anne," (attributed to 17th century composer William Croft) to which Watts' hymn is sung, recurs through the cantata like a series of pillars supporting the dramatic unfolding of Edward's sermon. Its rather chaotic first utterance reflects the state of flux in which hymn-singing found itself in Edwards' time. In some congregations, only the men sang, entering at their own tempo and key. In the more progressive churches all congregants sang and aspired to the European, schooled, four-part chorale style.

The austere opening theme in the strings represents Edwards' fierce, unswerving convictions. The variations on "St. Anne" follow and punctuate his evolving relationship with his flock, and "Steal Away," though an anachronism (and hopefully a forgiveable one) speaks for itself.—*Clifton J. Noble, Jr.*

TEXT

Part I – Now
*Our God, our Help in ages past,
Our Hope for years to come,
Our Shelter from the stormy blast,
And our eternal Home!

By the grace of God we have had our conversation in the world.
We live in a world of change where nothing is certain or stable.
And where a little time—a few revolutions—of the sun, brings to pass strange things, surprising alterations in particular persons in families, in towns and churches, in countries and nations. Those who seem most united, in a little time are most disunited and at the greatest distance.

*Time, like an ever-rolling stream,
Bears all its sons away;
They fly forgotten as a dream
Dies at the opening day.

There is one meeting more that they must have, and that is in the last great day of accounts. Now they meet together in a preparatory mutable state, but then in an unchangeable state. Then they shall meet together in a state of clear, certain, and infallible light!

Part II—Then
Tenor Solo: It will be pronounced:
Choir: He that is unjust, let him be unjust still—He that is filthy, let him be filthy still—He that is righteous, let him be righteous still—He that is holy, let him be holy still.

(1 Cor. 4:5)
Therefore judge nothing before the time until the Lord come, who . . . will bring to light the hidden things of darkness, and will make manifest the councils of the hearts:
And then shall every man have praise of God.

(Dan. 2:3)
And they that be wise shall shine as the brightness of the firmament, and they that turn many to righteousness, as the stars for ever and ever.

Dear children—I must bid you farewell—I leave you in an evil world.
May God in his mercy grant that . . . the Word of God, as it shall be hereafter dispensed to you, may prove as the fire and the hammer that breaketh the rock in pieces.

*Our God, our Help in ages past,
Our Hope for years to come,
Be Thou our Guard while troubles last
And our eternal Home!

Part III—Benediction
Tenor Solo & Choir: My desire and prayer is that the great Shepherd of the sheep [will] have a special respect to you, and be your guide . . . and that he who is the infinite fountain of light would open your eyes, and turn you from darkness unto light . . . that you may receive forgiveness . . . so in that great day, when I shall meet you again before your Judge and mine, we may meet in joyful and glorious circumstances, never to be separated any more.

All: I must leave you in the hands of God.

Steal Away. Steal Away. Steal Away. Steal Away to Jesus.
Steal Away. Steal Away home.
I haven't got long to stay here.
Steal Away. Steal Away. Steal Away. Steal Away to Jesus.
Steal Away. Steal Away home.
I haven't got long to stay here.

My lord calls me.
He calls me by the thunder.
The trumpet sounds within my soul.
I haven't got long to stay here.

My lord calls me.
He calls me by the lightning.
The trumpet sounds within my soul.
I haven't got long to stay here.

Steal Away, etc.

* "Our God, Our Help in Ages Past," text by Isaac Watts and tune *St. Anne* by Wm. Croft 1708.
"Steal Away"—traditional African-American spiritual.
All other texts from Jonathan Edwards' *Farewell Sermon,* including biblical texts cited by him.

IV. *String Quartet Number Two,* "Conversing with Some One Invisible" by Daniel Pinkham

I. Allegretto – Allegro energico
    II. Allegretto – Andante
       III. Vivo – Andantino – Presto scherzando
          IV. Andante tranquillo

PROGRAM NOTE

The quotation ". . . Conversing with some one invisible" is taken from a poem by Robert Lowell entitled "Jonathan Edwards in Western Massachusetts".

There is in my Second String Quartet no programmatic intention despite the work's borrowed literary title, ". . . Conversing with some one invisible."

In the *New York Times* Garry Wills, reviewing George M. Marsden's new biography, *Jonathan Edwards, a Life,* commented: "His words could thunder or soothe – scolding savagely, needling wittily or inspiring piously".

My attempt has been to present, in purely musical terms, a range of affects and colors that parallel the humors and dynamics of Edwards's literary contributions.

". . . Conversing with some one invisible" begins with a rising figure that not only introduces each of the four movements, but is heard in varied form throughout the entire work. After the introductory *Allegretto,* the first movement continues with an energetic fast section which features rapid meter changes. Despite lyrical intervals, the mood is blustery. The second movement, after a brief introduction, presents a serene *Andante,* a tranquil dialog between the second violin and the violoncello. The third movement, again introduced by the rising figure, is a lightning-quick scherzo. Highly mercurial, it presents a great range of affects. Many contrasting instrumental colors appear and vanish. The fourth movement is an epilog. It opens with the final statement of the rising figure. The viola is then assigned an extended and lyrical melody. The violoncello, playing on plucked strings, has a "walking-bass" *ostinato* and the violins are muted. At the very end there is a turbulent twelve-second improvisation. (Do you hear the rustle of wings?) The work ends with a gentle and reposed major chord.—*Daniel Pinkham*

COMPOSERS

DAVID KIDWELL is Minister of Music at the Edwards Church of Northampton, conductor of the Holyoke Civic Symphony and Guilford Festival Orchestra, and assistant to the conductor of the Springfield Symphony Orchestra. He holds degrees from Mary Washington College and the Hartt School of Music, and he has studied conducting at Tanglewood and the South Carolina Conductors Institute.

KEITH DIPPRE was born in Ancon, Panama in 1960. He received his undergraduate degree from Azusa Pacific University in California and his M.A. from California State University at Los Angeles. For roughly eight years, prior to beginning doctoral studies in composition at Ohio State, he played the resort and nightclub circuit on the West Coast and was a multi-keyboardist in the hip-hop oriented *Raw Nature*. Keith Dippre is a composer who enjoys combining sampled sounds with acoustic ensembles. It was during his stint as a road musician that he first developed into a "sampling junkie," trading and acquiring sounds with musicians all over the world. While living in California, he also had the privilege of doing studio work with some noteworthy players, among them popular jazz saxophonist, Boney James.

While at Ohio State, Dippre was the recipient of the Ruth Friscoe award for composition (1998) and was Composer-in-Residence with the Ohio State University Symphony Orchestra (1999). In 2000, the OSU Symphony Orchestra premiered his work *Soiree for 1999*. He made his festival debut as an accordionist in OSU's *Contemporary Music Festival 2001* playing the Lucas Foss piece *Curriculum Vitae with Time Bomb*. Dippre's composition, *Chorus of Cows*, was given its Columbus premiere during *Contemporary Music Festival 2000*. He has recently produced a piano concerto entitled *700 N. Electric* and a document, *Compositional Issues with Corigliano, Oliveros, and Kernis*. He is currently an Assistant Professor of Music at Methodist College, teaching courses such as music theory, ear-training, and survey of music. His most current orchestral work is entitled *Ikons*, which will be premiered by the Fayetteville Symphony (Fayetteville, North Carolina) next year. He has recently received a Regional Artist Project Grant from the Arts Council of Fayetteville and Cumberland County and was an artist-in-residence at the Artist's Enclave at I-Park (East Haddam, Connecticut). Dippre's work is also available through Musical Alchemy of Boulder, Colorado.

Still a jazz enthusiast at heart, he remains an active performer with musicians in the Fayetteville and Raleigh areas.

CLIFTON J. NOBLE, JR. is the Staff Accompanist at Smith College in Northampton, MA. For one year he served as organist (part of that time as choir director, in addition) at Edwards Church. His works have been performed throughout the United States and Europe by Smith, Mt. Holyoke, and Amherst College choral and instrumental forces, by the Boston Chamber Music Society, the Longmeadow Chamber Music Society, the Western MA Youth Orchestras, the Holyoke Civic Symphony, the Assabet Valley Mastersingers, pianist Rorianne Schrade, and flutist Carol Wincenc.

Noble was educated at Amherst College (B.A.,1983) and Smith College (M.A. 1988) and studied composition with Lewis Spratlan and Donald Wheelock. In addition to his coaching and performing duties at Smith College and numerous area performances with traditional jazz clarinetist Bob Sparkman, he writes classical reviews and features for the Springfield Republican newspapers.

DANIEL PINKHAM was born in Lynn, Massachusetts on 5 June 1923. He studied organ and harmony at Phillips Academy, Andover, with Carl F. Pfatteicher; then at Harvard with A. Tillman Merritt, Walter Piston, Archibald T. Davison and Aaron Copland (A.B. 1943; M.A. 1944). He also studied harpsichord with Putnam Aldrich and Wanda Landowska, and organ with E. Power Biggs. At Tanglewood he studied composition with Arthur Honegger and Samuel Barber, and subsequently with Nadia Boulanger. He has taught at Simmons College, Boston University, Dartington Hall (Devon, England), and was Visiting Lecturer at Harvard University (1957-58). In 1950 he was awarded a Fulbright Fellowship and in 1962 a Ford Foundation Fellowship as a choral conductor. He is a Fellow of the American Academy of Arts and Sciences. He is on the faculty of the New England Conservatory of Music, where he is senior professor in the Musicology Department. He is Music Director Emeritus of historic King's Chapel in Boston where he actively served from 1958 unto 2000. He is the recipient of six honorary degrees: Litt. D., Nebraska Wesleyan University, 1976; Mus. D., Adrian College, 1977; Mus. D., Westminster Choir College, 1979; Mus. D., New England Conservatory, 1993; Mus. D., Ithaca College, 1994; Mus. D., Boston Conservatory, 1998.

Pinkham is a prolific and versatile composer whose catalog includes four symphonies and other works for large ensembles; cantatas and oratorios; concertos and other works for solo instrument and orchestra for piano, piccolo, trumpet, violin, harp, and three organ concertos; theatre and documentary film works, chamber operas; songs, chamber music; and electronic music.

Pinkham's orchestral works have been played by major orchestras in the United States including the New York Philharmonic under the direction of Leonard Bernstein, The Buffalo Philharmonic (which he conducted in the premiere of his Organ Concerto Number One), the Boston Pops Orchestra under the direction of John Williams and by the composer himself. The Portland Symphony Orchestra, the Louisville Symphony Orchestra, the Orquestra Sinfonica Nacional de Mexico and many others. The London Symphony Orchestra has recorded his Symphony Number Three and Symphony Number Four, Serenades for Trumpet and Symphonic Wind Orchestra and Sonata Number Three for Organ and Strings with the American organist James David Christie as soloist.

In 1990 he was named Composer of the Year by the American Guild of Organists. In 1996 he received the Alfred Nash Patterson Foundation Lifetime Achievement Award for contributions to the Choral Arts.

MUSICIANS

Special thanks to Carol Huttar who assembled and coordinated the musicians for this concert.

CAROL HUTTER (Viola) was born in New Jersey, and began her musical studies at the age of 4 with the piano. She then studied violin and viola with Fredy Ostrovsky, Leopold Rybb, Maryanne Wallenberg and Toby Appel. She was a scholarship student to New England Conservatory of Music where she studied viola with Scott Nickrenz and Burton Fine, and chamber music studies with Eugene Lehner, Louis Krasner, and Eric Rosenblith. She played much 20th century chamber music under the tutelage of Gunther Schuller, and also was a student of Music History with Dan Pinkham. Carol also attended State University of NY at Binghamton, and received her Master of Music degree at UMASS AMherst where she was in the first post graduate string quartet in residence. She plays with the Springfield Symphony Orchestra and is principal viola of the Arcadia Players Baroque Chamber Orchestra. She has also performed as a member of the Hartford Symphony, the Sacramento Symphony, and is a founding member of the Bel Canto Chamber Players. Carol teaches violin and viola in Northampton, Springfield, and Amherst, and is a charter faculty member of both the Northampton and Springfield Community Music Schools.

Other Musicians:

ALEXA ADAMS (First Violin)
ROMINA KOSTARE (Second Violin)
NED SMITH SELAVKA (Tenor Solo)
ARTHUR COOK (Violoncello)

ACKNOWLEDGEMENTS

Special thanks are also due to David Kidwell and the Edwards Church Choir; and to Pastor Peter Kakos for graciously providing the Edwards Church for this performance.

The Bow of God's Wrath

for SATB chorus, a cappella

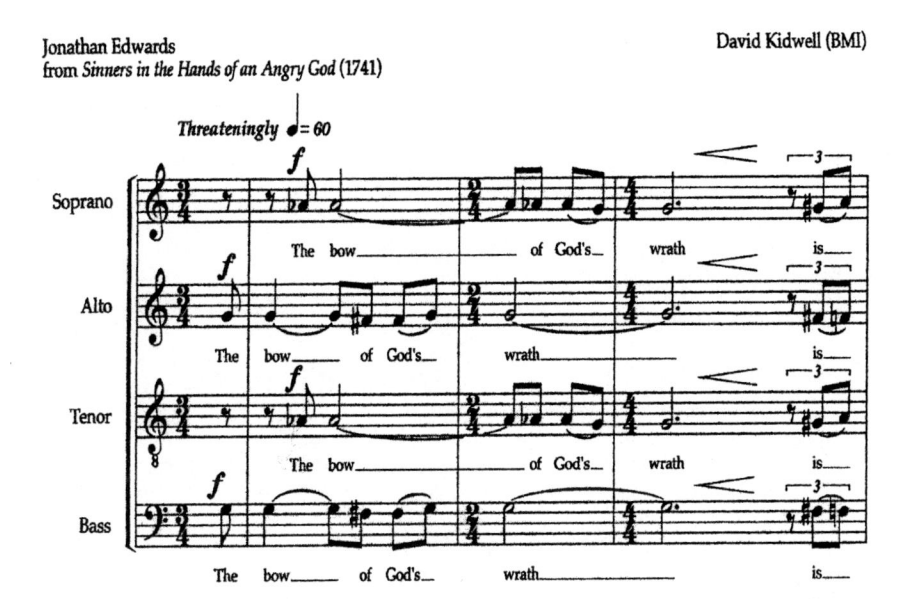

Jonathan Edwards
from *Sinners in the Hands of an Angry God* (1741)

David Kidwell (BMI)

© 2000, David Kidwell

KEITH DIPPRE

PILGRIM'S BLUES

Commissioned for the Jonathan Edwards Tercentenary
held in Northampton, Massachusetts in October 2003

for piano, violin, and cowbell
duration c. 8.5 minutes

Program note for *Pilgrim's Blues*

The summer of 1751 must have been excruciating for Jonathan Edwards. He had been ousted from his Northampton pulpit a year earlier and was now to undertake a journey that surely must have been filled with anguish and foreboding. He was going to laboriously transition his wife and eleven children to Stockbridge, Massachusetts and adopt the lifestyle of a wilderness missionary. What kinds of thoughts, even mental tortures, did this man experience on the road from Northampton to Stockbridge? Was he praying, panicking, attempting some kind of soothing mental diversion, or beseeching God for heavenly guidance? I suspect he experienced all of these, but in the end, bowed to a kind of severe, yet necessary spiritual refinement. *Pilgrim's Blues* is a sonic representation of the journey from Northampton to Stockbridge. The cowbell serves as a kind of cruel timekeeper, striping the inexorable steps of Edwards towards his new assignment. Towards the end of the piece there is an air of triumph and resolution, metaphorically pointing to Edward's great literary and theological accomplishments while residing on the frontier.

PILGRIM'S BLUES

*Commissioned for the Jonathan Edwards Tercentenary
held in Northampton, Massachusetts in October 2003*

Keith Dippre (2003)

24
Pno.
Perc.
Vln.
port.
sf
Ped.
27
a tempo
mf
con passione
f
31
35
p
ff

40
Pno.
sub. p
sub. p
Perc.
semplice, cantabile
Vln.
mf
46
jeté
f
con forza
sf
port.
52
a piacere
sff
sub. p
sf (senza pedale)
57
L.H.
ff

60
Pno.
Perc.
Vln.
sf
mf
64
Pno.
Perc.
Vln.
sf
mf
f
ff
68
Pno.
Perc.
Vln.
mf
cresc.
f
71
Pno.
Perc.
Vln.
f

5

84
leggiero
con espressione
Pno.
Perc.
Vln.
88 scherzando, più mosso
pizz.
95
101
solo

7

135
Pno.
Perc.
Vln.
p
142
arco
mf
mp
sf
148
a piacere, ad libitum
f
151
ff

154
Pno.
Perc.
Vln.
fff
157
mf
p
Ped.
f
mf
p
Play gestures in random order with very little space in between,
repeat section for about 15 seconds. Piano cues next section......
160
cowbell enters c. 5" after piano
pauses slightly longer for cowbell......
pizz.
arco
f
violin enters slightly after piano....

161
come prima, ♩ = 100
Pno.
Perc.
Vln.
ben marc.
166
170
sub. p
174
sub. p
sub. p

11

12

13

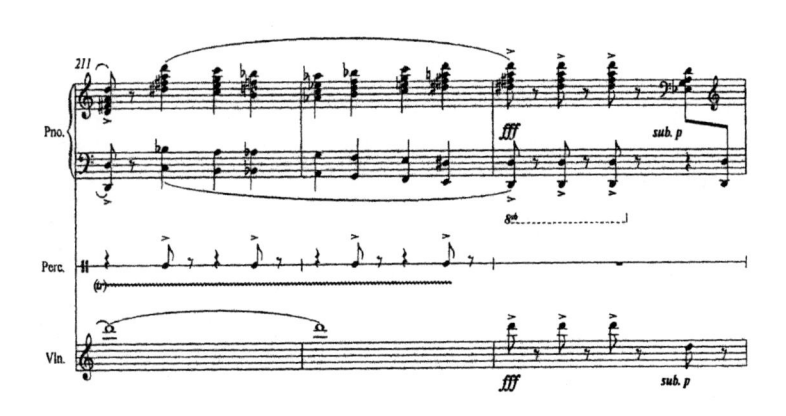

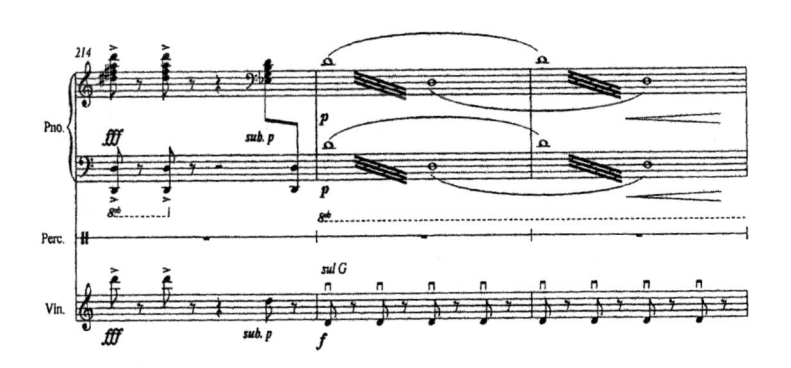

14

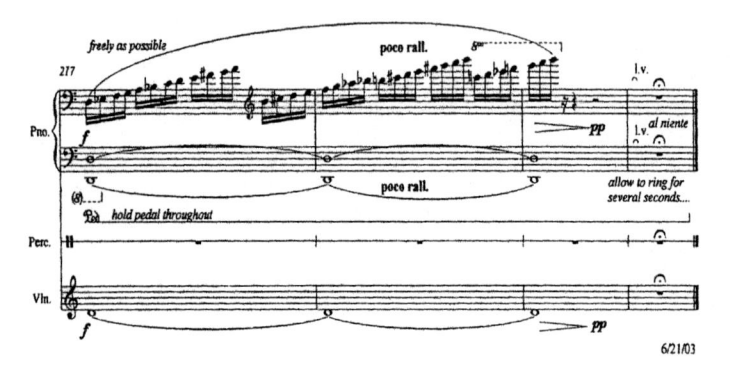

Parting Words

A cantata marking the tercentenary of Jonathan Edwards
Music by Clifton J. Noble, Jr.
2003

full score

PARTING WORDS

A Cantata, marking the Jonathan Edwards Tercentenary
For Mixed Voices, Tenor solo (may be from within the choir), and String Quartet

Part I -- Now

*Our God, our Help in ages past,
Our Hope for years to come,
Our Shelter from the stormy blast,
And our eternal Home!

By the grace of God we have had our conversation in the world.
We live in a world of change where nothing is certain or stable.
And where a little time – a few revolutions – of the sun, brings to pass strange things, surprising alterations in particular persons in families, in towns and churches, in countries and nations.
Those who seem most united, in a little time are most disunited and at the greatest distance.

*Time, like an ever-rolling stream,
Bears all its sons away;
They fly forgotten as a dream
Dies at the opening day.

There is one meeting more that they must have, and that is in the last great day of accounts.
Now they meet together in a preparatory mutable state, but then in an unchangeable state.
Then they shall meet together in a state of clear, certain, and infallible light!

Part II - Then

Tenor Solo: It will then be pronounced:
Choir: He that is unjust, let him be unjust still – He that is filthy, let him be filthy still, – He that is righteous, let him be righteous still – He that is holy, let him be holy still.

(1 Cor. 4:5)
Therefore judge nothing before the time until the Lord come, who…will bring to light the hidden things of darkness, and will make manifest the councils of the hearts:
And then shall every man have praise of God.

(Dan: 2:3)
And they that be wise shall shine as the brightness of the firmament, and they that turn many to righteousness, as the stars for ever and ever.

Dear children – I must bid you farewell – I leave you in an evil world.
May God in his mercy grant that…the Word of God, as it shall be hereafter dispensed to you, may prove as the fire and the hammer that breaketh the rock in pieces.

*Our God, our Help in ages past,
Our Hope for years to come,
Be Thou our Guard while troubles last
And our eternal Home!

Part III -- benediction

Tenor Solo & choir: My desire and prayer is that the great Shepherd of the sheep [will] have a special respect to you, and be your guide...and that he who is the infinite fountain of light would open your eyes, and turn you from darkness unto light...that you may receive forgiveness...so in that great day, when I shall meet you again before your Judge and mine, we may meet in joyful and glorious circumstances, never to be separated any more.

All: I must leave you in the hands of God

Steal Away. Steal Away. Steal Away. Steal Away to Jesus.
Steal Away. Steal Away home.
I haven't got long to stay here.
Steal Away. Steal Away. Steal Away. Steal Away to Jesus.
Steal Away. Steal Away home.
I haven't got long to stay here.

My lord calls me.
He calls me by the thunder.
The trumpet sounds within my soul.
I haven't got long to stay here.

Green trees are bending. Sinners stand a-trembling
The trumpet sounds within my soul.
I haven't got long to stay here.

My Lord calls me.
He calls me by the lightning.
The trumpet sounds within my soul.
I haven't got long to stay here.

Steal away, etc.

*"Our God, Our Help in Ages Past" text by Isaac Watts and tune *St. Anne* by Wm. Croft 1708
"Steal Away" – traditional African-American spiritual.
All other texts from Jonathan Edwards' Farewell Sermon, including biblical texts cited by him.

Marking the Jonathan Edwards Tercentenary

Parting Words
Part I -- now

Clifton J. Noble, Jr.

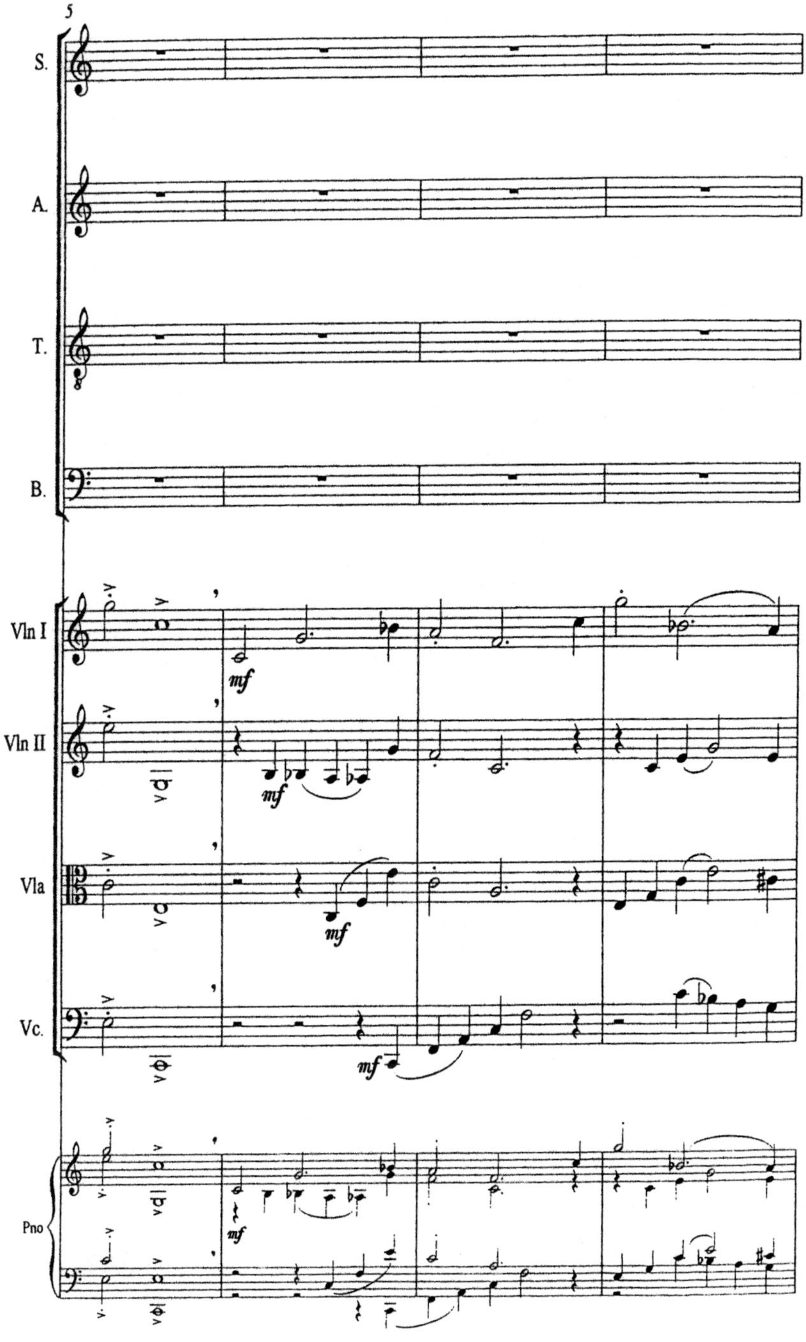
5
S.
A.
T.
B.
Vln I
mf
Vln II
mf
Vla
mf
Vc.
mf
Pno
mf

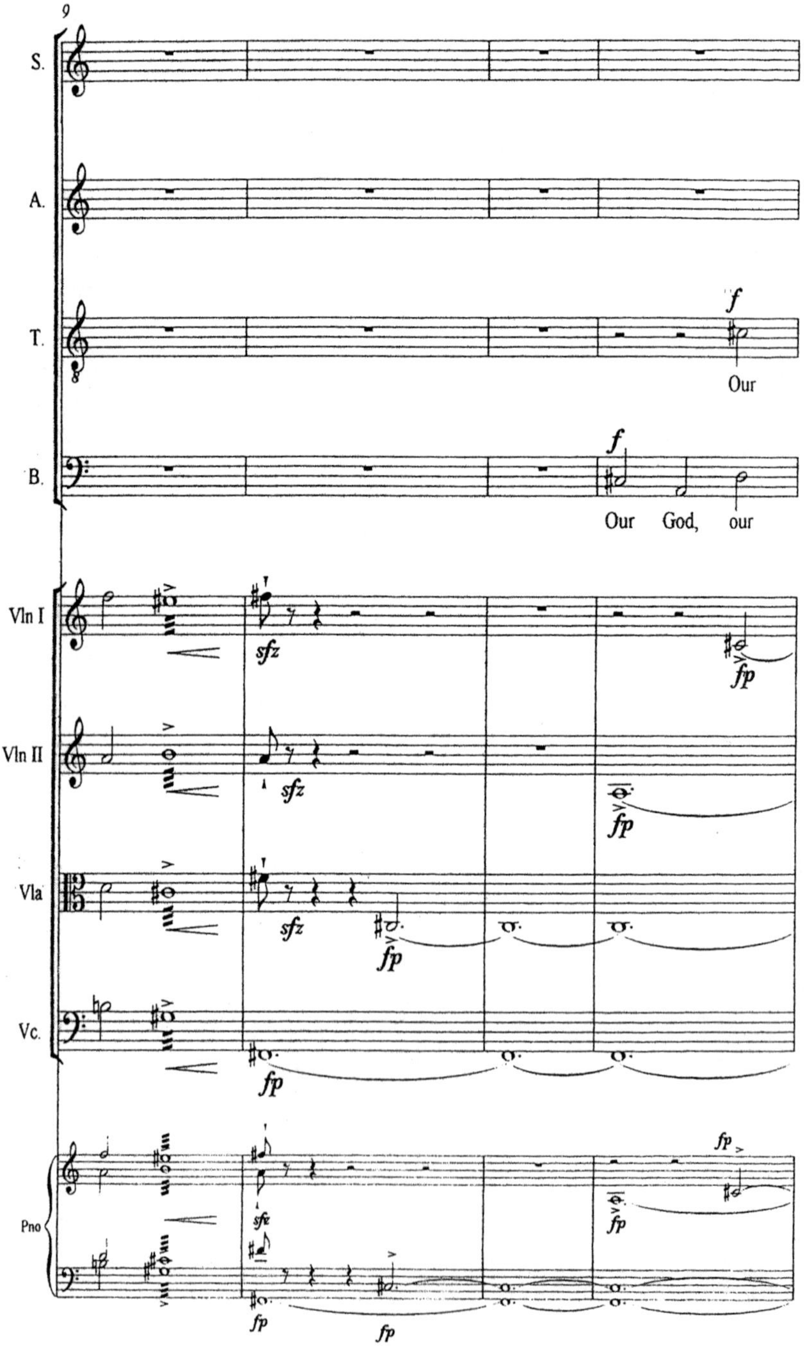
9
S.
A.
T.
B.
f
Our
f
Our God, our
Vln I
Vln II
Vla
Vc.
Pno
sfz
fp

13
S.
A.
T.
God, our help in a - ges past
B.
help in a - ges past
Vln I
Vln II
Vla
Vc.
Pno

17
S.
A.
T.
f
Our hope for years
B.
f
Our
Vln I
fp
Vln II
fp
Vla
fp
Vc.
fp
Pno
fp
fp
fp
fp

21
S.
A.
T.
B.
to come
hope for years to come
Our
Our
Our
Vln I
Vln II
Vla
Vc.
Pno
f
ff
6
tr

25
rit.
A tempo
mp
S.
And
A.
shel - ter from the storm - y blast, And
T.
shel - ter from the storm - y blast, And
B.
shel - ter from the storm - y blast, And
Vln I
Vln II
Vla
Vc.
Pno
rit.
A tempo
5

29
S.
our e - ter - nal home.
A.
our e - ter - nal home.
T.
our e - ter - nal home.
B.
our e - ter - nal home.
Vln I
pp
Vln II
pp
Vla
pp
Vc.
Pno
pp

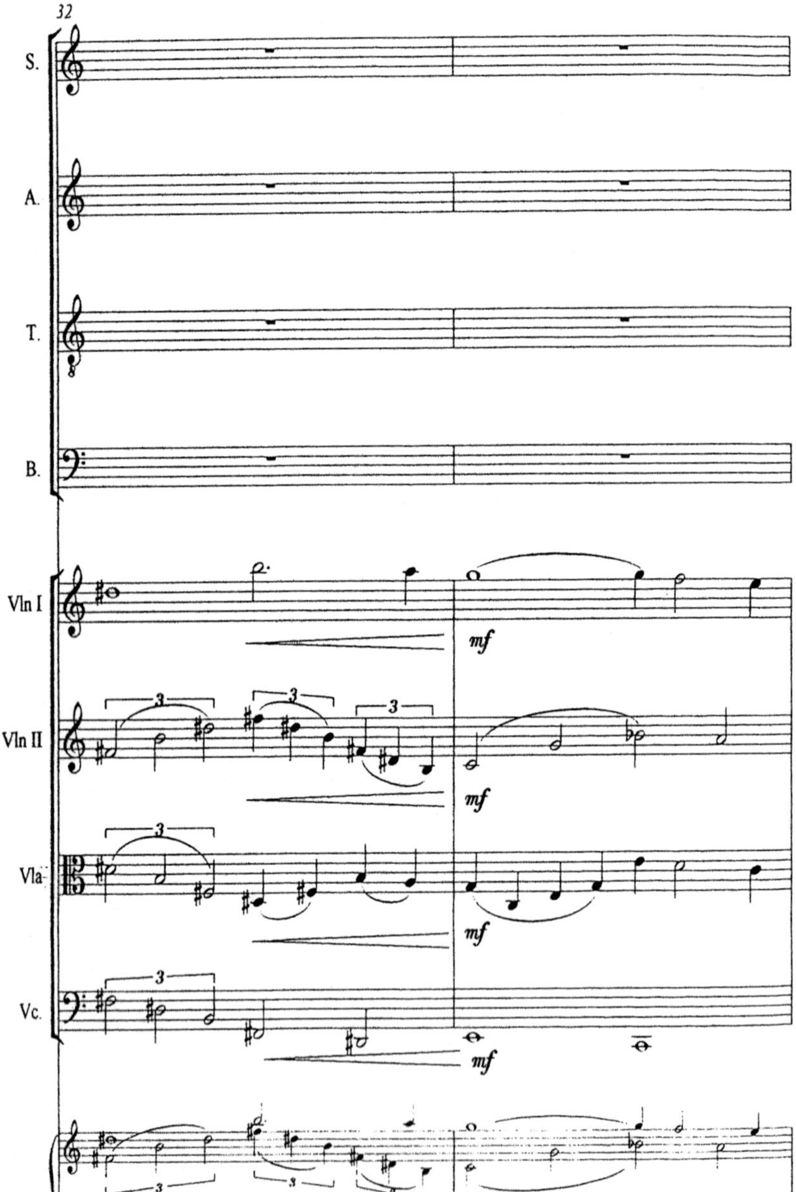
32
S.
A.
T.
B.
Vln I
mf
Vln II
3
mf
Vla
mf
Vc.
mf
Pno
mf

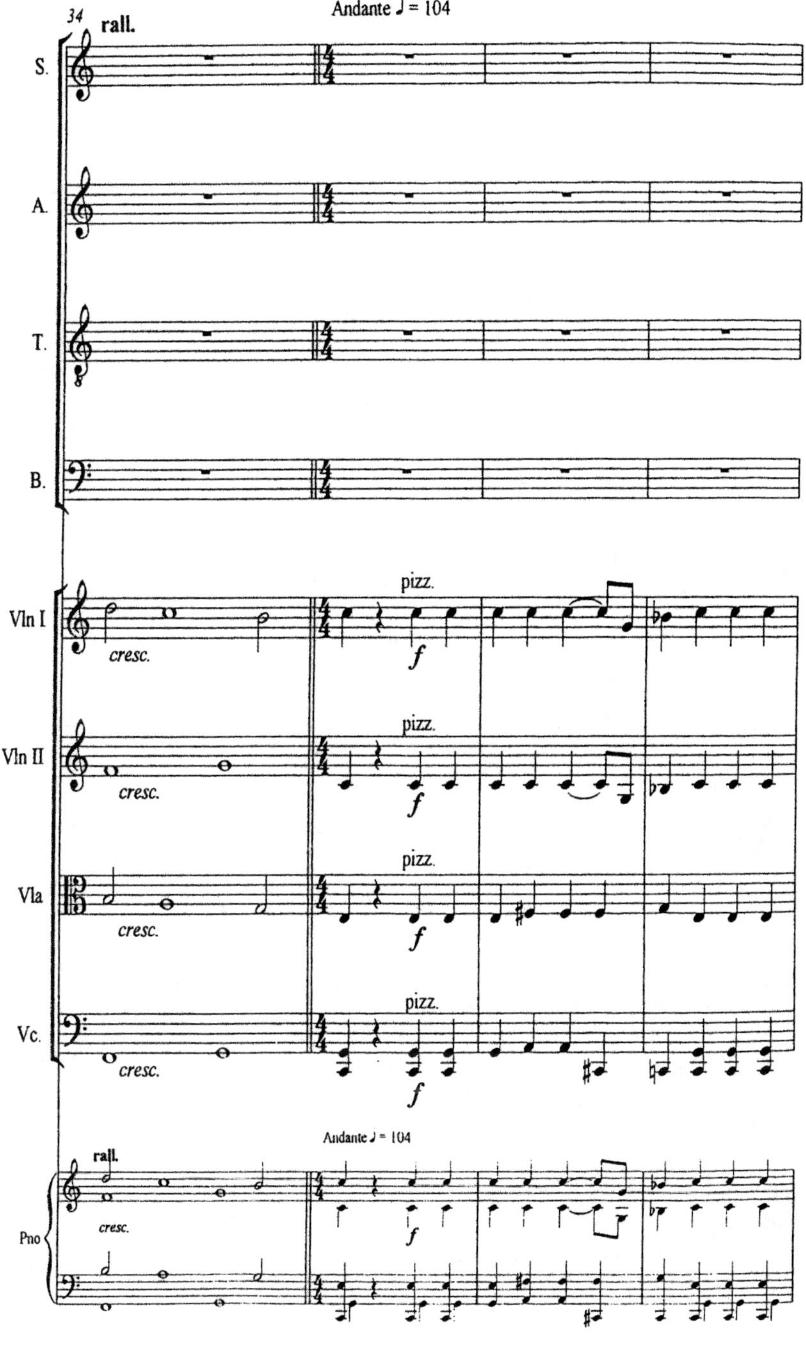
34
rall.
Andante ♩ = 104
S.
A.
T.
B.
Vln I
pizz.
cresc.
f
Vln II
Vla
Vc.
Pno

38
S.
mf
We live in a world of change where noth - ing is cer - tain
A.
mf
We live in a world of change where noth - ing is cer - tain
T.
mf
We live in a world of change where noth - ing is cer - tain
B.
mf
We live in a world of change where noth - ing is cer - tain
Vln I
Vln II
Vla
Vc.
Pno
3

42
S.
or sta- ble
A.
or sta- ble
T.
or sta- ble
B.
or sta- ble
Vln I
Vln II
Vla
Vc.
arco
f
Pno
arco
f

46
S.
A.
T.
B.
mf
And where a lit - tle time, a few___ rev - o - lu - tions_ of the
And where a lit - tle time, a few___ rev - o - lu - tions_ of the
And where a lit - tle time, a few___ rev - o - lu - tions_ of the
And where a lit - tle time, a few___ rev - o - lu - tions_ of the
Vln I
arco
mf
Vln II
arco
Vla
arco
Vc.
pizz.
arco
Pno
mf

49
S.
sun, brings to pass strange things, strange things.
A.
sun, brings to pass strange things, strange things.
T.
sun, brings to pass strange things, strange things.
B.
sun, brings to pass strange things, strange things.
Vln I
sul pont.
ord.
Vln II
sul pont.
ord.
Vla
sul pont.
ord.
Vc.
sul pont.
ord.
Pno

53
S.
mp
3
in par-ti-cu-lar
A.
mp
Sur-pri-sing al-ter-a-tions
in par-ti-cu-lar
T.
B.
Vln I
mp
Vln II
Vla
Vc.
Pno

56
S.
cresc.
per - sons, in fam - i - lies_ in towns and
A.
cresc.
per - sons, in fam - i - lies_ in towns and
T.
mp
cresc.
in fam - i - lies_ in towns and
B.
mp
cresc.
in towns and
Vln I
Vln II
Vla
Vc.
Pno

58
S.
church-es__ in coun-tries and na- tions.__
A.
church-es__ in coun-tries and na- tions.__
T.
church-es__ in coun-tries and na- tions.__
B.
church-es__ in coun-tries and na- tions.__
f
Vln I
cresc.
ff
Vln II
cresc.
ff
Vla
cresc.
ff
Vc.
cresc.
ff
Pno
cresc.
ff

62
S.
mp
Those who seem most u - ni - ted in a
A.
mp
Those who seem most u - ni - ted in a
T.
mp
Those who seem most u - ni - ted in a
B.
mp
Those who seem most u - ni - ted in a
Vln I
pizz.
mp
Vln II
pizz.
mp
Vla
pizz.
mp
Vc.
pizz.
mp
Pno
mp

66
S.
lit-tle time are most dis - u - ni-ted and at the great - est dis-tance.
A.
lit-tle time are most dis - u - ni-ted and at the great - est dis-tance.
T.
lit-tle time are most dis - u - ni-ted and at the great - est dis-tance.
B.
lit-tle time are most dis - u - ni-ted and at the great - est dis-tance.
Vln I
arco
Vln II
arco
Vla
Vc.
Pno

20

74
mf
S.
By the grace of God we have had our con - ver-
mf
A.
By the grace of God we have had our con - ver-
mf
T.
By the grace of God we have had our con - ver-
mf
B.
By the grace of God we have had our con - ver-
Vln I
Vln II
Vla
Vc.
Pno

77
poco allargando
S.
sa - tion in the world. Time,
A.
sa - tion in the world. Time,
T.
sa - tion in the world. Time,
B.
sa - tion in the world. Time,
Vln I
Vln II
Vla
Vc.
poco allargando
Pno

81
A tempo
S.
like an ev - er - rol - ling
A.
like an ev - er - rol - ling
T.
like an ev - er - rol - ling
B.
like an ev - er - rol - ling
Vln I
Vln II
Vla
Vc.
A tempo
Pno

stream, bears all her sons a - way.

88
S.
They fly for - got - ten as a dream
A.
They fly for - got - ten as a dream
T.
They fly for - got - ten as a dream
B.
They fly for - got - ten as a dream
Vln I
Vln II
Vla
Vc.
Pno
f
3

91
S.
— dies at the op - 'ning day.
A.
— dies at the op - 'ning day.
T.
— dies at the op - 'ning day.
B.
— dies at the op - 'ning day.
Vln I
Vln II
Vla
Vc.
Pno

27

S. There is one meet-ing more that

A. There is one meet-ing more that

T. There is one meet-ing more that

B. There is one meet-ing more that

28

S: we must have, and that is in the last great day____ of ac-

A: we must have, and that is in the last great day____ of ac-

T: we must have, and that is in the last great day____ of ac-

B: we must have, and that is in the last great day____ of ac-

102
S.
counts.
Nowwe meet to-ge- ther__ in a
A.
counts.
Nowwe meet to-ge- ther__ in a
T.
counts.
Nowwe meet to-ge- ther__ in a
B.
counts.
Nowwe meet to-ge- ther__ in a
Vln I
Vln II
Vla
Vc.
Pno

mu - ta - ble state__ but then, we shall meet to -

31

109
cresc.
S.
cer - tain and in -
cresc.
A.
cer - tain and in -
cresc.
T.
cer - tain and in -
cresc.
B.
cer - tain and in -
Vln I
Vln II
Vla
Vc.
Pno

33

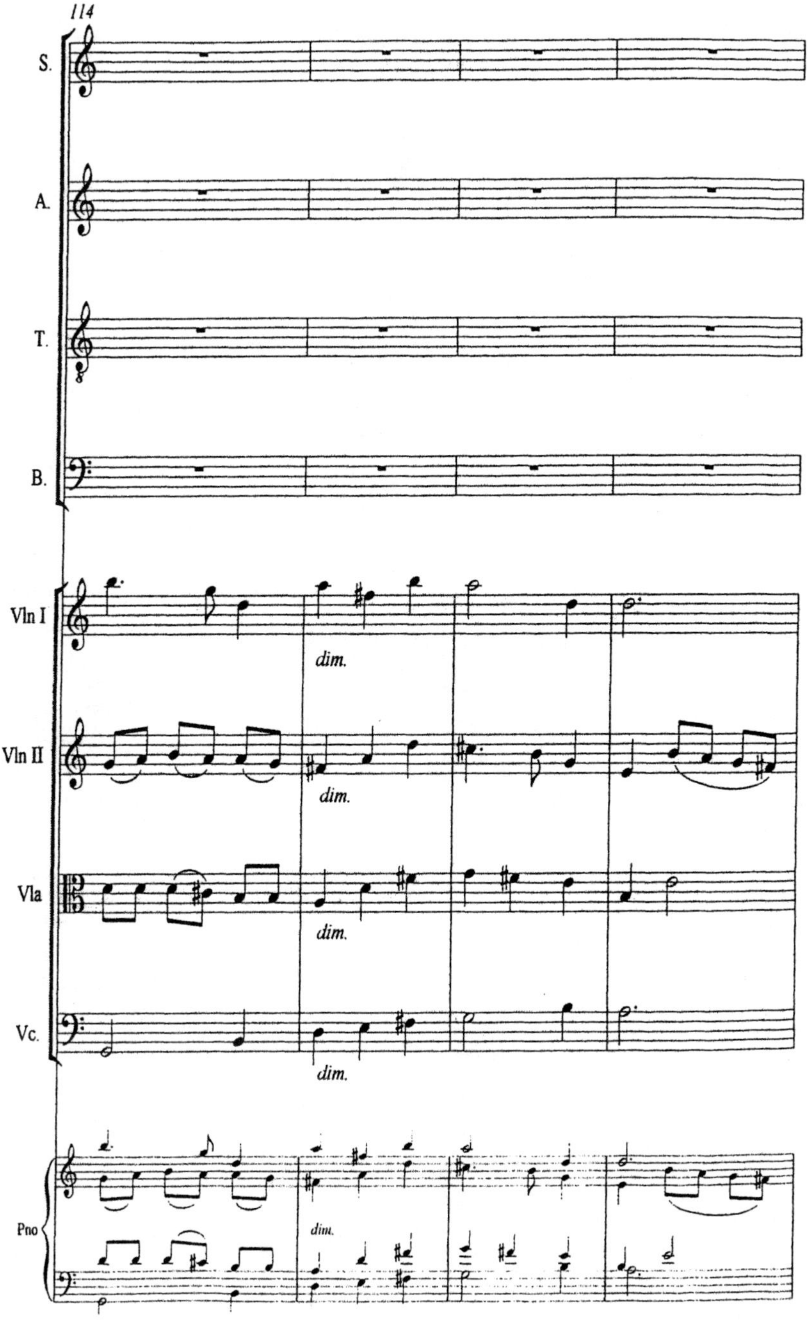
114
S.
A.
T.
B.
Vln I
dim.
Vln II
dim.
Vla
dim.
Vc.
dim.
Pno
dim.

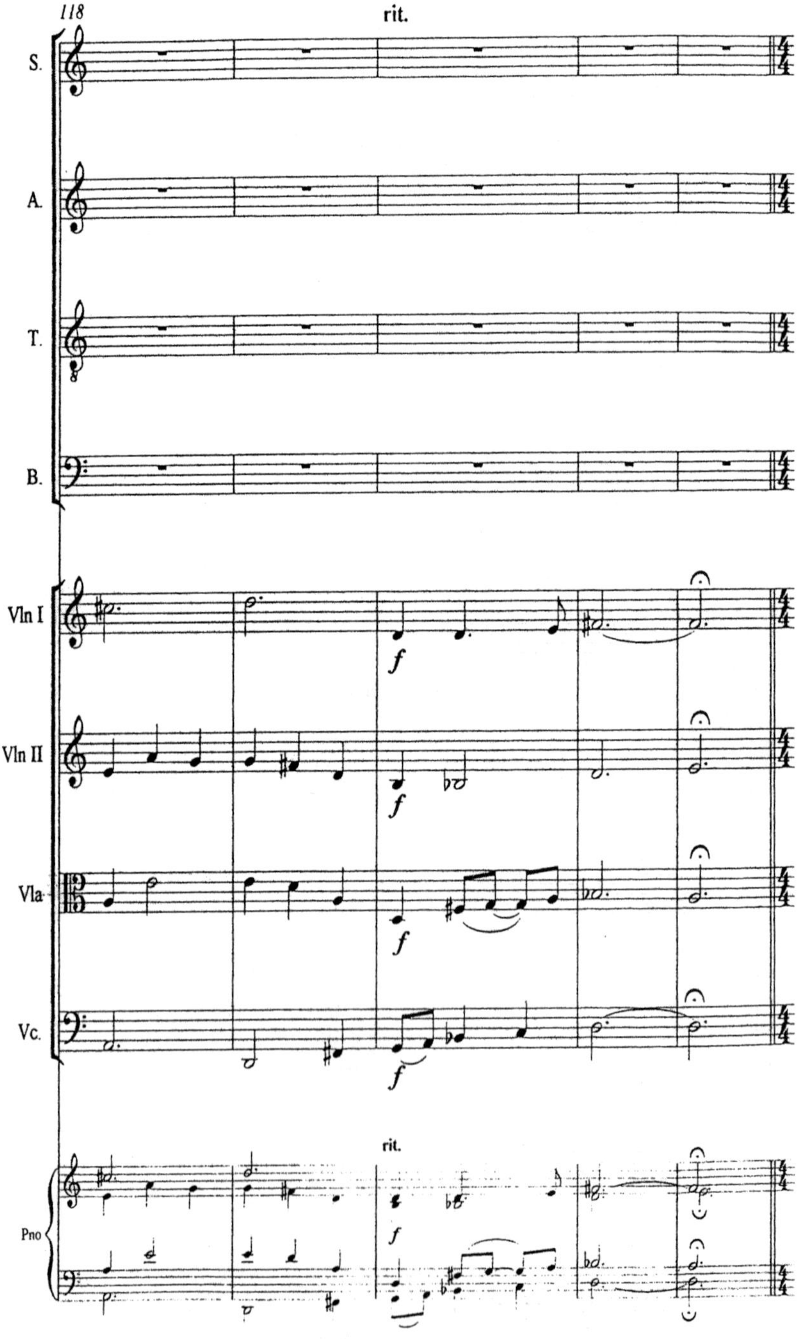
118
rit.
S.
A.
T.
B.
Vln I
Vln II
Vla
Vc.
rit.
Pno

Part II -- then

127
S.
him be un - just still, He that is filth - y
A.
him be un - just still, He that is filth - y
T.
him be un - just still, He that is filth - y
B.
him be un - just still, He that is filth - y
Vln I
Vln II
Vla
Vc.
Pno

130
S.
mf
let him be filth - y still, He that is
A.
mf
let him be filth - y still, He that is
T.
mf
let him be filth - y still, He that is
B.
mf
let him be filth - y still, He that is
Vln I
mf
Vln II
mf
Vla
mf
Vc.
mf
Pno
mf

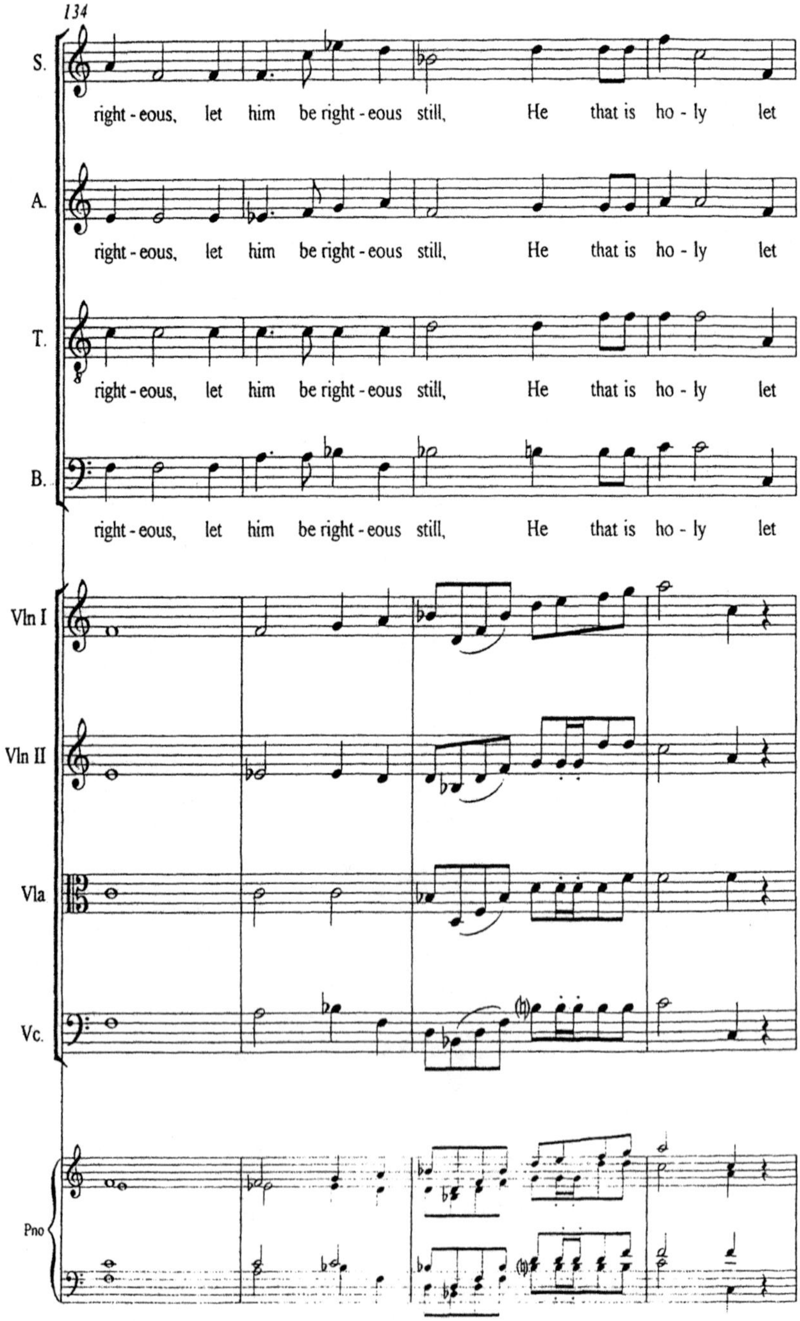
134
S.
right - eous, let him be right - eous still, He that is ho - ly let
A.
right - eous, let him be right - eous still, He that is ho - ly let
T.
right - eous, let him be right - eous still, He that is ho - ly let
B.
right - eous, let him be right - eous still, He that is ho - ly let
Vln I
Vln II
Vla
Vc.
Pno

138
S.
him be ho - ly still.
A.
him be ho-ly still.
T.
him be ho - ly still.
B.
him be ho-ly still.
Vln I
Vln II
Vla
Vc.
Pno

141
S.
He that is un - just, let him be un - just
A.
He that is un - just, let him be un - just
T.
He that is un - just,
B.
He that is un - just,
Vln I
f
mf
Vln II
f mp
Vla
mp
Vc.
f mp
Pno
f mp
mf

144
S.
still, He that is filth - y, let
A.
still, He that is filth - y, let
T.
let him be un - just still, He___ that is filth - y
B.
let him be un - just still, He___ that is filth - y
Vln I
Vln II
sim.
f mp
Vla
mp
Vc.
mp
Pno
sim.
f mp

147
S.
him be filth - y still, He that is
A.
him be filth - y still, He that is
T.
let him be filth - y, He that is
B.
let him be filth - y, He that is
Vln I
Vln II
Vla
Vc.
Pno

44

150

S: right - eous, let him be right - eous still, He that is

A: right - eous, let him be right - eous still, He that is

T: right - eous, let him be right - eous still, He that is

B: right - eous, let him be right - eous still, He that is

153
S.
ho-ly,
he that is ho-ly
he that is
A.
ho-ly,
he that is ho-ly
he that is
T.
ho-ly,
he that is ho-ly
he that is
B.
ho-ly,
he that is ho-ly
he that is
Vln I
Vln II
Vla
Vc.
Pno

157
S.
ho - ly, let___ him be ho - ly still.
A.
ho - ly, let___ him be ho - ly still.
T.
ho - ly, let___ him be ho - ly still.
B.
ho - ly, let___ him be ho - ly still.
Vln I
Vln II
f
Vla
f
Vc.
f
Pno
f

47

48

167
S.
There - fore judge no - thing be - fore the
A.
There - fore judge no - thing be - fore the
T.
There - fore judge no - thing
B.
There - fore judge no - thing
Vln I
Vln II
sul pont.
ord.
Vla
sul pont.
ord.
Vc.
Pno
ord.

170
S.
time un - til the Lord come,
A.
time un - til the Lord come,
T.
f
be - fore the time un - til the Lord come,
B.
f
be - fore the time un - til the Lord come,
Vln I
Vln II
Vla
Vc.
Pno

173
mf
S.
who will bring to light the hid - den things of
A.
who will bring to light the hid - den things of
T.
who will bring to light the hid - den things of
B.
who will bring to light the hid - den things of
Vln I
Vln II
Vla
Vc.
Pno

176
S.
dark - ness and will make man - i - fest the
A.
dark - ness and will make man - i - fest the
T.
dark - ness and will make man - i - fest the
B.
dark - ness and will make man - i - fest the
Vln I
Vln II
Vla
Vc.
Pno

53

182
allargando
f
♩ = 96
S.
And then shall ev - 'ry man have
A.
And then shall ev - 'ry man have
T.
And then shall ev - 'ry man have
B.
And then shall ev - 'ry man have
Vln I
Vln II
Vla
Vc.
cresc.
Pno
allargando
= 96

55

S. praise of God. And

A. praise of God. And

T. praise of God. And

B. praise of God. And

187
S.
then shall ev - 'ry man have praise of God.
A.
then shall ev - 'ry man have praise of God.
T.
then shall ev - 'ry man have praise of God.
B.
then shall ev - 'ry man have praise of God.
Vln I
Vln II
Vla
Vc.
Pno

189
S.
A.
T.
B.
mf
And they that be wise shall shine as the
And they that be wise shall shine as the
And they that be wise shall shine as the
And they that be wise shall shine as the
Vln I
Vln II
Vla
Vc.
Pno

192
S.
A.
T.
B.
Vln I
Vln II
Vla
Vc.
Pno
f
bright - - ness, the bright - - - - ness of the firm - a-

59

195

S: ment. Then shall ev-'ry man have

A: ment. Then shall ev-'ry man have

T: ment. Then shall ev-'ry man have

B: ment. Then shall ev-'ry man have

198
S.
praise of God.
A.
praise of God.
T.
praise of God.
B.
praise of God.
Vln I
Vln II
Vla
Vc.
Pno

61

S.: They that turn man-y___ to

A.: man-y___ to

T.: man-y to

B.: man-y ... man-y to

204
S.
right-eous- ness like the stars for- ev - er and ev - er.
A.
right-eous- ness like the stars for- ev - er and ev - er.
T.
right-eous- ness like the stars for-ev - er and ev - er.
B.
right-eous- ness like the stars for-ev - er and ev - er.
Vln I
Vln II
Vla
Vc.
Pno

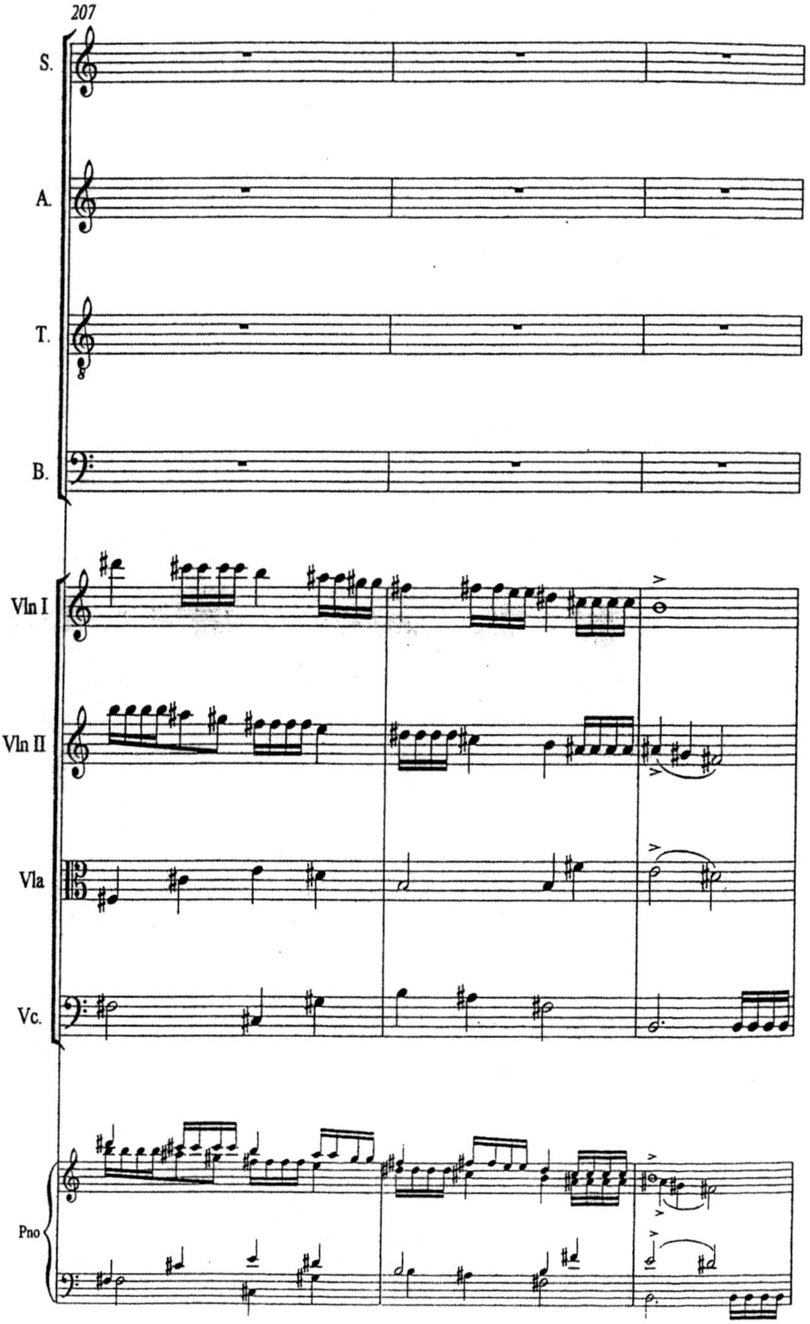
207
S.
A.
T.
B.
Vln I
Vln II
Vla
Vc.
Pno

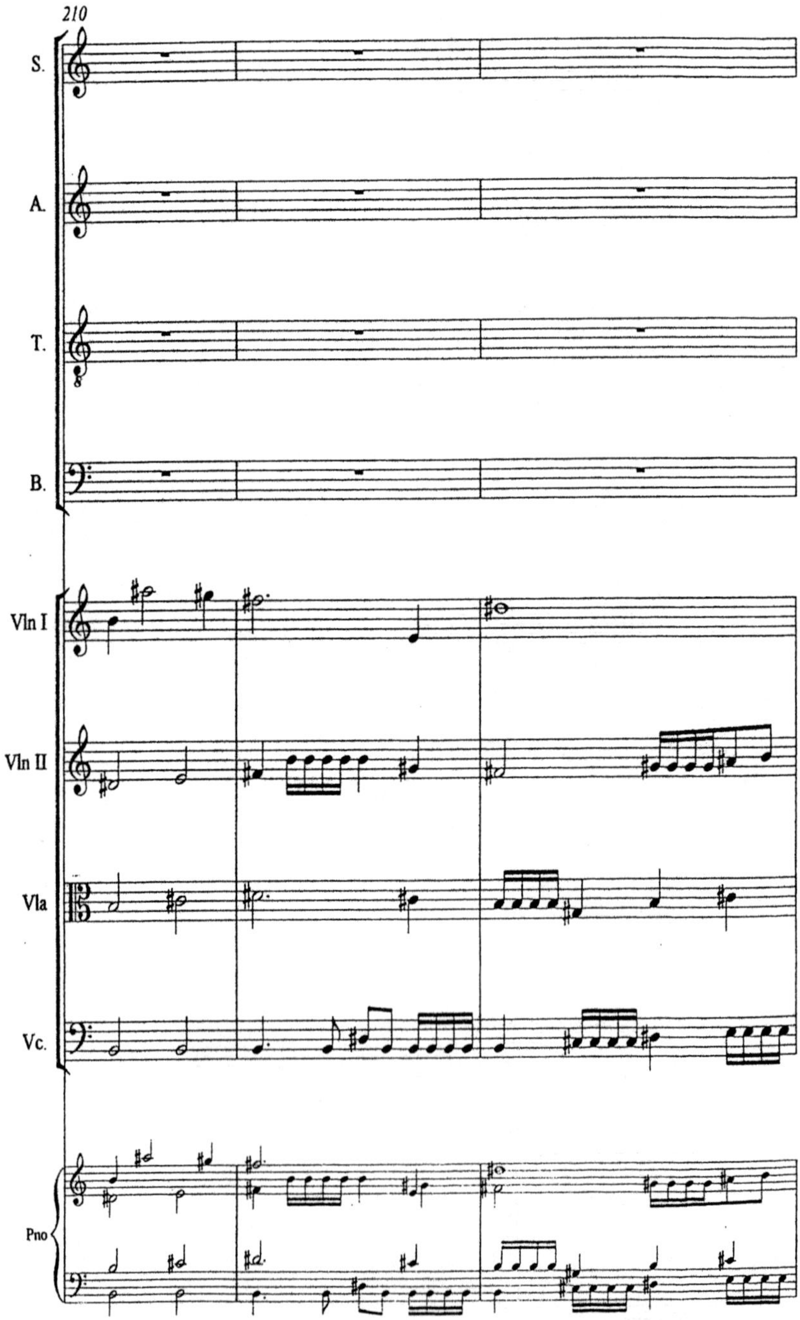

210
S.
A.
T.
B.
Vln I
Vln II
Vla
Vc.
Pno

213
subito
più mosso ♩ = 120
S.
A.
Tenor Solo
mf
T.
Dear chil - dren I must bid you fare - well
B.
Vln I
p
mf
Vln II
Vla
Vc.
colla voce
subito
più mosso ♩ = 120
Pno
colla voce

67

217

S. an e - vil world.

A. an e - vil world.

T. I leave you in an e - vil world. May

221
S.
in his mer - cy the word of
A.
in his mer - cy the word of
T.
God grant that the word of God
B.
in his mer - cy the word of
Vln I
Vln II
Vla
Vc.
Pno

225
S.
God
A.
God
T.
as it shall be here - aft - er dis - pens - ed to you May prove_ like the
B.
God
Vln I
Vln II
Vla
Vc.
Pno

228
S.
fire ham - mer that ham - mer that break - eth piec - es
A.
fire ham - mer that ham - mer that break - eth piec - es
T.
fire and the ham - mer that break - eth the rock in piec - es!
B.
fire ham - mer that ham - mer that break - eth piec - es
Vln I
Vln II
Vla
Vc.
marcato
Pno
marcato

231
mf agitato
S.
Our God our help in ag - es
mf agitato
A.
Our God our help in ag - es
T.
B.
Vln I
mp
Vln II
mp
Vla
mp
Vc.
mp
Pno
mp

234
S.
mf
past...
Be thou our
A.
mf
past...
Be thou our
T.
mf agitato
Our hope for years to come.....
Be thou our
B.
mf agitato
Our hope for years to come.....
Be thou our
Vln I
Vln II
Vla
Vc.
Pno

237
S.
A.
T.
B.
guide while life shall last and our e - ter - nal
guide while life shall last and our e - ter - nal
guide while life shall last and our e - ter - nal
guide while life shall last and our e - ter - nal
Vln I
Vln II
Vla
Vc.
Pno

74

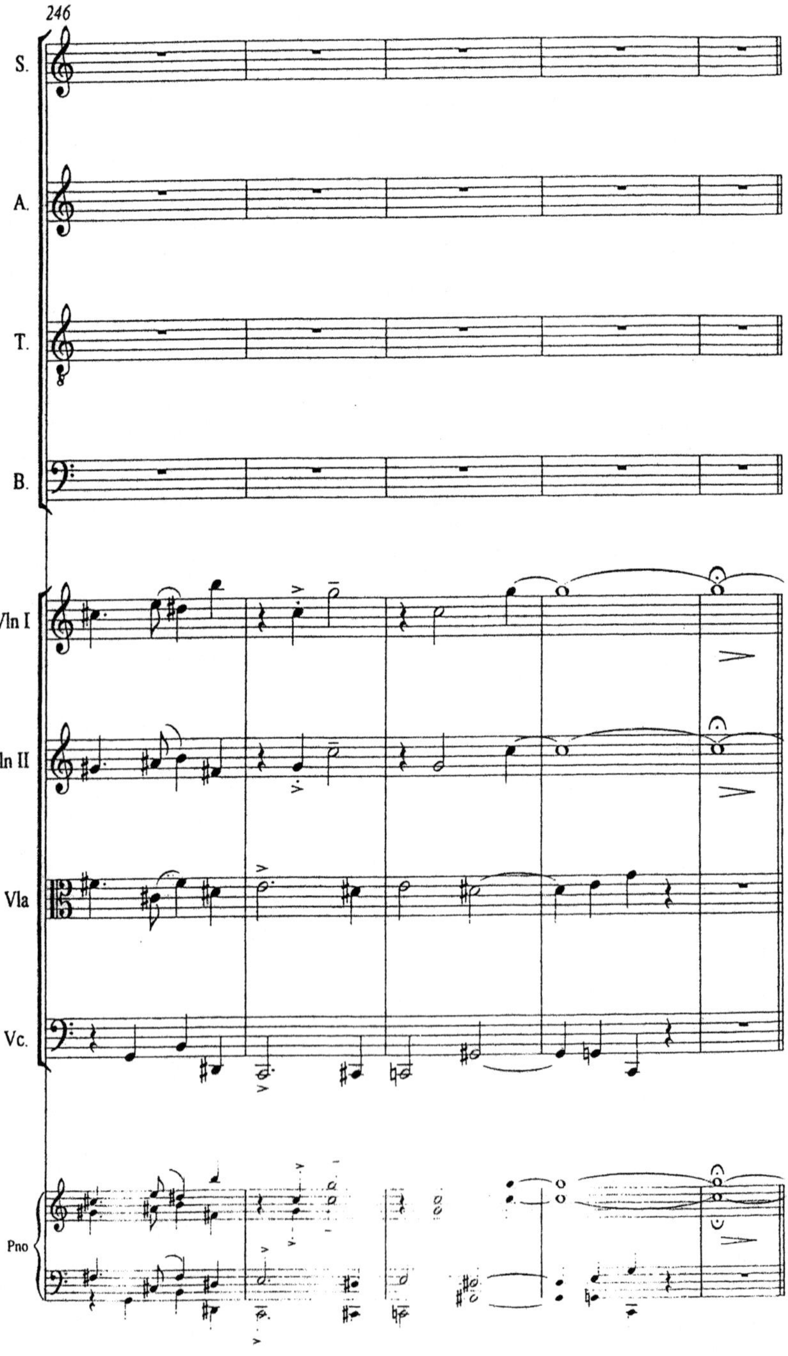
246
S.
A.
T.
B.
Vln I
Vln II
Vla
Vc.
Pno

Part III -- benediction

great Shep-herd of the sheep will have a spe-cial respect for you___ and be your guide.

And that He who is the in-fi-nite foun-tain of

light would o - pen your eyes and turn you from dark - ness un - to light that you

260
più mosso ♩ = 96
S.
mp
Great day
A.
mp
Great day
T.
may re-ceive for give-ness.
mp
So in that great day
B.
mp
Great day
Vln I
mp
Vln II
con sord.
mp
Vla
mp
Vc.
mp
più mosso ♩ = 96
Pno

265
S.
A.
great
T.
when I shall meet you a - gain be - fore your judge and mine
B.
great
Vln I
fp
Vln II
Vla
fp
Vc.
fp
Pno
fp

269
S.
great day
joy - ful,
mf
A.
day
joy - ful,
mf
T.
solo
We may meet in joy - ful
B.
day
joy - ful,
mf
Vln I
con sord.
fp
Vln II
fp
Vla
fp
Vc.
fp
Pno
fp

273
S.
glo - ri - ous,
great
day!
A.
glo - ri - ous,
great
day!
T.
glo - ri - ous
cir - cum - stan - ces
B.
glo - ri - ous,
great
day!
Vln I
Vln II
Vla
Vc.
Pno

84

poco meno mosso
♩= 88
279 rall.
S.
hands of God
A.
hands of God
T.
hands of God
B.
hands of God
Vln I
arco
dolce
Vln II
arco
dolce
Vla
arco
dolce
Vc.
arco
poco meno mosso
♩= 88
rall.
dolce
Pno
arco
dolce

284
S.
mp
Steal a-way, steal a-way, steal a-way to
A.
mp
Steal a-way, steal a-way, steal a-way to
T.
mp
Steal a-way, steal a-way, steal a-way to
B.
mp
Steal a-way, steal a-way, steal a-way to
Vln I
p
Vln II
p
Vla
p
Vc.
p
Pno
p

289
S.
A.
T.
B.
Je - sus. Steal a - way, steal a - way home I
Je - sus. Steal a - way, steal a - way home I
Je - sus. Steal a - way, steal a - way home I
Je - sus. Steal a - way, steal a - way home I
Vln I
Vln II
Vla
Vc.
Pno

292
S.
pp
have-n't got long to stay here. Steal a-way, steal a-
A.
pp
have-n't got long to stay here. Steal a-way, steal a-
T.
pp
have-n't got long to stay here. Steal a-way, steal a-
B.
pp
have-n't got long to stay here. Steal a-way, steal a-
Vln I
pp subito
Vln II
pp subito
Vla
pp subito
Vc.
pp subito
Pno
pp subito

296
S.
way, steal a - way to Je - sus, steal a -
A.
way, steal a - way to Je - sus, steal a -
T.
way, steal a - way to Je - sus, steal a - way,
B.
way, steal a - way,
Vln I
pizz.
Vln II
pizz.
Vla
pizz.
Vc.
pizz.
Pno

299
S.
pp
way home I have-n't got long to stay here.
A.
pp
way home I have-n't got long to stay here.
T.
3
pp
steal a-way home I have-n't got long to stay here.
B.
3
pp
steal a-way home I have-n't got long to stay here.
Vln I
arco
senza sord.
molto
Vln II
arco
senza sord.
molto
Vla
arco
senza sord.
pp
Vc.
arco
senza sord.
pp
molto
Pno
pp
molto

302
S.
My Lord calls me, he calls me by the thun - der The
A.
My Lord calls me He calls me by the thun - der The
T.
My Lord calls me He calls me by the thun - der
B.
My Lord calls me He calls me by the thun - der
Vln I
Vln II
Vla
Vc.
Pno

306
S.
trump-et sounds with - in my soul, I have-n't got long to
A.
trump-et sounds with - in my soul, I have-n't got long to
T.
have-n't got long to
B.
have-n't got long to
Vln I
mp
Vln II
mp
Vla
mp
Vc.
Pno
mp
mp

93

309

S. stay here, have-n't got long to stay here.

A. stay here, have-n't got long to stay here.

T. stay here, have-n't got long to stay here.

B. stay here, have-n't got long to stay here.

Vln I

Vln II   *mf*

Vla

Vc.

Pno   *mf*

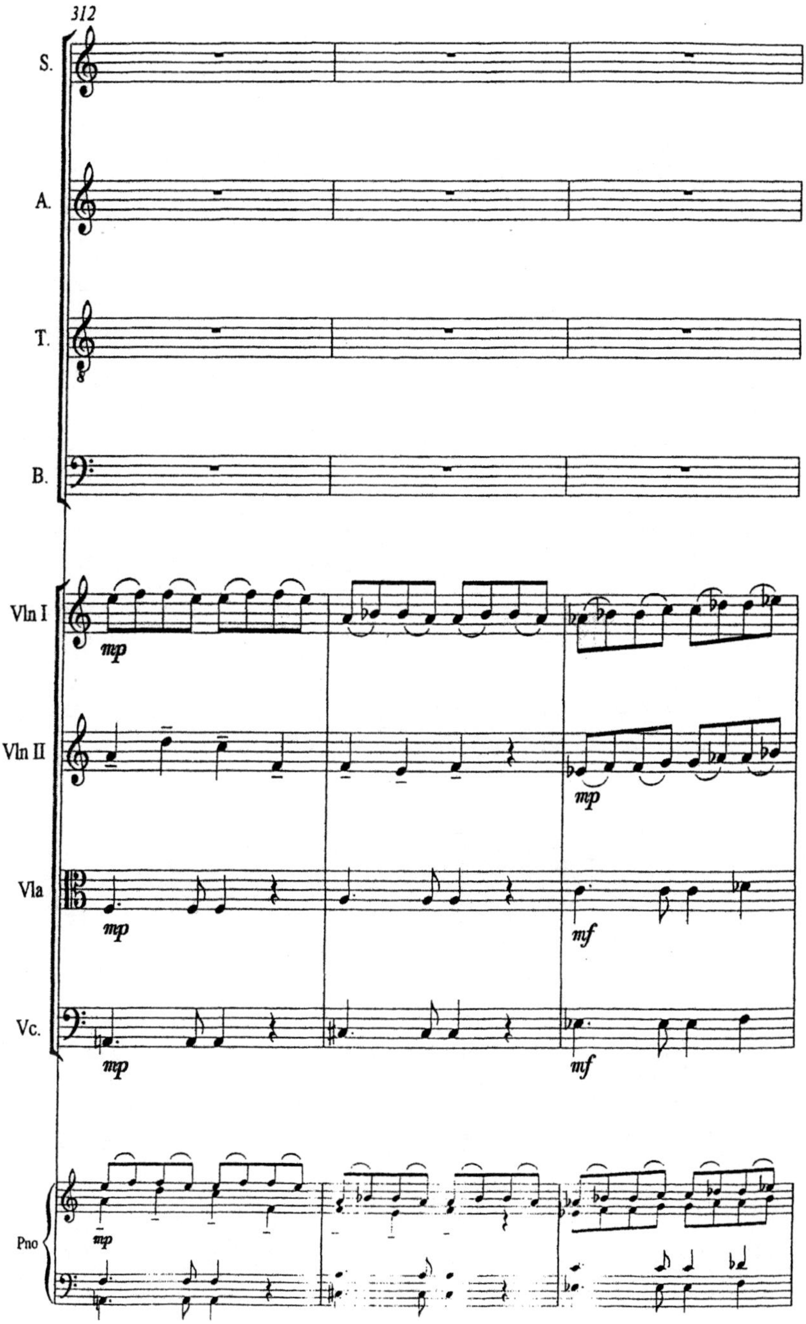
312
S.
A.
T.
B.
Vln I
mp
Vln II
mp
Vla
mp
mf
Vc.
mp
mf
Pno
mp

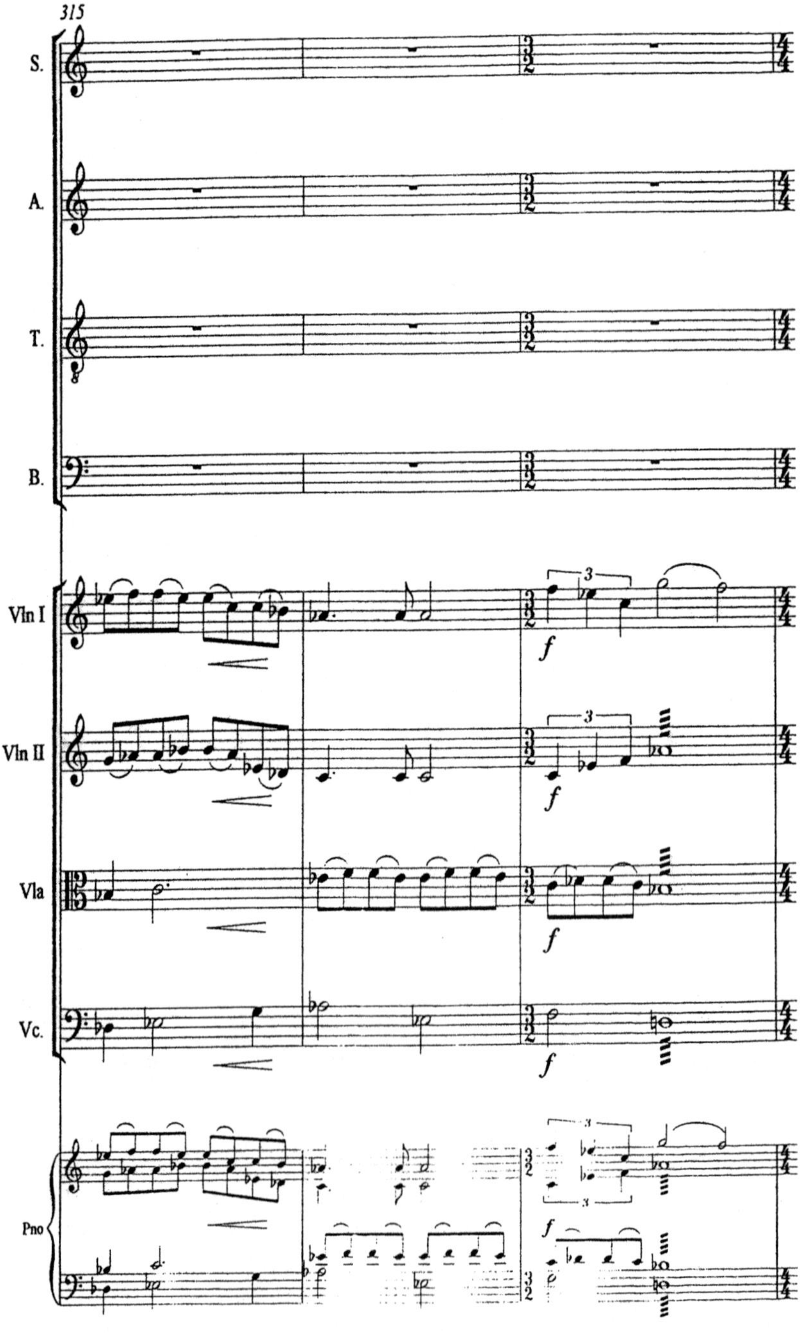
315
S.
A.
T.
B.
Vln I
Vln II
Vla
Vc.
Pno
f
3

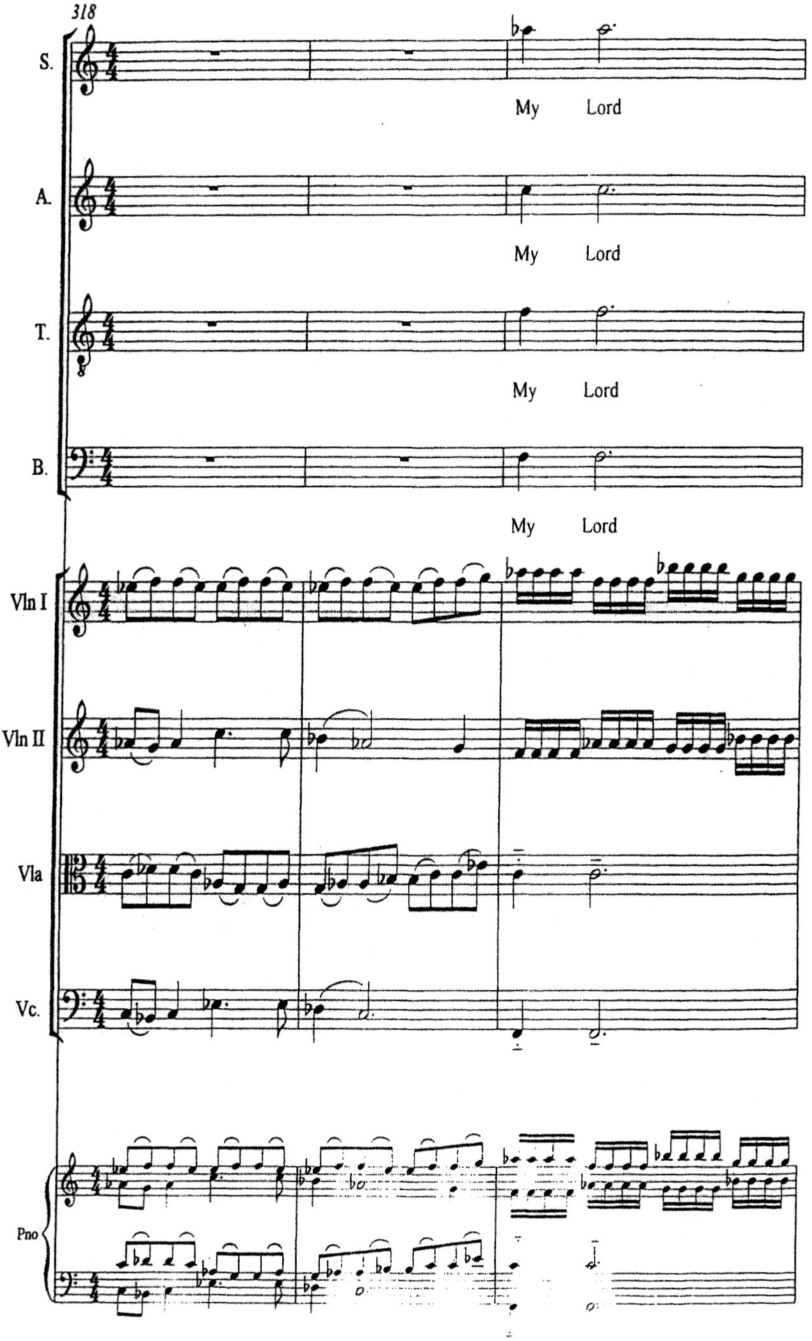
318
S.
A.
T.
B.
My Lord
My Lord
My Lord
My Lord
Vln I
Vln II
Vla
Vc.
Pno

97

S. calls me, He calls me by the

A. calls me, He calls me by the

T. calls me He calls me by the

B. calls me, He calls me by the

S. light - ning, I

A. light - ning, I

T. light - ning, The trump-et sounds with - in my soul, I

B. light - ning, The trump-et sounds with - in my soul, I

326
S.
have - n't got long to stay here, I have - n't got long to
A.
have - n't got long to stay here. I have - n't got long to
T.
have - n't got long to stay here, I have - n't got long to
B.
have - n't got long to stay here, I have - n't got long to
Vln I
Vln II
pizz.
Vla
pizz.
Vc.
pizz.
mp
Pno
mp

100

333
S.
Je - sus. Steal a - way, steal a - way
A.
Je - sus. Steal a - way, steal a - way
T.
oh steal a - way, steal a - way home, I
B.
oh steal a - way, steal a - way home, I
Vln I
Vln II
Vla
Vc.
Pno

336
S.
A.
T.
B.
Vln I
Vln II
Vla
Vc.
Pno
f
have - n't got long to stay here.
have - n't got long to stay here.
have - n't got long to stay here.
have - n't got long to stay here.

103

344
S.
gliss.
mp
Green trees bend - ing, sin - ners stand a -
A.
gliss.
mp
Green trees bend - ing sin - ners stand a -
T.
gliss.
mp
Green trees bend - ing sin - ners stand a -
B.
gliss.
mp
Green trees bend - ing sin - ners stand a -
Vln I
gliss.
Vln II
gliss.
Vla
mp
Vc.
mp
gliss.
gliss.
Pno
mp

105

trem-bling, The trump-et sounds with

350
S.
in my soul,
A.
in my soul,
T.
in my soul,
B.
in my soul,
Vln I
Vln II
Vla
Vc.
Pno
mf

107

108

36
allargando
Maestoso
S.
hands of God!
A.
hands of God!
T.
hands of God!
B.
hands of God!
Vln I
ff
Vln II
ff
Vla
ff
Vc.
ff
allargando
Maestoso
Pno
ff

110

SCORE

Photocopy of second proof, 20 July 2003

Catalog No. 6215

Daniel Pinkham

CONVERSING WITH SOME ONE INVISIBLE

(String Quartet Number Two)

I. Allegretto – Allegro energico
II. Allegretto – Andante
III. Vivo – Andantino – Presto scherzando
IV. Andante tranquillo

Ione Press, Inc. A division of ECS Publishing, Boston, MA

Commissioned by Richard A. S. Hall, acting on behalf of Herbert W. Richardson and the Edwin Mellen Press, for performance during the Northampton-Stockbridge Celebration of the Tercentenary of the birth of Jonathan Edwards.

The quotation "...*Conversing with some one invisible*" is taken from a poem by Robert Lowell entitled "Jonathan Edwards in Western Massachusetts".

The first performance took place on 5 October 2003 at The First Churches in Northampton, Massachusetts.

violin 1: Alexa Adams
violin 2: Romina Kostare
viola: Carol Hutter
violoncello: Arthur Cook

PROGRAM NOTE

There is in my Second String Quartet no programmatic intention despite the work's borrowed literary title, "...Conversing with some one invisible".

In the *New York Times* Garry Wills, reviewing George M. Marsden's new biography, *Jonathan Edwards, a Life*, commented: "His words could thunder or soothe – scolding savagely, needling wittily or inspiring piously".

My attempt has been to present, in purely musical terms, a range of affects and colors that parallel the humors and dynamics of Edwards's literary contributions.

"...Conversing with some one invisible" begins with a rising figure that not only introduces each of the four movements, but is heard in varied form throughout the entire work. After the introductory *Allegretto*, the first movement continues with an energetic fast section which features rapid meter changes. Despite lyrical intervals, the mood is blustery. The second movement, after a brief introduction, presents a serene *Andante*, a tranquil dialog between the second violin and the violoncello. The third movement, again introduced by the rising figure, is a lightning-quick scherzo. Highly mercurial, it presents a great range of affects. Many contrasting instrumental colors appear and vanish. The fourth movement is an epilog. It opens with the final statement of the rising figure. The viola is then assigned an extended and lyrical melody. The violoncello, playing on plucked strings, has a "walking-bass" *ostinato* and the violins are muted. At the very end there is a turbulent twelve-second improvisation. (Do you hear the rustle of wings?) The work ends with a gentle and reposed major chord.

Daniel Pinkham

Catalog No. 6215

CONVERSING WITH SOME ONE INVISIBLE
String Quartet Number Two

Duration: 13 minutes

Daniel Pinkham

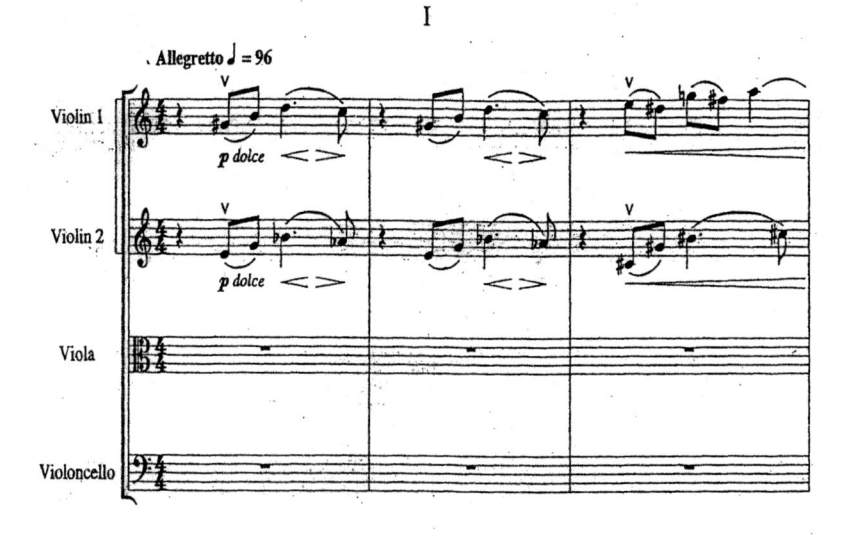

I

© Copyright 2003 by Ione Press, Inc.
A division of ECS Publishing, Boston, Massachusetts.
All rights reserved. Made in U.S.A.

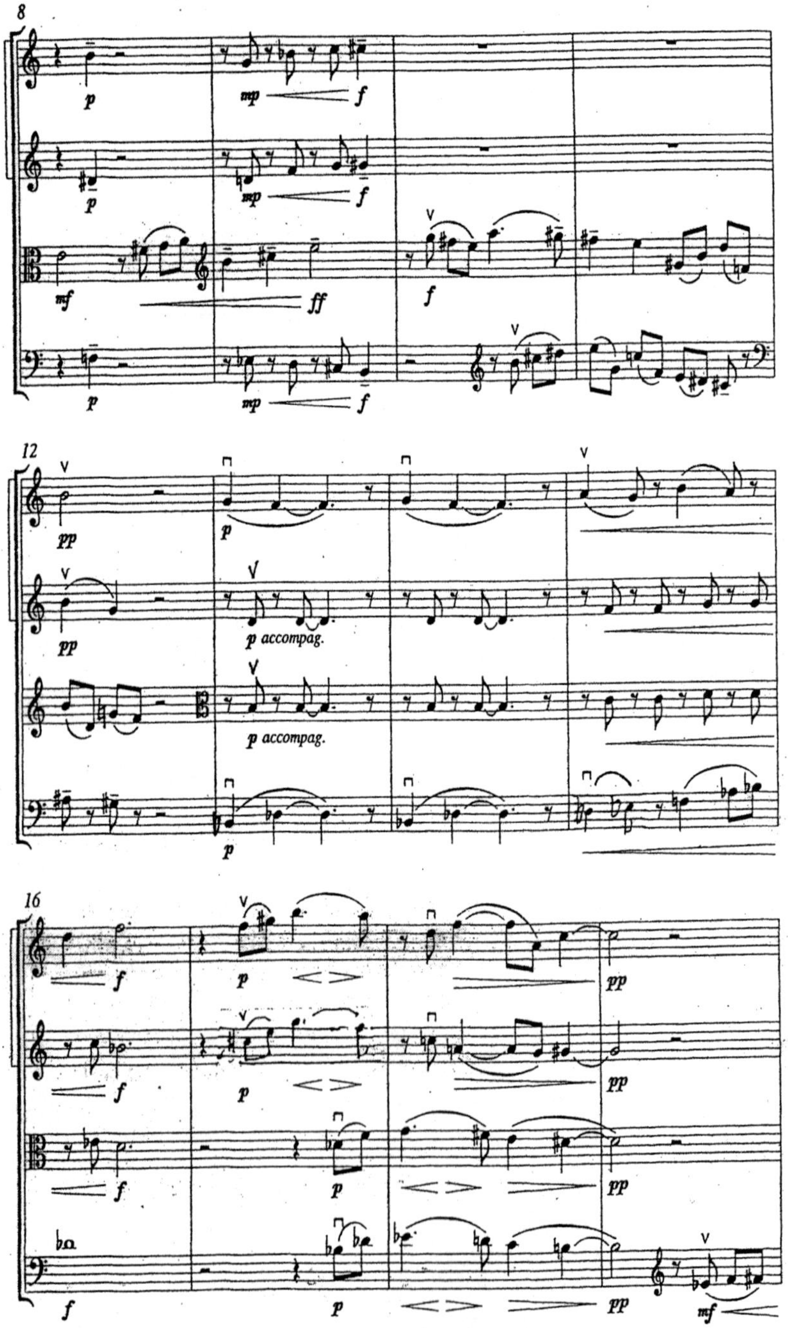
p accompag.
p accompag.

5

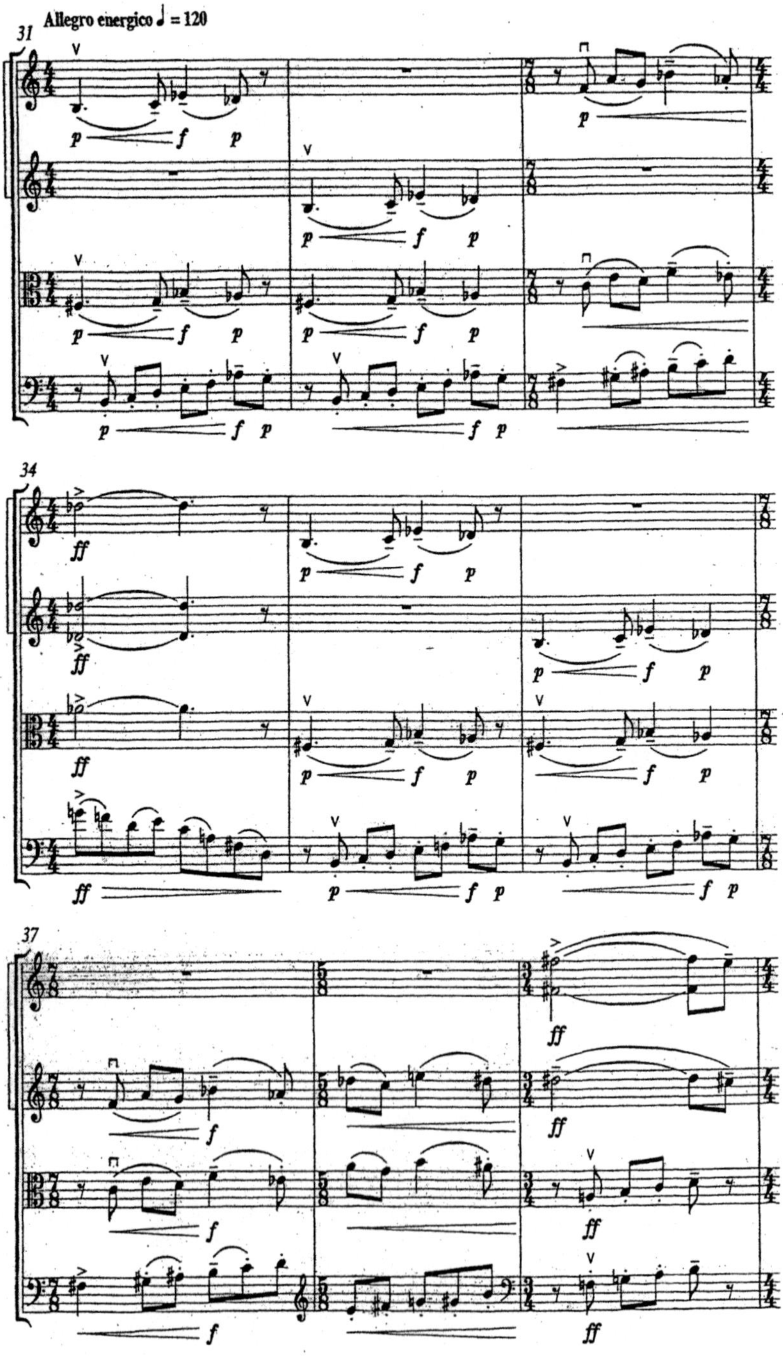
Allegro energico ♩ = 120

7

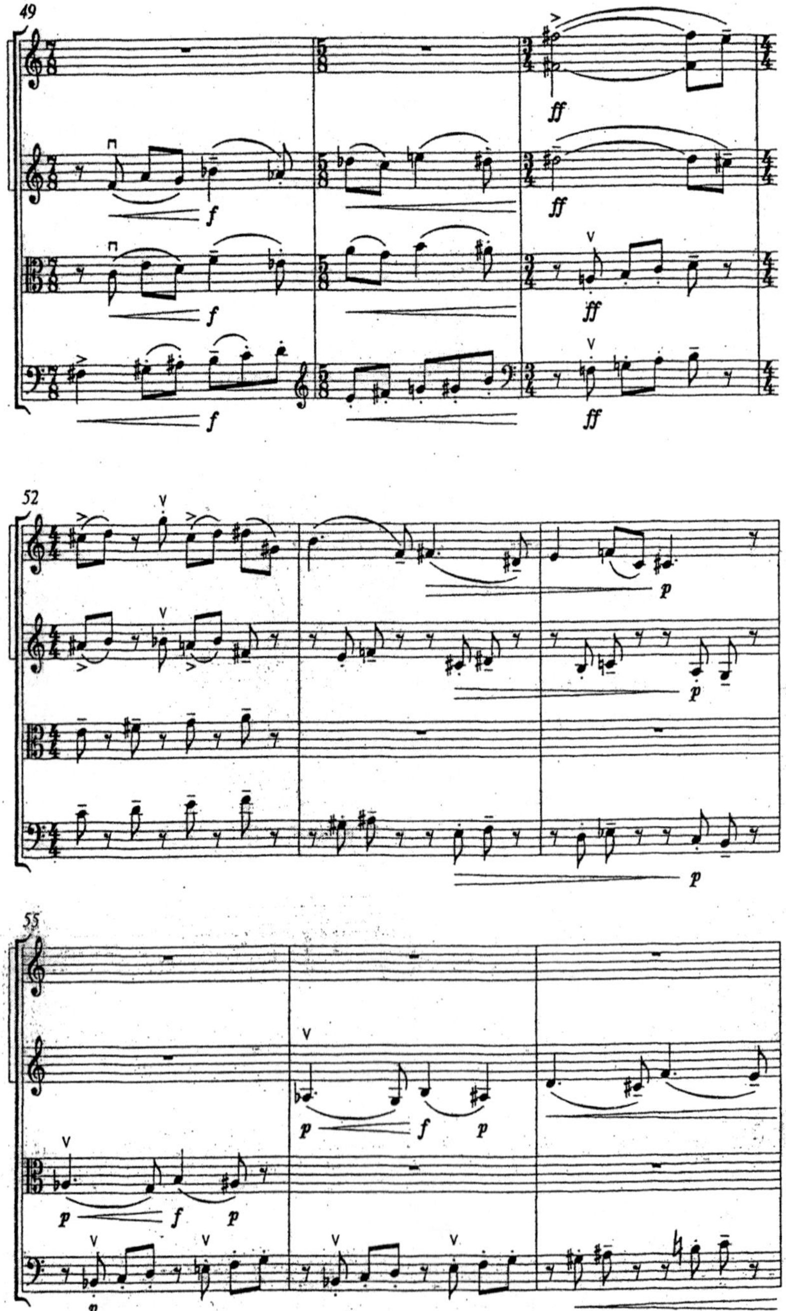
49
52
55

9

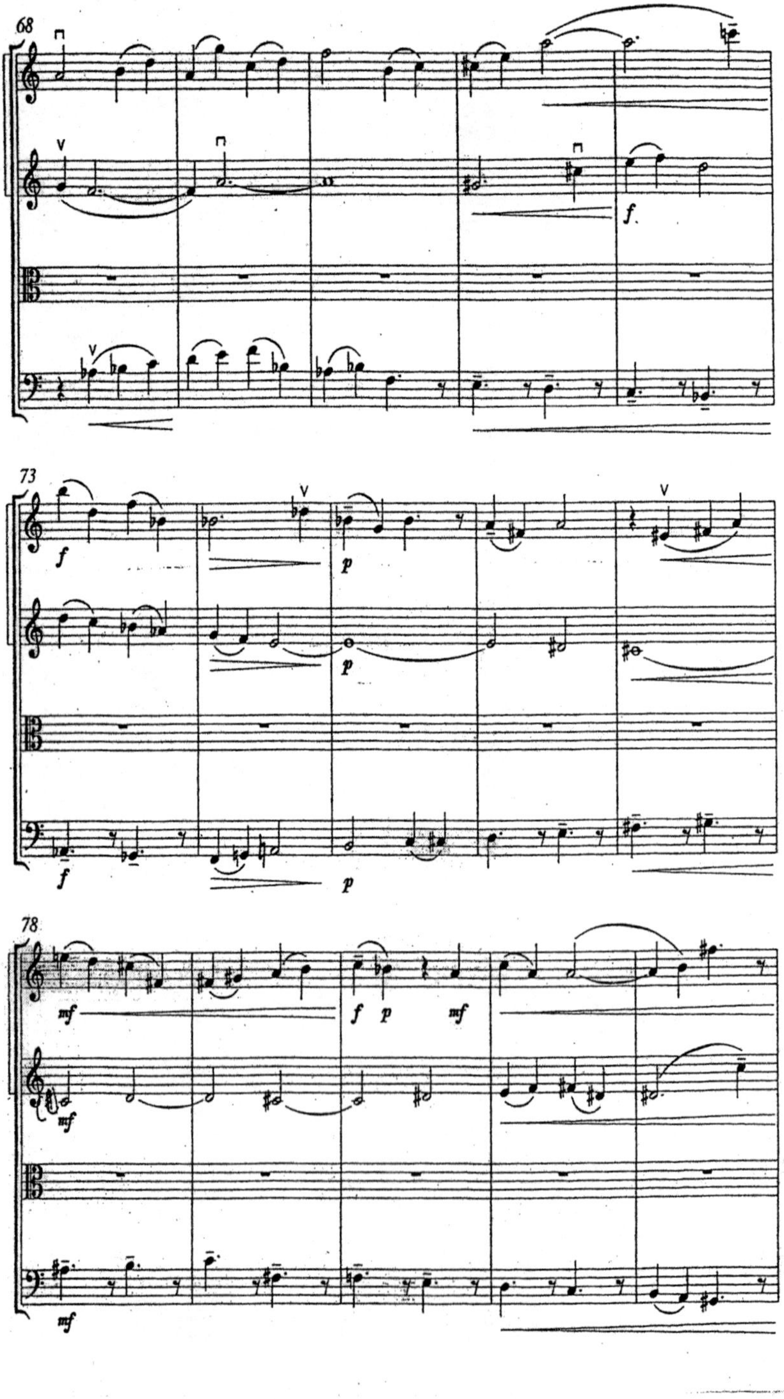
68
73
78

11

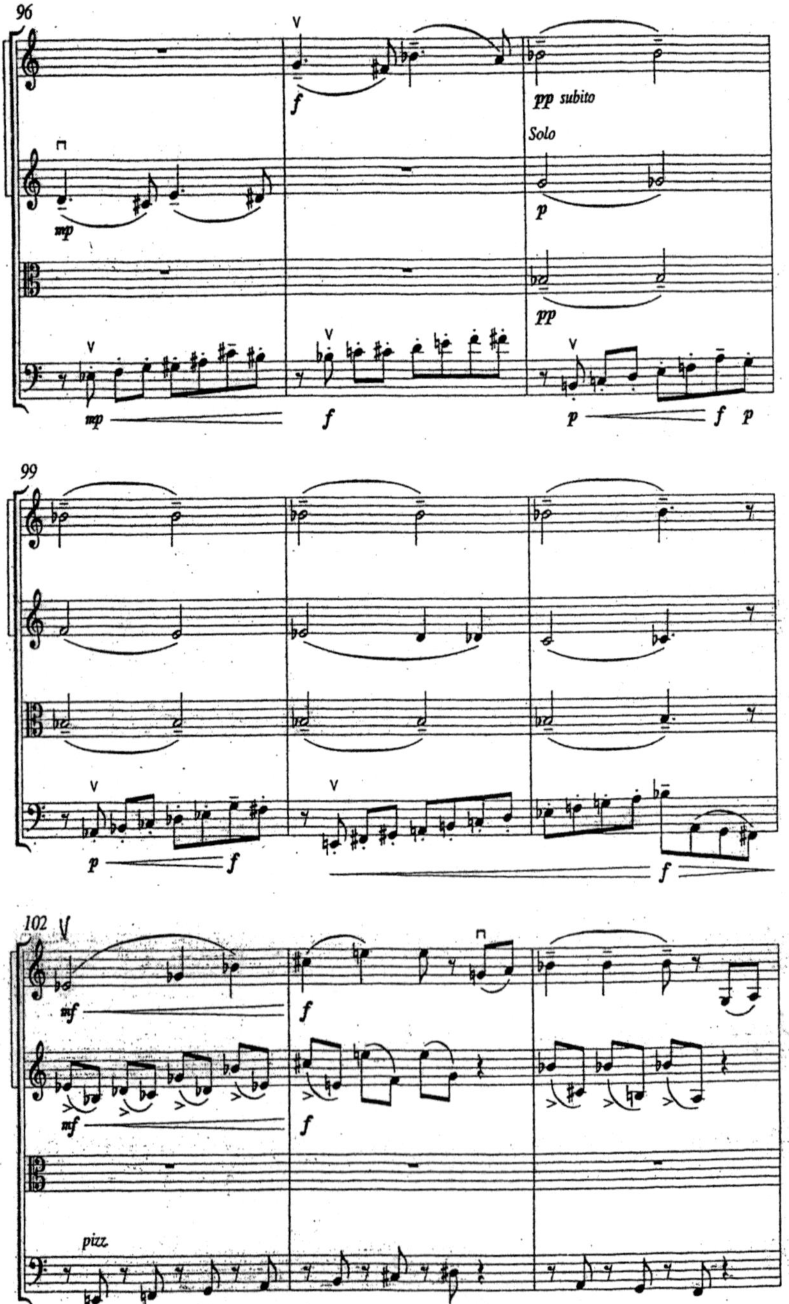
96
f
pp subito
Solo
mp
p
pp
mp
f
p
f p
99
p
f
f
102
mf
f
mf
f
pizz.
mf
f

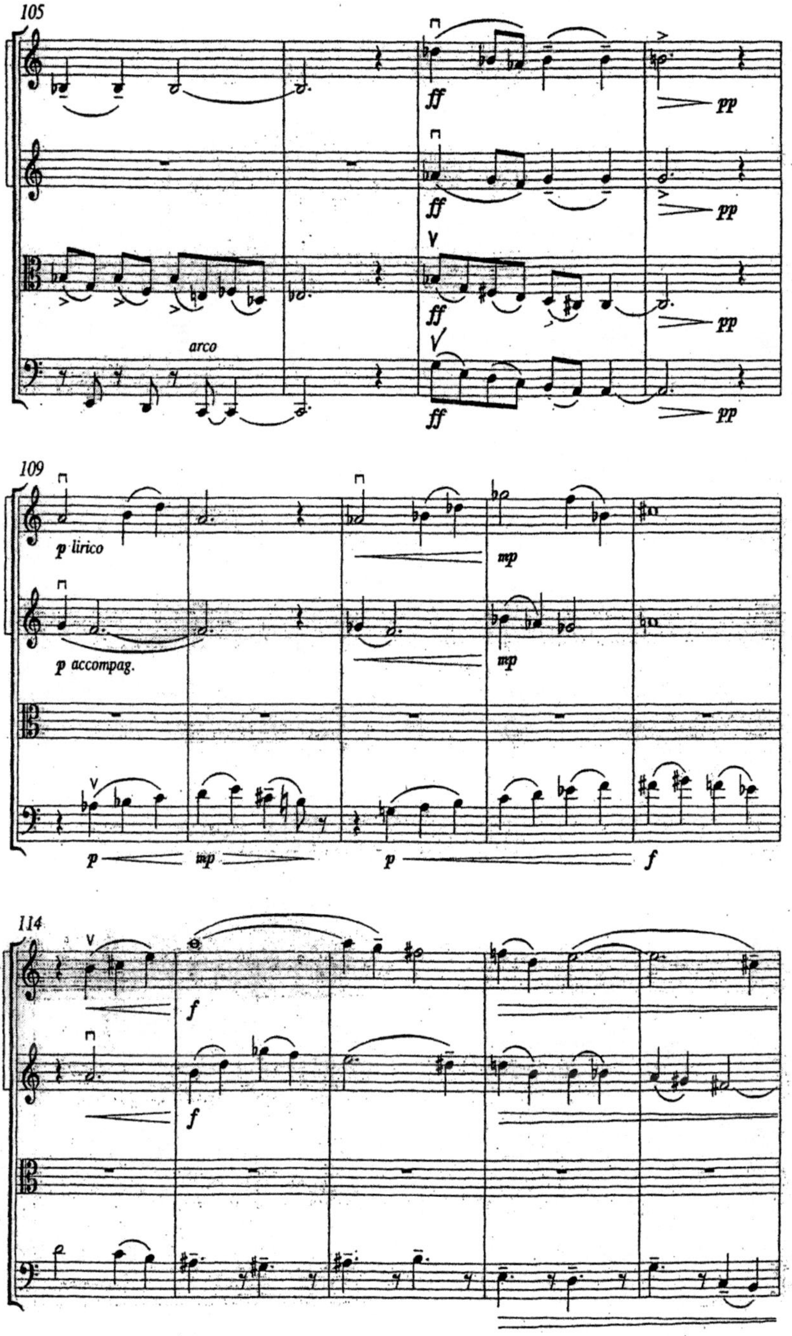
105
ff
pp
arco
109
p lirico
p accompag.
mp
p
f
114
f

119
p
p
p
124
pp
pp
Sola
mf espressivo
p
mf
pp
130
p
pp
p
Solo
mf
pp
ff
pp
p
pp
p
p
p

15

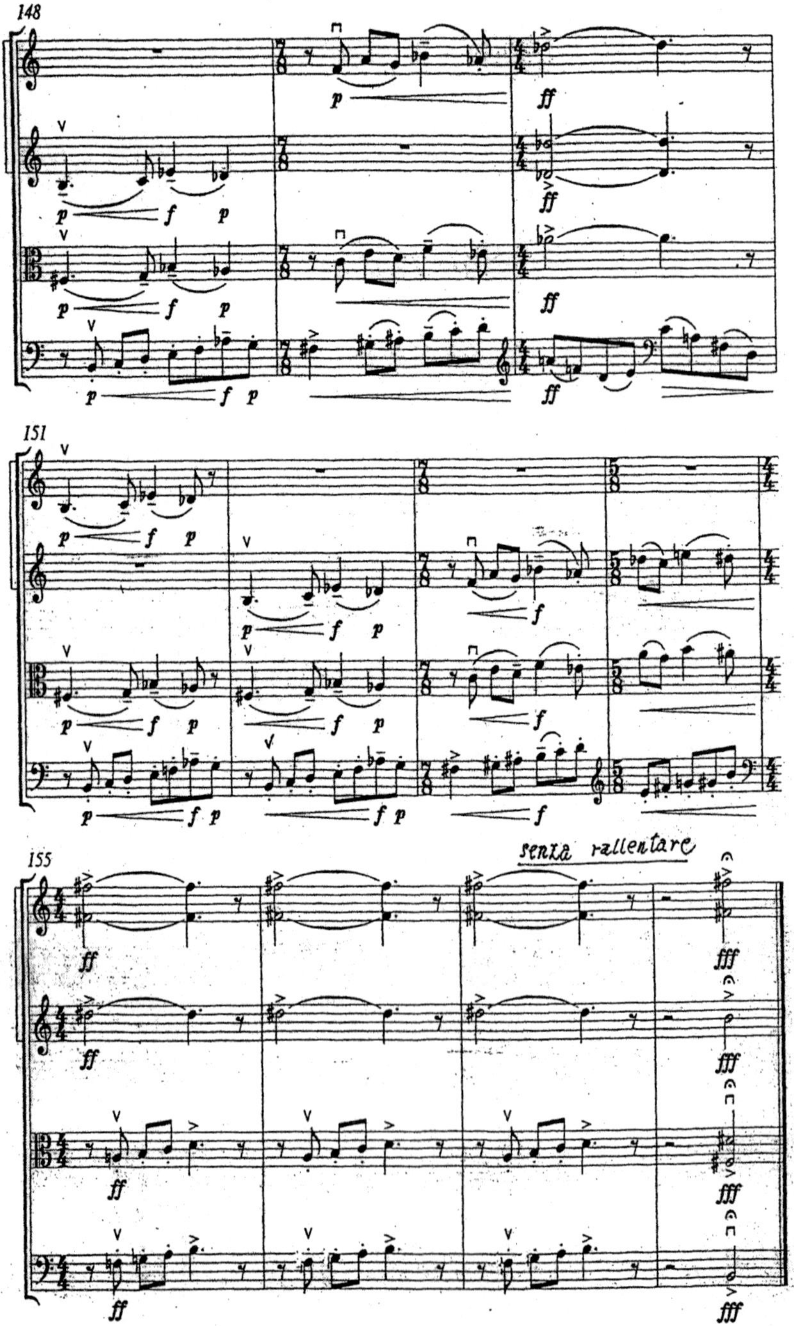
148
151
155
senza rallentare

II

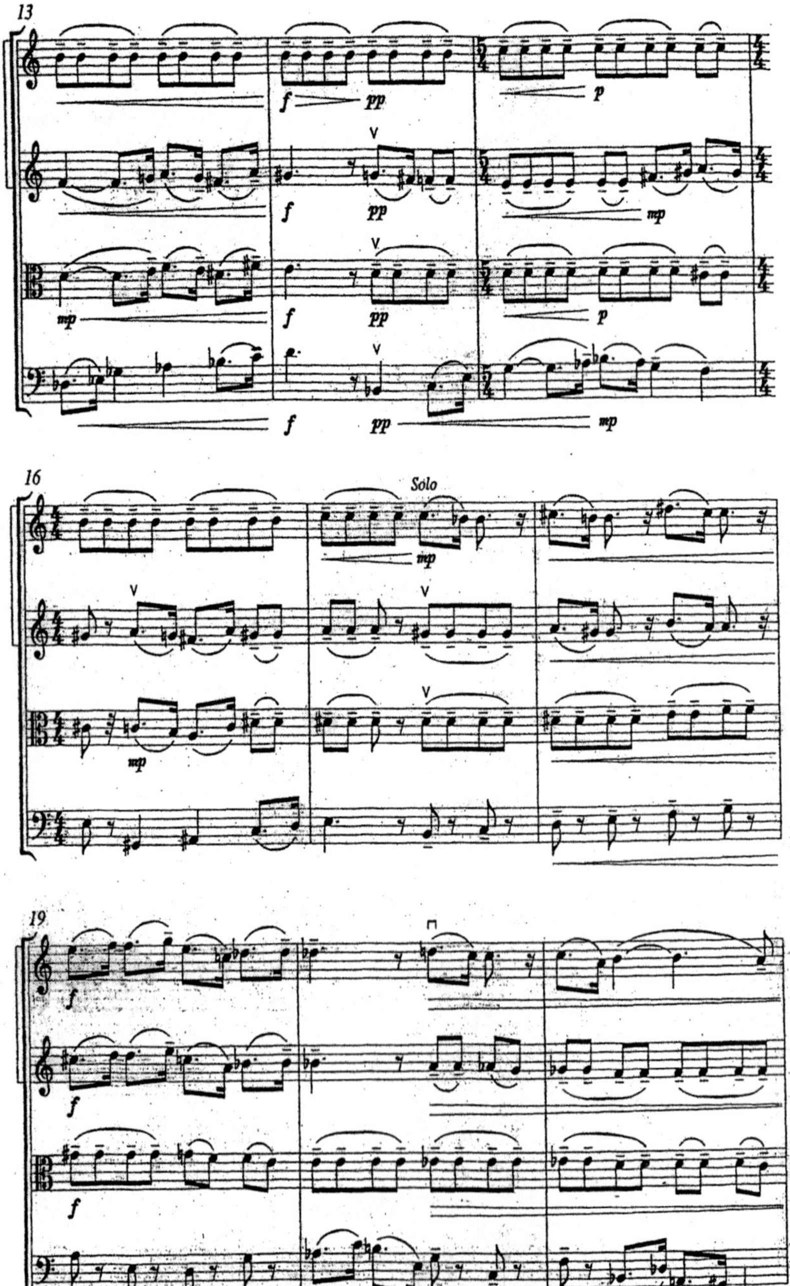
13
16
Solo
19

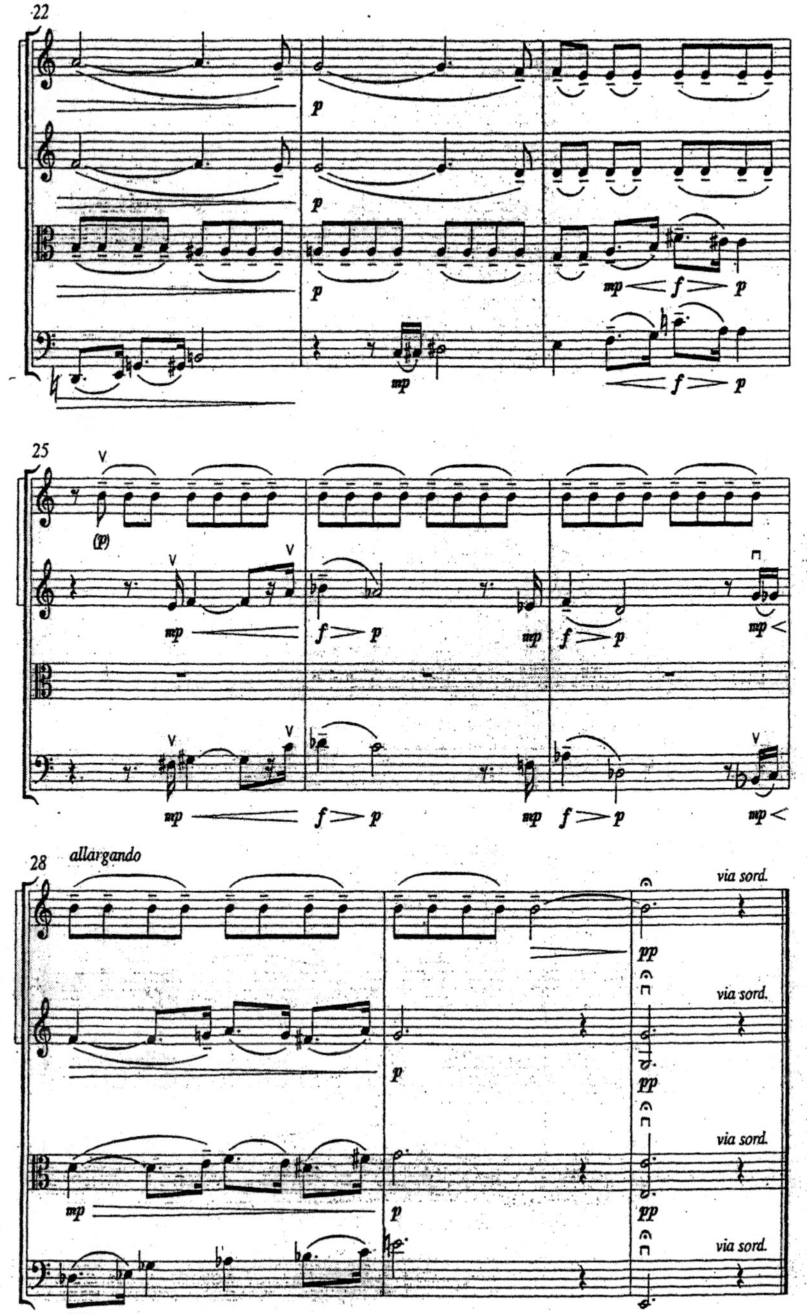
22
25
28
allargando
via sord.
via sord.
via sord.
via sord.

III

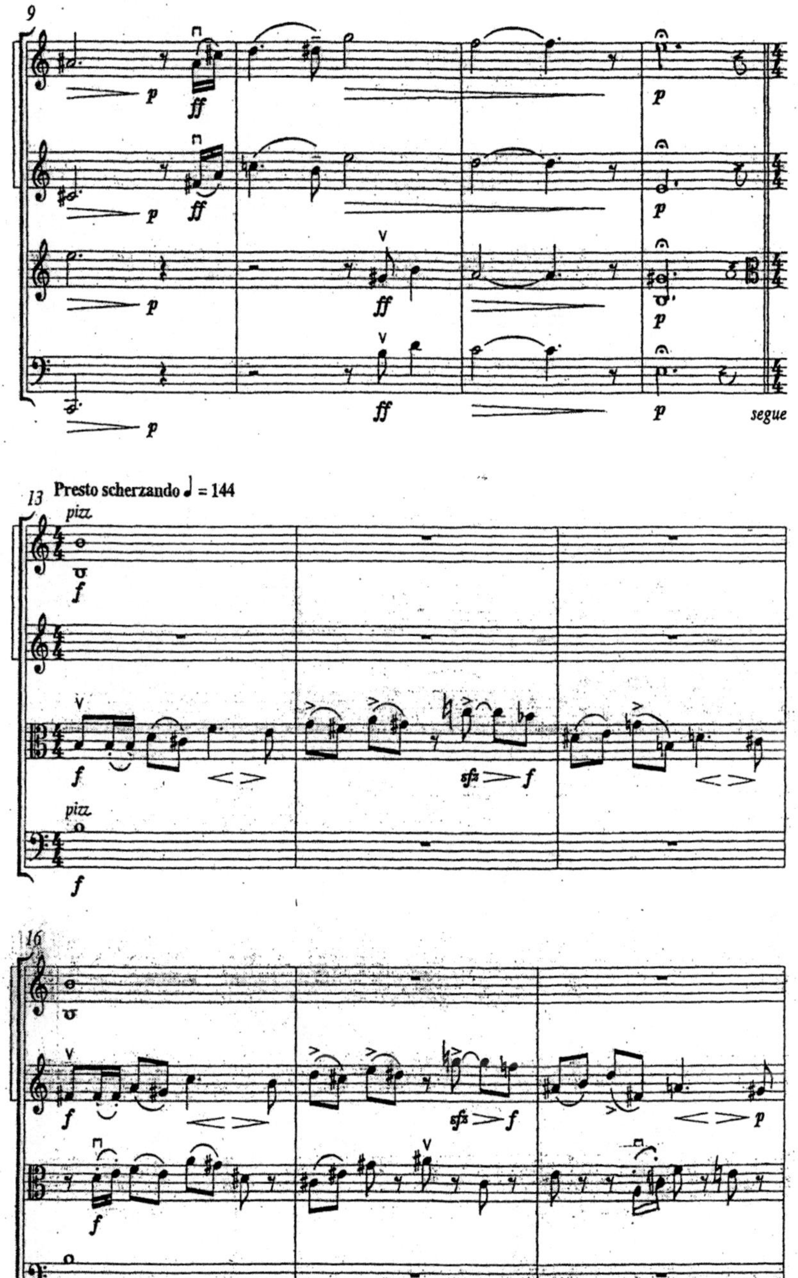
9
p
ff
segue
13
Presto scherzando ♩ = 144
pizz.
f
sfz
16

19
arco
f
ff
ff
ff
arco
f
ff
22
p
p
ff
25
Solo
mf
Solo
mf
p accompag.
p
p accompag.
pizz.
p

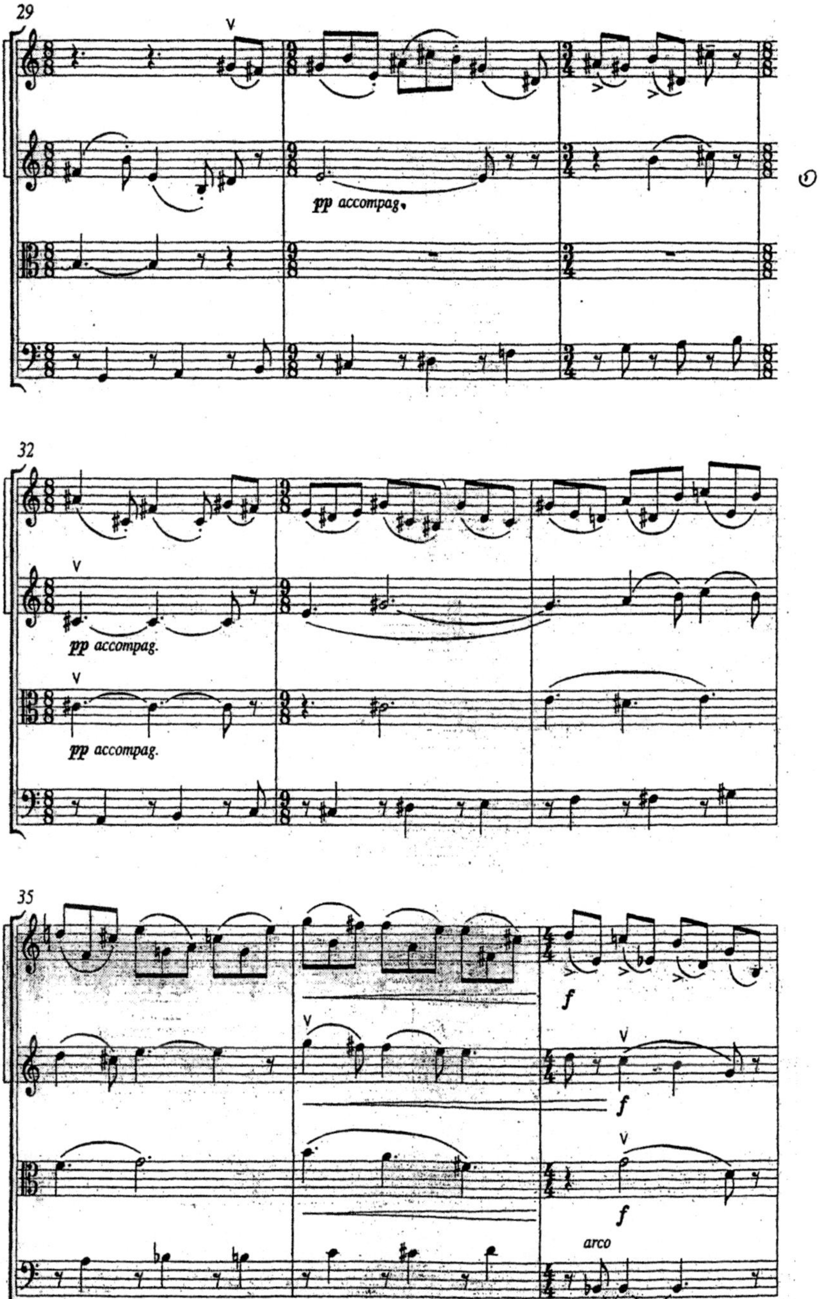
29
pp accompag.
32
pp accompag.
pp accompag.
35
f
f
f
arco
f

38
fp
mf
pp
pizz
Sola
arco
f
mf
pizz
mf
p
42
pp
pp
mf
mf
p
arco
mf
46
f
mf
f
mf
f
mf

25

26

27

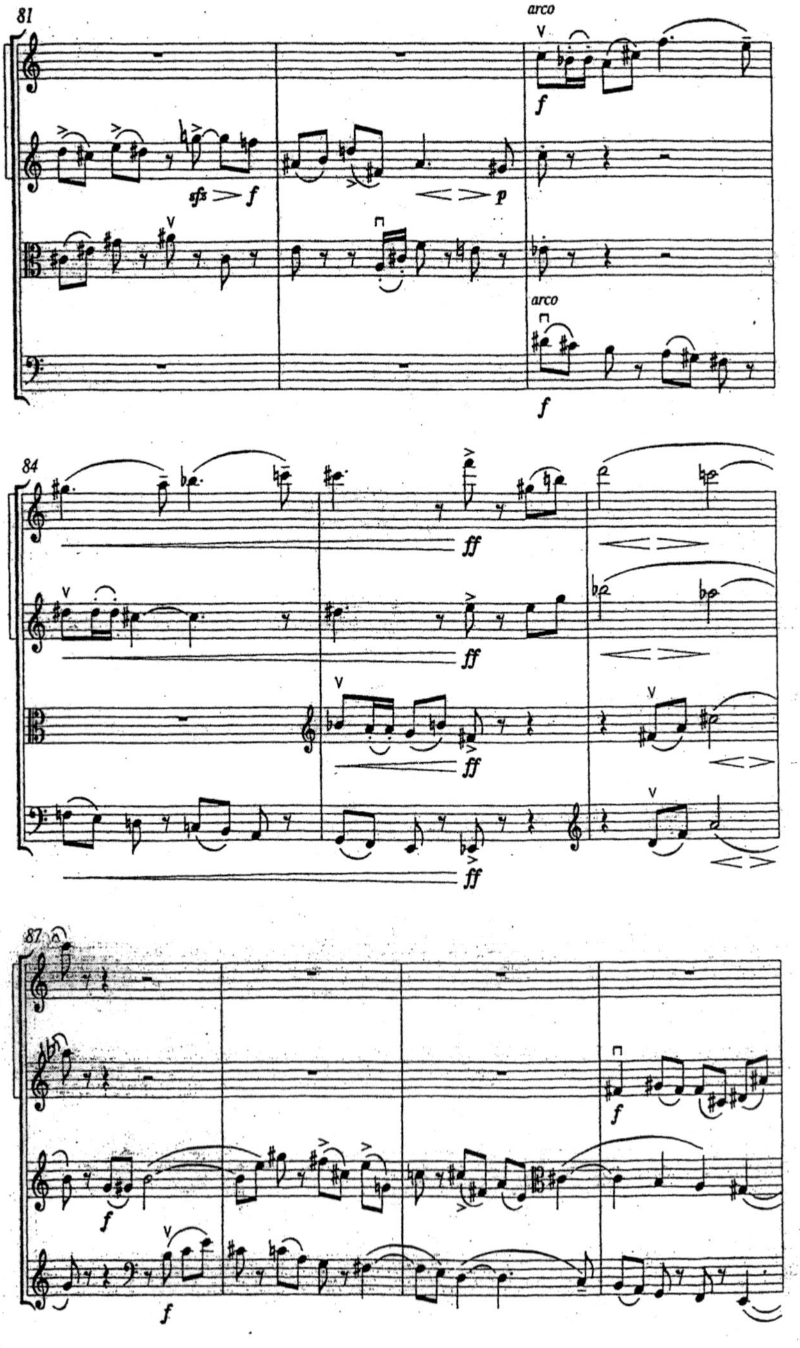
81
arco
f
sfz
f
p
arco
f
84
ff
ff
ff
ff
87
f
f
f

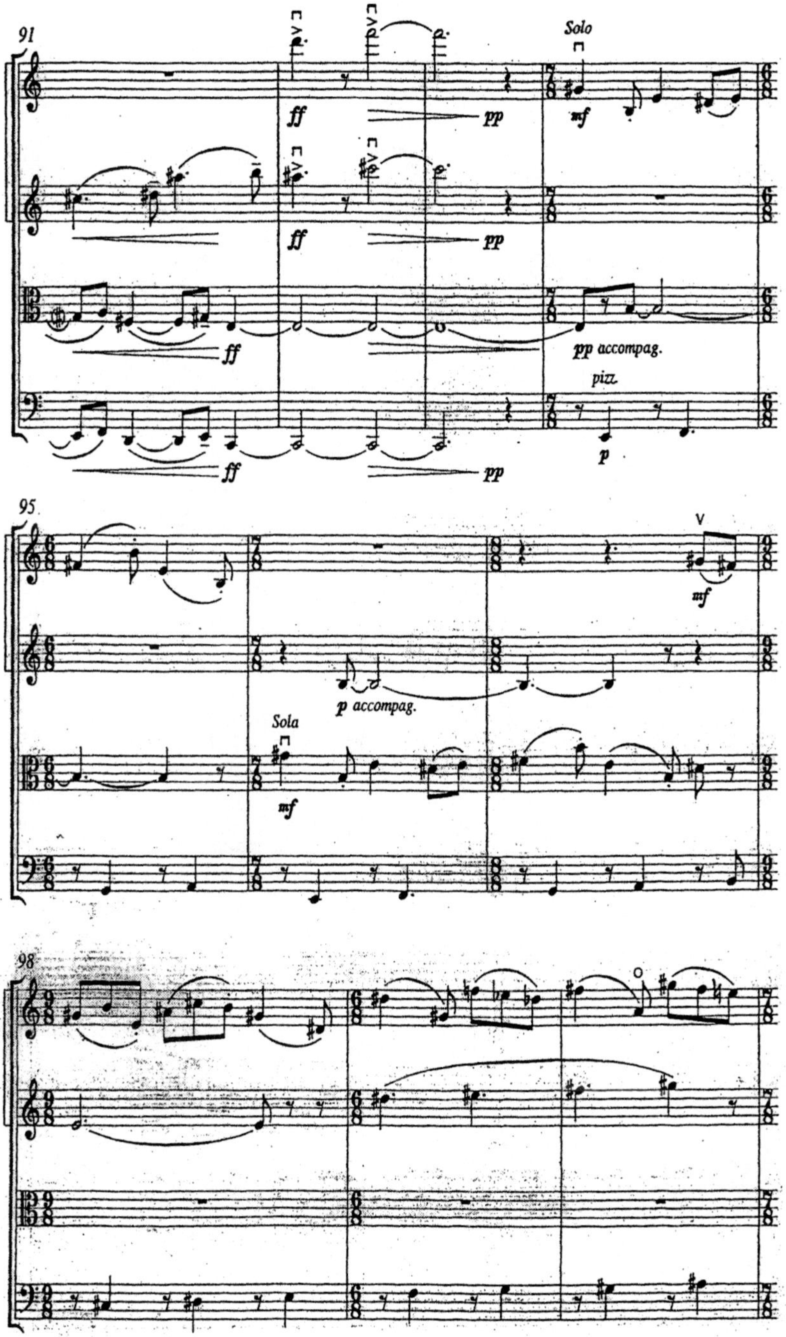
91
Solo
ff
pp
mf
pp accompag.
pizz.
p
95
p accompag.
Sola
mf
98

101
pp
Solo
mf
pizz.
p
arco
mp
Solo
arco
mf
105
f marcato
mf
109
pp
p
pp
p
pp
p

31

IV

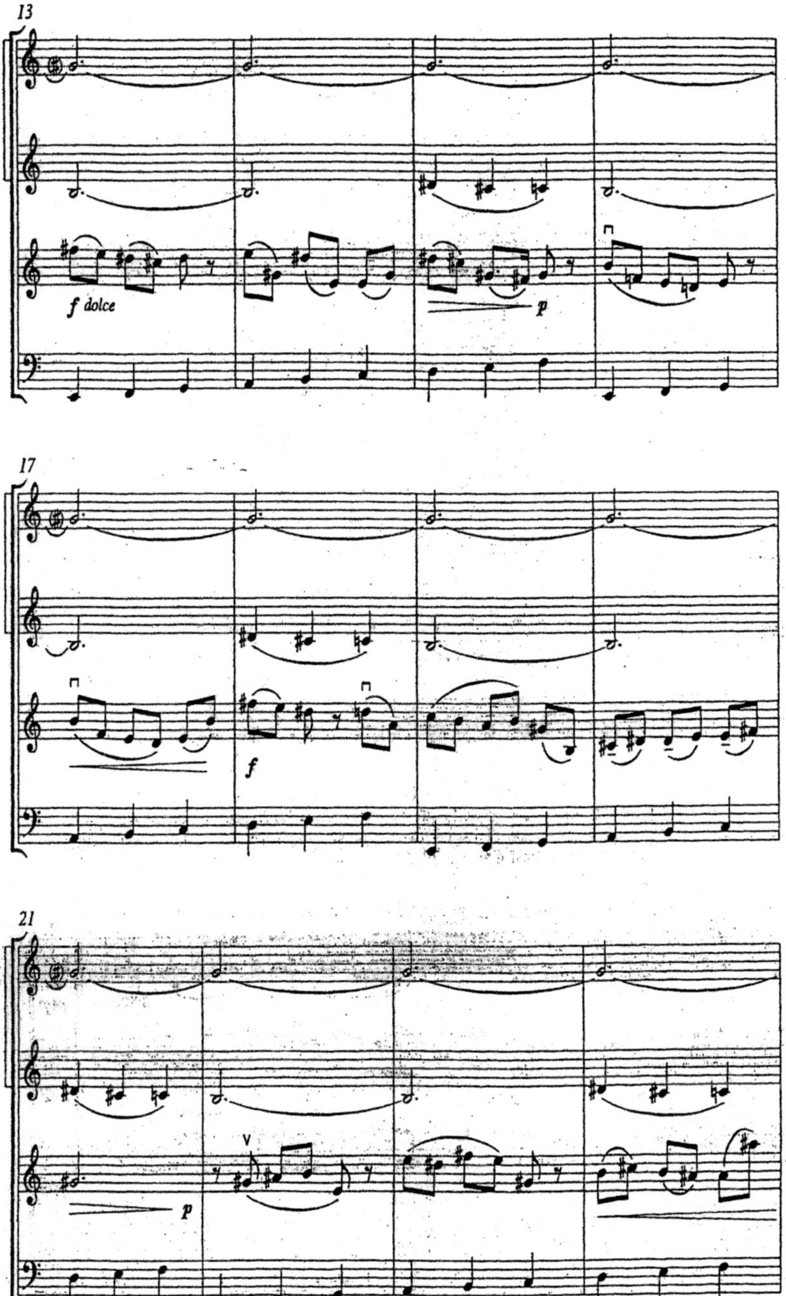
13
f dolce
p
17
f
21
p

During the following 12 seconds (4 measures), the violins and viola should play the assigned pattern as fast as possible, constantly repeating, and not synchronized with the other players. Begin ppp and crescendo to fff at the seventh second. Then begin a diminuendo. At a signal from the cellist at the twelfth second, leave the repeating pattern and skip to the final measure arriving at ppp.

Cambridge, Massachusetts
June 22, 2003

DANIEL PINKHAM was born in Lynn, Massachusetts on 5 June 1923. He studied organ and harmony at Phillips Academy, Andover, with Carl F. Pfatteicher; then at Harvard with A. Tillman Merritt, Walter Piston, Archibald T. Davison and Aaron Copland (A.B. 1943; M.A. 1944). He also studied harpsichord with Putnam Aldrich and Wanda Landowska, and organ with E. Power Biggs. At Tanglewood he studied composition with Arthur Honegger and Samuel Barber, and subsequently with Nadia Boulanger. He has taught at Simmons College, Boston University, Dartington Hall (Devon, England), and was Visiting Lecturer at Harvard University (1957-58). In 1950 he was awarded a Fulbright Fellowship and in 1962 a Ford Foundation Fellowship as a choral conductor. He is a Fellow of the American Academy of Arts and Sciences. He is on the faculty of the New England of Conservatory of Music, where he is senior professor in the Musicology Department. He is Music Director Emeritus of historic King's Chapel in Boston where he actively served from 1958 until 2000. He is the recipient of six honorary degrees: Litt D., Nebraska Wesleyan University, 1976; Mus. D., Adrian College, 1977; Mus.D. Westminster Choir College, 1979; Mus.D., New England Conservatory, 1993; Mus.D., Ithaca College, 1994; Mus. D., Boston Conservatory, 1998.

Pinkham is a prolific and versatile composer whose catalog includes four symphonies and other works for large ensembles; cantatas and oratorios; concertos and other works for solo instrument and orchestra for piano, piccolo, trumpet, violin, harp and three organ concertos; theatre and documentary film works; chamber operas; songs, chamber music; and electronic music.

Pinkham's orchestral works have been played by major orchestras in the United States including the New York Philharmonic under the direction of Leonard Bernstein, The Buffalo Philharmonic (which he conducted in the premiere of his Organ Concerto Number One), the Boston Pops Orchestra under the direction of John Williams and by the composer himself, The Portland Symphony Orchestra, the Louisville Symphony Orchestra, the Orquestra Sinfonica Nacional de Mexico and many others. The London Symphony Orchestra has recorded his Symphony Number Three and Symphony Number Four, Serenades for Trumpet and Symphonic Wind Orchestra and Sonata Number Three for Organ and Strings with the American organist James David Christie as soloist.

In 1990 he was named Composer of the Year by the American Guild of Organists. In 1996 he received the Alfred Nash Patterson Foundation Lifetime Achievement Award for contributions to the Choral Arts.

ECSPUBLISHING COMMITTED TO THE COMPOSER'S CRAFT

Jonathan Edwards
and the Environment

"The Oxbow," Thomas Cole's view of the Oxbow, Northampton, Mass, from Mt. Holyoke. *1836 oil on canvas, Metropolitan Museum of Art*

A conference to consider the relevance of the thought of Jonathan Edwards to our current environmental and ecological concerns.

October 5-7, 2007
Jonathan Edwards Meetinghouse
(the First Churches)
129 Main Street, Northampton, MA

Memorial Plaque of Jonathan Edwards unveiled on June 22, 1900 at The First Churches, Northampton, Massachusetts

Convener's Opening Remarks

On the very site where we are now convened, Jonathan Edwards ministered to his congregation for almost a quarter of a century. A memorial to him in the form of a bronze bas-relief sculpted by Herbert Adams is mounted on wall of the sanctuary, part of the fifth meeting house to occupy this site. It was formally unveiled on June 22, 1900 to commemorate the 150th anniversary of Edwards' dismissal. This memorial plaque, according to N. H. Gardiner who chaired the committee commissioning it, "represents more than the desire of this church to atone for the past; it represents rather a general sentiment of respect for the illustrious minister who belongs to no single church exclusively, but to the historic Church Universal."

We are convened here at The First Churches to consider the relevance of the thought of Jonathan Edwards to our current environmental and ecological concerns. Edwards was a keen observer of nature, and filled his voluminous notebooks with exact and sometimes poetic descriptions of a wide variety of natural phenomena. He conceived of the world Neo-Platonically as an emanation of God's external glory. He interpreted nature as a book of types or symbols, coordinate with scripture, which shadowed forth moral and spiritual lessons. He highly valued natural beauty since for him it was an image of divine beauty or love. His ethics of benevolence or "consent to being in general" morally enfranchises not only human but all other sentient beings. Clearly, then, Edwards has much to say to those working in the general fields of ecology, environmental philosophy and theology, and in the more specific fields of environmental ethics and aesthetics.

All the conferees are invited to join in establishing and contributing to the work of the Jonathan Edwards Society which is dedicated to promoting ongoing research on America's Spiritual Founding Father.

FRIDAY, OCTOBER 5TH, 2007

8:30-8:45 a.m. Convocation

- Introductions by The Rev. Peter Ives & Richard A. S. Hall

8:40-9:30 a.m.

- "The Glory of God and the Beauty of the Earth: Interpreting Ecology through Theological Aesthetics"
  --James McPherson

9:35-10:25 a.m.

- "Jonathan Edwards on the Beauty of the World: Ecological Themes"
  --Darrol M. Bryant

10:30-11:20 a.m.

- "Abusing Nature," A Manuscript Sermon"
  --Max Lesser

11:25-12:15 p.m.

- "More than Metaphors: Jonathan Edwards and the Environment in the Stockbridge Sermons"
  --Stephen J. Nichols

12:15-1:30 p.m. **LUNCH**

1:30-2:20 p.m.

- "'Benevolence to Being in general': The Universality of Edwards' Nature"
  --James Hewitson

2:25-3:15 p.m.

- "The Contemplative Nature of Jonathan Edwards' *Personal Narrative*"
  --Darryl Robert Frayne

3:20-4:10 p.m.

- "Jonathan Edwards and the Wilderness Tradition Of American Culture"
  --David R. Williams

4:15-5:05 p.m.

- "John Woolman--Quaker Divine: How His Life and Thought Might Contribute to Our Environmental Discussions"
  --Michael Thompson

5:10-6:00 p.m.

- "Jonathan Edwards as God's Gardener and Henry David Thoreau as God's Warrior: A Comparison and Contrast"
  --Vernice Cain

SATURDAY, OCTOBER 6TH, 2007

8:30-9:20 a.m.

- "Jonathan Edwards and the End of the World"
  --*Ken Minkema*

9:25-10:15 a.m.

- "A God-Haunted World: An Edwardsean Rationale for Saving the Creation"
  --*Robert Boss*

10:20:12:10 p.m.

- "Edwards and Ecology: An Accommodation"
  --*David E. White*

12:15-1:05 p.m.

- "Ecological Imagination"
  --*Steven Fesmire*

1:05-2:20 p.m. **LUNCH**

2:25-3:15 p.m.

- "The Transcendentalist Deduction of Goodness from Beauty"
  --*John Martin*

3:20-4:10 p.m.

- "Spider in a Tree"
  --*Susan Stinson*

4:15-5:05 p.m.

- "Human Values & Social Structures: An Edwardsean Reflection on the Moral Environment"
  --*John Taylor*

5:10-6:00 p.m.
- "Jonathan Edwards on the 'Flying' Spider: A Model of Ecological Thought in Microcosm"
  --*Richard Hall*

5:30-7:00 p.m. **RECEPTION (Forbes Library)**

SUNDAY, OCTOBER 7TH, 2007

10:00-11:00 a.m.
- Service of Worship
  The Rev. Peter Ives, Preacher

11:00-12:00 noon
- Coffee Hour

12:00-1:00
- Business Meeting: The Jonathan Edwards Society

LOCATION
All academic sessions of the conference will be held in The First Churches:
- Address: 129 Main Street, Northampton, MA 0160
- Phone: (413) 584-9392

I wish to thank the following individuals for their indispensable work in the planning and organization of this conference:

- *Peter Ives, Pastor at The First Churches, Northampton, MA*
- *Holly Martineau, Publicist with the Jonathan Edwards Meeting House, Northampton, MA*
- *Elise Bernier-Feeley, Local History & Geneology Librarian, Forbes Library, Northampton, MA*
- *Julie H. Bartlett, Archivist, Calvin Coolidge Presidential Library & Museum, Hampshire Room for Local History, Forbes Library, Northampton, MA*
- *Herbert W. Richardson, The Edwin Mellen Press, Lewiston, NY*

This conference is sponsored by The Edwin Mellen Press.

The Edwin Mellen Press is an international publisher of scholarly books acquired by research libraries throughout the world. The Press publishes specialized research: monographs, bibliographies, concordances, dictionaries, commentaries, translations, critical editions, methodological studies, criticism, conference proceedings, and multi-volume sets. The Press publishes approximately 425 new titles a year, over two dozen continuing series, academic journals, and the research generated by several scholarly institutes. It was established in Canada in 1974, the United States in 1978, and Great Britain in 1987.

Born October 5, 1703

THE FIRST CHURCHES OF NORTHAMPTON
First Church of Christ, UCC and First Baptist Church, ABC

Rev. Dr. Peter B. Ives, Minister   October 5, 2003
Rev. Kelly Gallagher, Asst. Minister   10:00 a.m.

JONATHAN EDWARD'S TERCENTENARY
Worship Service

PRELUDE MEDITATION

There in heaven this fountain of love, this eternal three in one, is set open without any obstacle to hinder access to it. There this glorious God is manifested and shines forth in full glory, in beams of love; there the fountain overflows in steams and rivers of love and delight, enough for all to drink at, and to swim in, yea, so as to overflow the world as it were with a deluge of love.

Jonathan Edwards' sermon "Heaven is a World of Love"

PRELUDE   "Jerusalem, My Happy Home"   Robert Law
Prelude on the American Folk Hymn, Land of Rest

WELCOME AND ANNOUNCEMENTS   Rev. Ives

INTROIT   "This Is the Day the Lord Hath Made"   Johann Cruger, 1647
           Text: Isaac Watts, 1719

This is the day the Lord hath made; The hours are all God's own;
Let heaven rejoice, let earth be glad, And praise surround the throne.
Hosanna in the highest strains The church on earth can raise!
The highest heavens in which God reigns Shall now resound with praise.

CALL TO ATTENTION (at the beat of the drum)   Kim Abell

*PROCESSING THE BIBLE   Paul Gibson
     The bible in Colonial times was taken from the "Bible box" and processed down the aisle of the Church and placed in position on the pulpit while the congregation stood.

*CALL TO WORSHIP (PILGRIM) (Psalm 95)   Rev. Dr. Peter Kakos

Leader: O come, let us sing to the Lord; let us make a joyful noise to the rock of our salvation.
ALL: Let us come into God's presence with thanksgiving, let us make a joyful noise to God with songs of praise!
Leader: O come, let us worship and bow down, let us kneel before the Lord our Maker.
ALL: For the Lord is our God and we are the people of God's pasture and the sheep of God's hands.

*HYMN #1 (PILGRIM)   "Our God, Our Help in Ages Past"

MOMENT OF REFLECTION   "The New Hymns"

*HYMN   "All People That on Earth Do Dwell"   (Old Hundredth)
In Colonial New England, churches did not have organs. Organs were called "the devil's bagpipes" and considered "unworthy for worship." Hymns were lined out by the Precentor.

Precentor (Holly Smith-Bove):

>All people that on earth do dwell,
>Sing to the Lord with cheerful voice
>Him serve with mirth, his praise forth tell
>Come ye before him and rejoice
>
>The Lord, ye know, is God indeed;
>Without our aid he did us make
>We are his folk, he doth us feed
>And for his sheep he doth us take
>
>O enter then his gates with praise,
>Approach with joy his courts unto
>Praise, laud, and bless his name always,
>For it is seemly so to do.

*Indicates: Please rise if it is comfortable for you to do so.

ANTHEM "David's Lamentation"   William Billings / Text: II Samuel 18:33
*Combined Edwards and The First Churches Choirs
under the leadership of David Kidwell*

David the King was grieved and moved, he went to his chamber and wept,
And as he went, he wept, and said, O my son, would to God I had died,
Would to God I had died for thee, O Absalom my son.

CHILDREN'S MESSAGE   Tessa Petersen

*HYMN #130 (PILGRIM)   "Joy to the World! The Lord is Come"

OFFERTORY   "We Sing the Mighty Power of God"
English / R.Vaughan Williams / Hopson   Text: Isaac Watts, 1674-1748
Cindy Naughton, flute

We sing the mighty pow'r of God, That made the mountains rise,
That spread the flowing seas abroad, And built the lofty skies.
We sing the wisdom that ordained The sun to rule the day;
The moon shines full at God's command, And all the stars obey.
We sing the goodness of the Lord, That filled the earth with food;
God formed the creatures with a word, And then pronounced them good.
Lord, how thy wonders are displayed Where e'er we turn our eyes;
If we survey the ground we tread, Or gaze upon the skies.
There's not a plant or flow'r below, But makes thy glories known;
And clouds arise, and tempests blow, By order from thy throne;
While all that borrows life from thee Is ever in thy care,
And ev'rywhere that we can be, Thou, God, are present there.
   Sing hallelujah. Praise the Lord.

*DOXOLOGY AND DEDICATION
(Children leave for Sunday School, including children from Edwards Church.)

Contemporary	Or	Traditional
Praise God from whom all blessings flow.		Praise God from whom all blessings flow.
Praise God, all creatures here below.		Praise him, all creatures here below.
Praise God above, you heavenly host.		Praise him above, ye heavenly host.
Creator, Christ, and Holy Ghost.		Praise Father, Son and Holy Ghost.

ORGAN REFLECTION

SCRIPTURE READINGS   Rev. Kakos

        I Samuel 2:3-8
        I Corinthians 13:4-13

*HYMN #177 (PILGRIM)   "When I Survey the Wondrous Cross"

SERMON   "Heaven is a World of Love"   Professor Ronald Story

ORGAN MEDITATION

PASTORAL PRAYER AND LORD'S PRAYER   Rev. Kakos

*PASSING THE PEACE
    Leader: "The peace of the Lord be with you"
    ALL: "And also with you"

*HYMN #202 (PILGRIM)   "Jesus Shall Reign Where'er the Sun"

EDWARDS' FAREWELL BLESSING   Rev. Ives

POSTLUDE   "Voluntary in A"   William Selby, 1738-1798
                                              Organist at King's Chapel, Boston

*Indicates: Please rise if it is comfortable for you to do so.

CALENDAR FOR THE WEEK OF OCTOBER 5-11

October 5	10 am Jonathan Edwards Service w/Edwards Church - Ron Story preaching 11:15 am (after service) Coffee Hour - Fellowship 2 pm Blessing of the Animals
October 6	6 pm Church Fair Meeting (parlor) 7 pm Discussion Series w/Edwards Church
October 7	10 am Staff Meeting (office)
October 8	7 pm Missions Mtg. (office) 7 pm Trustees Mtg. (Lyman)
October 10	7 pm Choir

Deacon of the Month: **Paul Gibson**
Ushers: Denise Karuth, Judy Sherman, Margaret Riddle, Peggy Whitham
Greeters: Doris Davis, Betty Barto

ANNOUNCEMENTS

WELCOME!

We welcome the members of the Edwards Church and the delegates of the Jonathan Edwards Tercentenary Conference to our service today. Our guest preacher is Ronald Story, professor of American History at the University of Massachusetts in Amherst.

MEMBERSHIP CLASSES begin next Sunday at 9:00 am in the Pastor's office.

LADIES LUNCHEON / DORCAS MEETING, Friday, October 10th
12:30 pm Ladies' Luncheon at Bickford's is being resumed. All women of the parish are invited to lunch together. Reservations may be made with Dot Swain (584-6930) or Marge Magner (584-7838).
2:00 pm Dorcas Meeting (at Bickford's) when the Dorcas Society will open its season with a presentation by Carolyn Benson on "Writing With Women in Prison". Carolyn, a member of First Churches, has an interesting

story to tell of her volunteer work. All are welcome to attend.

AMISTAD SHIP BUS TRIP
We invite you to sign up in Lyman Hall after the service for the Amistad Ship bus trip to Boston Harbor on Saturday, October 25. The bus will leave the Church at 8:30 am and return at 5:00 pm.

BLESSING OF THE ANIMALS - TODAY at 2:00 pm
The Blessing of the Animals will take place outside in front of the church today at 2:00 pm.

****

ENVIRONMENTAL COVENANT

We are an Environmentally Covenanted Church and promise to lift up care for God's earth through what we do in worship, education, individual and congregational lifestyle choices and in our church's community, national and global involvement.

STATEMENT OF WELCOME

We, the members of The First Baptist Church of Northampton and The First Church of Christ in Northampton, together known as "The First Churches," invite into our fellowship and membership all persons who love God and accept Jesus Christ as their Savior, without regard to such differences as race, ethnicity, age, gender, ability, sexual orientation, economic status, marital status, level of education, or any other difference that may be misunderstood as a barrier to Christian fellowship. We further welcome all who seek God, and we express our sincerest hope that in fellowship with the community of faith they may find the answers for which they search.

STAFF
Rev. Dr. Peter B. Ives, Minister
Rev. Kelly Gallagher, Assistant Minister for Outreach and Education
Janet Dahlberg & Dana Pasquale, Ministers of Music
Tessa Petersen, Director of Christian Education
Sheila Gilroy, Administrative Secretary
Laura Steinbock, Child Care Supervisor
Wendy Williams, Sexton

Born January 9, 1710